Taishinin's Judicial Behaviour in Corruption Cases

Kam Bill Wong · Steve Liang Fang

Taishinin's Judicial Behaviour in Corruption Cases

Japanese Body in Western Jacket

Springer

Kam Bill Wong
Hong Kong, China

Steve Liang Fang
Graduate School of Social Sciences
Chiba University
Chiba, Japan

ISBN 978-981-95-5822-3 ISBN 978-981-95-5823-0 (eBook)
https://doi.org/10.1007/978-981-95-5823-0

This Springer imprint is published by the registered company Springer Nature Singapore Pte Ltd.
The registered company address is: 152 Beach Road, #21-01/04 Gateway East, Singapore 189721, Singapore

Foreword

Today, when the crisis of democracy and democratic backsliding are frequently discussed around the world, the independence of the judiciary is often regarded as the last bastion for safeguarding democracy. Unlike the executive and legislative branches, the judiciary remains independent of the political powers of the day. By acting based on legal judgements rather than political ones, it can continue to uphold democratic values. Conversely, when movements emerge to undermine democracy, the judiciary is their primary target. Such movements have been visible in recent years across Central and Eastern Europe, the United States under the second Trump administration, and elsewhere in the world. By politicizing the judiciary, these politicians seek to neutralize the branch that stands against political power, thereby solidifying their domestic control. It is no exaggeration to say that the independence of the judiciary holds the key to the life or death of a nation's democracy.

However, there are limits to treating judicial independence as sacrosanct. Judges are often drawn from the upper echelons of society, ethnic majorities, males and older people. They are almost certainly highly educated individuals. They likely have little experience with manual labour. Judgements rendered by such individuals from the social elite carry the risk of becoming detached from common social norms and out of step with the sensibilities of ordinary citizens. The greater the independence of the judiciary, the more severe is this detachment. Might the judiciary also require a window open to society?

As outlined above, diverse perspectives intersect regarding the position of the judicial power. This book traces the evolution of Japan's *Taishinin*, illustrating how the judiciary has struggled within the interstices of politics, administration and society. At this juncture, where democracy stands at a crossroads, we must confront the fundamental question: How should judicial power be positioned? How can its independence be guaranteed while simultaneously allowing the winds of social change to influence it? As we tackle these difficult challenges, this book, which accurately depicts the historical development of judicial power, offers crucial insight.

Chiba, Japan
September 2025

Jiro Mizushima

Jiro Mizushima is Professor of Politics at Chiba University and the Leading Researcher of the Fair Society Studies Program. His research encompasses the welfare and labour reform movements unfolding across European nations, populist trends challenging established parties and destabilizing parliamentary politics, developments concerning minorities and the relationship between monarchies and democracy.

Preface

Corruption flouts rules of social fairness of equality, well-being and freedom in most nations. It is a persistent historical phenomenon eroding social justice, integrity of civil servants and the rule of law. The seriousness of it may also put lives and property at risk. There is little possibility that nations can escape the curse of corruption in the forms of bribery, extortion, rent-seeking, kickbacks and collusion. The roots of these deviant behaviours lie in abuse of public power for private gain. Power inequality provides a fertile breeding ground to abuse power and corruption. Institutionalized corruption reinforces more inequality and freedom in market. Prewar Japan is not an exception.

Not a casebook specifically for law students, this book explains *Taishinin*'s (former Supreme Court of Japan) judicial behaviour in narrative form and includes citations of judgements to substantiate two authors' arguments. No legal knowledge is needed to understand the major scandals analysed in content. The authors conduct review of Japanese anti-corruption laws and court's equitable judicial behaviour against it in the past 1,500 years as "Japanese body". Building on a nucleus of classic studies of it, the book also incorporates cultural and linguistic dimensions with descriptive richness, analytical thrust and conceptual framework. While corruption and bribery are assumed to be immoral and unethical, the arguments in this book support the proposition that some bribery may actually be ethical, depended on *Taishinin*'s judicial behaviour for rationalization.

The legal transplantation of Germanic anti-bribery legislation in the Meiji era is a "Western jacket" on this "Japanese body", which is not completely submissive and bowing down to Western legal values. As the final appellate court, it is largely in *Taishinin*'s courtrooms that the final judicial battles between corrupt bureaucrats and those preferring strict formal social control had played out. Utilizing prewar *Taishinin*'s judgements as a wealth of primary sources for justice marching with the truth, its legal values and judicial behaviour are confirmed innate. Through *Taishinin*'s judicial behaviour, legal transplantation of Western law as "jacket" sparked no outrage. Analysis of *Taishinin*'s rulings in respect of moral and illegal forms of corruption under different social conditions puts forth a clear illustration that anti-corruption values had developed throughout its history as "Japanese body", though

Taishinin operated in state polity which was originally created by Meiji Constitution. From Meiji Restoration, however, *Taishinin* began playing a role subordinated to politically powerful Ministry of Justice, which threatened efficacy of *Taishinin* on some occasions.

Hong Kong, China
Chiba, Japan
August 2025

Kam Bill Wong
Steve Liang Fang

Acknowledgements

The research and writing of this book, which traces the legal history of prewar Japan, focusing on the cases and judgements of *Taishinin* related to corruption, has been a profound journey, one that would not have been possible without the guidance, support and encouragement of numerous individuals and institutions.

Foremost, our deepest gratitude extends to the scholars and community of Fair Society Studies of Chiba University, Japan. This support programme provided not just an academic home but a vibrant intellectual environment where interdisciplinary ideas could flourish. As a research fellow (Steve) and an affiliated researcher (Bill) of this programme, we are profoundly thankful that this book could be one of the research outcomes supported by Fair Society Studies Program.

Our sincere thanks go to the researchers, especially Prof. Dixon Wong Heung Wah at the University of Hong Kong, and Prof. Mizushima Jiro, Prof. Kawase Takayuki at Chiba University.

This book is dedicated to the readers who are interested in sociolegal studies, Japanese history, and fair society studies. May your curiosity to building a more just world continue to draw inspiration from both the lessons and the warnings of law and history.

Hong Kong, China — Kam Bill Wong
Chiba, Japan — Steve Liang Fang
August 2025

Contents

About the Authors

Dr. Kam Bill Wong is a criminologist and researcher with a strong interest in Japanese studies. His academic background spans international human rights law, arbitration law, Japanese culture and history, business administration and marketing. He has extensive teaching and research experience at institutions in Hong Kong, Japan the United States, and mainland China. His current research focuses on the relationship between judicial behaviour and justice, particularly in relation to judgements in corruption cases adjudicated by the *Taishinin* in prewar Japan. Dr. Wong received his Ph.D. from the University of Hong Kong in 2008.

Dr. Steve Liang Fang is a researcher specializing in Japanese history, with a particular focus on pre-modern history and Japan's foreign relations in the nineteenth century. He is currently a research fellow at the Graduate School of Social Sciences, Chiba University, and a member of the Fair Society Studies group at the same institution. His work explores the historical factors contributing to social injustice, aiming to identify solutions to contemporary issues related to fairness and equality. Dr. Fang received his Ph.D. from Chiba University in 2022.

Chapter 1
Introduction

1.1 Judicial Response in the Dynamics of Bureaucratic Corruption

The term corruption is derived from the Latin term *corruptus*, which means "to spoil, pollute, abuse, or destroy". Thus, the term suggests a state of moral turpitude. The notion of corruption has demonstrated variability across different cultural contexts. However, it is predominantly associated with notions of unfairness and deviation from established norms, particularly those pertaining to religion (Holmes 2015, p. 27). Corruption is a persistent issue in Japanese society, with a long-standing presence that dates back to antiquity. Corruption has been demonstrated to result in unfair treatment and distributive injustice, as self-interested bureaucrats may engage in rent-seeking. The capacity of citizens to exercise autonomy is constrained by systemic inequities. In essence, individuals exhibit a pronounced aversion to unfairness resulting from corruption when it is disadvantageous to them. The book's primary focus is on the subject of Japanese court judgements concerning prewar bureaucratic corruption. The prevailing assumption is that anti-corruption laws are knowable, articulable and demystified by virtue of court judgements. This is a judicial phenomenon, and it is the most critical aspect of substantiative justice in ensuring a fair society.

The terms, bureaucrat and bureaucracy, are associated with at least three distinct connotations. Weber's perspective aligns with the conventional viewpoint. According to the Weberian model, ideal bureaucracy is characterized by several distinct features. These include a unified command structure that is organized according to a clearly delineated hierarchy of specialization, duties and regulations. Merit systems play a pivotal role in the recruitment and promotion processes within Weberian bureaucracy. The second meaning of bureaucracy refers to the structured missions, functions and processes of significant internal and external impacts on the environment of a public or private organization. The third perspective examines bureaucracy in its capacity to govern within public and private sectors, with a particular focus on military and security bureaucratic institutions. The delegation of power to bureaucrats

K. B. Wong and S. L. Fang, *Taishinin's Judicial Behaviour in Corruption Cases*,
https://doi.org/10.1007/978-981-95-5823-0_1

through a principal-and-agent relationship enables the implementation of a top-down model of governance, whereby political system maintenance is orchestrated by elite bureaucrats and organizational leaders (Farazmand 2009, p. 5, p. 8, p. 12).

The Japanese government has traditionally operated under a system of governance that is both entrenched and consolidated by its elite bureaucracy. The system under scrutiny is distinguished by the said three hallmark characteristics that are intricately linked to the concept of public power. Anti-bribery law in Articles 197 and 198 of the Penal Code 1907 was identified as a means of preventing corruption among bureaucrats as they exercised their public power. Besley elucidates that bureaucrats' authority is intricately intertwined with its exercise within the sociopolitical context, manifesting through the conduit of official duties (Besley 2006, pp. 10–11, p. 13.). Corruption can be conceptualized as a manifestation of substandard governance, which consequently results in suboptimal state performance within this specific power dynamic.

Massey's observations underscore a salient discrepancy between the comparatively diminutive nature of prewar Japan's bureaucracy and the expansive scope of its formal and informal power dynamics. This discrepancy is further accentuated by the considerable breadth of discretionary duties encompassed within these power relations (Massey 2012, pp. 298–299). These include licencing and approval powers, as well as various means relevant to local governments' maintenance of public order. It is common assertion that the statutory scope of civil servants' powers during their official duties was not clearly delineated. This appeal was frequently made in the context of each *Taishinin* judgement on a corruption case.

The primary concern pertains to the implementation of measures aimed at curtailing the potential for bureaucrats to exploit their authority for personal gain and to violate the fundamental principles of their profession. This is of paramount importance in maintaining public trust and ensuring governmental oversight. The extensive history of Japanese anti-corruption legislation underscores the significance of this enduring question in the context of formal social control. As elucidated in Chap. 3, the Japanese legal system offers little clarity on the definition of bribery or corruption. In order to combat bureaucratic corruption, it is essential to mobilize the efforts of the general public and implement a comprehensive array of policies. The implementation of such policies is expected to enhance public accountability and transparency. Furthermore, it is imperative that they guarantee a just society through legal mechanisms (Hough 2013, p. 7). The court's obligation to respond in a fair manner of substantiative justice is contingent upon the rendering of a judgement.

It is debatable that prewar Japanese court judgements are not readily discernible, explicable, or demystified for non-specialists. All prewar court judgements were written exclusively in *kanji* and *katakana*, lacking the punctuation marks such as quotation marks, periods and commas that are commonly used in modern Japanese language. Furthermore, the intricacies of Japanese legal terminology and the judicial reasoning process can prove overwhelming for individuals lacking a foundation in legal studies. The credibility and validity of prewar Japanese court judgements may not be bolstered by legal reasoning that adheres to this traditional style. The Japanese legal culture exerts a significant influence on this classic style, thereby shaping the role perception of well-educated Japanese judges. Consequently, contemporary Japanese law students exhibit a marked reluctance to engage with prewar judicial rulings. The judgement analysis in this book intentionally overcomes these difficulties by presenting key court rulings in ordinary English with citation of the original Japanese text. It is not necessary to possess specialized legal knowledge, classical Japanese grammar, or an understanding of social conditions to reap the benefits of this book.

The two authors hope that the court judgement analysis contained in this book will be of broad interest, not only to law students, but also to readers with a penchant for prewar Japanese society, legal history, public administration, social policy and fair society studies. For the convenience of the reader, special law terms and Japanese terms are provided with Roman pronunciation and English translation. In Japanese naming conventions, surnames are placed before given names.

The book under review employs a research methodology that is primarily rooted in doctrinal judicial behaviour, drawing upon anti-corruption legislation and the judicial thought and adjudication of *Taishinin* judges in their efforts to eradicate corruption. In addition to the interpretation of statutes, they traversed uncharted seas, navigating the intricate labyrinth of internal experiences, emotions and attitudinal beliefs.

1.2 *Taishinin*'s Judgements as Primary Data

It is hypothesized that traditional Japanese legal values were incorporated and reflected in *Taishinin*'s judgements as "Japanese body". The rationale underlying this phenomenon is evident. Judicial knowledge of the community is developed within socially established norms and values. The concept of transplanted law as "Western jacket" is, in this context, assimilated to the Japanese "body" of ideology. This integration is concomitant with the legal system, political values, legal cultures, power relations, social hierarchy and the structure of governance (Gillespie 2001, pp. 286–311). Prior to the enactment of the National Public Service Ethics Law in 1999, Japan lacked a comprehensive, codified legislative framework to address bureaucratic corruption, with the exception of Articles 197 and 198 of the Penal Code of 1907. These articles, derived from Germanic law, were intended to prevent bribery by bureaucrats. The criminalization of corruption in Japan differs from the practices observed in most other nations. In most countries, anti-corruption laws are designed to criminalize various *modus operandi* (methods to commit crime). However, in Japan, the criminalization of corruption was dependent on court rulings regarding these two articles in the prewar Penal Code 1907. *Taishinin* was the precursor to the present-day Supreme Court of Japan and was at the forefront of the prewar Japanese judiciary in the domain of European civil law jurisprudence. The court's decisions were characterized by its judicial behaviour and expertise concerning these two articles, and they were regarded as definitive and conclusive. The judgement rendered by *Taishinin* had a significant impact on each Japanese individual.

The study of organizational behaviour has reached a point of maturity within the domain of business studies. Despite its status as a judicial institution, the extant research on *Taishinin*'s behaviour from an organizational perspective remains underdeveloped. A judge can be regarded as a judicial bureaucrat. In the context of judicial corruption, this phenomenon can result in miscarriage of justice and even wrongful conviction. The judicial decision-making process can profoundly influence the principles and collective moral responsibility that underpin the concept of a fair society. This influence is particularly evident in the context of studies on fair society, where it is evident that the well-being of individuals, the enjoyment of freedom under public power, equality, and, most notably, social justice is of paramount importance.

1.3 Judicial Behaviour and Fair Society

In this book, readers may encounter intermittent references to fundamental concepts in the study of fair societies. These concepts include, but are not limited to, the notions of freedom, democracy, equality of opportunity, collective well-being and labour justice (Chandler 2024, pp. 28–88). These provide a framework for further consideration of the most challenging issue, namely the role of *Taishinin*'s justice in prewar Japanese society. John Rawls dedicated his life to the development of a seminal concept concerning justice in the context of his renowned social justice theory. The foundation of his theory is the conceptual framework of fairness (Rawls 1971). Meiji Constitution is widely regarded as a "social contract" that established prewar Japanese society as a state polity system, rather than a fair system of cooperation. However, it is important to consider whether the mission of *Taishinin* was solely focused on justice. If not, why not? If yes, why?

To this end, the five *Taishinin* judgements selected in this book, offer a multidimensional analysis of *Taishinin*'s judicial behaviour. The objective of the conclusion in Chap. 10 of this book is to evaluate *Taishinin*'s judicial behaviour in various perspectives. An evaluation of its judicial behaviour, as presented in this book, offers insights that facilitate multidimensional contemplation on academic inquiries. It is unfortunate that research on prewar judicial behaviour in corruption cases, as assessed by the framework of a fair society, remains absent from the existing literature. The absence of a universally applicable metric for assessing the fairness of judicial behaviour is attributable to the cultural relativism inherent in legal principles. The present volume employs the most recent conception of an ideal fair society to assess the fairness of *Taishinin*'s judicial behaviour.

1.4 Corruption as Dark Figure of Crime in Prewar Japan

Corruption is a nebulous form of criminal activity. The number of corruption cases may be underreported, undetected, or undiscovered. It is impossible to compile a database of actual figures for corruption offences to facilitate categorization and understanding of the extent of corruption. The initial challenge pertains to the absence of a universally accepted definition of corruption. For instance, the act of bestowing a gift can be interpreted as a form of bribery or as a component of a social ritual. The majority of corruption cases are likely to be concealed within customary practices. Other prevalent factors have been identified as contributors include a lack of awareness regarding criminal activity, the concealment of truthful information, rationalization in accordance with social norms, misleading information presented in surveys, memory deterioration, the telescoping of past events in favour of more recent cases and inadequate knowledge, as well as an unsuitable questionnaire design that affects interviewees' willingness and ability to provide answers. The conditions and environment during the interview may also affect the quality of research findings (Newburn 2017, p. 63). In Japan, the criminal acts of corruption and bribery are typically kept hidden due to the norm of Japanese shame culture, as defined by Benedict. This cultural norm is characterized by the belief that shame is a significant sanction, leading to feelings of guilt and self-reproach in individuals who engage in certain behaviours (Benedict 1954, pp. 222–223). This phenomenon results in the absence of relevant data from official statistics (Tierney 2006, p. 27; Maxfield and Earl 2015, p. 149, p. 161.). The extent of its severity in prewar Japan remains unknown; however, an examination of *Taishinin*'s assessments offers insight into its implications within the context of prewar social structures.

1.5 Japanese Terms and Idioms Denoting Corruption

Language socialization affects emotional expressions in Japanese shame culture. The Japanese term *hazukashii* is usually translated as shameful in English, which is a tool for the language socialization of children to know shame in Japanese-speaking society (Takada 2019, p. 1, p. 3). The intersection of law and language has been a tool for judicial behaviour studies. Examples are phrases used in everyday discourse and courtroom discourse (Conley et al. 2019, p. 8).[1] *Kanyōku* (Japanese terms and idioms) can provide some hints of *modus operandi* for corruption as a social phenomenon in Japanese society. Other than *wairo* for bribery, the following Japanese terms and idioms denoting corruption and bribery can provide some profiles:

---

[1] See "Linguistic anthropology" at https://www.britannica.com/science/anthropology/Linguistic-anthropology#ref839712. Accessed 1 September 2025.

a. *Sodenoshita* (under the sleeve) can also be stated explicitly as *sodenoshita wo watasu* (pass under the sleeve). As a vulgar way of speaking, the hidden meaning is secretly handing over money and goods by hiding it under the sleeve, which is bribe. The word implies a sense of immorality.
b. *Mainai* is from the combination of *mai* (bribe) with *nai* (currency). It means bribery with gifts. Originally, it also has a neutral meaning of giving something as a gift or only indicating particular something in this transaction. *Mai* also has a positive meaning of offering something for God or simply gifts for another person.
c. *Uragane* means money that is secretly paid and not recorded as a transaction in order to make things go smoothly, which is used in the sentence of *uragane ga ugoku* as bribery behaviour. Conceptually, it is like the lubricant theory in corruption studies, which is inappropriate but not sinful.
d. *Hanagusuri* is an *ingo* (jargon) that literally means nasal medicine. And the act of using nasal medicine, *hanagusuri wo kagaseru* was negatively used for bribery. Usually, the amount is comparatively small.
e. *Amai shiru wo suu* literally mean sucking the sweet juice and is currently used for doing nothing by oneself but benefiting from others' hard work. It can be used to indicate organizational corruption with the similar meaning of *wairo wo chōshū* (Collecting bribes). In Japanese term, the certain amount of *Amai shiru wo suu* is likely to constitute *kōzōoshoku* (structural corruption).
f. *Shifuku wo koyasu* (filling one's personal stomach) is a very shameful sentence due to the poor integrity and damage to public interest. For example, *wairo nado wo uketotte, shifuku wo koyashite ita* (He took bribes to enrich his private pocket).
g. *Oshoku* is the most commonly used term for corruption in Japanese. It has implications of criminality and bears similarity with *tokushoku*. Two terms have overlapping area of *shokken-ran'yō* (abuse of authority). *Fuhai* is also translated as corruption in English, but this Japanese term of immorality is about the mental degradation of the substance of a system or organization.
h. *Hainin* (breach of trust) and *haininzai* (breach of trust offence) indicate higher seriousness than corruption. *Haininzai* is disobeying duties entrusted by others, which is one of the criminal acts under Article 247 in current Penal Code, and it is an act that damages an objective to which one should contribute, such as breaching the trust of a company for the benefit of oneself or a third party.

   A breach of fiduciary duty occurs when the fiduciary acts in the interest of themselves, rather than the best interest of the employer or principal.
i. *Tankanori* means officials abusing one's authority to commit evil. *Kan* and *ri* refer to bureaucrats or officials. This word negatively describes greedy filthy bureaucrats and corrupt officials.
j. *Reisen* means money given as a *sharei* (reward). It initially meant money presented to the Shogunate on specific celebrations in the Muromachi period. *Sharei* is an expression of appreciation and one of the common terms used in appeal grounds for exculpation.

It is noteworthy that *Taishinin* used *sharei* repeatedly in its judgements to criminalize inappropriate acceptance of money or gifts as corruption offence.

k. *Kanagutsuwa wo hameru* literally means putting in a gold ring, which is currently used for giving money as bribes to have no complaint or keep them silent. This is a very functionalist approach.
l. *Jitsudan* (live ammunition) is also an *ingo* that is used in electoral corruption. As a term invented in 1919, it currently means the monetary things used as the lubricant for bribery in elections.
m. *Seikyū* was the demand for bribe, which is used commonly as bill or invoice in daily Japanese now. *Kyūmon* and *kyūka* are old Japanese *ingo* that are similar to *Seikyū* for bribery request.

Linguistic discourse is commonly applied to judicial behaviour research. Overall, (a) to (m) reflect social phenomenon of corruption and indicate the profile of socialization against corruption and bribery in Japanese language. All these common terms and idioms of Japanese language have negative implications against corruption as a deviant behaviour. Other than linguistic discourse, profiling by personality traits and social background of court case also provides hints to analyse *Taishinin*'s judicial behaviour in respect of corruption (Kocsis 2007, pp. 263–265).

In order to further understand the impacts of internal and external factors on *Taishinin* judicial behaviour, it is necessary to consider the possibility of conducting interviews with *Taishinin* justices and attending court hearings. It is evident that *Taishinin* is no longer a viable entity. Research on *Taishinin*'s judicial behaviour through analysis of its judgements against social conditions is a feasible methodology, albeit one that is time-consuming. Consequently, social conditions are incorporated into the analysis of each court judgement in this book. Moreover, the book under consideration herein extends to cover the personal and family backgrounds of *Taishinin* Chief Justices. This is due to the fact that childhood socialization has been demonstrated to have the capacity to determine a person's attitudinal model for or against a particular behaviour.

1.6 Cost of Corruption in Prewar Japan

Despite the advancements in artificial intelligence and quantitative methods in economics and statistics, accurately quantifying the hidden costs of corruption remains a formidable challenge. The societal cost of crime is not confined to the economic expense of a single offender. It encompasses the financial implications of law enforcement responses and the anticipation of criminal activity. Corruption has the potential to compromise the government's authority and the stability of social relationships. The assessment of the severity of corruption is invariably derived from the results of opinion polls that gauge the subjective perception of corruption among the domestic population of a particular nation. The annual Corruption Perception

Index of Transparency International serves as a widely accepted metric for evaluating perceptions of corruption.[2] The prewar Japan had not conducted a nationwide opinion poll that addressed the perception of damage caused by corruption. The financial impact of corruption was inherently challenging to ascertain, further compounding the opaque nature of the situation.

The notion of corruption is not confined to a single theoretical framework. The economic value of corruption has the potential to provide a rationalization for its occurrence. The "lubricant" advantage of corruption is that it may facilitate the bypassing of bureaucratic regulations and expedite economic transactions. As elucidated in Chaps. 4 and 5, the compensation case and the railway company case, respectively, pertain to circumventing inefficient bureaucratic procedures by leveraging political factions within the Tokyo City Assembly. Bureaucratic corruption, defined as the utilization of illicit means to attain a lawful objective, constitutes a grave form of social injustice (Edelbacher et al. 2016, p. 2). The improvement of people's well-being, living conditions and welfare could be achieved by increasing the compensation amount and enhancing the railway network. In the context of fair society studies, this approach has been shown to enhance residents' perception of well-being and quality of life. However, this has been achieved by allocating public funds and restricting individuals' freedom to select the most efficient railway firm in the context of fair competition and equality. Although the economic rationality of corruption may be acknowledged, its high moral cost may ultimately outweigh any advantages it may offer.

It is evident that history is repeating itself. Throughout the Showa era, a series of political corruption scandals plagued the dominant factions within the ruling Liberal Democratic Party, as well as the opposition parties, which included the Japanese Socialist Party, Komeito and the Democratic Socialist Party. The Japan Communist Party demonstrated a comparatively low degree of involvement in allegations of corruption (Babb 2005, p. 186). This situation bears a striking resemblance to the grand corruption case involving the Tokyo City Assembly, which is thoroughly examined in Chaps. 4 and 5.

In Chaps. 6 to 8, the acceptance of hospitality by teachers and police officers were focused. The public held elevated expectations for the conduct and discipline of these individuals as teachers and police officers. The criminalization of corruption is predicated on the assumption that corruption is inherently detrimental to social justice, freedom and equality. These phenomena have the potential to hinder harmonious social cooperation and the realization of a fair society. In Chap. 6, *Taishinin* presents a moralistic attitudinal model of judicial behaviour, under which corruption is criminalized as a breach of social trust. This social fabric links citizens in a society together. In order to effectively combat corruption, it is essential to implement a multifaceted approach that incorporates legislation, the establishment of a politically impartial anti-corruption institution and the judicious application of the law by an independent judiciary. This strategy is predicated on the recognition that

[2] On this see "Corruption Perception Index" at https://www.transparency.org/en/cpi/2020/index. Accessed 1 September 2025.

the judicious application of the law is instrumental in targeting corrupt bureaucrats and ensuring the integrity of the judicial system (Babb 2005, pp. 176–177). In accordance with the Japanese language profile against corruption, traditional Japanese legal consciousness, as delineated in Chap. 3, also substantiates the elevated ethical implications of corruption. As citizens of the country and as moral beings in the prewar Japanese state polity, they were entitled to demand social justice from the perspective of a fair society. In the period preceding the war, the mass media functioned as the watchdog of society in Japan. They supported this social consciousness by labelling it as a scandal in headline news.

1.7 *Taishinin* in Historical Institutionalism

Historical institutionalism is defined as a methodological framework that analyses the impact of institutions on politics and society. It facilitates a more profound comprehension of the origins, evolution and ramifications of humanly constructed institutions over time and geographically distinct regions (Plaček et al. 2022). *Taishinin*, the precursor to the contemporary Supreme Court of Japan, is also pronounced *Daishinin*. This judicial system can be characterized as a tepid reform of the judicial system. The institution's establishment was in accordance with a specific mission that was oriented towards the facilitation of governance within the state polity. The development of the Ministry of Justice's institutional infrastructure was closely intertwined with the institution's establishment in Meiji Restoration.

1.7.1 Taishinin's Establishment

Hōmushō, also known as the Ministry of Justice, was previously referred to as the *Shihōshō* in prewar Japan. The scope of responsibility for this ministry encompassed a wide range of legal and judicial affairs, including the supervision of courts and court-related affairs, representing a significant aspect of the ministry's mandate. As the Tokugawa era drew to a close, the Japanese body of legal tradition was characterized by a lack of separation between legislative power and the administration of justice. The establishment of a court of open judicial independence was incongruent with Japanese legal tradition. According to Japanese intellectuals, the Japanese body of traditional judicial behaviour under neo-Confucianism was considered legitimate.

In Meiji Japan, *Daijōkan* or *Dajōkan* (Great Council of State) was the highest administrative organ of Japanese Imperial government up to early Meiji era. On 9 July 1871, under *Dajōkan* Promulgation No. 337 to 340, *Shihōshō* was established as the Ministry of Justice to replace both *Gyōbushō* (Ministry of Criminal Justice) and *Danjōdai* (Inspection Agency). With *Dajōkan* Promulgation No. 491 dated 27 September 1871, the Meiji Government set up *Meihōryō* (legal training school). For internal judicial socialization and legal training for staff of in *Shihōshō*, it was evolved from a combination of *Banshozusho* (Foreign Book Examination Institute) with a medical school at Izumi Kandabashi, Tokyo in 1877 (Takami 2001, p. 807).

In 1874, *Meihōryō* employed French law professors, Gustave Émile Boissonade de Fontarabie (1825–1910) and Georges Hilaire Bousquet (1846–1937) to teach the first intake of seven students. This is the landmark start of training with the Western legal culture. *Dajōkan* then arranged all of them to study in France. The second intake in 1876 had 100 students for the eight-year course. In 1884, both the preparatory course and regular course of the law school were transferred to the Law School of Tokyo University. The graduates became the backbone of human resources supply to judiciary in Meiji and prewar Showa era, including *Taishinin* Chief Justices.

The *Shihō-shokumu-teisei* (Judicial Duties System) of twenty-two chapters prepared by the Ministry of Justice in 1872 was mainly about the power and structure of Ministry of Justice, but part of it was a blueprint of the court structure afterwards in 1890. It was an unsystematic way to tailor a judicial jacket for "Japanese body". It outlined very simple civil and criminal procedures. For the first time in Japanese legal history, it introduced the legal qualifications of *shōshohito* (decree issuer), *daishohito* (scriber) and *daigenjin* (spokesman). In today's Japanese terms, *shōshohito* is *kōshōjin* (notary), and *daishohito* is *shihō-shoshi* (judicial scrivener). The noteworthy was the establishment of *meihōryō* in chapter 19, the *shōrinji-saibansho* (Temporary Court of Ministry of Justice) and the regulations in chapter 11 to chapter 18. The whole judiciary and judicial administration were under the transformational leadership of *kyō* (Minister of Justice) who doubled up the post of *saiban-shochō* (Chief of Court) in *Shihōshō*. As the judge of highest rank, *daihanji* (the grand judge) was his subordinate of one lower rank. However, no intention for the establishment of *Taishinin* is found in *Shihō-shokumu-teisei.* As of October 1872, courts were set up in Osaka, Kyoto and thirteen prefectures under the administration of the Ministry of Justice. In January 1874, the Ministry of Justice and the Ministry of Interiors had their own judicial police and administrative police, respectively (Fukuyama 2017, p. 738, p. 749), which was also the main focus in Chaps. 7 and 8 in this book. As a matter of historical institutionalism, it structurally paved the way for the subsequent undue influence of the Ministry of Justice on the judiciary, in which the Minister owned judicial administration power for the whole judiciary of state polity. Under the Ministry, Tokyo Court had jurisdiction on final appeal before the establishment of *Taishinin* (Ukai 1959, p. 55). However, the blueprint for the evolution of *Taishinin* was still non-existent.

After Osaka Conference of the Meiji leaders from January to February 1875, the Emperor founded *Taishinin* as the final appeal court in with his *Oshōchokusōan* (Draft of Imperial Rescript) dated 14 April 1875, which was promulgated on government gazette as No. 59 of *Dajōkan-fukoku* (Proclamations issued by *Dajōkan*). Therefore, the roles of *Taishinin* and *Motorōin* (Senate) were formed in a constitutional state polity. With Gustav's advice, *Taishinin* was structurally designed by the Ministry of Justice officials in 1875 as a copy of the independent French Court of Cassation (or Great Court of Cassation). It was established in Tokyo to replace the old *saibansho* and assumed to have independence from the Ministry of Justice. It was a faithful transplantation of French judicial system of magistrates' courts, courts of first instance and appellate courts (Ministry of Justice 1900, p. 31).

After the organization of *Taishinin* was established under the issue of *Taishinin-shosaibansho-shokusei-shōtei* (Chapters on Organization of *Taishinin*) on 24 May 1875, *Saiban-jimu-kokoroe* (Knowledge of Court Affairs) of five articles was issued under *Dajōkan-fukoku* No. 103 on 8 June 1875 to clarify the judicial standards of trials. It consisted of legal guidelines of applicability to limit *Taishinin*'s scope of judicial behaviour when the legal system was in institutional transformation in 1875. *Saiban-jimu-kokoroe* was considered an important step in the Meiji legal development. Articles 1 and 2 are common to both civil and criminal cases, prohibiting the suspension of a trial due to asking a higher court for clarification on doubts about proceeding to a trial. Trial should be conducted without delay. An appeal against a judgement should be lodged to a higher court within a specified time limit. With respect to civil trials, Article 3 stipulates that if there is neither written law nor customary law, the case should be decided according to *jōri* of reasonable principles.[3] In specific chapters of *Taishinin-shosaibansho-shokusei-shōtei* related to *Taishinin*'s appeal procedures, further operational details of *Taishinin* were provided, including appeal proceedings, conditions for bail, *Shūjinkyūyo-kisoku* (prisoner salary regulation), travel allowance for witness and acquitted defendant and rules for court adjudication.

The legal transplantation of Western judicial "jacket" was compelled by Western pressure, and the Meiji government's objective to terminate unequal treaties with Western powers embodied extraterritoriality. The establishment of *Taishinin* and a judicial system in a Western style, along with legal transplantation and codification of various laws derived from Western jurisprudence, was imperative for the realization of this objective (Spaulding 1967, pp. 4–5, p. 34).

1.7.2 Hidden Agenda and Isolation of Taishinin

After *Taishinin*'s initial establishment, the *Jitsumihō* (Penal Code) issued in July 1880 addressed that the judicial structure tentatively composed of *Taishinin, Kōso-saibansho* (Court of Appeal), *Hajimeshin-saibansho* (Court of First Instance) and *Chian-saibansho* (Court of Public Order). At the time, a separate statute for judicial structure had not yet been established. The initial intention behind the establishment of a Japanese judiciary was merely symbolic at this stage. The clandestine objective was to demonstrate to foreign powers that Japanese legal justice was not barbaric, without rejecting the principles of justice as established in traditional Japanese jurisprudence. As per *Daijōkan-fukoku* No. 53 in 1881, this structure was confirmed to be implemented in 1882. With further authorization under *Daijōkan* Promulgation No. 420 dated 18 August 1881, the Ministry of Justice first took

[3] The original text of Article 3 in *Saibanjimu-kokoroe*: 民事ノ裁判ニ成文ノ法律ナキモノハ習慣ニ依リ習慣ナキモノハ条理ヲ推考シテ裁判スヘシ。

over the criminal and civil jurisdiction of Tokyo Prefecture, established its Prison Division, Sentencing Division, Law Division, Indemnification Division and General Affairs Division. The Ministry of Justice was positioned as a central judicial organ of government controlling both criminal and civil jurisdiction. The whole criminal justice system was under his domination except *Taishinin*. Unlike most courts of final appeal which are vested with the power of final adjudication and management of the whole judiciary, *Taishinin* was only for appellate jurisdiction. Its administration was limited to its own judges. There was no preparation for *Taishinin* to have independence from the government in the organizational structure at the outset.

The *Saibansho-kōseihō* (Court Structure Code), which was codified in 1890, stated that the *Shihō-daijin* (Minister of Justice) possessed absolute power to monitor all courts, as outlined in Article 135. This power, referred to as *shihō-gyōsei*, pertained to the minister's authority over judicial administration. According to Article 134, the judicial administration power for *Taishinin* was held by *Taishininchō* (*Taishinin* Chief Justice) (Nakamura 2008, p. 277, pp. 285–286). Therefore, from a statutory and administrative standpoint, the prewar judiciary was under the jurisdiction of the Minister of Justice, with the exception of the *Taishinin*. From a historical institutionalist perspective, *Taishinin* was completely isolated from the criminal justice structure. The phenomenon observed was not an instance of independence in judicial behaviour, but rather one of isolation. The Emperor's status as the supreme entity within the state political structure is paramount. As delineated in Article 57 of the Meiji Constitution, the judicial authority of the court is to be exercised in accordance with the legal principles stipulated in the Emperor's name.

1.7.3 Taishinin's Kenri

At the inception of the judicial reform, *Taishinin* occupied a lower historical institutionalist status relative to the administrative status of the cabinet within the state polity structure. The establishment of a new supreme court with the objective of ensuring judicial independence and facilitating a system of checks and balances within the government's organizational structure was not a primary intention. Conversely, its original conception was for the purpose of serving *kenri* (authority権理).

In early 1885, the *kanji* term 権理, instead of 権利 of same pronunciation, was used in the mission of legal reform discussed in *Ōsaka-kaigi-mōshiawasōan* (Draft of Proposal for the Osaka Conference) in 1885. It can be traced to 権理通議 (*kenritsūgi*) when Fukuzawa Yukichi to tried to interpret the Western concept of *right* in Japanese, in his famous *Gakumon-No-Susume* (*An Encouragement of Learning*). Nevertheless, *Kenri* (authority権理) was more likely to imply the traditional Japanese *dōri*, which was a common sense or authority and behaviour guideline based on social norms and ethnic principles. The concept denoted a voluntary compliance with state domination under the authority of the Emperor but did not signify formal legal sanction. It was also different with the Western conception of individual rights or contemporary human rights that are subject to legal protection. Even Fukuzawa found *kenri* (right 権

利) in Japanese language could not fully express *right* which was very individualistic (Yanagibu 1982, pp. 149–172). The concept of individual *right* was totally unfounded in Japanese legal history. In the subsequent *Seifu-kaikakuzuan* (Government Reform Plan), *Taishinin* was institutionally designated to be under the power of the Emperor and the cabinet at the service of Japanese jurisprudence of *kenri* (authority権理). In the perspective of historical institutionalist model, linguistic discourse confirms that the original mission of *Taishinin* was not at the service of Japanese nationals' *kenri* (right 権利) but the domination of state polity with *kenri* (authority権理). Accordingly, *Taishinin*'s judicial behaviour was assurance of loyalty to the Emperor as *dōri*, or simply speaking, a common sense.

In the Japanese Penal Code 1907 transplanted from Germany, the Germanic law term *recht* for criminal justice could not be fully transplanted and adopted. The term *recht* from "*rccht*" is evolved from the Roman "*jus*", considering as the foundation of all rights instead of one right fully owned by state or monarchy. Therefore, *recht* is not merely *kenri* (right 権利). Traditional Japanese "body" of legal justice had no connectivity with Roman law origin. Even *right* in English is not exactly identical to the Germanic term *recht. Kenri* (authority権理) is an examination of the traditional legal consciousness that is ingrained in the Japanese mindset based on *dōri*. It is noteworthy that in the context of Japanese legal culture, the concept of *dōri* as the "Japanese body" has historically played a significant role in the determination of deviance, which is one of the main concerns in this book and will be discussed in greater detail in the subsequent chapters. *Dōri* has been employed to encourage individuals to voluntarily adhere to the prevailing norms and values of Japanese society, particularly within the context of its shame culture (Iwatani 2008, pp. 38–40).

In the early Meiji era, a group of prominent Meiji intellectuals published their ideas in the influential magazine *Meiroku-zasshi*. These intellectuals advocated for the combination of Japanese *kokka-kenryoku* (Japanese state power) with law to discharge the responsibility of *kenri* (authority権理) (Izuhara 1982, pp. 72–73). The proposal was made in light of the shortcomings of the Meiji Constitution in its role as a social contract, particularly with regard to the promotion of democratic principles and the maintenance of a balanced distribution of power within a fair society. Japanese intellectuals expressed support for the utilization of state power in lieu of individualism, as a means of achieving *kenri* (authority権理)in the context of state polity. This phenomenon aligned with the prevailing Japanese equity within the framework of Japanese legal culture. From the outset, *Taishinin* was conceptualized as a component of the "tailored Western jacket", designed to envelop the Japanese physique. The aforementioned behaviour exhibited by the judicial system was characterized by the interpretation of facts and the application of law as *jittaihō* (substantive law) in conjunction with this Japanese body. The implementation of a binding court ruling could potentially contribute to the establishment of a stable social order with the *kenri* (authority権理) (Nakamura 1971, p. 10, pp. 15–16). In the context of neo-Confucianist influence, the objective of criminal law enforcement transcended the realm of mere criminal justice. Law with *kenri* (authority権理)was a rigorous instrument intended to inform the Emperor's subjects of His Majesty's benevolence and the reestablishment of His Majesty's direct rule over the new government (Kobayashi

1943, pp. 115–162). The phenomenon may be considered an additional application of *wakonyōsai* (Japanese spirit and Western talent) to protect the Emperor's hegemony against corruption and bribery.

1.7.4 Taishinin Chief Justices

A distinguishing feature of historical institutionalism is the notion that bureaucracy serves as a conduit for the dissemination of values and oversees the implementation of policy or the formulation of policy. Judicial behaviour, particularly in instances where legal ambiguity prevails, is profoundly influenced by the values held by the presiding judge. In accordance with the tenets of historical institutionalism, the personal history background posits that a judge's personal attributes and past experiences, including, but not limited to, race, gender, education and professional history, shape their perspective and, consequently, their rulings. Social background theory posits that prior socialization experiences exert an influence on subsequent behaviour. In the attitudinal model of the judicial behaviour paradigm, this influence is evident (George 2008). The Chief Justice of a final appeal court or constitutional court is responsible for the legal reasoning that underlies the values of the judicial and political systems. This reasoning ultimately leads to the implementation of rulings as a strategy with cultural implications for national policy. However, the presence of institutional or political constraints on the judicial leadership can impede a judge's ability to strategically guide the political system (Tushnet 2009).

The socialization process for judges' personal values typically commences during their formative years, encompassing both the educational and familial environments. A thorough examination of the socialization and backgrounds of three *Taishinin* Chief Justices preceding the Court Structure Code of 1890 is instrumental in comprehending *Taishinin*'s judicial conduct in the nascent stages of its historical institutionalism.

1.7.4.1 *Tamano Seiri*

The inaugural *Taishinin* Chief Justice was Tamano Seiri, who was born on 3 September 1825 in a samurai family in Iwakuni Domain, which corresponded to the present-day southern Yamaguchi Prefecture. A comparative analysis of the service records of early *Taishinin* Chief Justices reveals that Tamano's tenure at *Taishinin* was the most protracted, spanning a duration that exceeded that of his counterparts. His early education included the study of neo-Confucianism at the governmental school. Subsequently, he transitioned to the study of pragmatic neo-Confucianism at *yomeigaku*, and then pursued a comprehensive examination of Western studies. In 1869, at the age of 45, Tamano served as a representative for Iwakuni, travelling to Kyoto in support of the Meiji Restoration. This endeavour led to his appointment by the Meiji government as a junior judge for civil litigation. In 1874, Tamano was elevated to the rank of *shihōken-daihanji* (senior justice). He was initially appointed acting *Taishinin* Chief Justice in 1875, and subsequently received formal confirmation of the appointment in 1878. In 1879, he was transferred to the position of *Shihō-Daisuke* (Vice-Judicial Minister) of *Motorōin* (Senate), a position he held until his formally reappointment as the Chief Justice in 1881. In 1886, he committed suicide, though the motivation behind this action remains shrouded in mystery. Tamano was lauded as an impartial and ethical magistrate, devoid of any taint of dishonesty. A particularly salient aspect of his career was his close working relationship with the Minister of Justice, Yamada Aakiyoshi, in the drafting of Japanese laws during the period of legal transplantation. A notable similarity between the two was their shared lineage from samurai families and their lack of formal training in Western jurisprudence. Despite these differences, they collaborated in the codification of various civil laws. Yamada, a conservative legal draftsman, could be considered as a pioneer to apply "Japanese body in Western jacket" by adhering to Japanese tradition and customary practices in his legislative behaviour. He was also the founder of two universities in Japan (Iida 2018, pp. 1–7; Watanabe 1994, p. 214).

1.7.4.2 Kishira Kaneyasu

Like Tamano, Kishira Kaneyasu was also born in a samurai family. In 1868, he started his civil servant career as *giseikanshikan* (council historian) of *Daijōkan* status in the *giseikan,* which was a legislative advisory body established by Meiji government in 1868. Since then, he had worked at various law enforcement posts with one-year legal training in Paris from 1872 to 1873. He was then appointed as *shihō-daikenji* (Chief Prosecutor of Ministry of Justice) and Prosecutor of *Taishinin* in 1873 and 1875, respectively. With French legal education, Kishira was openminded, advocating adversarial legal system, evidentiality of proof and the abolishment of torture during investigation. In 1877, he headed the Prosecution Bureau of Ministry of Justice. After his service as *Taishinin* Chief Justice ended in 1881 for Tamano's resumption of the same post, he returned to Ministry to Justice as *Shihōkyō* (Minister of Justice). This rank was higher than *Taishinin* Chief Justice. In 1883, he was appointed as councillor of *Motorōin* but passed away in the same year. Kishira was an openminded senior judicial bureaucrat but with a strong sense of loyalty to the Emperor. Especially, *seishi* (Emperor's holy order) twice appeared in his opinions on necessity of judicial reform and the necessity of judicial and administrative police for state polity in 1875.

1.7.4.3 Ozaki Chūji

Ozaki Chūji served as *Taishinin* Chief Justice from 1886 until 1890 when *Saibansho-kōseihō* (Court Structure Law) was promulgated. He was born in 1831 as the second son of a samurai family in Tosa. He also succeeded his father's *hanshi* (samurai belonging to a clan) status after feudal education. In 1870, he joined the Department of Criminal Law under the Ministry of Justice. In 1870, he worked as *Keihō-daikaibu* (senior official handling criminal litigation), which was a very feudalistic title for a high-ranking official of the Ministry of Justice to handle litigation. His duty was responsible for interrogating suspects in criminal cases. In 1872, Ozaki was appointed as a judge by the Minister of Justice. One year later, he was promoted to *Shihō-kenchū-hanji* (judge of intermediate rank). Although it was the early stage of the Meiji Restoration, the very old fashion post titles of *daikaibu* and *hanji* remained, which had been used and recorded in *Ryonogigei* (Collection of Commentary on the *Ritsuryō* Code) in the Japanese judicial historical institutionalism since 833.

In 1877, Ozaki was the justice in charge of Nagasaki High Court. Thereafter, he served in various cities as a judge until his *Taishinin* Chief Justice appointment in August 1886. In 1888, he doubled down the post of the President of the High Court under the Minister of Justice simultaneously. Soon after his retirement from *Taishinin* in 1890, he accepted the job offer of *Sūmitsukomon-kan* (Privy Councillor offering advice to the Emperor) and was honoured as *danshaku* (baron) of *kazoku* (nobility clan). It is noteworthy that after Ozaki's retirement in 1890, there was still no specific formal legal qualification requirement for the post of *Taishinin* Chief Justice before the codification of Article 70 of *Saibansho-kōseihō* in the same year (Konakamura 1903, p. 91).

1.7.4.4 Education Background and Bureaucrat Career

As an institution of its own organizational culture, the Ministry of Justice, like most similar institutions in other countries, had its own law school for internal socialization and legal education (Cook 1971, p. 253–254). Among the twenty *Taishinin* Chief Justices appointed after Ozaki Chūji and *Saiban-shokōseihō* in 1890, Nishi Narinori, Nanbu Mikao, Kojima Korekata and Namura Yasuzō mainly received the traditional neo-Confucian education. Miyoshi Taizō and Yokota Kuniomi were graduates of Keio University. Hayashi Raizaburō graduated from Chuo University. The last *Taishinin* Chief Justice, Hosono Nagayoshi was a graduate of Kyoto University. The remaining 12 Chief Justices were either graduates of *Shihōshō-hōgakkō* (Law School of the Ministry of Justice) which was under the direct command of the Ministry of Justice, or Tokyo University. The thirteenth, Tomitani Shoutarou was the first *Taishinin* Chief Justice graduated from *Shihōshō-hōgakkō*, where some students were even sent abroad for legal study, especially France (Okubo 1998, p. 1–18).

Some *Taishinin* Chief Justices who laid the foundation of *Taishinin*'s working culture after 1890 were actually former bureaucrats of the Meiji Government. The most symbolic example is Nishi Narinori. With a family background of samurai in Fuchu Domain, Nishi debuted his civil service career with the post of *Gaikoku-bugyō-shihai-kumigashira* (Head of the Diplomatic Affairs Group). At the end of the Edo era, *Gaikoku-bugyō* was the shogunate official handling diplomatic affairs, especially trade relationship and other actions under the shogunate guideline of traditional

Japanese legal value of *dōri*[4], which as a Japanese jurisprudential concept, was integrated with the interpretation of international treaty law. This post existed during 1854 to 1868. In 1871, Nishi changed his job to a class-six official of the Ministry of Justice as a *sanji* (councillor) of Shizuoka Domain. Afterwards, he climbed up his judicial career ladder through the post as the chief justice of Tokyo Appeal Court. In August 1890, he became *Taishinin* Chief Justice after Ozaki Chūji.[5]

Nanbu Mikao became the acting *Taishinin* Chief Justice in 1891 due to the sudden death of Nishi. He was a politician and a member of the conservative *Tosakin'nōtō* (Tosa Loyalist Party) before the Meiji Restoration. His first job was *hyōbu-shōroku* (army officer of intermediate rank) which was irrelevant with law. With the honour of *danshaku*, in June 1896, he was awarded his second appointment as the eleventh *Taishinin* Chief Justice and his term continued for ten years. In July 1906, he was further promoted to *Sūmitsukomon-kan* (Privy Councillor).[6]

Namura Yasuzō had been the acting *Taishinin* Chief Justice for six months from 24 August 1892 to 3 March 1893. His bureaucrat career started as a *bakushin* (vassal or stateman) of the bakufu and acted as a senior interpreter of Nagasaki Prefecture and professor of the Bureau of French Studies with his language proficiency in Dutch, English, German and French. In 1872, he joined the Ministry of Justice as an official and participated in the legal research in Europe with the minister, Eto Shinpei. In 1874, he accompanied Okubo Toshimichi to Qing China for diplomatic negotiation of *the Taiwan Incident* in 1874 when the Meiji government sent troops to the island of Taiwan. He was then shifted to the legal job of *Shihō-daishokikan-kenji* (senior judicial prosecutor).

It is noteworthy that the tenth, Miyoshi Taizō, was the first *Taishinin* Chief Justice who completely received formal legal education in a private university and graduated from Keio University. Miyoshi was also a former bureaucrat in *Taishoukyoku* which was a government department that received and processed citizens' grievances and opinions. As a bureaucrat, he was transferred to the Ministry of Justice. He was appointed as *shihō-shōfu*, the third rank judicial official which was one rank lower than the senior judge in the organization. Additionally, he engaged in a European travel for the purpose of conducting research on the judicial system under the supervision of Ito Hirofumi.[7]

1.7.4.5 Socialization in Samurai Family

It has been demonstrated that the majority of *Taishinin* Chief Justices had undergone samurai family socialization during their childhood. Socialization is defined as the process by which individuals, including judges, internalize the norms, values,

[4] The original text of the *dōri* principle of shogunate: 交易筋は勿論,条約相振候儀は道理を詰,幾応も穏申論。On this see Shimamura (1994, p. 31).

[5] On this see Asahi Shimbun Publishing (1994).

[6] Ibid.

[7] Ibid.

customs and ideologies of their respective communities and broader societies (Clausen 1968, p. 5). In the attitudinal model of judicial behaviour, socialization is understood to relate to the motivational assumption that judicial decisions are motivated by a judge's sincere attitudes and values concerning the facts of a case. Legislation has been demonstrated to exhibit a positive correlation with prevailing dominant attitudes. This phenomenon prompts individuals to reevaluate their beliefs concerning the approval or disapproval of deviant behaviours and to align their actions accordingly (McAdams 2000, pp. 339–340, p. 343).

The early Meiji era was a period marked by the overturning of regional domains under daimyo and the entire removal of class privileges associated with samurai status. Following the three pioneering Chief Justices in 1890, all subsequent *Taishinin* Chief Justice similarly had socialization through traditional samurai families. Family, school and religion are non-legal institutions that are organized around vertical hierarchies of different authorities. These hierarchies are characterized by their phenomenologically similar structure. It is the process by which values, attitudes and beliefs about the legitimacy of a behaviour are developed (Fine and Trinkner 2020). It is not possible to eliminate the possibility of a connection between *Taishinin* Chief Justices' childhood socialization in samurai families and their conservative attitudinal judicial behaviour in corruption cases.

1.8 *Taishinin*'s Judicial Behaviour and Hegemonic Governance in State Polity

In the field of legal studies, the terms positivist and positivism are often employed in a rather expansive manner. Positivists tend to argue that the legal system in a society is dependent on administrative structures of governance, rather than the extent to which it satisfies such canon ideals as justice, democracy, and/or the rule of law.[8] In the context of positivism, *Taishinin* and the Ministry of Justice were functionalist institutions that functioned as instruments of governance, rather than as instruments of legal justice. Justice is not always coterminous with rule of law in the Western sense. At times, it is rather its own distinctive domain. The objective of prewar hegemonic governance in Japan was not to guarantee equal freedom, human rights, democratic elections, or the autonomy of individuals. Rather, it was to ensure the loyalty and obedience of the populace to the Emperor and the stability of governance. The earliest documented instance of a legendary social relation in Japanese vertical society, which was based on the divinity of the hegemonic Emperor at the peak, can be traced back to the third century (Toby 1984, p. 213). In the context of prewar Japan, the paramount concern was the preservation of the prevailing social order, characterized by a strong sense of social hierarchy and authority (Bellah 1970, pp. 114–117). The prewar Japanese legal system, characterized by its adherence

[8] See "Legal Positivism" at https://plato.stanford.edu/entries/legal-positivism. Accessed 1 September 2025.

to constitutional monarchic jurisprudence, sought to ensure widespread acceptance by focusing on the legitimacy of governance. *Taishinin*'s judicial behaviour aimed at law enforcement against bureaucratic corruption. It played a significant role in this endeavour, with the purity of hegemonic power originating from the Emperor being strictly regulated. The role of *Taishinin*, serving as the final appellate court, was subject to the undue influence of the Ministry of Justice. This book elucidates the manner in which the Ministry of Justice wielded disproportionate influence over *Taishinin*'s judicial conduct within the context of a state polity characterized by an absence of genuine separation of powers.

The term, state polity, adverse to democracy appears frequently hereinafter in most chapters of this book. The original thought of state polity for restoration of imperial rule was advocated in the historical book Hoken Daiki written by a Confucian Kuriyama Senpō, alias Kuriyama Gen, in 1689 though similar term had been used in Chinese classics and ancient Japan (Satomi 1942, p. 123). Both officials and subjects should have *hōtai* (reverential acceptance) of the Emperor's governance and protection of *tennō-shuken* (imperial sovereignty). The Privy Councillor Motoda Eifu's *Kensei Ikensho* (Constitutional Opinions) in June 1879 suggested national Shintoism to integrate within state polity in order to rationalize the Emperor as a living God (Numata 1986, pp. 3–5). The seeds of a nationwide bureaucracy under the Emperor in state polity were finally sown through the Meiji Constitution (Carpenter 2003, pp. 53–54), which stipulated the whole judiciary and all government officials to be under the Emperor. Therefore, *Taishinin* was not granted exemption.

1.9 Judicial Behaviour of "Japanese Body in a Western Jacket"

This book makes a contribution to the academic discourse on the judicial phenomenon of "Japanese body in a Western jacket". In the context of prewar Japan, the Penal Code of 1907 emerged neither as a product of domestic legal development over the preceding 1500 years nor as a result of a popular referendum following extensive public discourse. Despite the absence of significant criticism regarding its implementation, *Taishinin*'s assessments, when considered in their entirety, exhibited a notable degree of rationality and fairness. These assessments align with the established Japanese legal principles against corruption, as outlined in Chap. 3. In order to avert the potential for being constrained by illegitimacy in this particular context, *Taishinin*'s exercise of judicial authority to criminalize corruption in the five cases examined in this book was found to be sufficiently rational to individuals outside the legal community.

For many decades following the implementation of the Penal Code of 1907, *Taishinin* confronted challenges concerning legal principles and traditional Japanese legal values as articulated in Articles 197 and 198 of the Penal Code, which had been adopted from Germanic legal traditions. In the event that Germanic criminal law concepts are expressed in such general terms as those found in Penal Code 1907, there should be ample room for conceptual differences with regard to *Taishinin*'s judicial behaviour in terms of criminalizing it. This judicial receptivity in legal transplantation is often referred to as the "Japanese body in a Western jacket", yet there is a paucity of literature that provides a comprehensive account of its functionality. The book tries hard to provide it.

1.10 Chapter Outline

The book is composed of ten chapters. This chapter functions as an introduction, in which the overarching framework of the book is delineated. Chapter 2 delineates the scope and methodologies employed in the examination of corruption theories, neither of which enjoy universal acceptance. Chapter 3 offers a comprehensive examination of the phenomenon of bribery and corruption within the context of Japanese legislation from the ancient era to the Meiji period.

In Chaps. 4 through 8, examinations of five corruption cases are conducted. It is evident that no two *Taishinin* cases are precisely analogous. The appellants in the five cases under consideration belong to a diverse group, including Tokyo City Assembly members, media professional, politicians from major political parties, administrative and judicial police officers, as well as teachers, brothel owners and fishmongers. The case backgrounds also vary. For instance, the reconstruction of Tokyo in the aftermath of the Great Kantō earthquake, as well as the development of the prewar sex industry, are notable cases in point.

After the in-depth case analysis is conducted, Chap. 9 elucidates the multi-faceted factors that exert a significant influence on *Taishinin*'s judicial behaviour in the decision-making process. The factors under consideration ranged from judges' personalities to *Taishinin*'s special role in the social hierarchy of state polity. The conclusion of the study made specific reference to fair society studies in Chap. 10. At present, an absolute standard for assessing judicial behaviour that is agreed upon by all is lacking. The concept of a fair society is predicated on the notion that it represents the pinnacle of societal ideals, wherein each individual is entitled to their fair share of resources and opportunities.

1.11 Impacts of *Taishinin* Judgements Remain

Taishinin's judicial behaviour with regard to corruption is socially responsive to prewar Japan. This is achieved through overt legal reasoning, which integrates divergent and dissenting opinions to confront legal and moral principles. This perspective aligns with a historical institutionalist framework, offering an analysis of law as a historical artefact and the ongoing discourse between societal entities and judicial institutions. Judicial behaviour of rule of law is widely regarded as a hallmark of the modern democratic state. It is considered a fundamental pillar of a fair society.

In stark contrast to the more individualistic postwar Constitution of 1947, *Taishinin*'s judicial behaviour under the "social contract" of the Meiji Constitution played no special role in checking and balancing power. In Chap. 9, the authors cite incidents to illustrate the undue influence exerted by the Ministry of Justice and its manipulation of *Taishinin*'s judicial behaviour. *Taishinin*'s judicial behaviour can also be understood as a response to the persistent social injustice inherent in the prewar state polity. The elements of social order that were in place under the state polity have now been rendered non-existent by the new Constitution of 1947. However, the legal influence of rulings in *Taishinin* judgements remains in effect until they are overruled by new court rulings. In next chapter, the nature and categorization of judicial behaviour models is explored.

References

Babb, J. (2005) Corruption and governance in Japan (pp. 174–191). In: Glenn D. Hook (ed.), *Contested Governance* (1st ed.). Routledge.

Bellah, R. (1970) *Beyond belief: Essays on Religion in a Post-Traditionalist World*. University of California Press.

Benedict, R. (1954) *The Chrysanthemum and the Sword*. Charles E. Tuttle Company.

Besley, T. (2006) *Principled Agents? The Political Economy of Good Government*. Oxford University Press.

Britannica "Linguistic anthropology". https://www.britannica.com/science/anthropology/Linguistic-anthropology#ref839712. Accessed 1 September 2025.

Carpenter, S. (2003) *Special Corporations and the Bureaucracy: Why Japan Can't Reform*. Palgrave Macmillan.

Chandler, D. (2024) *Free and equal: a manifesto for a just society*. Alfred A. Knopf.

Coney, J. M., O' Barr W. M., and Riner, R. C. (2019) *Just Words: Law, Language, and Power* (3rd ed.). University of Chicago Press.

Cook, B. B. (1971) The Socialization of New Federal Judges: Impact on District Court Business. *Washington University Law Quarterly*, Vol. 1971 (2), 253–279.

Edelbacher, M., Bojan, D., Peter, C. K. (2016) *Corruption, fraud, organized crime, and the shadow economy*. CRC Press.

Farazmand, A. (2009) *Bureaucracy and Administration*. CRC Press.

Fine, A. D., Trinkner, R. (2020) Legal Socialization. In Gurung, R. ed. *Routledge Psychology in the Real World. Routledge.*

Fukuyama, M. (2017) Shihō Shokumu Seitei kara Daishin'in Secchi-go made no Keiji Saiban Seido to Shihōshō (The Criminal Justice System and the Ministry of Justice from the Establishment of Judicial Duties to the Establishment of the Supreme Court). *Fukuoka Daigaku Hōgaku Ronsō (Fukuoka University Law Journal)*, Vol. 67 (3), 735–774.

George, T. E. (2008) *From Judge to Justice: Social Background Theory and the Supreme Court*, 86 North Carolina Law Review, 1333-1366.

Gillespie, J. (2001) Globalization and Legal Transplantation: Lessons from the Past. *Law Review* 6(2), 286-311.

Holmes, L. (2015) *Corruption A Very Short Introduction*. Oxford University Press.

Hough, D. (2013) *Corruption, Anti-Corruption and Governance*. Palgrave Macmillan.

Iida, Y. (2018) Tamano Seiri and Yamada Akiyoshi. *Hōmu Kenkyū(Legal Research)*, No. 15 (1), 1–9.

Iwatani, J. (2008) Dejitaru de Tsumugu Fukuzawa Yukichi no Hō no Kotoba: Kenri, Kenri, Tsūgi (The Legal Words of Yukichi Fukuzawa Digitally Spinned: Rights, Rights, and Common Senses). *Keio University Media Center MediaNet*, No. 15, 38–40.

Izuhara, M. (1982) Meiji Shoki ni okeru Kenri Kannen ni tsuite (On the Concept of Rights in the Early Meiji Era). *Social Science of Research Institute for Humanities, Doshisha University*, No.29, 63–94.

Kocsis, R. N. (2007) *Criminal Profiling: International Theory, Research, and Practice.* Humana Press Inc.

Konakamura, K. (1903) *Ryō no Gige Kōgi (Lecture on Ryōnogige).* Yoshikawa Kobunkan.

Massey, A. (2012) *International Handbook on Civil Service Systems.* Edward Elgar.

Maxfield, M. G., Earl R. B. (2015) *Research Methods for Criminal Justice and Criminology.* Wadsworth Publishing.

McAdams, R. H. (2000) An Attitudinal Theory of Expressive Law. *Oregon Law Review*, Vol. 79 (2), 339–390.

Nakamura, H. (2008) Kindaiteki Shihō Seido no Seiritsu to Gaikokuhō no Eikyō (Establishment of the Modern Judicial System and the Influence of Foreign Laws). *Waseda Hōgaku (Waseda Legal Studies)*, Vol. 42 (1–2), 261–304.

Newburn, T. (2017) *Criminology.* Routledge.

NHK Broadcasting Culture Research Institute. ed. (2005) Kotoba no Handobukku Dai 2-han (The Language Handbook, 2nd ed.). NHK Broadcasting Culture Research Institute.

Okubo, T. (1998) Meiji Shoki, Pari Daigaku Hōgakubu Nihonjin Gakusei no Ryūgaku Kiroku (1): Shihōshō Hōgakkō Seito o Chūshin to shite (Records of Japanese students studying abroad at the Faculty of Law at the University of Paris in the early Meiji period (1): Focusing on students at the Ministry of Justice Law School). *Tōkyō Daigakushi Kiyō (Bulletin of the University of Tokyo)*, Vol. 16, 1–19.

Plaček, M. et al. (2022) Historical institutionalism: a tool for researching the nonprofit sector in times of pandemic. *Innovation: The European Journal of Social Science Research*, 37(4), 926–940.

Rawls, J. (1971) *A Theory of Justice* (Original Ed.). Belknap Press of Harvard University Press.

Shimamura, M. (1994) Bakumatsu Tsūshō Gaikō Seisaku no Tenkan (Changes in trade and foreign policy at the end of the Edo period). *Kanagawa Kenritsu Hakubutsukan Kenkyū Hōkoku: Jinbun Kagaku (Kanagawa Prefectural Museum Research Report: Humanities)*, No. 20, 28–53.

Stanford Encyclopedia of Philosophy "Legal Positivism" https://plato.stanford.edu/entries/legal-positivism Accessed 1 September 2025

Toby, R. P. (1984) *State and Diplomacy in Early Modern Japan: Asia in the Development of the Tokugawa Bakufu.* Princeton University Press.

Transparency International "Corruption Perception Index" https://www.transparency.org/en/cpi/2020/index Accessed 1 September 2025

Takada, A. (2019) Socialization Practices Regarding Shame in Japanese Caregiver–Child Interactions. *Frontiers in Psychology* 10(1545), 1-14.

Takami, K. (2001) Kōza Tantō-sha kara Mita Kenpoku Gakusetsu no Shosō: Nihon Kenpōgakushi Kenkyū Josetsu (Aspects of Constitutional Theory from the Perspective of a Course Instructor: An Introduction to Research on the History of Japanese Constitutional Law). *Hokudai Hōgaku Ronshū (Hokkaido University Law Review)*, Vol. 52 (3), 803–840.

Tierney, J. (2006) *Criminology: Theory and context* (2nd ed.). Longman.

Tushnet, M. (2009) Judicial Leadership. In Kane, J. et al ed. *Dispersed Democratic Leadership: Origins, Dynamics, and Implications* (pp. 141–160). Oxford University Press.

Watanabe, T. (1994) Chihōkan Kaigi to Chihōmin Kai (Local Government Meeting and Local People's Association). *Sundai Shigaku (Sundai Historiography)*, Vol. 90, 214–253.

Chapter 2
Literature Review of Judicial Behaviour Models

2.1 Introduction

The question of whether judges consider law and justice when making decisions in court cases is complex. Judges frequently assert their independence, claiming the capacity to make decisions based on legal principles to achieve justice. This concept is sometimes referred to as the "judicial autonomy of the rule of law", which posits that the law should be adhered to and not employed to make unjust decisions. This chapter elucidates the limitations of our ability to ascertain the attainment of this objective. This understanding, among other things, is evidenced by the findings court decision may involve judges' personal bias, stereotypes, injustice and reverse causality. Reverse causation is defined as the interaction between two variables in which the observed relationship between one variable does not align with the expected causal direction (Staton 2018, pp. 598–620). The outcome of a court case is influenced by numerous factors. On occasion, the court's actions fall short of the standard of excellence that is generally anticipated. This chapter mainly delineates three basic models of judicial behaviour: attitudinal, strategic and historical institutionalist. These models facilitate comprehension of the exploration, description and explanation of *Taishinin*'s judicial behaviour in corruption cases presented in this book. Research on judicial behaviour originated in the United States. However, this research field is still in its developmental stages in Japan. This chapter is principally concerned with research on the judicial behaviour studies in the United States.

2.1.1 Model of Judicial Behaviour and Judicial Decision-Making

Researchers have long been perplexed and intrigued by the manner in which judges arrive at their decisions. The field of judicial behaviour studies is concerned with

K. B. Wong and S. L. Fang, *Taishinin's Judicial Behaviour in Corruption Cases*,
https://doi.org/10.1007/978-981-95-5823-0_2

the analysis of the decision-making processes undertaken by courts in the context of judicial proceedings. This concept also functions as a legal theory. Tate proposed a methodology for the study of judicial behaviour. His approach involves the consideration of the study's purpose, the unit of analysis and the time dimension (Tate 1983, pp. 52–53). Judges are expected to articulate their decisions as the optimal choice within the framework of legal rules and doctrines or the legislative intent inherent in each court case. The particulars of this approach are subject to variation, depending on the jurisdiction and the circumstantial factors of the case (Segal 2008, pp. 19–33). For instance, court martial and its case natures are distinct from other courts in the judicial hierarchy. *Taishinin* also played a distinctive role in prewar Japanese society.

It is a misconception to assume that judges make decisions solely based on legal principles and principles of justice. Donald Black expounds on the notion that the societal milieu in which a judge operates exerts a significant influence on the judicial decisions rendered by him. Black proposes that we should examine how other factors influence the court's judicial behaviour. He defines it as "the amount of governmental authority brought to bear on the judicial decision of a person or group". The legal system is contingent upon the cultural, political organizational and social control mechanisms inherent within a given society. His research focuses on the legal decision-making processes of judges in various social contexts (Black 1976, p. 63, p. 86, p. 107). Judges' decisions are influenced by a multitude of factors that extend beyond a superficial understanding and application of legal principles to the facts of a case. Ultimately, the judge-made laws and court decisions on a particular type of case may establish a model for how judges behave in various situations (Posner 2005, p. 1259).

Early research on judicial behaviour facilitates comprehension of the interplay among law, politics and culture. These phenomena are addressed within the framework of either legal realism or legal formalism. Legal formalism, a type of jurisprudence, is predicated on rules and laws, eschewing considerations such as intuition, policy and non-legal elements. During the early twentieth century, prominent scholars such as Edward Corwin regarded it as a means to comprehend justice, rather than as a field of legal study (Murphy and Tanenhaus 1972, p. 13). This approach is referred to by political scientists as the "legal model" of judicial decision-making. The legal formalism model is predicated on the principle of rules that are derived and applied through a neutral legal reasoning process for the purpose of judicial decision-making. According to this model, court decisions are value-free and have no necessity for judge-made law. Factors such as a judge's political beliefs, the political party they belong to, their personal traits and their social background are not considered.[1] It is a set of rules for understanding, explaining and assessing legal decisions. In essence, the legal framework under scrutiny encompasses a precise enumeration of legal terms, with the offender being exonerated from the requirement of intentional or awareness-based engagement with these terms (Green 2005, pp. 2–3). Illegal parking is an offence without checking the driver's intention. This scenario bears resemblance to a strict liability offence in legal studies. *Taishinin*

[1] On this see Segal and Spaeth (1993, 1996a and 1996b).

also employed the "strict liability model" to adjudicate cases of corruption through Chaps. 4 to 8 in this book.

2.1.2 Legal Realism and Judicial Behaviour

Conventional legal research is predicated on legal formalism, which is defined as the study of the formulation and implementation of legal instruments. Legal realism is another distinct concept, as it examines the impact of unacknowledged courtroom practices on judicial decisions (Llewellyn 1930, pp. 443–445, p. 448, p. 464). Legal realism is the concept that judges arrive at legal decisions prior to examining the established rules. In common law countries such as the United States and the United Kingdom, judicial policy principles are often employed to formulate new court rulings, thereby establishing legal precedent. Judges have been known to justify their pre-decided decisions by presenting them as formal court rulings with legal authority. This is a judicial strategy to achieve a goal. Personal factors have been demonstrated to exert influence on the decisions rendered by courts. The personal qualities and political views of the judge can influence their decision (Tumonis 2012, p. 1362, pp. 1365–1366). Bingham offers the earliest summary of the characteristics of realists' judicial behaviour. These characteristics include arguments within the purview of government, objectivity for the analysis of legal institutions and judge-made law. Judge-made law is a strategic toolkit that facilitates the categorization and communication of legal knowledge (Bingham 1912, pp. 109–120). In Japan, the late Dando Shigemitsu serves as a prime example of this phenomenon. He previously served as Chief Justice of the Supreme Court of Japan. He is renowned for his advocacy against capital punishment, a position he had steadfastly upheld. Fair society studies demonstrates that the judicial behaviour of strategic legal realism can be utilized to enhance democracy and freedom for fair social cooperation.

Early American legal realists, including Karl Llewellyn and Jerome Frank, pioneered a synthesis of legal scholarship with the social sciences. This prompted further investigation into the behavioural patterns exhibited by judges (Ingersoll and Karl 1996, p. 264). Judges are constrained not only by the particular institutional context, but also by social constraints, particularly the sociopolitical environment within which the judicial institution is situated (Gibson 1983). To illustrate, the social, political and legal environment of *Taishinin* is unsurprisingly and considerably divergent from that of contemporary Supreme Court of Japan. In their work, Epstein and Weinshall explore the judicial decision-making process. Judges are known to deliberate on the actions they wish to pursue, the desires of the individuals involved and the established principles of the institutions and other groups (Epstein and Weinshall 2021, p. 3). This cognitive approach mirrors the theoretical frameworks and methodologies that are typically explored within the domain of business education, especially organizational behaviour studies. The association of this approach is like legal behaviouralism in the United States (Segal and Spaeth 1993, pp. 65–69).

An example is legislation facilitating the formal recognition of same-sex partnerships through legal frameworks, such as "civil union" exemplifies the tenets of legal realism. The establishment of these legal provisions was precipitated by the evolution and interaction of both the judicial system and societal norms.

2.1.3 Judicial Behaviour as Quantitative or Qualitative Research

Quantitative research method for studying how judges make decisions seems straightforward. This statistical approach facilitates the comparison and verification of court decisions, ensuring that they are grounded in rational reasoning. Lijphart classified this methodology into the following categories: experimental, statistical, comparative and case study methods (Lijphart 1971).

Conversely, qualitative methodologies are often regarded as superior. Harry Thomas Edwards, the former Chief Judge of the United States Court of Appeals for the District of Columbia Circuit in Washington, D.C., shared his insights on the subject of judicial behaviour analysis: "It is reasonable to hypothesize that judicious statistical analysis, when interpreted with precision, can elucidate the decision-making processes of judges. However, scholars of a serious disposition who wish to study the work of the courts cannot disregard the judges' personal experiences. It is imperative to acknowledge the significance and veracity of these experiences (Edwards 1998, pp. 1337–1338)". In order to comprehend the thought processes and emotional states of judges within the judicial system, as well as their interactions with each other, it is imperative to undertake a thorough examination of the terminology employed in judicial opinions and rulings. For analysis of *Taishinin* judgements from Chaps. 4 to 8 in this book, the two authors of this book also adopt linguistic discourse method of Harry Thomas Edwards accordingly.

If each judge makes decisions solely based on what he/she believes is right for a particular case, without being influenced by outside factors, we can expect a variety of outcomes under different beliefs. This approach, rather than one influenced by external pressures or group dynamics, will yield a set of results that is more random and individualized. The composition of this book is not imperative. A seminal group of researchers in the field of judicial behaviouralists, including Herman Pritchett, Robert Dahl, Walter Murphy, Sydney Ulmer, Glendon Schubert and Martin Shapiro, initiated the study of judicial behaviour as a distinct hybrid sub-discipline of law and political science. Nancy Maveety has categorized judicial behaviour studies into three primary classifications. These categories facilitate easy comprehension of the rationale behind judicial decisions and their ramifications for society. The categories under consideration are the attitudinal, strategic and historical institutionalist models (Maveety 2006, pp. ix-viii). The following review will examine the contributions of early scholars in the field of judicial behaviour, as they pertain to Maveety's three models.

2.2 The Attitudinal Model

Attitudinalism posits that the behaviours exhibited by the legal system can be elucidated by examining the prevailing norms and values. This encompasses the notion that judges' individual political inclinations may influence their judicial decisions in court cases (Cameron and Kornhauser 2017, p. 536). The utilization of law for the purpose of obscuring political motivations rather than fostering justice through the attitudinal model has been a subject of considerable debate. The attitudinal model, in its essence, repudiates the notion that legal decisions are influenced by ideological factors. Judges are granted a significant degree of discretion in determining the outcome of legal cases. This suggests that judicial decisions may be influenced by personal beliefs or values. This phenomenon is referred to as "judicial politics" (Perino 2006, pp. 497–498). The objective nature of legal decisions is not universally upheld. The decision is influenced by the personal beliefs of the judges. Judges are often accused of a lack of impartiality, particularly in cases involving moral issues such as abortion. The influence of mass media and public opinion is especially significant in the legal reasoning process in abortion cases (Geyh 2021, p. 1107, p. 1079, pp. 1081–1083).

The attitudinal model is a conceptual framework that elucidates the cognitive processes underlying judicial decision-making. This approach is predicated on the assumption that judges consider legal facts as well as their own personal beliefs and values. Legal facts are defined as statements regarding an event, occurrence, or state of affairs that have been formally declared to have occurred within the context of a court case. Judges utilize these facts to inform legal decisions. The veracity of legal facts is not absolute; they may be partially true or false, or a combination of both. In the attitudinal model, case-specific factors influence judges' ideologies. If the majority of judges in analogous cases adhere to analogous ideas and values, it is likely that they will reach similar conclusions, resulting in a discernible pattern in their behaviours. The majority of judges exhibit analogous preferences when making judicial decisions, thereby facilitating the anticipation of the outcomes of analogous court cases. A prominent illustration of this phenomenon is *giri-ninjō*, a concept in Japanese culture that underscores a profound sense of responsibility and respect for others. However, it is important to note that the legal system in another part of the world may not necessarily adhere to the same cultural values. Gibson elucidates that the decisions rendered by judges are indicative of their conception of what is optimal for society (Gibson 1983, p. 9).

2.2.1 Herman Pritchett's Attitudinal Model

In the late 1930s, the political scientist Herman Pritchett initiated a research project on the Justices of the Supreme Court of the United States. During the 1930s, the Supreme Court of the United States expressed opposition to President Roosevelt's New Deal policies. Roosevelt's triumph in the 1936 election was characterized by a substantial margin, thereby bestowing upon him the capacity to exert significant influence over the rulings of the US Supreme Court (Jeff 2010, p. 12). He endeavoured to appoint judges to the Supreme Court who would concur with his ideologies (Pritchett 1948, p. 57, p. 92). The manner in which judges executed their duties was influenced by the political authority wielded by Roosevelt.

Pritchett's research revealed that the life experiences of US Supreme Court Justices influenced their legal decision-making and legal interpretation. Judges interpreted the laws in a manner influenced by their personal experiences (Pritchett 1941, p. 895, p. 898). Pritchett conducted additional research on specific factors related to each case and the lives of individual judges. He presented a summary of how Supreme Court Justices' political preferences affected their interpretation of the Constitution for Roosevelt's policies (Pritchett 1948, p. xi, p. xiv). Pritchett's finding is logical, as decisions are informed by experience and cognitive frameworks. Similarly, graduates from law schools at Japanese imperial universities prior to the war also wielded significant influence over the appointment of judges. A significant proportion of these individuals attended the same educational institutions and hailed from comparable familial backgrounds. As mentioned in Chap. 1, these individuals were raised in samurai families under the impact of similar culture.

Pritchett's research on Supreme Court justices' decisions in national security and personal rights cases is widely regarded as a seminal landmark in judicial behaviour studies. The conservatism of his work is evidenced by his unwillingness to acknowledge the significance of judicial decisions that promote human rights. He even stigmatized these decisions as "sects and schisms" (Pritchett 1961, p. viii, p. 168). The efficacy of Pritchett's employment of statistical data is called into question, as it does not provide a clear indication of the prevalence of human rights abuses (Pritchett 1968, pp. 152–155). Utilizing quantitative analysis, a specific type of data analysis, the researcher examined the relationship between judges' personal histories and their influence on public policy (Pritchett 1968, pp. 484–487, pp. 490–491, pp. 499–509). It is erroneous to assume that judges arrive at decisions based solely on their personal convictions regarding political, social and economic matters (Pritchett 1948, p. 263). Researchers must examine social conditions in greater detail to ensure the reliability of statistics. The number itself is incomplete without additional evidence from a qualitative analysis. Pritchett's stance on human rights issues is a matter of concern. He perceives these groups as discrete entities, and he does not advocate for the concept of a fair society in which all individuals possess the autonomy to exercise their own discretion regarding matters of significant importance to the sustainability of society.

2.2.2 Glendon Schubert's Attitudinal Model

Schubert's seminal works in 1958, 1959, and 1963 marked a significant shift in his legal scholarship, transitioning from a focus on public law analysis to a more behavioural study of judicial decision-making.[2] His approach incorporated a mathematical statistical analysis. Pritchett's methodology for the analysis of judicial voting patterns in higher education issues served as the foundational framework for his subsequent academic work, entitled *Quantitative Analysis of Judicial Behaviour*.[3] In *The Judicial Mind*, Schubert examined the actions of the US Supreme Court over a lengthy period of 17 years. He employed a synthesis of conservatism, liberalism and a pragmatic conservatism that was moderate to elucidate political judgement. This objective was pursued by means of an examination of the economic circumstances of both the affluent and the impoverished (Schubert 1965, p. 101, p. 295). And he employed an attitudinal model to examine the legal decisions of the Australian Dixon High Court from 1951 to 1961.[4] Pritchett and Schubert are engaged in a discourse regarding the extent to which quantitative research can adequately capture the attitudes of judges. This methodological problem is of consequence. He further elaborated: "The fundamental purpose of the opinion-writing ritual is to furnish justifications that will shield the justices from both personal criticism and personal accountability for their decisions" (Schubert 1965, p. 14). Opinion writing that seeks to elucidate legal decisions is predominantly concerned with the articulation of ideas and arguments, rather than with the mere presentation of numerical data.

2.2.3 Power in Attitudinal Model

Pritchett and Schubert rarely discuss the fact that Supreme Court judges possess unchallengeable power to make decisions, a distinction that distinguishes courts from other social institutions. Spaeth asserts that the Supreme Court's authority to adjudicate legal disputes frequently rests on the discretion of the judges (Spaeth 1962, p. 54). In the course of the initial eight terms of US Supreme Court Justice Warren's tenure (1953–1960), a total of 52 civil liberties cases were adjudicated. Of these, seven cases were determined on the basis of the Supreme Court's judicial activism of new rulings. This indicates that the court exercised its discretion, deviating from the precedent established in case laws (Spaeth 1962, p. 56). Judicial attitudes may be influenced by political factors or personal responses to specific issues. This phenomenon constituted a fundamental component of the judicial discretion and judicial activism paradigm (Spaeth 1962, p. 55, p. 82). In this particular instance, *Taishinin* similarly exercised its judicial power for judicial activism to determine how customary gift-giving be criminalized and contingent upon the fulfilment of the stipulated legal criteria.

The attitudinal model's application extends beyond the mere analysis of political preferences. *The Study of Public Law*, authored by Murphy and Tanenhaus, elucidates the utilization of law in decision-making processes, the mechanisms by which judges

[2] On this see Schubert (1958, 1959 and 1963).

[3] On this see Schubert (1960).

[4] On this see Schubert (1969).

are selected and the subsequent impacts on society. This objective is pursued by means of an examination of public law. Murphy and Tanenhaus concur with Pritchett and Schubert on the significance of deliberating on the distinction between right and wrong. The consensus was similarly reached that judges' attitudes exert a significant influence on the manner in which they exercise their discretionary judicial power.[5]

In their influential work, Segal and Spaeth advanced the hypothesis that the political inclinations of US Supreme Court justices accounted for 70 per cent of their decisions, a claim that was substantiated by statistical data rather than factors from qualitative analysis. The study's primary focus was on the manner in which judges' attitudes influence their personal ideological policy preferences and the extent of their power in judicial decision-making process within the Supreme Court. This notion is thoroughly delineated in their book, *The Attitudinal Model Revisited*. A study of Supreme Court judges revealed that they possess a high degree of autonomy in making judicial policy decisions (Spaeth and Segal 2002, p. 10, p. 12, p. 44). The government's public policy and its judicial policy preferences interact directly with each other. Attitudinal judicial behaviour is defined as a set of beliefs about an object or situation that persist over an extended period. The determination of judicial policy preferences for the involved parties is determined by the judge and is always based on the available evidence (Spaeth and Segal 2002, pp. 76–77, pp. 91–96, pp. 99–111).

Segal and Cover's study employed an innovative methodology to assess the ideological inclinations of US Supreme Court justices. Utilizing a content analysis of editorials published in four prominent newspapers, the researchers examined the sentiments expressed regarding the nominees upon their nomination as judges.[6] This method of analysing newspaper content is discarded in this book due to its inherent structural deficiencies. It is not professional for judges to openly specify their judicial stance and ideological preference for all legal issues. This topic remains highly sensitive for judges and ministers of justice in both the United States and Japan. On 11 November 2022, the Japanese Minister of Justice, Hanashi Yasuhiro, submitted his resignation. He was criticized for stating that he was against capital punishment.[7]

Epstein, Landes and Posner's findings indicated that the influence of ideological preferences increased from the lower echelons of the US federal judiciary to its highest ranks. The researchers confirmed the importance of the attitudinal model of ideological effects on the US Supreme Court. However, the research did not address how judges' personal goals of job satisfaction, salary, outside income and leisure interacted with this model (Epstein et al. 2013, pp. 48–50, pp. 274–281). Two authors of this book also find that *Taishinin* justices received lower compensation compared to individuals employed in other government ministries. Despite the fact that *Taishinin* Chief Justice possessed a respectable social standing, the Minister of Justice held a higher rank. This phenomenon did not align with the concept of separation of powers inherent in the prewar state system. Details are provided in Chap. 9.

[5] On this see Murphy and Tanenhaus (1972).

[6] On this see Segal and Cover (1989).

[7] On this see Radio France Internationale (2022).

The concept of "solidarity of blocs of judges" signifies that judges exhibit congruence in their stance toward a decision, shared objectives, comparable bargaining power and analogous dispositions. This phenomenon is a recurring subject in the academic study of organizational behaviour but now it is applied to judicial behaviour studies. Changes in membership have been demonstrated to exert a significant influence on the formation and solidarity of groups. The judicial administration of recruitment, remuneration, practices, procedures, conduct and discipline is associated with bloc membership and solidarity (Guimaraes et al. 2018, pp. 477–478). Ulmer's analysis focused on the voting patterns of US Supreme Court Justices during the 1958 term in cases pertaining to civil liberties. The objective of his study was to ascertain whether the judges' interpersonal relationships and the extent of their mutual support might have influenced their judicial behaviour during the court proceedings.

To assess the collaborative efficacy of diverse judicial groups, he employed a "Solidarity Index". The research findings indicated that judges' divergent opinions, values and backgrounds exerted a significant influence on their capacity to reach group decisions.[8] Changes in bloc membership had the potential to precipitate alterations in ideological preference and solidarity (Spaeth and Segal 1999, pp. 18–20). In a display of collective power of judges through such judicial behaviour, judges expressed their power of solidarity.

Spaeth and Segal's collection of data from US courts spanned over 60 years. The prevailing belief among judicial behaviour scholars was that the majority of US judges operated on the basis of rational motivation. The objective of judicial policy is not the sole motivating factor.[9] Farbman rejected the notion that a judge's decision might be influenced by team solidarity and spirit. He held the opinion that US judges exhibited a higher degree of independent professionalism than their counterparts in foreign countries (Farbman 2022, p. 9).

Beverly Blair Cook has gained reputation for her proficiency in conducting multidisciplinary research on a myriad of subjects related to jurisprudence. Her academic pursuits have encompassed case studies, the impact of prior court decisions on contemporary cases, in-depth interviews, the biographies and memoirs of judges, social surveys, the historical evolution of law, the interplay between the social and psychological dimensions of the law and methodologies for the collection and analysis of voluminous data sets. Eclecticism can be defined as the combination of different ideas and the attitudinal model is but one component of this multifaceted concept (Lewis 1970, pp. 362–363, pp. 463- 465). Judges' attitudes towards legal issues may exhibit both similarities and differences. The process of making legal decisions can be more readily comprehensible by examining how judges' attitudes are influenced by political, legal, social and cultural institutions (Geyh 2012, p. 204; Agustin 2016, pp. 61–66). The scope of Cook's academic and research interests is multifaceted and unprecedented in judicial behaviour studies. These include the manner in which gender identity influences the decision-making processes of female judges, the historical and geographical variances in the conduct of courts

[8] On this see Ulmer (1960).

[9] On this see Epstein and Knight (2013).

across different eras, the impact of socialization and judges' personal beliefs on their decision-making, the role of political culture and public opinion in shaping judicial decisions, and the examination of challenging legal cases that have been adjudicated by the U.S. Supreme Court.

Cook's research on Georgia Bullock, the inaugural female career judge in California, illuminates the nexus of moralistic attitudinalism and gender injustice within the attitudinal model of judicial behaviour (Mather 1994, pp. 76–78). In *Public Opinion and Federal Judicial Policy*, Cook employs the study of the social and psychological aspects of society to understand how judges' sentencing behaviour. This phenomenon illustrates the impact of public perception on the judges' attitudes. Cook's most significant discovery was that political preferences or ideological preference merely constituted one of many factors that influenced judicial behaviour. The attitudinal model proved to be an inadequate representation of specific external factors (Cook 1977, pp. 591–592, p. 594). In this connection, two authors of this book apply hybrid judicial behaviour model to analyse Taishinin judgements.

2.2.4 Shortcomings of Attitudinal Model

The study of judicial behaviour has incorporated the examination of judges' political preferences since Pritchett's work, *The Roosevelt Court*, published in 1948. However, it is crucial to acknowledge the possibility that judges may have distinct objectives and varied perspectives on what constitutes legal justice. Five common personal objectives have been identified as factors that influence the judicial behaviour of judges. These objectives encompass the extent of a judge's workload, the degree of visibility and esteem accorded to the judge, the utilization of court decisions as a medium for communication with the public, the reluctance to be overtaken by a higher court and the advancement in one's professional career. In the context of this list, the cultivation of an optimistic outlook might not be prioritized (Baum 2006, pp. 9–22). It is more job satisfaction and selfish career development than legal justice.

The attitudinal model's primary focus is on ideology and policy implications. However, its impact on attitudes is not as straightforward as that of legal formalism. The prevailing notion that individuals' political preferences are immutable is a fallacy. The attitudinal model is incapable of utilizing past behaviours to formulate and distort political stereotypes regarding liberalism or conservatism of judges. Songer's research revealed that the Warren Court of the US Supreme Court initially exhibited a liberal judicial tendency. However, following the appointment of a new judge by President Nixon between May 1969 and October 1971, the court shifted to a conservative stance. The attitudinal model should encompass more than just people's political attitudes and beliefs (Songer 2012, pp. 340–344, p. 357). For instance, the observable characteristics of judges, such as their gender, race, religion and ethical background, may be associated with their judicial behaviour and professional independence.

Interest groups also wield significant influence in the selection process for the Supreme Court. If the selection of judges is deemed a judicious undertaking, then the political inclinations of a political party are hypothesized to exert a substantial influence on public sentiment (Segal et al. 1992, p. 114). However, it is not possible to ascertain the court's ultimate decision until the judges' legal reasoning process and judicial decision are observed. While the judges' attitudes toward the law constituted the primary focus of the study, Spaeth's analysis revealed that the judges exhibited strategic behaviours in multiple dimensions concurrently (Spaeth 2004, p. 143, pp. 156–157). Spaeth's observation that two distinct judicial behaviours can coexist is further exemplified by *Taishinin*'s hybrid judicial behaviour model. For example, attitudinal model can be combined with strategic model for understanding the rationales behind *Taishinin*'s judicial decision.

In *Law, Ideology and Collegiality: Judicial Behaviour in the Supreme Court of Canada,* Songer, Johnson, Ostberg and Wetstein raised the question of whether political preferences in the attitudinal model constituted the most salient factor in the Supreme Court of Canada's judicial behaviour. The study's findings revealed that judges' votes were not consistently aligned with either the liberal or conservative ideological leanings. A team of researchers examined the decisions made by 23 judges from 1984 to 2002. The findings indicated that female judges exhibited a greater propensity to favour individuals from lower-class backgrounds. The influence of gender identity on courtroom judicial behaviour supersedes political affiliation or ideological preference, as it is a distinct phenomenon that influences an individual's conduct (Songer et al. 2012, p. 4). It is evident that *Taishinin* was not associated with any female judges. This book does not address the question of whether *Taishinin*'s judicial behaviour is consistent with their gender identity or human right of gender justice.

The attitudinal model is a retrospective analysis and "postediting", rather than utilizing current data. The utilization of post-edited qualitative outcomes for the purpose of predicting current judicial behaviour carries an inherent risk.[10] Post-edited attitudinalism is the doctrine that judges are incapable of altering their initial conclusions. In the context of attitudinal model research, ideology can be a particularly salient factor, with the potential to be exaggerated or discarded through quantitative analysis (Howard 1968, p. 43, p. 44, p. 48, pp. 55–56). It is imperative to acknowledge that any model of judicial behaviour must be founded on the particulars of each judicial decision (Ruger et al. 2004, p. 1154, p. 1158). To comprehend the situation, it is necessary to consider both external factors and internal factors (Howard 1981, p. 175, p. 185). Therefore, an exposition of the social conditions of the five *Taishinin* cases in this book is warranted. From Chaps. 4 to 8, social conditions are provided to help readers understand what was happening in prewar Japan while *Taishinin* was making judicial decision on that particular case.

[10] On this see Emmert (1992).

2.3 Strategic Model

The strategic judicial behaviour model is a plan to achieve a goal or interest, which may be public or personal nature. The political preference of the attitudinal model is but one of numerous factors considered in this strategy of judge. This theoretical framework could be designated as a hybrid strategic attitudinal model. In this model, judges demonstrate a willingness to compromise their own objectives and even selfish personal interests in pursuit of a more optimal beneficial outcome (Perino 2006, p. 498). The manner in which a judge approaches these issues may prove advantageous only to that judge. A prime example of this phenomenon is the attainment of a professional reputation and/or promotion within a legal institution or court. According to Rhode and Spaeth, while judges' decisions are influenced by their beliefs, this influence may not the dominant factor in their judicial decision-making. Judges who make decisions based on strategy are not only concerned with justice; they are also adept at making rational calculations. In order to comprehend the judges' approach to legislation, it is necessary to consider the extent of their knowledge regarding their colleagues, the legislative process and the consequences of their decisions. After a thorough consideration of all the relevant factors, a strategist arrives at a decision. The strategic decision is influenced by the factors selected by the strategist, as well as the decisions made by other judges within the same institution. Collegiality in the court refers to the practice of all judges voting together to reach a final decision. This phenomenon can be characterized as a type of mutual dependence and interaction among judges working in the same court. Judges operate in a collaborative manner as a collective entity. They are more likely to demonstrate a strong sense of solidarity.

In the United States, the most significant factors influencing the society are political parties, Congress and the President. A strategic judge must consider the judicial administration policy, judicial accountability, the judge's actions and discipline, transparency and social ethics. In certain instances, social conditions have been observed to exert an influence on the decisions made by judges, resulting in outcomes that align with the personal objectives of the judges in question. Black asserts that these limits encompass "the amount of power the government uses against a person or group".[11] These elements exceed the scope of the variables present within the attitudinal model. The strategic model does not provide a free pass. Utilizing data from 1947 to 1992, Bergara, Richman, and Spiller ascertained that approximately one-third of US Supreme Court decisions were influenced by political factors, personal traits and beliefs. The legitimacy of these decisions could be called into question by various external factors, including the actions of Congress, the Supreme Court, or prevailing public opinion, which could cast doubt on the extent of justice in court's decision-making process.[12]

The strategic model and the attitudinal model can be utilized together as a hybrid model in tandem to facilitate a comprehensive understanding of judges' objectives,

---

[11] See Black (1989, p. 8, p. 20, p. 28, p. 39).

[12] See Posner (2008, pp. 30-31), Perino (2006, p. 498), Bergara et al. (2003, p. 249, p. 267).

the established principles of the court and the prevailing circumstances, thereby assisting us to understand how judges make informed decisions.[13] The strategic judicial behaviour model of *Taishinin* is one main tool in the toolkit for judgement analysis of this book.

2.3.1 Danelski's Qualitative Analysis

Danelski is an expert in qualitative analysis of intra-court leadership, judicial decision-making and judicial opinion assignment processes. His *A Supreme Court Justice is Appointed* delves into the background of US Supreme Court Justice Pierce Butler, examining his formative years and the influence of socialization on his judicial philosophy, which led him to adopt a conservative stance in judicial decision-making. Danelski's research revealed that Butler's leadership style was characterized by strategic model of judicial behaviour, with the purpose of fostering team solidarity in the context of collegial judicial decision-making (Danelski 1964, p. 45). In his study, Danelski pioneered a novel approach to the analysis of strategic judicial behaviour, asserting that attitudinal elements should be regarded as a comparatively negligible variable within the broader ambit of judicial behaviour studies. Presently, the relevant files of *Taishinin* cases are unavailable for perusal, with the exception of judgements. As an alternative approach, this book examines the social context of each judgement to ascertain whether *Taishinin* exhibited strategic judicial behaviour in corruption cases.

2.3.2 Legalism of Epstein and Jacobi

Epstein and Jacobi concur that judges are motivated by factors beyond politics and personal traits. Moreover, their actions are driven by pragmatic and rational considerations, guided by the principles of legality and the precedent set by prior cases (Epstein and Jacobi 2010, pp. 342–346). Judicial behaviour of this kind is like *stare decisis* in common law jurisprudence. Consequently, judicial legalism and judicial realism can be integrated into a unified plan to achieve a shared objective. Judicial legalism posits that rights and duties are of paramount importance and must be observed. This phenomenon is frequently observed within the domains of politics, society and culture.[14] The theoretical underpinnings of judicial legalism, as a political philosophy, are predicated on its capacity to provide a rationale for judicial conduct characterized by impartiality. This theoretical underpinning posits that judges, in their capacity as legal experts, are able to apply the principles of justice with objectivity by adhering to established legal precedents and the dictates of legislation.

---

[13] On this see Rhode and Spaeth (1976).

[14] See Shklar (1986), pp. 15-16, pp. 30-31, pp. 33-35, p. 106, pp. 222-224.

Judicial decision-making can be influenced by a judge's desire for personal reputation, sense of self and perceived influence, potentially impacting legal decisions based on legalism.

Cohen's position is that legalism and realism can coexist as valid perspectives, contingent upon prevailing social conditions. In order to formulate a realistic theory of judicial decisions, it is imperative to acknowledge that each decision is not merely an expression of an individual's personality; rather, it is the result of social influences and interaction with other factors (Cohen 1935, p. 843). The strategic model is a methodical approach that rationally involves the systematic balancing of all the relevant factors to achieve a desired objective. Furthermore, it is imperative to exercise effective time management when formulating legal decisions that have the potential to influence public opinion (Epstein and Weinshall 2021, pp. 26–29). The notion of "timing" can be defined as the ability to execute the appropriate course of action at the most opportune moment. This model strikes a balance among all the salient factors and the extent to which it contributes to the promotion of freedom, equality and well-being in a fair society is contingent upon the specific circumstances in each case. An illustration of this phenomenon is provided by *Taishinin*'s judicial behaviour in support of "justice under militarism" in the late 1930s. This kind of judicial behaviour did not provoke public outrage regarding the perceived injustice under militarism. *Taishinin*'s judicial behaviours were politically astute, as they were aligned with the optimal strategy for the prevailing political culture.

2.3.3 Murphy's Judicial Strategy

Walter Murphy's book, *Elements of Judicial Strategy*, discusses the manner in which judges reach decisions, thereby contributing judicial decision to the formulation of public policies.[15] Murphy's work indicated that political influences impact the behaviour of judges. Additionally, he demonstrated the challenges associated with navigating the intricate relationships prevalent within the judicial system. The prevailing approach to address this issue entailed the court's collaborative adjudication. This was achieved through the use of mediation and the cultivation of personal friendships for consensus. Murphy's discourse encompasses a range of methodologies through which interest groups may endeavour to exert influence over judges. These tactics encompass a range of strategies, including cajolery, flattery, promises of future rewards and even political pressure.

Murphy's strategic model is often characterized as a form of jungle theory and Social Darwinism of survival of the fittest. Murphy's observations suggest that US Supreme Court Justices adhere to legal principles, particularly the Constitution and procedural regulations. Judges divulged their personal convictions regarding societal and political matters to the general public. Consequently, the Supreme Court's rulings were rooted in the prevailing public policy. In order to ensure the efficacy

[15] On this see Murphy (2016).

of the court, the Chief Justice of the US Supreme Court typically selects judges who share his ideological perspective and cultivates relationships with the President. This enables the Chief Justice to persuade the President to appoint judges who align with his preferences for candidates. The abilities of Supreme Court Justices in this process were constrained by the established procedural guidelines that govern the selection of Justices (Murphy 2016, pp. 176–210). The bluffing strategy employed in Supreme Court decision-making proved to be a source of tension, both personally and professionally, among the judges. This tension hindered the ability of the judges to collaborate efficiently and effectively (Brenner and Whitmeyer 2009, p. 95, pp. 110–111).

Murphy's analysis fails to consider the legal culture influenced by the constitution, legal professionals, judges and legal academics. This culture imposes constraints on the court's strategic model. Cultural differences have been shown to result in a lack of support from the public and the elite, which is a critical factor in the acceptance of judicial decision (Rosenberg 1991, pp. 10–11, p. 16). The impact of this phenomenon on judges' behaviour in abortion cases is the most evident. It is conceivable that certain judges in the United States might exercise discretion and decline to preside over cases that pertain to contentious public policies. A decade later, Shepherd's research yielded analogous results.[16] In an effort to circumvent the potential for denial of reappointment, judges might resort to the utilization of low judges' trails for cases pertaining to public policy-oriented abortion. The subjects did not wish to act in opposition to the government's policies or the prevailing opinions of the general public. *Taishinin*'s methodology in addressing judicial matters involving corruption is also evidently centred on public policy, with the primary objective being the preservation of purity of public power. Nevertheless, there is an absence of evidence substantiating the strategy employed by the *Taishinin* justices for reappointment or career advancement.

2.3.4 Epstein and Knight's Exogenous Constraints of Strategy

The strategic model provides a framework for comprehending the various factors that influence judges' objectives and the hidden agendas that underpin their decisions. Epstein and Knight concur that the actions of the US Supreme Court were influenced by the limitations of the system designed to prevent the government from abusing its power. These constraints are influenced by social and political factors. Consequently, the manner in which judges conduct themselves ought to be contingent upon the shifting tides of societal and political transformations. Shifts in societal priorities and the regulatory framework that governs it can impede the capacity of judges to ensure the administration of justice. The government's alignment with court decisions

[16] On this see Brace et al. (1999) and Shepherd (2009).

also influenced judges' strategic decision-making.[17] In a manner analogous to the US Supreme Court, *Taishinin* was constrained by Meiji Constitution and de facto the Minister of Justice. It did not meaningfully contribute to the equilibrium of power in the prewar state political system. Notwithstanding, there had been instances in the past when *Taishinin* had expressed disagreement with the government regarding the matter of judicial independence.

Exogenous constraints may emerge from politicians' strategic utilization of the courts for political ends. It is possible that political leaders could make use of the constitution as a legal strategy, leveraging the judicial behaviour of the US Supreme Court to invalidate legislation. Politicians may also strategically utilize the judicial system to advance their objectives. The appointment of judges who share the same beliefs by the president could potentially result in the utilization of the courts as a political weapon. In instances where individuals find a judge's approach to be unsatisfactory, Garber asserts that judges possess the autonomy to modify their strategy in a manner that conforms to the prevailing sentiment (Graber 1993, pp. 72–73). The dynamics of political competition from external entities can also influence the retention of Supreme Court Justices. Brenner and Cohen's study of US courts in 14 states from 1950 to 1990 demonstrated that judges were meticulously deliberating on the potential influence of politicians on court decisions and the question of whether the courts would maintain their judicial autonomy.[18] In Chap. 9 of this book, it is not surprising for readers to read that some *Taishinin* judges behaved in a manner consistent with prewar political trends.

The external factors that influence Congress's legislation, in addition to the political constraints it faces, are a subject of interest for researchers in judicial behaviour studies. The President or Congress may disapprove of the court's assertive approach to adjudication. In the Grove City College Case, the US Supreme Court strategically altered the interpretation of legislation to align with their own judicial objective of profound political implications. Subsequently, the House of Representatives counterattacked by legislative behaviour to codify new legislation aimed at overturning the court's ruling (Marks 2015, p. 845–848, pp. 871–872). In order to gain the upper hand in a legislative stalemate, the Supreme Court has the ability to set new rules for all lower courts (Gely and Spiller 1990, p. 263, p. 296). A parallel can be drawn between the European Court of Justice's approach and that of the aforementioned court. EU member-state governments had indicated their intention to disregard court rulings. This course of action was implemented as a political strategy to combat what was perceived as the court's "strategic judicial activism" (Carrubba et al. 2008, pp. 449–450, p 452).

[17] See Epstein and Knight (1998, p. 138, pp. 142-143, p. 157, p. 172, pp. 185-186).

[18] See Brenner and Cohen (2016, p. 335, p. 355, p. 359).

2.3.5 Strategic Model to Serve Self-Interest

Judges of US junior courts are not guaranteed permanent job protection. However, they are able to leverage their position to advance their careers selfishly (Baum 1994, pp. 749–750). In order to circumvent the possibility of review or reversal by the Supreme Court, it is incumbent upon junior court judges to recalibrate their judicial behaviour. This would result in a lower reversal rate, which would be beneficial for job reappointment or advancement.[19] The repercussions of such actions may have deleterious effects on one's professional trajectory and standing within their respective professional judicial fields. Even appeal court judges have been known to modify their legal decisions in order to avoid being overturned (McNollgast 1995, p. 1673).

In 39 states within the United States, trial judges are obligated to stand for reelection. Huber and Gordon's study examined the behaviour of judges during their reelection campaigns. The study's findings indicated that trial judges in Pennsylvania exhibited a heightened propensity to impose more substantial sentences prior to their reelection.[20] Boyd and Spriggs conducted a study on the utilization and comprehension of Supreme Court rulings by US district courts.[21] District court judges frequently cited and concurred with Supreme Court decisions that espoused analogous beliefs. This is an intelligent strategic approach to leveraging legal mechanisms to selfishly advance one's professional aspirations.

Another objective of strategic judicial behaviour is a judge's self-serving electoral funding. In the majority of states, it is considered an anomaly to hold elections for state Supreme Court justices. The impacts of temporal correlation between funding for reelection in the 1990s and the judicial votes of a judge for a funder who had financially contributed to the trial judge's reelection campaign was found to be statistically significant (Waltenburg and Lopeman 2008, p. 257). McCall's analysis focused on court decisions made by conservative judges of the Texas Civil Supreme Court between January 1994 and June 1997. The judges were found to have demonstrated a greater propensity to rule in favour of the plaintiff if the plaintiff had donated campaign money (McCall 2003, pp. 314–315, pp. 330–331). A comparable relationship is observed between funding for judges and their rulings in arbitration cases within the Alabama Supreme Court (Ware 1999, pp. 683–684).

To ensure the integrity of the judicial system, the Wisconsin Supreme Court has established regulations governing the financial resources that political parties are permitted to allocate for the purpose of campaigning. This decision contributed to fostering public confidence in the Supreme Court's autonomy. The legal monetary sum was insufficient to alter the manner in which judges would adjudicate (Cann 2002, p. 272).

In Japan prior to the war, the legal decisions of *Taishinin* were not significantly influenced by direct funding and election, due to the absence of such democratic

---

[19] See Bowie and Songer (2009, pp. 393-394, pp. 405-406), Shepherd (2011, p. 1755, p. 1758).

[20] See Huber and Gordon (2004, pp. 247-248, pp. 261-262).

[21] See Boyd and Spriggs (2009, p. 41, p. 78).

processes. However, *Taishinin* existed under the undue influence of Minister of Justice in prewar state political structure. As delineated in the Meiji Constitution, the prerogative to appoint judges for the court of *Taishinin* resided with the Minister of Justice in the name of Emperor. Historically, *Taishinin* has, at times, engaged in resistance against governmental control in an effort to preserve the autonomy of its own legal system. However, it is important to note that the majority of the population also expressed support for the prewar government (details are in Chap. 9).

2.3.6 Strategy of Dynamic Interpretation and Vague Opinions

In the absence of conflict with governmental or judicial policy and if the relevant upper court judges are in agreement upon voting for judicial decision, a flexible legal reasoning and interpretation of laws can serve as a strategic means for judges to balance the interests of all parties involved. In circumstances where legal opinions are ambiguous, it is advisable to exercise caution and refrain from succumbing to political pressures. This approach ensures that the court's decisions are adhered to, thereby safeguarding the integrity and image of the legal system (Epstein and Jacobi 2010, pp. 351- 353). The ambiguity of legal terminology and the lack of clarity in legal opinions can lead to a degree of flexibility and subjectivity, thereby allowing readers to interpret them in a variety of ways (Christie 1964, p. 890). In common law jurisdiction, a lot of law terms are Latin confusing laymen without legal knowledge.

In the European civil law tradition as a "Western jacket", *Taishinin*'s judgements are composed in classical Japanese, omitting punctuation such as commas or full stops. At present, this ambiguous style is discarded in Japan. However, the research method of linguistic discourse finds that it was not an uncommon characteristic of *Taishinin*'s judicial behaviour to apply concise moralistic terms as legal methodology. They demonstrated a capacity to adapt their unclear interpretations and vague opinions to shifting circumstances. This approach was a customary method for the Japanese court to reach decisions prior to the war. For example, in Chap. 8, the key term for criminalization was the vague phrase of *ippan-no-kengen* (general authority), but the clear scope of it in police duty was unexplained.

2.3.7 Shortcomings of Strategic Model

The strategic judicial behaviour model employs a systematic approach, examining various methods of leveraging legal mechanisms to achieve specific objectives in a coherent manner. These approaches typically encompass the perspectives of other judges, the range of available options, the organizational structure, the assessment of social benefit, the principles of justice and the potential for feedback through legislative behaviour (Epstein and Knight 1998, pp. xii- xiii, pp. 80–81). Judges frequently implement a rational strategy that involves allocating funds to their own campaigns and pursuing reappointment. However, the veracity of this assertion remains challenging to substantiate (Bergara et al. 2003, pp. 248–249, p. 267.). The question that must be addressed is how to achieve a balance between competing goals and interests of all relevant stakeholders with a judicial strategy. The strategic model offers no clear guidance on establishing the boundary and objective for the rationality of it. It varies from case to case. In prewar Japan, judicial strategy for hegemonic governance of state polity was paramount.

2.4 Historical Institutionalist Model

The historical institutionalist model is predicated on legal history and documents intrinsic to the judicial decision-making process (Gaffney 1976, p. 215). Adopting a historical-oriented approach, this model encompasses the realism of empirical questions, government institutions, the social structures of a nation, politics, traditional interest groups and stakeholders, informal social control and formal social control as outcomes of historical development. It also includes standardized operational practices, rules and procedures that establish structural relationships among individuals. The common research fields include the origins, evolution and impacts of social institutions across time and place, especially legal institutions, political institutions, public policy and political and economic relations.[22] The historical institutionalist model is a complex concept that is challenging to present in a succinct manner. In prewar Japan, the historical institutionalist Meiji Constitution and organizational structure of government handcuffed room for *Taishinin*'s judicial behaviour.

Judicial behaviour studies also examine the context of norms, powers and ideological preferences that influence judicial behaviour and interactions among actors within the institution. The historical institutionalist model facilitates comprehension of the manner in which these elements have influenced the court's judicial behaviour in bygone eras (Maveety 2006, pp. 285–286). The majority of the initial research conducted on this model was focused on the US Supreme Court and its conception of substantive justice (O'Brien 1983, pp. 558–563). It is recommended that a multifaceted approach be considered, encompassing the consideration of rules, standards and political analysis. Smith proposed a research approach aimed at enhancing comprehension of judicial decision-making processes. This research is an examination of the historical evolution of ideas, rules and values pertinent to the judicial function.[23] Following Smith's methodology, the Japanese historical evolution of anti-corruption laws and judicial behaviours in respect of corruption are presented in Chap. 3 of this book.

Edward S. Corwin also took legal history as a methodology for judicial behaviour studies. His legacy of academic works is considered a classic of historical institutionalism in law, such as *The Doctrine of Judicial Review* (1914), *John Marshall*

---

[22] See Steinmo et al. (1992, p. 2) and Fioretos et al. (2016, pp. 2-3).

[23] See Smith (1988, p. 90, pp. 96-98, pp. 101-103, pp. 106-107).

and the Constitution (1919), *The Worship of the Constitution* (1920), *Understanding the Constitution* (1949) and *The Presidency Today* (1956, with Louis Koenig). In *Constitution v. Constitutional Theory* (1925), he debunked the myth of popular veneration for the US Constitution and its political legislative intent. His *The Twilight of the Supreme Court: A History of Our Constitutional Theory* (1934, with Jack W. Peltason) suggests judicial behaviour analysis to understand and interpret the US Constitution as a living document: "It is the plain duty of the Court a super-constitution which, in the name of the Constitution, repeals and destroys that historic document…Having done this the Court will be free to assume again the role, so powerfully claimed for it by Chief Justice Marshall, of pillar and supporter of the national power and its supremacy (Corwin and Peltason 1934, pp. I82-183)". In *The Commerce Power versus States Rights* (1936), he continued to criticize US Supreme Court's judicial behaviour of strict legal interpretations of Congress' interstate powers and the ideological preference of constitutional federalism. *The President: Office and Powers* in 1940 established Corwin's "institutional model" of the American President's historical legal functions and powers as an institution in historical institutionalism. *The Presidency Today* (1956, with Louis Koenig) is about the persistent cause of presidential autocracy in relation to Congress and the judiciary. With historical precedents, they were uncertain about the methods for managing the legislature and judiciary in the United States. Corwin's most influential work on judicial behaviour, *The Constitution and What It Means Today*, was first published in 1920. The 13th edition was published in 1974. With succinctness and accuracy of the analysis of court judgements, Corwin confirmed that the US Supreme Court's judicial behaviour in the Constitution pertaining to labour justice, the human right of religious freedom and the right to a fair trial were under political pressure.[24] According to Corwin, justice is not a static concept, but the outcome of an evolutionary process historically. The evolution of anti-corruption law in Japan revealed by Chap. 3 of this book proves the same.

Pnina Lahav's *Judgement in Jerusalem: Chief Justice Simon Agranat and the Zionist Century* is about historical institutionalism of Israeli Supreme Court. As Lahav notes, the unintentional judicial behaviours of Chief Justice Simon Agranat of the Israeli Supreme Court in the 1950s has "pushed its frontiers beyond Agranat's wildest imagination" (Lahav 1997, p. 252). Thereafter, the later Israeli Chief Justices followed Agranat's judicial activism to interpret the Israeli Declaration of Independence to rationalize legal rights. Lahav's work provided self-evident historical information on the institutional evolution of the judicial behaviour of the Israeli Supreme Court (Lahav 1997, pp. 161–162).

Robert Alan Dahl regards politics as the exercise of power and coercion for influence (Dahl and Stinebrickner 2003, p. 32). His *Decision Making in a Democracy: The Supreme Court as a National Policymaker* in 1957 was a pioneering pathfinding work in historical institutionalism about the role and impact of the US Supreme Court. It was far earlier than McCloskey's *The American Supreme Court* in 1961 (In 2016, the sixth edition appeared), *The Impact of Supreme Court Decisions: Empirical*

[24] See Corwin (1929, p. 572, p. 586, p. 589) and Corwin (1974).

Studies edited by Theodore L. Becker in 1969 and Donald Horowitz's *The Courts and Social Policy* in 1977. Dahl wrote socio-politically for judicial behaviour in *Democracy and Its Critics*. Dahl did not agree that US Supreme Court had judicial power to strike down legislation by judicial review. He believed that "the most reliable means for protecting and advancing the good and interests of all the persons subject to collective decisions of presiding judges" (Dahl 1989, pp. 188–192, p. 322). Dahl consistently assumed minorities of the general population can fight for rights through court decisions in favour of them. The Supreme Court was thus not only a judicial institution historically, but also a political institution of its judicial behaviour in respect of controversial national policy issues. Like the attitudinal and strategic models, Dahl also considered the impact of the political selection and appointment of Supreme Court Justices historically.[25]

Robert Green McCloskey historically traced American conservativism facilitated by a degeneration of democracy formulated by Thomas Jefferson and Andrew Jackson (McCloskey 1951, p. xiii, p. I93) and subsequently extended it to judicial behaviour studies. In *The Modern Supreme Court* (1972), McCloskey analysed judicial behaviours of US Supreme Court's Justices, public opinion and public policy, especially during the term of Justice Stone (1940–45), Justice Vinson (1946–52) and Justice Warren (1953–69). His concern was whether evolving judicial behaviour in civil rights might develop as a new jurisprudence and legal culture. His essay *Civil Liberties, Civil Rights and the Supreme Court* elucidated the role of the Supreme Court as an instrumental institution in the US governance instead of simply legal justice.[26]

In the 1990s, Howard Gillman and Cornell Clayton wrote in self-styled "new institutionalism", also known as neo-institutionalism. They focused on the historical analysis of the judicial behaviour of the US High Court, in which conflict among competitive interest groups for limited social resources was frequent. New institutionalism rejected quantitative analysis, but "sought to emphasize the cognitive structures that attached courts and judges in general to culture and society". They referred to particular court decisions and its political effects, confirming that the overall judicial behaviour of American courts was in transformation from protecting corporate capitalism to justice for individual and group rights. They labelled this judicial behavioural pattern as "human agents developing their very capacity for meaningful interaction" (Gillman and Clayton 1999, pp. 4–5, p. 78).

2.4.1 *Martin Shapiro as a Bridge*

Shapiro is widely recognized as a preeminent scholar in judicial behaviour studies. He combines "old" and "new" institutionalism, which are based on the historical

---

[25] See Dahl (1957, p. 279, pp. 281-284, pp. 292-294).

[26] On this see McCloskey (1972).

institutionalism of Corwin and McCloskey. Shapiro's treat judiciary as a sociopolitical institution rather than pure judicial. He examined the efficacy of judicial decision-making processes, focusing on their adherence to legal principles and the potential for enhancement of this procedural justice. According to Shapiro, the legal system functions as a political tool utilized by competitive interest groups within the political domain. Interest groups employ this mechanism to formulate strategy and operationalize policies. Interest groups do not utilize legal mechanisms to advance abstract legal principles without concrete outcome (Maveety 2006, pp. 387–390, pp. 393–394).

Shapiro's term "political jurisprudence" appears in his first book *Law and Politics in the Supreme Court* in 1964. The idea of political jurisprudence is that judges are like legal technicians and government agencies that take political power for themselves in the US federal system. Political jurisprudence moved from the traditional approach, which focused on the law, to the court's actions in a competition for power to achieve a goal. This is the most important part of Shapiro's new institutionalism, which combines the rational choice, sociopolitical and historical institutionalist approaches. It is a hybrid role of judges and bureaucrats. Shapiro's work *Courts: A Comparative and Political Analysis* in 1981 attacks court's traditional stereotypical image of impartiality for justice. Shapiro wrote: "In a startling number of instances…a person who draws little or no distinction between administering and judging……The basic social logic, or perceived legitimacy, of courts rests on the mutual consent of two persons in conflict to refer that conflict to a third for resolution (Shapiro 1981, p. 20, pp. 36–37)".

To understand the power relationship in constitutional interpretation and judicial behaviour, Shapiro examined pragmatic political jurisprudence surrounding "the power of one segment of a government vis-'a-vis other segments of that government and the public".[27] The court has policymaking power. It is a channel for those who are unable to find representatives to help them secure their social interests. The court's judicial behaviour can play a role in this power matrix of "many centers of political decision-making". Judiciary should be integrated in the operation and interaction in this matrix of government and politics.[28]

The court in this matrix has to rely on the government to implement its judicial decisions, in which its judicial behaviour may add, subtract, or modify public policy or administrative order. Court in fact does not have its own police to enforce its judicial decision. Shapiro regarded the judicial behaviour of the Supreme Court as a "repeated" behaviour based on "looking for an answer to the political power question": "which government department should have the legal power to take action under court order and judicial policy? Court order to this government department is for contribution to well-rounded representation of social interests (Shapiro 1964, pp. 10–11, p. 40, p. 46.)". Shapiro's *The Supreme Court and Administrative Agencies* (1968) further crystalized the operation and interaction in this political power

[27] On this see Shapiro (1963).

[28] See Shapiro (1961a, p. 181, pp. 184-85, pp. 189-90, pp. 196-97, p. 200, p. 204).

matrix. To Shapiro, the US Supreme Court is effective in facilitating political integration through its judicial behaviour linking legal disputes with bureaucrats' decision-making.[29] He deemed the court's judicial behaviour as a political process in the political power matrix. His *Morals and the Courts: The Reluctant Crusaders* examined moralistic judicial behaviours by assessment of moral turpitude, law and obscenity.[30] Shapiro's historical institutionalism has not underestimated the impacts of exogenous factors on judicial behaviour as a political process. His model integrates exogenous and endogenous facets into a complete picture of the judicial behaviour of political power implications (Shapiro 1963, pp. 294–298). Shapiro's works inspired the two authors of this book to integrate exogenous and endogenous facets in their analysis of *Taishinin*'s judicial behaviour. In addition to the prewar social conditions of Japanese society, the personal backgrounds of *Taishinin* Justices are therefore covered. *Taishinin* was also found in the power matrix of "many centers of political decision-making", but it had cognitive consistency to have social administration policy in support of state polity (refer Chap. 9).

2.4.2 Shep Melnick's Political Jurisprudence

With the application of courts' judicial behaviour in a matrix of power of political institutions and policy making processes like Shapiro's new institutionalism, in *Regulation and the Courts: The Case of the Clean Air Act*, Melnick portrayed how judicial behaviour shapes the expansion of bureaucratic institutions and policy through statutory interpretations. He mentioned a court order under the Clean Air Act to support his argument. The US Supreme Court's order led to the creation of new bureaucratic units to meet the requirements outlined in the court order. After the court's review, bureaucrats got appointments, political influence, career advancement and job satisfaction. So, they praised the court's actions in the perspective of a newly created interest group in political power matrix (Melnick 1983, p. 153, pp. 379–380). The court has actually created a new group of people who have a shared interest.

Melnick's case study is a methodology in historical institutionalism. Melnick furthered his political jurisprudence in *Between the Lines: Interpreting Welfare Rights* by screening three American social welfare court cases in detail. Melnick concluded that the court's judicial behaviour gave no deference to bureaucrats' influence on its judicial behaviour to adopt strict narrow statutory interpretation. Through historical institutionalist analysis, Melnick emphasized that lower courts could also participate in the political power matrix by ruling to create new legal rights for handicapped children under *The Education for All Handicapped Children Act*. Congress' subsequent legislative amendment was under the jurisprudential influence of lower courts' humanistic judicial behaviour (Melnick 1994, p. 135). Neither Melnick nor historical institutionalism is perfect. In *Between the Lines: Interpreting Welfare Rights*,

---

[29] On this see Shapiro (1980).

[30] On this see Shapiro (1961b).

Melnick did not explore whether unfairness in educational opportunities was due to bad behaviour by Congress or bad actions by bureaucrats. While new legal rights are created by humanistic judicial behaviour in the matrix as political jurisprudence, it is necessary to do empirical follow-up analysis for or against them. This is concrete research into ideas about the law in politics and moral reflection. Smith's analysis of law and politics includes three fundamental ideas: historical institutionalism, attitudinalism and strategic considerations. The three models can be used together and are a good fit for each other.[31] Inspired by Smith, this book also uses these three basic judicial behaviour models to analyse *Taishinin*'s judgements. As abovementioned, *Taishinin* was a participant in the matrix of power of political institutions. *Taishinin* could formulate judicial policy for disciplinary management of civil servants.

2.4.3 Judicial Biography

A judicial biography is defined as a written account of a judge's public life and judicial duties. The document contains information regarding the judge's legal background, duties, relationships with other judges, personal background and the judge's training (Frank 1949, pp. 375–380). Alpheus Thomas Mason is arguably the most suitable individual to compose a treatise on judges within the historical institutionalist paradigm. The examination of legal biographies and autobiographies provides a valuable insight into the evolution of the legal system through the ages. Furthermore, it demonstrates the evolution of legal frameworks, court decisions and the prevailing legal cultures. Mason's literary contributions, which encompass a substantial corpus on the subject of US Supreme Court justices, stand as a testament to his profound engagement with the intricacies of the judicial system. In her book, Mason discusses how judges have been influenced by politics in the legal system (Loughlin 2018, p. 140).

Mason's works *Brandeis: A Free Man's Life* (1946), *Harlan Fiske Stone: Pillar of the Law* (1957), and *William Howard Taft: Chief Justice* (1964) are masterpieces of judicial biographies of legal realism. All these works genuinely record how all laws have historically originated from prevailing social interests and public policy like an evolutionary process. In Mason's historical institutionalism, judicial decisions also emerged from interactions among the justices of US Supreme Court, social factors, self-interest and normative persuasion. In *Brandeis: Lawyer and Judge in the Modern State*, Mason recorded Brandeis's biography as evidence to prove Brandeis's judicial behaviour was out of his personal devotion to liberalism and humanitarianism. In *Bureaucracy Convicts Itself*, Mason advocated a balance between procedures and techniques contributing to the economy and more new effective safeguards for individual libertism (Mason 1941, p. 20). In *Brandeis: A Free Man's Life*, he presented Brandeis' development of philosophical and normative legal arguments to explain origins of his judicial behaviour. He detailed the whole socialization in Brandeis' life

[31] On this see Smith (1989).

history, including emigration to America until he became a justice of the US Supreme Court and the influence of such socialization on Brandeis' judicial behaviour.

Because of the growing influence of multinational businesses on the legal system, Mason was worried that the independence of the courts would be threatened. He talked about how the Supreme Court of the United States has handled balancing wartime needs and limits on people's rights during wartime. Mason used the example of the Marshall and Hughes courts to talk about how Supreme Court justices behaved. He did this by talking about how Franklin Delano Roosevelt and Thomas Jefferson's thoughts affected the behaviour of the Supreme Court justices.[32] Mason's biographies about judges clearly show how the US Supreme Court have used the law to influence politics. This book covers Mason's approach by including short biographies of the three earliest *Taishinin* Chief Justices.

Another influential historical institutionalist is Roger K. Newman's judicial biography. Newman unprecedentedly took twenty-six years and more than one thousand interviews for his *Hugo Black: A Biography*. Justice Black had been a United States senator for ten years before his 34-year service on the Supreme Court from 1937 to 1971. With primary data of Justice Black's personal letters and oral history spanning his entire political and judicial career, Newman described Black as a justice imbued with "boundless self-confidence" (Newman 1994, p. 169). Newman applied history and linguistic discourse to analyse Black's judicial behaviour in his fifth longest-serving record in the US Supreme Court. He attitudinally labelled Black as "a southern liberal in the populist tradition" (Newman 1994, p. 127), and detailed Black's personality, relationships with fellow justices, the controversy of Black's Supreme Court appointment and Black's judicial behaviour in collegiate judicial decision-making. He was the Warren Court's "chief philosopher" with his own ideological preference (Newman 1994, pp. 435–436, p. 537).

2.4.4 Shortcomings of Judicial Biography

The biography of judges constitutes an element of the study of the functionality of institutions over a specific period of time in the past. While researching a judge's life can provide insights into the court, law and history, it may not fully help predict how a judge will behave in court. This phenomenon can be attributed to a variety of factors, including personal traits, childhood socialization, upbringing, political preferences and relationships with other judges. The primary strength of judicial biography, as a methodology in historical institutionalism, lies in its ability to provide explanations for the past decisions made by judges. Honesty is an integral quality for a judge to possess. Authenticity in judicial biography contributes to the public's confidence in the judicial system and the perception of real fairness or unfairness among the legal community. In order to provide a compelling account of a judge's lifespan, it is imperative to undertake an objective and factual examination of the factors that are intrinsic

[32] On this see Mason (1955, 1957 and 1962).

to the judge, as well as those that are extrinsic to the judge. A significant challenge in the study of judicial biography is the difficulty in verifying authenticity of psychological factors and incidents.[33] The author may unintentionally incorporate personal beliefs into the description of the judge's background through moral teaching in the attitudinal model. For instance, in *Justice Lewis F Powell Jr.*, law scholar John Jeffries Jr. described Justice Powell with "long string of achievements were not the fruits of easy confidence, but of ceaseless struggle against self-doubt. Fiercely ambitious, yet ineradicably unsure, Powell always had to prove himself". With concrete proof of incidences, Jeffries confirmed Justice Powell's judicial behaviour to mitigate racial tension in court and Southerners' social tension under court order (Jeffries 1994, p. 8, pp. 507–508, p. 561). Usually, concrete evidence for such descriptions in court is not easy to find to substantiate judicial behaviour studies.

In *Learned Hand: The Man and the Judge*, Gerald Gunther traced the origins and nature of Justice Hand's ideology. Hand's decisions were "within the confines set by the executive and legislative branches". Hand's judicial behaviour took place in Shapiro's political power matrix. Gunther attributed it to "Hand's personality of fervent commitment to judicial restraint" (Gunther 1994, p. xvi, p. xvii). However, Gunther's perception of a judge's personality can be subjective. Without hybrid training in legal, humanistic and social-scientific techniques, a trustworthy and reliable judicial biography is unlikely. Law schools usually do not provide courses specializing in biographical writing for the literary authorship of judicial behaviour.[34] Interdisciplinary training for writing the legal lifespan of a judge intertwining legal history, law and sociolegal studies is essential but academic programmes of this kind are unpopular nowadays (Sugarman 2015, pp. 9–10).

2.5 Brief Remarks

Research on judicial behaviour is interdisciplinary in nature. This chapter provides a bird's-eye view of judicial behaviour studies as a developing academic subject, examining three predominant models of judicial behaviour which are adopted for case analysis from Chaps. 4 to 8 of this book. These three models offer a total of four ways to understand judicial behaviour. In order to comprehend the rationale behind judicial decisions, it is imperative to examine the legal justifications that underpin them. Additionally, it is important to elucidate the processes by which judges are selected and promoted, the evolution of legal precedents over time and their interaction with social conditions as a manifestation of historical institutionalism.

The second way involves the conceptualization of the court's judicial behaviour as "a small group of solidarity". This objective is pursued by means of a meticulous examination of the court's operational dynamics as a cohesive entity, with a particular focus on the interrelationships that exist among its judges. It is significant to identify

[33] On this see Josev (2017).

[34] See Posner (1995, pp. 511-516, pp. 519-20, p. 523).

and examine groups of judges, with a particular focus on their voting patterns and the cultural milieu of their institutions. This phenomenon bears certain parallels with the manner in which organizational behaviour is examined.

The third is understanding how judges are influenced by their education, beliefs, personal qualities, social backgrounds and reaction to external influences. This chain of socialization processes is of particular significance when examining how it impacts their courtroom decisions strategically. The present study combines elements of strategic management in business studies and sociopolitical research.

The fourth type is the attitudinal way, which identifies judges' attitudes toward public policy issues, political consciousness, moral standards, norms, values and judicial decision-making (Peck 1967, pp. 2–4). This chapter confirms judicial behaviour under scrutiny is apparently multifaceted, involving a confluence of social, legal, political, organizational and cultural factors. The following chapters of this book utilize these methodologies to study how *Taishinin* justices behaved in corruption cases. The *Taishinin* cases examined in this book transpired from the mid-1920s to the 1930s. Consequently, the macro-quantitative methodology characteristic of social science is not employed. This is due to an absence of primary statistical data. Maveety's three judicial behaviour models, particularly historical institutionalism, elucidate the determination of *Taishinin*'s role within the prewar state political system under the jurisdiction of the Minister of Justice, among other factors. Readers will read how judges in prewar Japan had strict legal interpretations to create a "Japanese body" to fit into the "jacket of transplanted Germanic law".

Two authors introduce a new strict liability model to elucidate *Taishinin*'s judicial behaviour, complementing Maveety's three models. Two authors also posit that the study of judicial behaviour can be advanced by integrating the insights of judicial behaviour researchers with the ethical commitments of fair society studies. The rationale underlying this phenomenon is evident. The universal standard for the assessment of the fairness of the legal system is not a straightforward task. The study of fair societies represents a recent development in academic research. A close examination of these two academic fields reveals their shared adherence to legal realism. The concept of fairness is predicated on the principle of justice, which is defined as the guarantee of each individual's fundamental needs for a life of happiness and personal autonomy.[35] Analysis of *Taishinin*'s judicial behaviour reveals its extent of fairness to prewar Japanese society. Fair society studies, universality/universalism and cultural relativism are imperative to generate new novel concepts about judicial behaviour, as detailed in Chapter 10 of this book.

In the following chapter, an examination is conducted on historical evolution of Japanese anti-corruption legislation and the conventional legal principles associated with *Taishinin*'s judicial behaviour models.

[35] On this see Chandler 2023.

References

Agustin, E. D. (2016) Arguments for or against an emerging eclectic theory of law. *International Comparative Jurisprudence*, Vol. 2 (2), 61–130.

Baum, L. (1994) What Judges Want: Judges' Goals and Judicial Behavior. *Political Research Quarterly* Vol. 47 (3), 749–768.

Baum, L. (2006) *Judges and Their Audiences: A Perspective on Judicial Behavior*. Princeton University Press.

Becker, T. L. (1969) *The Impact of Supreme Court Decisions: Empirical Studies*. Oxford University Press.

Bergara, M., Barak R., Pablo T. S. (2003) Modeling Supreme Court Strategic Decision Making: The Congressional Constraint. *Legislative Studies Quarterly*, Vol. 28 (2), 247–280.

Bingham, J. W. (1912) What is the Law. *Michigan Law Review*, Vol. 11 (1), 109–121.

Black, D. J. (1976) *The Behavior of Law*. Academic Press.

Black, D. J. (1989) *Sociological Justice*. Oxford University Press

Bowie, J. B., Songer, D. R. (2009) Assessing the Applicability of Strategic Theory to Explain Decision Making on the Courts of Appeals. *Political Research Quarterly*, Vol. 62 (2), 393–407.

Boya, C. L., Spriggs, J. F. (2009) An Examination of Strategic Anticipation of Appellate Court Preferences by Federal District Court Judges. *Washington University Journal of Law and Policy*, Vol. 29, 37–81.

Brace, P. et al. (1999) Judicial Choice and the Politics of Abortion: Institutions, Context, and the Autonomy of Courts. *Albany Law Review*, Vol. 62 (4), 1265.

Brenner, D., Cohen, A. (2016) Ideology and Strategy among Politicians: The Case of Judicial Independence. *Review of Law and Economics*, Vol. 12 (2), 333–375.

Brenner, S., Whitmeyer, J. M. (2009) *Strategy on the United States Supreme Court*. Cambridge University Press.

Cameron, C. M., Kornhauser, L. A. (2017) Rational choice attitudinalism? A review of Epstein, Landes and Posner's The behavior of federal judges: a theoretical and empirical study of rational choice. *European Journal of Law and Economics*, Vol. 43 (3), 535–554.

Cann, D. M. (2002) Campaign Contributions and Judicial Behavior. *The American Review of Politics*, Vol. 23, 261–274.

Carrubba, C. J. et al. (2008) Judicial Behavior under Political Constraints: Evidence from the European Court of Justice. *American Political Science Review* Vol. 102(4), 435–452.

Chandler, D. (2023) *Free and Equal: What would a fair society look like?* Penguin Random House.

Christie, G. (1964) Vagueness and Legal Language. *Minnesota Law Review*. Vol. 48, 885–1011.

Cohen, F. S. (1935) Transcendental Nonsense and the Functional Approach. *Columbia Law Review*, Vol. 35 (6), 809–849.

Cook, B. B. (1977) Public Opinion and Federal Judicial Policy. *American Journal of Political Science*, Vol. 21 (3), 567–600.

Corwin, E. S. (1929) The Democratic Dogma and the Future of Political Science. *The American Political Science Review*, Vol. 23 (3), 569–592.

Corwin, E. S. (1974) *The Constitution and What It Means Today* (13th ed). Princeton University Press.

Corwin, E. S., Peltason, J. W. (1934) *The Twilight of the Supreme Court: A History of Our Constitutional Theory*. Yale University Press.

Corwin, E. S., Louis W. K. (1956) *The Presidency Today*. New York University Press.

Dahl, R. A. (1957) Decision-Making in a Democracy: The Supreme Court as a National. Policy-Maker. *Journal of Public Law*, Vol. 6 (2), 279–295.

Dahl, R. A. (1989) *Democracy and Its Critics*. Yale University Press.

Dahl, R. A., Stinebrickner, B. (2003) *Modern political analysis* (6th ed.). Prentice Hall.

Danelski, D. J. (1964) *A Supreme Court Justice is Appointed*. Random House.

Edwards, H. T. (1998) Collegiality and Decision Making on the D.C. Circuit. *Virginia Law Review* Vol. 84 (7),1335–1370.

Emmert, C. F. (1992) An Integrated Case-Related Model of Judicial Decision Making: Explaining. Supreme Court Decisions in Judicial Review Cases. *Journal of Politics*, Vol. 45, 543–552.
Epstein, L., Knight, J. (1998) *The Choices Justices Make*. CQ Press.
Epstein, L., Jacobi, T. (2010) The Strategic Analysis of Judicial Decisions. *Annual Review of Law and Social Science*, Vol. 6, 341–358.
Epstein, L., Landes, W. M., Posner, R. A. (2013) *A review of Epstein, Landes and Posner's The behavior of federal judges: a theoretical and empirical study of rational choice*. Harvard University Press.
Epstein, L., Knight, J. (2013) Reconsidering Judicial Preferences. *Annual Review of Political Science*, Vol. 16, 11–31.
Epstein, L., Weinshall, K. (2021) *The Strategic Analysis of Judicial Behavior: A Comparative Perspective*. Cambridge University Press.
Farbman, D. (2022) Judicial Solidarity. *Yale Journal of Law and the Humanities*. Vol. 33 (1), 1–58.
Fioretos, O. et al. (2016) *The Oxford Handbook of Historical Institutionalism*. Oxford University Press.
Frank, J. P. (1949) Ingredients of Judicial Biography. *Indiana Law Journal*. Vol. 24 (3), 374–381.
Gaffney, E. M. J., (1976) History and Legal Interpretation: The Early Distortion of the Fourteenth Amendment by the Gilded Age Court. *Catholic University Law Review*, Vol. 25 (2), 207–249.
Gely, R., Spiller, T. (1990) A rational choice theory of Supreme Court statutory decisions with applications to the State Farm and Grove City cases. *Journal of Law, Economics, and Organization*, Vol. 6 (2), 263–300.
Geyh, C. G. (2012) Can the Rule of Law Survive Judicial Politics. *Cornell Law Review*, Vol. 97 (2), 191–254.
Geyh, C. G. (2021) Judicial Independence at Twilight. *Case Western Reserve Law Review*, Vol. 71 (3), 1045–1109.
Gibson, J. L. (1983) From Simplicity to Complexity: The Development of Theory in the Study of Judicial Behavior. *Political Behavior*, Vol. 5 (1), 7–49.
Gillman, H., Clayton, C. (1999) *The Supreme Court in American Politics: New Institutionalist Interpretations*. University Press of Kansas.
Graber, M. (1993) The Nonmajoritarian Difficulty: Legislative Deference to the Judiciary. *Studies in American Political Development*, Vol. 7 (1), 35–73.
Gunther, G. (1994). *Learned Hand: The Man and the Judge*. Alfred A. Knopf.
Green, S. P. (2005) Six Senses of Strict Liability: A Plea for Formalism. In Simester, A. (ed.) *Appraising Strict Liability Get access Arrow*. Oxford University Press.
Guimaraes, T. A. et al. (2018) Administration of justice: an emerging research field. *RAUSP Management Journal*, Vol. 53 (3), 476–482.
Horowitz, D. (1977) *The Courts and Social Policy*. Brookings Institution Press.
Howard, W. J. (1968) On the Fluidity of Judicial Choice. *The American Political Science Review*, Vol. 62 (1), 43–56.
Howard, W. J. (1981) *Courts of Appeals in the Federal Judicial System: A Study of the Second, Fifth, and District of Columbia Circuits Courts of Appeals in the Federal Judicial System*. Princeton University Press.
Huber, G. A., Gordon, S. C. (2004) Accountability and Coercion: Is Justice Blind When It Runs for Office? *American Journal of Political Science*, Vol. 48 (2), 247–263.
Ingersoll, D. E., Karl, L. (1996) American Legal Realism, and Contemporary Legal Behavioralism" *Ethics*, Vol. 76 (4), 253–266.
Jeff, S. (2010) *Supreme power: Franklin Roosevelt vs. the Supreme Court*. W.W. Norton & Company.
Jeffries, J. J. (1994) *Justice Lewis F Powell, Jr*. Charles Scriber's Sons.
Josev, T. (2017) Judicial Biography in Australia: Current Obstacles and Opportunities. *University of New South Wales Law Journal*, Vol. 40 (2), 842.
Lahav, P. (1997) *Judgement in Jerusalem: Chief Justice Simon Agranat and the Zionist Century*. University of California Press.

Lewis, O. C. (1970) Systems Theory and Judicial Behavioralism. *Case Western Reserve Law Review*, Vol, 21 (3). 361–465.
Lijphart, A. (1971) Comparative Politics and the Comparative Method. *American Political Science Review*, Vol 65 (3), 682–693.
Llewellyn, K. N. (1930) A Realistic Jurisprudence-the Next Step. *Columbia Law Review*, No. 30, 431–65.
Loughlin, M. (2018) *Political Jurisprudence*. Oxford University Press.
Marks, B. A. (2015) A model of judicial influence on congressional policy-making: Grove City College v. Bell. *The Journal of Law, Economics, & Organization*, Vol 31 (4), 843–875.
Mason, A. T. (1941) *Bureaucracy Convicts Itself*. The Viking Press.
Mason, A. T. (1955) *Security through freedom: American Political Thought and Practice*. Cornell University Press.
Mason, A. T. (1957) *Harlan Fiske Stone: Pillar of the Law*. The Viking Press.
Mason, A. T. (1962) *The Supreme Court: Palladium of Freedom*. The University of Michigan Press.
Mather, L. (1994) Introducing a Feminist Pioneer in Judicial Politics: Beverly Blair Cook. *Political Science and Politics*, Vol. 27 (1), 76 – 78.
Maveety, N. (2006) *The Pioneers of Judicial Behavior*. University of Michigan Press.
McCall, M. (2003) The Politics of Judicial Elections: The Influence of Campaign Contributions on the Voting Patterns of Texas Supreme Court Justices, 1994–1997. *Politics and Policy*, Vol. 31 (2), 314–343.
McCloskey, R. G. (1951) *American Conservatism in the Age of Enterprise: A Study of William Graham Sumner, Stephen J. Field, and Andrew Carnegie*. Harvard University Press.
McCloskey, R. G. (1961) *The American Supreme Court*. University of Chicago Press.
McCloskey, R. G. (1972) *The Modern Supreme Court* (Shapiro, M ed.). Harvard University Press.
McNollgast (1995) Politics and the courts: A positive theory of judicial doctrine and the rule of law. *Southern California Law Review*, Vol. 68 (6),1631–1683.
Melnick, S. R. (1983) *Regulation and the Courts: The Case of the Clean Air Act*. Brookings Institution.
Melnick, S. R. (1994) *Between the Lines: Interpreting Welfare Rights*. Brookings Institution.
Murphy, W. F. (2016) *Elements of Judicial Strategy*. Quid Pro Books.
Murphy, W. F., Thnenhaus, J. (1972) *The Study of Public Law*. Random House.
Newman, R. K. (1994) *Hugo Black: A Biography*. Pantheon Books.
O'Brien, D. M. (1983) Reconsidering Whence and Whither Political Jurisprudence. *The Western Political Quarterly*, Vol. 36 (4), 558–569.
Peck, S. R. (1967) A Behavioural Approach to the Judicial Process: Scalogram Analysis. *Osgoode Hall Law Journal*, Vol. 5 (1), 1–28.
Perino, M. A. (2006) Law, Ideology, and Strategy in Judicial Decision Making: Evidence from Securities Fraud Actions. *Journal of Empirical Legal Studies*, Vol. 3 (3), 497–524.
Posner, R. A. (1995) Judicial Biography. *New York University Law Review*, Vol. 70 (3), 502–523.
Posner, R. A. (2005) Judicial Behavior and Performance: An Economic Approach. *Florida State University Law Review*, Vol. 32 (4), 1259–1279.
Posner, R. A. (2008) *How Judges Think*. Harvard University Press.
Pritchett, H. C. (1941) Divisions of opinion among justices of the U.S. Supreme Court, 1939–1941. *American Political Science Review*, No.35 (5), 890–898.
Pritchett, H. C. (1948) *The Roosevelt Court: A Study in Judicial Politics and Values 1937–1947*. The Macmillan Company.
Pritchett, H. C. (1961) *Congress versus the Supreme Court*. University of Minnesota Press.
Pritchett, H. C. (1968) Public Law and Judicial Behavior. *The Journal of Politics*, Vol. 30 (2), 480–509.
Radio France Internationale (2022) Japan minister resigns after criticism over death penalty remarks, 11 November 2022. https://www.rfi.fr/en/international-news/20221111-japan-minister-resigns-after-criticism-over-death-penalty-remarks. Accessed 26 January 2023.
Rohde, D. W., Spaeth, H. J. (1976) *Supreme Court Decision Making*. W. H. Freeman.

Rosenberg, G. (1991) *The Hollow Hope: Can Courts Bring About Social Change?* University of Chicago Press.
Ruger, T. W. et al. (2004) The Supreme Court Forecasting Project: Legal and Political Science Approaches to Predicting Supreme Court Decision-making. *Columbia Law Review*. Vol. 104 (4), 1150–1210.
Schubert, G. A. (1958) The Study of Judicial Decision-Making as an Aspect of Political Behavior. *American Political Science Review*. Vol. 52 (4), 1007–1025,
Schubert, G. A. (1959) *Quantitative Analysis of Judicial Behavior*. The Free Press of Glencoe.
Schubert, G. A. (1960) *Quantitative Analysis of Judicial Behavior*. The Free Press of Glencoe.
Schubert, G. A. ed. (1963) *Judicial Decision-Making*. The Free Press of Glencoe.
Schubert. G. A. (1965) *The Judicial Mind: The Attitudes and Ideologies of Supreme Court Justices 1946–1963*. Northwestern University Press.
Schubert, G. A. (1969) Judicial Attitudes and Policy-Making in the Dixon Court. *Osgoode Hall Law Journal*, Vol. 7 (1), 1–29.
Segal, J. A., Cover, A. D. (1989) Ideological Values and the Votes of U.S. Supreme Court Justices. *American Political Science Review*, Vol. 83 (2), 557–565.
Segal, J. A. et al. (1992) A Spatial Model of Roll Call Voting: Senators, Constituents, Presidents, and Interest Groups in Supreme Court Confirmations. *American Journal of Political Science*, Vol. 36 (1), 96–121.
Segal, J. A., Spaeth, H. J. (1993) *The Supreme Court and the Attitudinal Model*. Cambridge University Press.
Segal, J. A., Spaeth, H. J. (1996a) The influence of stare decisis on the votes of United States Supreme Court justices. *American Journal of Political Science*, Vol. 40 (4), 971–1003.
Segal, J. A., Spaeth, H. J. (1996b) Norms, dragons and stare decisis: a response. *American Journal of Political Science*, Vol. 40 (4), 1064–1082.
Segal, J. A. (2008) Judicial Behavior. In Gregory, A. C. et al. ed. *The Oxford Handbook of Law and Politics* (pp. 19–33). Oxford University Press.
Shapiro, M. (1961a) Judicial modesty, political reality, and preferred position. *Cornell Law Review*, Vol. 47 (2), 175–204.
Shapiro, M. (1961b) Morals and the courts: the reluctant crusaders. *Minnesota Law Review*, Vol. 45, 897–961.
Shapiro, M. (1963) Political Jurisprudence. *Kentucky Law Journal*, Vol. 52 (2), 294–345.
Shapiro, M. (1964) *Law and Politics in the Supreme Court*. The Free Press of Glencoe.
Shapiro, M. (1980) Appeal. *Law and Society Review*, Vol. 14 (3), 629–662.
Shapiro, M. (1981) *Courts: A Comparative and Political Analysis*. University of Chicago Press.
Shepherd, J. M. (2009) Are Appointed Judges Strategic Too? *Duke Law Review*, Vol. 58, 1589–1626.
Shepherd, J. M. (2011) Measuring maximizing judges: Empirical legal studies, public choice theory and judicial behavior. *University of Illinois Law Review*, Vol. 2011 (5), 1753–1766.
Shklar, J. N. (1986) *Legalism: Law, Morals, and Political Trials*. Harvard University Press.
Smith, R. (1988) Political Jurisprudence, the "New Institutionalizing and the Future of Public Law". *American Political Science Review* Vol. 82 (1), 89–108.
Smith, R. (1989) The new institutionalism and normative theory: reply to Professor Barber. *Studies in American Political Development*, Vol. 3, Spring, 74–87.
Songer, D. R. (2012) The dog that did not bark: Debunking the myths surrounding the attitudinal model of Supreme Court decision making. *The Justice System Journal*, Vol. 33 (3), 340–363.
Songer, D. R. et al. (2012) *Law, Ideology, and Collegiality: Judicial Behaviour in the Supreme Court of Canada*. McGill Queen's University Press.
Spaeth, H. J. (1962) Judicial Power as a Variable Motivating Supreme Court Behavior. *Midwest Journal of Political Science*, Vol. 6 (1), 54–82.
Spaeth, H. J., Segal, J. A. (1999) *Majority Rule or Minority Will: Adherence to Precedent on the U.S. Supreme Court*. Cambridge University Press.
Spaeth, H. J., Segal, J. A. (2002) *The Supreme Court and the Attitudinal Model Revisited*. Cambridge University Press.

Spaeth, H. J. (2004) An Unexamined Feature of Supreme Court Decision Making. *The Justice System Journal*, Vol. 25 (2), 143–158.

Staton, J. K. (2018) Judicial Independence Research Beyond the Crossroads. In Howard, R. M., Kirk, A. R. ed. *Routledge Handbook of Judicial Behavior*. Routledge.

Steinmo, S. et al. (1992) *Structuring politics Structuring Politics: Historical Institutionalism in Comparative Analysis*. Cambridge University Press.

Tate, N. C. (1983) The Methodology of Judicial Behavior Research: A Review and Critique. *Political Behavior*, Vol. 5 (1), 51–82.

Sugarman, D. (2015) From Legal Biography to Legal Life Writing: Broadening Conceptions of Legal History and Socio-legal Scholarship. *Journal of Law and Society*, Vol.42 (1), 7–33.

Tumonis, V. (2012) Legal Realism and Judicial Decision-Making. *Jurisprudence*. Vol. 19 (4), 1361–1382.

Ulmer, S. (1960) Analysis of Behavior Patterns on the United States Supreme Court. *The Journal of Politics*, Vol. 22 (4), 629–653.

Waltenburg, E. N., Lopeman, C. S. (2008) Tort decisions and campaign dollars. *Southeastern Political Review*, Vol. 28 (2), 241–263.

Ware, S. J. (1999) Money, Politics and Judicial Decisions: A Case Study of Arbitration Law in Alabama. *Journal of Law and Politics*, No. 15, 645–685.

Chapter 3
Historical Evolution of Japanese Anti-Corruption Law

3.1 Introduction

This chapter has two objectives. First, it examines the evolution of Japanese values, norms and legal concepts related to corruption over time. This approach forms the foundation of *Taishinin*'s methodology for adjudicating corruption cases. Secondly, before analysis of *Taishinin*'s judgements in the following five chapters, it is crucial to understand the historical evolution of corruption as a criminal act in Japan. Anti-corruption legislation had endeavoured to prevent corruption from eroding social fairness and the rule of law in Japan for more than 1500 years. Building upon the review of anti-corruption legislation in Japan since 512, this chapter highlights the forces driving the evolution of judicial behaviour against corruption until the transplantation of Germanic Penal Code in 1907. It is unsurprising that *Taishinin*'s judicial behaviour was of nostalgia for traditional Japanese legal values.

3.2 Legal Consciousness Against Corruption

The legal framework under discussion is markedly distinct from that of *hōishiki*, which is often referred to as legal consciousness. *Hōishiki* is a system that analyses the thought processes and behaviours of individuals in relation to their experiences, comprehension of the world, actions, emotions and cultural practices. The "identity school" places emphasis on legal awareness and the identity of a group that comes together and exerts influence on one another. The "hegemony school" of legal thought posits that legal consciousness functions as a potent instrument employed by nations to exercise control over their populace. The "mobilization school" conceptualizes legal awareness as a means to comprehend the utilization of legislation for the enhancement of society (Chua and Engel 2019, pp. 337–343). Without *hōishiki*, the general public may not be cognizant of the legal ramifications associated with

K. B. Wong and S. L. Fang, *Taishinin's Judicial Behaviour in Corruption Cases*,
https://doi.org/10.1007/978-981-95-5823-0_3

corruption in their daily lives. This phenomenon can result in practices that initially appear to be lawful, but upon closer scrutiny, are found to be in violation of established legal statutes. The Japanese tradition of gift-giving serves as a prime example of this phenomenon. This phenomenon has the effect of normalizing and rationalizing corruption by portraying it as a collective societal practice.[1] The codification of legislation aimed at deterrence against deleterious conduct represents merely the initial phase in a broader societal endeavour (Rawls 1999, pp. 24–46).

The subsequent tier involves the establishment of rules and terms of authorization or empowerment to enforce it for formal social control (MacCormick 1998, pp. 316–317). Judicial behaviour for the efficient and effective enforcement of legislation in a legal culture belongs to the second tier.[2] The legal system and the culture surrounding it interact with social forces (Friedman 1987, p. 2). Additionally, it fosters a more profound comprehension of the legal system, encompassing *hōishiki* for its practical application in real-life scenarios and the significance of adhering to legal principles in addressing illicit actions (Galanter 2005, p. 5).

Judges' judicial behaviour wields a considerable degree of influence in shaping the public's comprehension of the law as *hōishiki*. Nevertheless, they are not immune to its sway themselves. Judges are continually reinterpreting and commenting on legislations, thereby updating social understanding of the law (Levon 2014, p. 18). Furthermore, the phenomenon is subject to variation based on social hierarchies and the experiences, relationships and attitudes of different social groups (Nielsen 2000, pp. 1055–1056, p. 1086). According to Bellah, social relationships represent a fundamental component of Japanese culture (Bellah 1970, pp. 114–115). This approach bears a striking resemblance to the structuralism espoused by the renowned French anthropologist Claude Lévi-Strauss. Lévi-Strauss placed significant emphasis on the notion of cultural diversity. He posited that this diversity could facilitate our comprehension of local interpretations of social facts and their evolution.[3] The legal culture of a society exerts a significant influence on the extent of its members' interactions with the law. The concept of legal consciousness exerts a significant influence on individual behaviour, self-regulation and adherence to social norms (Nadareishvili and Chkheidze 2015, pp. 123–124).

During the Meiji era, Japanese laws and social relations had long embraced the idea that corruption was totally wrong. Corruption can be defined as the abuse of the principal-agent relationship of power between the emperor or ruling class and officials. Furthermore, the study found that social relationships also played a role in the criminalization of corruption (Silbey 2001, pp. 8626–8627). The most evident illustration of this phenomenon is the exclusion of bribery within "private-to-private" social relations from the contemporary iteration of the Japanese Penal Code. The aforementioned legislation against "private-to-private" bribery is codified in three current Japanese laws: the Japanese Companies Act, the Financial Instruments and Exchange Act and the Bankruptcy Code. In Japan, the distinction between bribes and

[1] On this see World Bank Institute (2008, p. 4).

[2] On this see Treisman (2003).

[3] On this see Darnell (1995).

gifts can be challenging to discern. A review of prewar Taishinin's judicial behaviour in Chap. 8 reveals that it employed its own unique interpretation and expansive legal reasoning, effectively criminalizing midyear gift-giving.

3.3 Bribery in *Nihonshoki*, *Taihō-Ritsuryō* and *Asukakiyomihara-Ryō*

The practice of bribery has been deemed illicit in Japan since the term *mainai* (bribe) was documented in Volume 17 of *Nihonshoki*.[4] The crime of bribery in Japan has a history that is more than 1500 years old in historical institutionalism. According to Japanese law, the term *mainai* was originally employed to denote gifts of money or goods that are bestowed for inappropriate reasons, such as the pursuit of personal financial gain. The earliest extant references to Japanese divinity being corrupted are from the third century. Nonetheless, the earliest Japanese record of it is found in Volume 17 of Emperor Keitai in *Nihonshoki*.

In December 512 (*Keitai* 6), the kingdom in the North Korean peninsula, *Kōkuri* (Goguryeo), expelled another kingdom in the west, *Kutara* (Baekje), to move southward. In order to safeguard its domains, Baekje drafted a request to Yamato (Japan) for the land of four regions of *Mimana* (a small nation in the south of the peninsula), Okoshitari, Aroshitari, Sada and Muro which were considered under the Japanese regime. *Nihonshoki* wrote that the request was eventually achieved with the help of the powerful and influential *Ōmuraji* (severed as the emperor's regent), Ōtomono Kanamura and Hozumino Omioshiyama, who was the *kokushu* (head of state) of Okoshitari accepted Baekje's *mainai* (bribe). This was the first bribery behaviour in Japanese written history, especially it was given to someone in the upper social hierarchy.[5] However, no legal punishment was recorded for this immoral act. In *Nihonshoki*, *mainai* refers to gifts given to people directly. In the current study of corruption, this case is considered a form of "grand corruption", which is defined as the misuse of significant power that benefits a small group of people while causing significant harm to many others, which often goes unpunished.[6]

In June 527 (*Keitai* 21), the Yamato court attempted to send troops to *Mimana* for the protection of Baekje resisting the extension of Shiragi (or Shinra, the powerful kingdom in the east of the Korean peninsula). However, it was blocked by the *Gōzoku* (powerful regional family) of Iwai at Tsukushi (or Chikushi) of Kyūshū. Shiragi learnt of this rebellion and secretly bribed Iwai in order to encourage his interference with

[4] *Nihonshoki* (Chronicles of Japan), text that, together with the *Kojiki*, comprises the oldest official history of Japan, covering the period from its mythical origins to AD 697.

See "*Nihonshoki*" at https://www.britannica.com/topic/Nihon-shoki. Accessed 1 September 2025.

[5] The original text in *Nihonshoki*: 於是或有流言曰大伴大連與哆唎國守穗積臣押山受百濟之賂矣。See Uematsu (1920, pp. 24–26).

[6] On this see "*What is grand corruption and how can we stop it?*" at https://www.transparency.org/en/news/what-is-grand-corruption-and-how-can-we-stop-it. Accessed 17 July 2022.

the Yamato arm led by Ōminokena.[7] The word *mainai* was used again in *Nihonshogi* for Shiragi's bribery behaviour (Aston 2023, pp. 282–299). Bribery in this case is strategical in the game theory of corruption, which is about officials' rationales for corrupt decisions and strategy after a calculation of pros and cons and interactions among agents of interest. Game theory helps in the manipulation of social controls (Birmingham 1970, pp. 57–73). Bribery in Iwai Rebellion is a case of this kind.

Nihonshoki does not record any law that criminalized bribery or corruption. The earliest Japanese legislation that criminalized it was the *Taihō-ritsuryō* of 17th articles codified by Prince Shōtoku (574–622). It was nicknamed the Seventeen-Article Constitution as the earliest constitution in the world. *Ritsu* means criminal law and *ryō* means administrative law under the influence of the Tang Dynasty of China. In Japan, the earliest *ryō* was the *Ōmi-ryō* complied by Fujiwara Kamatari during the reign of the Emperor Tenchi in 671 (*Tenchi* 10). The *Ōmi-ryō* was issued in the form of imperial court decrees. And the main content was the Emperor's order, especially information on the decree for posting and administrative ranking of officials (Hasunuma 2006, pp. 1–4). This traditional judicial function of the Emperor's imperial decree was a source of law in the Japanese legal tradition, which affected judicial behaviour of judiciary lasted until the end of the Pacific War. The term "Imperial Rescript" is often used in English translation.

Before the full completion of the *Taihō-ritsuryō* in 701, the *Asukakiyomihara-ryō* was compiled under the order of the Emperor Tenmu in 681 and completed in 689. The *Asukakiyomihara-ryō* was considered to mark the initial administration structure under official, also the household registration and eligibility to receive arable land. The judicial enforcement of the *Asukakiyomihara-ryō* was difficult as it contradicted against the social reality of lack of an effective criminal justice system, social relations for formal social control and economic conditions in the Heian period. It had merely become a nominal enforcement by the mid-Heian period (Naoki 1999, pp. 4–5, pp. 10–13). Both the *Ōmi-ryō* and the *Asukakiyomihara-ryō* were never in place but simply set a legislative model for the *Taihō-ritsuryō*, in which Article 5 was an anti-corruption provision formalizing the legal consciousness against corruption.

The *Taihō-ritsuryō* is always misunderstood as an independently codified legislation. In fact, *Nihonshoki* first mentioned it in the section on the personal history of the Emperor Suiko in April 604 (*Suiko* 12) (Masamune 1930, pp. 311–312). Although criminal law was modelled on the legal value of the *Eiki-ritsuryō* (*Yonghuiling*) of the Tang Dynasty of China, administrative law and the legal order for trials were legislative attempts to adapt to the social reality in Japan. It was extensively modified until 701 in order to achieve its legislative intent.[8]

With the full completion of the *Taihō-ritsuryō* in 701, the entire national code was completed in Japan for the first time. Article 5 stigmatized corruption and emphasized the importance of judicial behaviour for justice as *Shin-dō* (the duty or proper way of a person in a subordinate position to another). It states, "Officials should not indulge

[7] The original text in *Nihonshoki*: 新羅知是密行貨賂于磐井所而勸防遏毛野臣軍。See (Uematsu 1920, pp. 35–36).

[8] See Yamakawashuppansha (2018, p. 41).

in sumptuous feast and desire. They should administer citizens' litigation fairly and efficiently though there may be thousands of such litigation cases. Nowadays, those officials who administer justice always accept bribes and undue interest and ignorant of what a vassal should behave and what a bureaucrat should act as *Shin-dō* in social relations. Litigation is thereby like a meaningless act of throwing a stone into water."[9] The legal consciousness against bureaucratic corruption embedded in Article 5 was out of people's experience, understanding, actions and feelings in a corrupt social reality. The harm of corruption on the stability of social relations was sensed.

Article 5 was against "private-to-public" bribery. Corruption as an issue for the administration of justice implied that the judicial behaviour of the court was suffering from institutionalized judicial corruption. Deviant organizational culture and the abuse of power delegated through the "principal-agent" social hierarchy of *Shin-dō* (臣道, the duty or proper way of a person in a subordinate position to another) were common. In the typology of corruption, judicial corruption targeted by Article 5 is the most fatal. Judicial corruption is more than just abuse of official duty or power for personal or private gain. It can distort justice to be injustice and vice versa. The linguistic discourse of the term *tsunemi* (regularly seen) in Article 5 also reflects that the social reality was systemic corruption, also known as endemic corruption. The independent-minded judges' judicial behaviour of proper integrity and ethics is rare. This occurs when political leaders fail to manipulate administrative institutionalism to control corruption in judicial behaviour. Systemic corruption in the judiciary means that channels in the social hierarchy facilitate corruption upwards to contaminate the judicial behaviour of elite judges. This type of corruption usually originates from bribe collectors at the bottom (Langseth 1999, p. 5). In other words, judicial corruption is the lawlessness of no control by judicial behaviour.

3.4 Hegemonic Emperor, Principal-Agent Theory and Punitive *Taihō-Ritsuryō*

According to the *Taihō-ritsuryō*, the Emperor was the principal of all powers under the principal-agent theory. All officials were his agents for exercising power delegated by him (Rose-Ackerman 2006, p. xiv–xxxviii). Persson, Rothstein and Teorell argue that the principal-agent theory of corruption is based on the assumption of goal conflict between principals and agents and that agents have more information for abusing power than the principal (Persson et al. 2013, p. 456). Information asymmetry between them creates a loophole for the abuse of power for private gain, because the principal does not have such information to identify loopholes. Article 5 of the *Taihō-ritsuryō* was the first legal provision in Japan for the formal social control of judicial officials who were agents of the powers delegated by the principal Emperor

[9] The original text in *Nihonshoki*: 五曰絶饗棄欲明辨訴訟其百姓之訟一日千事一日尚爾況乎累歳須治訟者得利爲常見賄聽讞便有財之訟如石投水乏者之訴似水投石是以貧則不知所由臣道亦於焉闕。See Hayashi (1939, pp. 6-7).

Suiko. Anti-corruption judicial behaviour is expected from an equitable fair body administrating justice that fights corruption, not the other way around (Gloppen 2014, p. 73).

For this objective, the punishments stipulated in the rules for officials of the *Taihō-ritsuryō* were severe as the acceptance of bribe was punishable by exile. In case of acceptance of bribes and commission of crime as *ōhōzō* (an aggravating factor), the maximum punishment was death penalty. The cost of crime has increased significantly for deterrence. Although the central government copied laws along the lines of Tang China to consolidate the Emperor's imperial rule, the Chinese social relation of the Mandate of Heaven, which might potentially be used by another for the potential justification of a revolution, was discarded in the entire *Taihō-ritsuryō*. This meant that no one could thereafter use the law to claim a legitimate social relationship with the Mandate of Heaven except the Emperor, whose hegemony was thus easily resumed in the Meiji Restoration. The *Taihō-ritsuryō* indoctrinated the political ideology of conformity to group interest, integrity and loyalty to superiors, which were essences embedded in traditional Japanese legal consciousness against corruption (Bolz 1980, pp. 95–96). The same legal consciousness against corruption can be read between the lines in *Taishinin* judgements as part of its judicial behaviour.

3.5 Bribery Recorded in *Shokunihongi*

After the *Taihō-ritsuryō*, the compilation of *Shokunihongi* (history text coming directly after *Nihonshoki*) was started in early Heian period and completed in 797 (*Nobereki* 16) mainly by Fujiwara Tsugutada and Sugano Mamichi, covering the historical events from the first year of Emperor Bunbu to 791 (*Nobereki* 10). Volume 39 of *Shokunihongi* records that during the reign of Emperor Kanmu in 793 (*Nobereki* 12), "citizens complained against corruption and unfairness of bureaucrats' performance of official duties. They were notorious for being sly, and perpetually annoyed citizens. They used to drink wine and did not care about their duties. They indulged their subordinates to be solicited by selfish private gains upon discharging their official duties".[10]

This historical record shows that government officials at all levels were involved in widespread structural corruption. This corruption was the organizational part of a system that was designed to self-protect the organization from outside scrutiny for transparency. Their working culture did not care about their responsibility to the Emperor.[11] The idea that corruption is the result of people acting together can be used to understand what happened in *Shokunihongi*. A large group of dishonest government officials took over an institution by convincing each other that being

[10] The original text in *Shokunihongi*:在官貪濁處事不平肆行姦猾以求名譽畋遊無度擾乱百姓嗜酒沈湎廢闕公務公節無聞私門日益放縱子弟請託公行。See *Keizaizashisha* (1897).

[11] The original text in *Shokunihongi*:於事商量甚乖道理。See *Keizaizashisha* (1897); also see Thompson (1995, pp. 7-8).

corrupt was normal for the organization (Olson 2002, pp. 125–128). *Shokunihongi* saw it as a big problem in Japanese culture. It was a behaviour deviant from the legal idea of *dōri* (divine principle). This deviation was caused by a large number of greedy bureaucrats. The court was expected to punish these bureaucrats.[12]

3.6 Importance of *Dōri* in Social Control

Today, bribery is a *tsumi* (crime) under the Japanese Penal Code. In April 718 (*Yōrō* 2), *Shokunihongi* formally applied equitable *dōri* (on "*dōri*" see "*Taishinin*'s *Kenri*" in Chap. 1) as a legal consciousness against corruption.[13] *Dōri* is synonymous with *jōri* (natural reason) (Sato 2001, p. 73). Under *dōri*, crime in ancient Japan was religiously associated with the impurity of the soul contaminated by dirt instead of merely being an offence punishable by court. *Dōri* in traditional Japanese legal consciousness was rooted in the hybridity of religious belief of Buddhist Law and Shintō belief. Breach of *dōri* was *prima facie* a conflict of ideological consciousness between two Japanese religions, one indigenous and the other was imported Buddhist Law.[14] *Dōri* can also be seen in *Ōharaenonorito* that is important in Shintō ritual prayers for exorcism or ceremonial chants, also known as *Ōharaenokotoba*, complied in volume eight of *Engishiki* (a book about Japanese laws and customs completed in 927). *Engishiki* was completed in 905 (*Enki* 5) by a team of eleven, led by Fujiwara Tokihira and Fujiwara Tadahira in the Heian era. During the long Heian period, on the eve of June and December each year, the *Nakatomi* (a religious ritual official),[15] made a presentation of it at the *Suzakumon* gate to purify the crimes and impurities committed as a *dōri* matter. The Buddhist and Shinto religious origin of *dōri* made *dōri* like nature law of relation to positive law. Natural law is system of right or nature justice which was originated from nature, reason and morality instead of law codified by legislature in a society. Natural law derived from nature and reason is common to every human being and oblige human behaviour. Legal development of similarity to *dōri* as natural law can also be found in Bologna, Italy, where Gratian, a Benedictine monk and scholar in the twelfth century, equated natural law with divine law by both juristic and scholastic approaches for canon law.[16]

Dōri was the most important equitable legal consciousness of morality and unwritten law of religious implications that reinforced the ultimate necessity to end crime by punishment. Religious elements of Shinto gradually further reinforced *dōri*

[12] The original text in *Shokunihongi*:今乃苟貪公廨徵求以甚。See *Keizaizashisha* (1897).

[13] The original text in *Shokunihongi*:於義商量甚違道理。See *Keizaizashisha* (1897).

[14] On this see Brown (2006).

[15] See "Nakatomi Hara" at https://www.city.hirosaki.aomori.jp/gaiyou/bunkazai/shi/shi55.html. Accessed 15 September 2025.

[16] See "Natural Law" at https://www.britannica.com/topic/natural-law. Accessed 15 September 2025.

with more moral principles, circulating in self-regulation, performance of normative behaviour, social relations and legal interpretation in Japan (Arai 1967, p. 296). During the Kamakura Shogunate (1185–1333), the number of disputes increased in the absence of effective nationwide statutory law enforcement to settle them. Samurai control was mainly based on informal social control of flexible *dōri*, which was applied to adjudication without being limited by the rigidity of *ritsuryō-hō* and *kuge-hō* (court noble law) (Kawamura 1982, p. 79). Legislators cannot foresee all *modus operandi* of crime commission. *Dōri* was an equitable legal consciousness of a far-reaching moralistic discretionary power to soften the rigidity of statute. This is very similar to equity softening statutory rigidity in common law jurisprudence. *Dōri* is the most important in *Goseibai-shikimoku,* which is collection of precedents.

Goseibai-shikimoku is also known as *Sadanaga-shikimoku* or *Kantō-oshikimoku.* It was enacted in the Kamakura period (1192–1333) based on precedent case laws since Minamotono Yoritomo (1147–1199), and the customs and morals in samurai society as part of the legal consciousness under equitable *dōri. Dōri* preserved the correct and intended operation of law for adjudication in unforeseeable situations. In today's terms, it intertwined with a system of precedents of judge-made law, which became the first samurai law enforceable on 10 August 1232. *Goseibai-shikimoku* was also the first codification of customary practices in samurai families, cultivating samurai's legal consciousness. Through the implementation of judge-made-law, *dōri* of strong moral tone thereby dominated society by *Goseibai-shikimoku,* which was subsequently enforced beyond the samurai class to formal social control of Japanese society. It socially became a well-accepted morality in practice through judicial behaviour in attitudinal and historical institutionalist models (Takeshita 1992, pp. 1527–1528), rational beings were in the habit of obeying. The compilation of *Goseibai-shikimoku* is very similar to the common law practice of codifying case laws as statutes to guide judicial behaviour in adjudication.

Goseibai-shikimoku has a total of 51 articles which is triple the number of 17 articles in the *Taihō-ritsuryō*, stipulating the authority of shrines as important social institutions, Buddhist services, *shugo* (a post of samurai status) and *jitō* (land stewards), control of territories, criminal law, transfer of territories, litigation procedures and so on. Articles 9 to 17 are penal code while articles 6, 28–31, 35, 41, 44, 45,49–51 are for penal procedure. The codification of moralistic *dōri* as enforceable basic statutory laws helped strive for equitable judicial behaviour in administering justice. Legislative behaviour to control court trials and procedures can help achieve both procedural and substantive justice.[17]

[17] On this see Ikeuchi 1962.

3.7 *Kenmu-Shikimoku* Criminalizing Gift-Giving for Bribery

Emperor Go-daigo's (1288–1339) Kenmu Restoration (1337–1335) occurred after the fall of the Kamakura Shogunate (1185–1333). On 7 November 1336 (*Kenmu* 3), *Kenmu-shikimoku* of 17th articles were released as the administrative policy and guidelines instead of the formal legal provisions of the Muromachi Bakufu. *Kenmu-shikimoku* had a lot of moralistic consensuses interacting with the moralistic *dōri* of *Goseibai-shikimoku*. Article 1 was about the necessity of being frugal. Article 2 prohibited group wine drinking and luxury entertainment. Together with prohibition of bribery in Article 10, Article 11 specifically criminalized the modus operandi of giving bribes under the cover of gifts. It disallowed luxury gifts. Article 13 reminded social relations and hierarchy, the importance of position (or status) in social stratification and due respect to superiors, while Article 14 repeated righteousness, uprightness and loyalty for the conduct and discipline of bureaucrats. Article 15 was about fair and equitable court trials without corrupt malpractice.[18]

While *Goseibai-shikimoku* had the elements of moralistic consensus as *dōri*, all these guidelines in *Kenmu-shikimoku* were for individual moralistic integrity. It was about individual official's integrity, loyalty, simple frugal life, disapproval of bribery under the package of gifts and anti-corruption. Article 15 is the most noteworthy for its objective of ensuring justice in judicial behaviour. The frugal simple life of high integrity as a moral standard set by *Kenmu-shikimoku* is instrumental in controlling corruption. An extensive control of officials' integrity on official duty and their private life is its strategic goal. A lifestyle audit is a tool for the detection and prevention of corruption. Luxury standards of living can raise red flags, warranting the loophole of abusing power for private gain (France 2021, p. 2). The nature of anti-corruption in *Kenmu-shikimoku* is state responsibility together with moral consensus of *dōri* imposed on the state apparatus, but public officials administering the state are also citizens as duality of the public (Toeba 2019, pp. 168–171). *Kenmu-shikimoku* is a reasonable strategy to control both private life and public duty to prevent corruption. As it was codified, judicial behaviour had to follow it moralistically as attitudinal institutionalism in judicial behaviour.

3.8 *Dōri* and *Tendō*

Hirihōkenten (a commandment to act according to the way of heaven) was printed on the banner of the military commander Kusunoki Masashige (1294–1336) in the Nanbokuchō period (1337–1392). It was a flexible commandment to act according to the equitable divine way of heaven. *Hirihōkenten* was the abbreviation of four short

[18] The original text in *Kenmu-shikimoku*: 一、可被行儉約事;二、可被制群飲佚遊事;十、固可被止二賄貨事;十一、殿中付二内外可被返諸方進物事;十三、可専禮節事;十四、有廉義名譽者殊可被優賞事;十五、可被聞食貧弱輩訴訟事。See Nikaidō 1563.

sentences: *hi* (deviance or illegality) cannot override *dōri*, and *dōri* cannot override *hō*; *Hō* cannot override *ken* (authority), and *ken* cannot override *tendō* (heaven's way); *Tendō* cannot be deceived. Without a fixed definition of these five types, the best way in this hierarchy is to act according to *tendō* equitably and conscientiously. While *dōri* was divine principle at the second hierarchy, *tendō* was above all as the paramount standard for ultimate justice.

Such notion of a hierarchy of five types had impacts on the subsequent Japanese jurisprudential concept and legal consciousness in judicial behaviour. An example is that military commander Saitō Tokugen in the Edo period repeated *hirihōkenten* in the second volume of his *Mottomono-sōshi*, which was originally published in 1634 (*Kanei* 11). As a samurai of the *hatomoto* (military strategist or commander) status in the middle of the Edo period, Ise Sadatake also mentioned exactly the same in his work *Isesadatakekakun* (Ise Sadatake Family Precepts) (Yoshiwara 2017, p. 48). *Tendō*, as a paramount divine principle, has similarity with the notion of natural law affecting judicial decision-making in Western jurisprudence. It represents a flexible legal consciousness of law enforcement of an unchallengeable ultimate equitable moral standard. Both *tendō* and natural law have similarity of legal consciousness by holding that God gives natural law which is authoritative over all humankind. Both are synonyms for revealed divine law as well as infallible normative value. In the attitudinal model of judicial behaviour, normative values can be deduced to court's judicial behaviour according to legal facts (Murphy 2019, pp. 305). In *Taishinin*'s judgement analysis hereinafter, we will read moralistic but flexible and equitable judicial behaviour of *Taishinin*.

3.9 *Dōri* in Muromachi Bakufu and Tokugawa Bakufu

In the *shikimoku* (law) of Muromachi Bakufu (1336–1573), the predominance of *dōri* was also a mixture of justice, morality and customary practice. Law was not merely the *ryō* of *han* (clan) in feudal state of bakufu. The spirit of *hirihōkenten* was heightened to the status of law through legal reasoning. It is said that the judicial behaviour of the court should not be bound substantively by the codified *ryō*. From the perspective of judicial behaviour, judges' decision-making should be based on equitable *dōri* in order to attain the highest moralistic standard of *seken no daihō* (the great law of the world) as the natural law of *tendō*. This provided a larger room for discretionary judicial decision-making. Judicial behaviour for substantive justice of fairness could thereby be achieved (Matsuzono 2020, pp. 47–49). In this connection, *Taishinin*'s judicial behaviour of expansive legal reasoning and interpretation in its attitudinal model of judicial behaviour is "old wine in new bottle".

After the Muromachi Bakufu (1336–1573) and the Toyotomi family perished, Tokugawa Ieyasu (1543–1616) appointed himself as *Seii-taishōgun* and founded the Edo Bakufu in 1603 (*Keichō* 8). During the Tokugawa Bakufu (1603–1867), there were six *Buke-shohatto* (Samurai Laws) with anti-corruption implications. On 7 July 1615 (*Genna* 1), the first *Buke-shohatto* law as *Genna-rei (the decree of Genna 1)*, consisting of 13 articles, was promulgated under the name of Tokugawa Hidetada. *Genna-rei* had implications for the moralistic legal consciousness of *Kenmu-shikimoku*. Tokugawa Ieyasu ordered the daimyo to have loyalty to him and prohibited drinking and playing in groups, precepts of lasciviousness and gambling. *Kenmu-shikimoku* encouraged thriftiness after a lengthy social turmoil. By such laws, Tokugawa Ieyasu wanted to ensure loyalty in social relations and keep subordinates' integrity of high moralistic standards free of corruption.[19]

The *Kan'ei-rei* of 19 articles was issued by Tokugawa Iemitsu on 21 June 1635 (*Kan'ei* 12). The legislative intent was to ban daimyo's luxurious life of private navigation with large boats and foreign transportation. To prevent potential judicial corruption in breach of this ban, non-officials were kept off-limits during its execution of punishment. *Chigyosho* (government office) was strictly ordered to have assurance for no corruption during performance of official duty. It reinforced anti-corruption by ordering officials to have a simple lifestyle of no conspicuous consumption, extravagant house and luxury culinary enjoyment.[20] Like *Kenmu-shikimoku*, *Kan'ei-rei* made use of a frugal, simple life to facilitate lifestyle audits as an anti-corruption strategy.

On 3 May 1663 (*Kanbun* 3), the fourth generation Shogunate Tokugawa Ietsuna issued *Kanbun-rei* of 21 articles. Article 21 of it imposed *Buke-shohatto* nationwide in Japan. It eliminated the disparity of different daimyos' different standards of procedural and substantive justice. That meant the assurance of standardized procedural justice before judicial decision-making to keep bribery under control of Article 21 as substantive justice.[21] In the Kanbun era, *bugyō* (government office) was delegated power to enforce laws, including civil construction law and anti-corruption law (Tsumaki and Aoyama 1999, pp. 281–288). On 25 July 1683 (*Tenwa* 3), Tokugawa Tsunayoshi issued *Tenwa-rei*, also known as *Hōei-rei*, of 15 articles for law amendment. Special moralistic emphasis was placed on loyalty, filial piety, politeness and literalism as a transition to the administration of justice for social control under Confucian thought of benevolence. As an agent of government power, the corruption of an official is always a breach of loyalty in the principle-agent relationship. [22] Loyalty was the most important moralistic *dōri* hidden and embedded in *Taishinin*'s judicial behaviour in respect of corruption. Readers of this book will sense it from Chaps. 4 to 8.

The Genroku period from 1688 to 1707 enjoyed a long period of prosperity in Japanese history. Junior officials used lengthy economic prosperity to exacerbate corruption at the local level. Merchants usually had a willingness to give bribes for higher business profitability. Corruption occurred in the area overlapping private gain

[19] On the original text see Ministry of Justice (1959a, pp. 61–62).

[20] The original text in *Kan'ei-rei*: 知行所務清廉ニコレヲ沙汰シ非法致サズ国郡衰弊; 贈答嫁娶リ儀式或ハ饗応或ハ家宅営作等当時甚ダ華麗ノ至リ自今以後簡略タルベシソノ外万事倹約ヲ用フルベキ事。See Takayanagi and Ishii (1934a, pp. 1–2).

[21] The original text in *Kanbun-rei*: 万事応江戸之法度於国々所々可通行事。See Ministry of Justice Research Division (1932, p. 107).

[22] On the original text see Ministry of Justice Research Division (1932, pp. 109–110).

of wealth and officials' misuse of public power and discretion. This scenario is similar to the collective action theory of corruption. Bribers gave bribes to senior bakufu officials (Nakase 1935, pp. 9–11), corrupting the entire administrative organization through institutional corruption. Officials abused their official power for private gain in an institutional context. It could stimulate economic growth by creating productive chances and assets, but it was also a vehicle for rent-seeking by politicians and officials.[23]

In 1710 (*Masanori* 1), the sixth generation of Shogunate Tokugawa Ienobu issued *Masanori-rei* of 17 articles in an attempt to keep institutional corruption under control. Ienobu made efforts to reinforce townspeople's legal consciousness against corruption by strict liability of fixed penalty (Kukita 1980, pp. 63–64). Bribery of government officials was strictly and explicitly disallowed in order to prevent petty corruption of small amount and sporadic corruption at the local level. For this purpose, the net of criminalization was extended to disallow the social ritual of gift-giving for *aino mimai* (expression of concern) to officials of ranking *rōjū* (a government official of Edo Bakufu who reported directly to shōgun) and *wakadoshiyori* (a government official of Edo Bakufu whose rank was only next to shōgun) at the management level by law.[24] The legislative intent especially aimed to prevent bribery from perverting justice in litigation and control officials' integrity (Nakase 1989, p. 9).

During this period, the new strict anti-corruption legal provision of Article 17 in *Masanori-rei* had a certain extent of deterrence against corruption (Takayanagi and Ishii 1934b, p. 21).

Fixed penalties and strict liability limited the flexibility of legal reasoning in judicial behaviour. *Taishinin*'s judicial behaviour in the strict liability model from Chaps. 4 to 8 in this book was thus nothing new in prewar Japan. Notwithstanding heavy punishment as the cost of crime, institutional judicial corruption still persisted among the judicial behaviours of local *bugyō*, who had the power for judicial decision-making at the local level (Arai 1968, p. 260). *Masanori-rei* lasted for only six years because of officials "acquiesce" to bribery and institutional corruption. As of the Meiji era, bribery for undue influence on judicial behaviour in "litigation" proceedings was still widespread. It existed among high-ranking bureaucrats to low-ranking officials at both local and central institutions.[25] In view of judicial corruption, the applicability of equitable *dōri* to judicial behaviour was limited.

The last *Buke-shohatto* was issued by the eighth *Seii-taishōgun* Tokugawa Yoshimune in 1717 (*Kyōho* 2) as *Kyōho-rei* for the strict observance of old customary moralistic practice in order to maintain officials' integrity and morality. In Japanese language, this is labelled *kyūkan-bokushu* (adhere strictly to old practices). In 1742 (*Kanpo* 2), Tokugawa Yoshimune ordered to compile *Kujikata-osadamegaki* of two volumes as the basic code of the Edo Shogunate. The first volume contained 81 *rei* as procedural regulations and decrees, such as the standardized working rules of the appraisal office, judiciary, police, notices, letters and lawsuit procedures. It thereby

---

[23] See Rose-Ackerman (2010).

[24] On the original text see Ministry of Justice (1959b, p. 340).

[25] On this see Ōhira (1996).

limited the abuse of procedural justice by misusing discretionary power for private gain. Article 3 (No. 2 and 5), Article 22 and Article 26 were for anti-corruption and punishment in order to protect the purity and legitimacy of the bakufu's administrative power under the principal-agent relationship (Fujioka 1979, p. 43). The second volume was also called *Osadamegaki-hyakkajō* (the Edicts of 100 Articles), consisting of 103 articles as *ritsu*, which were the standards for judicial behaviour covering adjudication and judgements such as lawsuits, trial procedures and penal regulations. From today's perspective, it is about both procedural and substantive justice. Article 26 was specifically codified to address bribery. The term *wairo* for bribe was clearly used for criminalization by statute.[26] At the end of *Osadamegaki-hyakkajō*, a reminder of its secret law nature was added: "The foregoing having been duly reported [to the Shōgun], it is hereby decreed. It is not to be allowed to be seen by anyone except the magistrates."[27] Citizens were not supposed to know how bakufu's secret law was codified and enforced in the criminal justice system, let alone the details of judicial behaviour in such a system.

The Tokugawa Bakufu had a criminal justice system based on the social hierarchy of *mibun sekinin* (status responsibility) to determine the proportionality between culpability and punishment. The status system involved hierarchical social relations of samurai and commoners, parents, masters and children, servants, or women and *eta* or *hinin* (literally means non-human, people ranked the lowest in the social hierarchy) as a ruling principle in Tokugawa society. Officials received heavier punishment than ordinary citizens (Shirota 2015, pp. 224–226). The judicial behaviour of Tokugawa Japan was not independent of the administrative apparatus but was an integral part of it in determining conviction and proportionality for punishment. Minister of Justice's undue influence on *Taishinin*'s judicial behaviour in prewar Japan was therefore not a new phenomenon.

According to Bourdieu's idea that the law can be used as a tool, secret law was a way for judges to exercise power in a strategic way. In secret law, shōgun and daimyo could directly determine and express the hierarchical status of all social groups and punish people based on that status (Ooms 1996, p. 314, p. 324). This was also the case for corruption offences. The Tokugawa secret system clearly stated that the severity of punishment for crimes was related to a person's social responsibility. As a matter of *dōri*, great social responsibility should be punished more severely. The legal case was based on whether or not someone had a certain status, which was a key part of Bakufu criminal law (Nishihara 1967, pp. 57–58). Accordingly, juveniles, women, those with mental illness, and the elderly were subject to different criminal liabilities and punishments (Ōkubo 1995, p. 43–70). Judges had to follow the government's policy of legal discrimination, which was based on the social hierarchy.

In Tokugawa society, law enforcement and a strong moral legal system worked together. *Dōri* was used to make the laws less strict. Corruption was seen as a serious offence against the lord. This *dōri* was absolute, but it differed depending on one's

[26] On the original text see Nihon University (1905, p. 15).

[27] The original text in *Osadamegaki-hyakkajō*: 右の趣上聞に達し相極め候。奉行中の外他見有るべからざるもの也。See Nihon University (1905).

rank in the government and social hierarchy (Steenstrup 1996, pp. 121–123, p. 151). In 1615, the *Kinchu-narabini-kuge-shohatto* (Laws of Court Nobles) was issued. This document had 17 articles that further consolidated the social hierarchy. Article 1 and Article 2 explain how important the Emperor and the court nobles under him were (Takano 1989, pp. 2–4). The position of the Emperor in the Japanese government did not suddenly appear in the Meiji Constitution. The Emperor expected all bureaucrats to be loyal to him. The Meiji Constitution was just a reaffirmation of this *dōri*, which affected the way *Taishinin* acted in court (as discussed in the analysis in Chap. 9).

3.10 Unsuccessful Anti-Corruption Law of Tokugawa Bakufu

During the Edo Shogunate, Tanuma Okitsugu (1719–1788) and Tanuma Okichi (1749–1784) were important government officials. They joined bureaucracy because they wanted to help the government collect taxes and improve the economy. They changed the government's farming policy to mercantilism to help the economy get better. However, the period between 1769 and 1786 under their leadership saw some of the worst corruption in Japanese history. The people who sold the most products were allowed to monopolize how those products were marketed. They did this by bribing government officials to disallow other people to sell similar products. The government made improvements to its social services, economy and financial management, but widespread repugnant bribery and corruption distorted market mechanism and undermined these anti-corruption efforts. Many of Tanuma's policies affected the interest group of businessmen.[28] Tanuma then pushed for the production of other goods besides rice and started a trade union. The development of new rice fields and the increase in the annual tax rate were successful. However, Tanuma Okitsugu was accused of being a corrupt politician who was involved with bribery by merchants. Merchants' dishonest actions (for example, exchanging something good for something of poor quality) were a way to get ahead and manipulate market. Bribery was like grease or lubricant in an illegal market mechanism for the merchants' selfish goal of no sense of social responsibility (Venkatesan 2015, p. 4).

During this period, the term *kimiyuki* originally meant public deed, but it implied *oshokuseiji* (political corruption) due to the widespread corruption. It turned bakufu into a dysfunctional kleptocratic state, discrediting hegemonic governance (Martinsson 2021, pp. 267–271). For example, Matsudaira Sadanobu, as a senior bakufu official, reversed mercantilism back to agrarianism for curtailing corruption. With frugality and strict discipline in institutional administration, Matsudaira kept market-driven corruption under control (Ōfuchi 2021, p. 1).

In the subsequent *Kansei-kaikaku* (Kansei Reform) between 1789 and 1790 (*Kansei* 1–11), a large number of 352 legal decrees had been issued in order to uproot corruption, in order to improve citizens' quality of life, sense of well-being,

[28] On this see Hall (1955).

fairer distribution of resources and ensuring officials' integrity and discipline. This is similar to legislative behaviour controlling judicial behaviour by codifying legislation. However, judicial officials were not competent enough to apply *dōri* to legal facts as case laws (Igata 1973, pp. 3–6). Though the intrinsic incompetency of judicial officials limited further development of judicial behaviour during this period, a vast morass of flexible customary laws co-existed like *dōri* with decrees in pre-Meiji legislation. Moralistic customary practices had all along beende facto observed as *dōri* and a source of law. Legislation could prevail over *dōri.* In case of no legislation, moralistic *dōri* could dominate. Lords in their own domains enforced their own moralistic customary practices and local legislation (Henderson 1952, p. 91, p. 107).

Even though it was hard to stop corruption, the samurai who had paid work managed the Edo community in a way that was advantageous to the Shogunate administration. This made it hard for dangerous daimyo to take control. Farmers could focus on farming when social order was stable (Enta and Ogawa 2011, pp. 91–92). Before the Meiji era, Japanese law was based on Chinese law (Takizawa 2005, pp. 182–183). No transplantation of foreign law had a similar impact on Japanese legal culture. Professional lawyer was an unknown term (Noda 1976, p. 145). Before the American black ships arrived in 1854, the judicial system in Japan treated corruption cases fairly. Its judicial behaviour applied with equitable customary practice and morality as *dōri* was socially acceptable.

3.11 Karikeiritsu, Shinritsukōryō and Kaiteiritsurei

After *Taiseihōkan* (restoration of imperial rule) on 9 November 1867, the *Karikeiritsu* (Provisional Penal Code) or *Kariritsu*, was enacted in 1868. It copied the *ritsuryo* system and compilation of Qing and Ming laws of China (Arai 2013, p. 1352), stipulating four types of punishment: *muchi* (flogging), *to* (servitude), *ryū* (exile) and *shi* (death). *Karikeiritsu* functioned as judicial guidelines for issuing directives in response to legal inquiries from daimyo's domains. Under the shadow of *Keihōsōsho* (drafted Penal Code) of *Higokumamoto-han*, ancient laws of *Yōrō-ritsu* and *Kujigata-osadamegaki*, *Karikeiritsu* was merely an old law by new promulgation. This "old wine" handcuffed the development of judicial behaviours by uniformity and standardized legal interpretation, limiting judicial activism (Tezuka 1950, pp. 1–7).

In 1870 (*Meiji* 3), *Shinritsukōryō* (New Code of Law) was promulgated as a comprehensive penal code. It inherited the principal categorization of criminal offences of *hachigyaku* (eight heinous criminal offences), namely *muhen* (treason), *mutaigyaku* (conspiracy for high treason), *muhon* (rebellion), *akugyaku* (atrocity), *fudo* (barbarity), *daifukyō* (great disrespect), *fukō* (lack of filial piety) and *fugi* (unrighteousness). The first article under sub-categorization of *juzōritsu* (the offence of receiving loot) was *kanrijuzai,* which aimed at strict prohibiting officials from bribe acceptance. It endorsed judicial behaviour to retroactively enforce the penal code. Retroactivity of law is the imposition of *ex post facto* laws, which means law looking backward or contemplates the past.[29] Retroactivity of law was not rule of law because law is non-existent before criminal act. In case of insufficient applicability of *Shinritsukōryō*, the judge could even refer to previous laws in order to meet the requirement of *zaikeihōtei-shugi* (the doctrine of no law, no crime and no punishment). *Ruisuitekiyō* (analogy application) was disapproved and excluded from the judicial behaviour. *Shinritsukōryō* was a summary and enforcement of previous codes transplanted from the Chinese jurisprudence of limitation to judicial behaviour. This legislative behaviour protected the hegemonic monarchy and social hierarchy. Since 1870, there had been requests for revisions and additions to improve the shortcomings of *Shinritsukōryō*. The Ministry of Justice accepted it upon the legislation of *Kaiteiritsurei* as a revised version of *Shinritsukōryō* (Hōjō and Miyahira 2009, p. 26).

Under *Daijōkanfukoku* (Daijokan Proclamation) No. 206 in 1873 (*Meiji* 6), *Kaiteiritsurei* of 318 articles had been enforced since 10 July 1873. *Kaiteiritsurei* had a "fatal" shortcoming "handcuffing the hands of judicial behaviour". In terms of judicial applicability, it was not easy for a judge to criminalize an act with unclear constituent elements of crimes in it. *Kaiteiritsurei* was confusing vis-à-vis Western criminal laws. By the middle of the first decade of the Meiji Restoration, a new penal code of drastic change was urged (Hedinger 2012, p. 146).

3.12 Penal Code 1880

Under the pressure of the urgent call for abolishing the unequal treaties signed by the Edo bakufu, time was not allowed to accumulate case laws to copy British common law jurisprudence, although case laws could reflect judicial behaviour. Under the influence of French legal scholar Gustave Emile Boissonade, the French Code Pénal was selected as the first Penal Code1880 (nicknamed Old Penal Code) by Meiji leaders, taking effect on 1 January1882. Article 3 was *hō-no-fusokyū* (prohibition of retroactive punishment). Article 2 of it codified "*nullum crimen sine lege*" as "no punishment without law",[30] which had also been incorporated as Article 23 of Meiji Constitution 1889.[31] Analogous application was disallowed, but the judicial behaviour of expansive interpretation with *dōri* was legitimate. The application of "*nullum crimen sine lege*" made the "constituent element" of *shokumu* (official duty) a threshold to criminalize bribery and/or corruption. Non-official duty was the most common appeal ground for seeking exoneration from conviction in *Taishinin* judgements.

[29] The original text in *Shinritsukōryō*: 新律依テ擬断シ旧律援引スルコトヲ得ス。

[30] On the original text see *Hōrei Zensho (Compendium of laws and regulations)* (1880, p. 106).

[31] The Original text of Article 2 in the Penal Code 1880: 法律ニ正条ナキ者ハ何等(なんら)ノ所為ト雖(いえど)モ之(これ)ヲ罰スルコトヲ得ス。See *Hōrei Zensho (Compendium of laws and regulations)* 1880.

The Penal Code of 1880 stipulated the crime of *Kanritokushokuzai* (corruption of public officials) in Chap. 9 of Articles 273 to 291, which narrowly criminalized different types of *tokushokuzai* (corruption or malfeasance offence) as damages inflicted on public interest, people and property. The legislative intent was not only anti-corruption but also the control of malfeasance. The constituent elements of the bribery offence in Penal Code 1880 were closely related to a specific *modus operandi* and act of public officials.

Article 278 of Penal Code 1880 was about an official's arrest without authority. Article 284 was limited to the acceptance of bribery to follow the instructions of the briber. In case of no evidence to prove the briber's instruction, the defendant should be found not guilty. Conviction of bribery under Articles 285 and 286 were only applicable to judicial corruption in civil and criminal adjudication respectively. Article 287 was acceptance of bribes applicable to judges, prosecutors and police officers for false accusations. Article 288 prescribed punishment for conviction under Article 287. Articles 289 and 290 related to an official's embezzlement of public property and excessive charges of land tax for private gain. Electoral corruption was separately codified in Article 234 with the constituent element fixed at voting behaviour.[32]

Under the limitation of strict constituent elements together with the applicability of *nullum crimen sine lege* in Article 2, the dimension for judicial behaviour of expansive legal reasoning based on *dōri* was very narrow. This was different from the pre-Meiji attitudinal judicial behaviour. Expansive legal reasoning to criminalize according to the new circumstances of *modus operandi* was nearly illegitimate under the "*nullum crimen sine lege*" principle. In *Taishinin* judgement dated 9 November 1908 on a corruption case, Article 284 of Penal Code 1880 was applied because the criminal act occurred before the implementation of Penal Code 1907. This *Taishinin* case was about the secretary of a primary school as an official's acceptance of a bribe for the leakage of examination questions. His official status had to be proven exactly identical to the constituent elements stipulated in Penal Code 1880 (Koaze 1910, pp. 151–152). Otherwise, the legal test of *nullum crimen sine lege* could not be passed.

The most serious shortcoming of Penal Code 1880 was the strict limits directly imposed on judicial behaviour by classifying crimes into felonies, misdemeanours and police offences. This strictness invalidated judges' discretionary power. Judicial activism was, therefore, nearly impossible. In theory, this could prevent judges' judicial misbehaviour of arbitrary punishments. The demerit was the difficulty in understanding complex French legal concepts and integrating them into the traditional Japanese body of expansive legal reasoning with *dōri*. This structural shortcoming led to lenient sentences and a dramatic increase of crime rate. Opponents criticized Penal Code 1880 for not considering Japanese customary practice and equitable *dōri*. Some Japanese even feared that French-style laws might invoke a French-style revolution. They turned to Germanic penal code to solve this dilemma.

---

[32] On the original text see *Hōrei Zensho (Compendium of laws and regulations)* (1880, p. 104, pp. 141–144).

Law should assimilate into the lives of Japanese nationals and judicial behaviour upon law enforcement.[33]

Apparently, Japanese needed to accommodate *dōri* in judges' attitudinal judicial behaviour. Influential Confucian legal scholars of the Meiji era such as Tomii Masaaki, Yokota Kuniomi (a former *Taishinin* Chief Justice appointed in 1906), Kuratomi Yuuzaburō and Makino Eiichi supported application of moralistic Confucian ethic for formal social control. Judges thus could apply *dōri* as social well-accepted nature justice and their ideological preferences to judicial behaviour (Posner and Grover 2008, pp. 19–20). All these constitute messages to Japanese society about what right and wrong is (Friedman 1987, pp. 25–28). This is the background of Penal Code 1907.

3.13 *Tokushokuhō*

In order to mitigate the limitations of judicial behaviour in corruption cases, *Tokushokuhō* (Anti-corruption Code) was specifically codified in 1901 (*Meiji* 34). Article 1 of *Tokushokuhō* limited the scope of its applicability to elections or appointments based on laws and regulations, assembly members, committee members, representatives and so on. The *modus operandi* covered giving, offering and promise of bribe. In the early Meiji era, some judges received English and French legal training in order to integrate Western legal theory with Japanese social conditions.[34] Judicial behaviour aimed at protecting the Meiji state polity belonged to the strategic model. This strategic goal of *Tokushokuhō* can be seen in *Taishinin*'s judgement on electoral corruption dated 5 March 1907 (Meiji 40). *Taishinin* covered the status of an elected assembly member as a constituent element. In another *Taishinin* case dated 28 May 1908, the unclear scope of official duty was clarified and confirmed through expansive legal reasoning for net-widening of criminalization. The briber's unilateral offer of a bribe was strictly considered bribery, even though the bribee neither gave consent nor knew about it (Koaze 1910, pp. 343–348). Without consideration of the bribee's guilty intent, this early *Taishinin*'s hybrid judicial behaviour of the strategic model and strict liability model set a precedent for subsequent judicial behavioural factors. It was an integration of Western law as a "jacket" with the "Japanese body" of *dōri* under social, economic, cultural, factual situations and traditional Confucian morality.[35] Judicial behaviour of strict liability is explained through Chaps. 4 to 8 in this book.

---

[33] On this see Meyers (1950, p. 131, p. 161), Noda (1976, p. 39, pp. 47–52, pp. 58–60).

[34] On this see Hamilton and Young (2001, pp. 2–10).

[35] On this see Tanaka (1976, p. 124, p. 191, pp. 215–216, p. 240).

3.14 Penal Code 1907 as a Germanic Jacket

Both Penal Code 1880 and *Tokushokuhō* were replaced by the new Penal Code (Law number 45) promulgated by *Kanpō (Gazette)* on 24 April 1907 (*Meiji* 40). After many amendments, the current version of Penal Code 1907 is different from the original one. Articles 197 and 198 of Penal Code 1907 are for bribery offences. The term "bribe" is used in these two articles, but the word "corruption" is not.[36] The gazette version of it on 24 April 1907 is tabulated and analysed as follows[37]:

1. The first part of Article 197 addresses the crime of simple acceptance of a bribe. When a public servant or arbiter receives, demands, or agrees to a bribe in connection with his duties, he is sentenced to three or fewer years of penal servitude.

   This is the most basic offence of accepting an offer of bribe. The legal formula for criminalization under Article 197 is the constituent element of a public servant or arbiter, bribe, plus an act of receipt, demand, or agreement. Ostensibly, "public servant" and "bribery" are the two most important constituent elements for the threshold of *nullum crimen sine lege*.

   In reality, social change can lead to new categories of job natures. The variety of legal orders for "public servant" and "bribery" at different times needs to be well understood additionally. As a matter of *dōri*, *Taishinin* judges adopted expansive legal reasoning in their judicial behaviour for criminalizing or decriminalizing a behaviour under change of social conditions. As a judicial behaviour of such legal interpretivism, it is about how judges offer an explanation for the deviant behaviour of impacting legal rights and obligations. This modification can be either positive or negative. Accordingly, judicial behaviour helps identify the legal principles in question and the normative implications.[38]
2. Article 197, the latter part: The crime of accepting a bribe in return for promised services. A public servant or arbiter who has received, demanded, or agreed to a bribe in connection with his duties in return for a promised service, should be sentenced to a minimum of one year and a maximum of ten years penal servitude.

   The salient constituent element in the latter part of Article 197 is the additional culpability of "in return for service promised". It indicates premeditation and conspiracy to commit a bribery offence and a conspiracy between the briber and bribee beforehand. For this aggravating factor, the penalty range is between one year and ten years imprisonment. Pre-mediation and conspiracy imply a higher degree of moralistic blameworthiness for the more serious harm

---

36 On the English translation of the Penal Code (Act No.45 of 1907) see Japanese Law Translation by the Ministry of Justice at https://www.japaneselawtranslation.go.jp/en/laws/view/3581. Accessed 15 September 2025.

37 On the original text see *Kanpō(Gazette)*, 24 April 1907.

38 See "Legal Interpretivism" at https://plato.stanford.edu/entries/law-interpretivist/. Accessed 7 September 2022.

inflicted on social interest. Heavier punishment is proportional to blameworthiness. The Imperial Diet intentionally left the determination of "seriousness" open for judicial behaviour.

The prewar Japanese Penal Code did not define the unfair practice of omitting or negligence of one's reasonable duty. The Imperial Diet's legislative behaviour of vague definition gave a free hand for *Taishinin*'s expansive legal reasoning to criminalize it according to legal facts and *dōri*. The wordings "received, demand or agreed ...... in return for service promised" highlighted the fact that the unfair practice of an "omission or negligence of reasonable behaviour" was implied as an actualized and completed act that related to a specific corrupt consideration. This gave room for the judge to determine with equitable *dōri*.

3. Paragraph 4 of Article 197 concerns the forfeiture and pursuit of bribes. In addition to fines and imprisonment, forfeiture and pursuit of bribes are another form of punishment for an offence under Article 197 but not for "giving" a bribe in Article 198. This is understandable because "giving bribe" is assumed to be a completed act.
4. Article 198 is about the crime of giving a bribe. A person who gave or agreed to a bribe provided in the crime of the acceptance of a bribe shall be punished by three or less years of penal servitude or with a fine not exceeding 300 *yen*. Confession is a mitigating factor for lighter punishment or exemption from punishment.

Neither Articles 197 nor 198 is specific or descriptive enough. Both articles have legislative silence on the quality and quantity of bribes and the nature and scope of public servants' official duties. Other than confession, statutory mitigating factors for the severity of the criminality of bribery offences are not available. There is no mention of a deterministic reference to customary practice for evidentiality and convictability. All of these are left to the court's judicial decision-making and discretionary judicial power. Penal Code 1907, consisting of 264 articles, is a legal transplant of its Germanic counterpart. The number of articles in Penal Code 1907 is in fact small and concise, considering the comprehensive stipulation of all crimes in the original Germanic version. As a result of the huge gap between Germanic and Japanese legal culture and social development, the enforcement of Penal Code 1907 is undoubtedly an integrated entity of "body of Japanese legal culture in a Germanic jacket". Legal culture refers to the extent of social integration with the law. Legal consciousness exists in social relations, self-discipline and the performance of normative behaviour (Nadareishvili and Chkheidze 2015, pp. 123–124).

3.15 The United Nations Convention Against Corruption (UNCAC)

In the legalistic approach, corruption is an act explicitly identified by the legislative behaviour of the Japanese Diet. The only universal anti-corruption instrument legally binding on Japan is the UNCAC. The UNCAC is endorsed by United Nations

General Assembly resolution 58/4 of 31 October 2003 as "the only legally binding universal anticorruption instrument". Japan signed the UNCAC in December 2003. Diet approved it in June 2006.

The UNCAC extensively covers different constituent elements of corruption, including bribery (Article 15), trading in influence (Article 18), abuse of functions (Article 19), illicit enrichment (Article 20), corruption in the private sector (Articles 21 to 23), concealment after the commission of any of these offences (Article 24), obstruction of justice (Article 25), liability of legal persons (Article 26), participation and attempt (Article 27), knowledge, intent and purpose as elements of an offence (Article 28).

Article 15 of Chapter III of the UNCAC defines the bribery of national public officials as follows:

Each State Party shall adopt such legislative and other measures as may be necessary to establish as criminal offences, when committed intentionally:

a. The promise, offering or giving, to a public official, directly or indirectly, of an undue advantage, for the official himself or herself or another person or entity, in order that the official act or refrain from acting in the exercise of his or her official duties.
b. The solicitation or acceptance by a public official, directly or indirectly, of an undue advantage, for the official himself or herself or another person or entity, in order that the official act or refrain from acting in the exercise of his or her official duties (United Nations 2004, p. 17).

Article 15 is far from straightforward. It is universally endorsed that a state functionary who accepts bribes for personal enrichment is corrupt. As a signatory in the UNCAC, Japanese courts can integrate it with Penal Code 1907 for judicial behaviour together with *dōri*.

3.16 *Dōri* as the Body of Judicial Behaviour

A robust correlation exists between social rituals, customary practice and instances of corruption. These rituals are employed to serve the local interests of state machinery (Lomnitz 1995, p. 41). When individuals in positions of authority engage in the exchange of bribes, it signifies a transaction that transcends the mere exchange of monetary or material assets (Lomnitz 1971, pp. 93–106; Lomnitz 1988, p. 44.). To determine criminality of transaction, *dōri* affects judicial behaviour under the influence of legal consciousness and a prevailing moralistic social consensus. Before the Meiji era, *dōri* was an unwritten equitable rule aimed at controlling the samurai community through the criminal justice system for formal social control. It inextricably and flexibly bound all legal facts together.

Dōri covers *giri*, but *giri* is not fully equivalent to *dōri*. In comparison with *dōri*, *giri* also exists as a fact of the natural right way to behave and to follow as a person (Genryo 1971, p. 41). *Giri* includes morality, the act for expressing regret for a mistake in relationships, and the same relationship as blood relatives that people who are not blood relatives. After the latter half of the Kamakura era, it extended horizontally from the duty of loyalty in the master-servant relationship to the relationship of in-laws. A parent-adopted child who has no blood relationship is called *giri no oyako* (Karita 1958, p. 130). The breach of *giri* is a particular type of shame. Braithwaite labels shame in Japan as reintegrative shaming because of its coupling with a formal collectivity to which the individual belongs, such as family and the titular head of the collectivity (Braithwaite 1989, p. 63). Bribery offences can be held against both *dōri* and *giri,* depending on the judge's attitudinal judicial behaviour. *Giri* in *Taishinin*'s judicial behaviour will be explained further with reference to *Taishinin* judgement.

Unsurprisingly, laws that work in Western society might not necessarily be successfully enforced in prewar Japan in the absence of corroboration with equitable Japanese judicial behaviour. Below the surface of the Japanese adversarial legal system of judges, courts and criminal justice agents transplanted from Western countries in the Meiji era, it retains *dōri*, which has been practiced for more than 1500 years.

Dōri, giri and *jori* have overlapping area in Japanese legal culture. Article 3 of the Directions for the Conduct of Judicial Affairs 1875 stated that where no written law or custom existed, cases should be adjudicated "by way of deduction from *jori* (natural reason)". *Jori* originated from *dōri* found in the judicial decisions of feudal Japan (Dean 2002, p. 134). In corruption offences, the target of bribery is a bureaucrat or a person of similar capacity. To Tokugawa bureaucrats, Confucianism was a holistic *jori* for statecraft, which had no demarcation among polity, economy and social conditions. A bureaucratic monolith was absolute loyalty to the feudal lord at the top of the bureaucratic hierarchy (Mass 1999, p. 2). The feudal lord fulfilled his moral obligation to govern his domain and bureaucrats with benevolence (Sagers 2006, p. 15). Matsunaga Sekigo, an influential Confucian scholar in the Edo period, elaborated Confucian learning to social control. Matsunage criticized the slaying of selfish desires and treated humaneness as *tenri* (principles of heaven) in terms of *giri*. This is the essence of *shin no sei* (regulating the mind), thereby making things in *gi* (correct) order. This is similar to the Western legal concept of natural justice that everyone is born with it naturally in one's original mind for making moralistic judgement equitably. Everyone is endowed with *giri honshin* (principles of rightness inherently in one's mind). Without *giri honshin,* human beings live like beasts, because this is the fundamental wisdom and ability to understand *banbutsu no giri* (the right principles of the ten thousand things) (Tucker 2014, pp. 46–48).

Against this background of social conformity to *giri* and *dōri*, Japanese elite bureaucrats of the feudalistic Tokugawa military regime ruled Japan from 1603 to 1867. Their judicial behaviour operated independently of legal sanctions without legal limitations, let alone a balance of power. In contrast, the seeds of historical institutionalism in the conduct and discipline of bureaucracy in the Meiji era were sown.

Bureaucrats' organizational culture valued honour, integrity, pride and unmaterialistic affluence in order to avoid infringement against *dōri, giri* and *jori.*[39] At the dawn of Meiji era, Japan's longest legal cultural commitment was its equitable *dōri*, which was historically embedded in a well-preserved social hierarchy of vertical obligation rather than supportive of individual human rights in social relations. *Dōri* continued to hide in *Taishinin*'s judicial behaviour for the social construction of corruption in prewar Japan. Financial interest, gifts and favours are in fact morally neutral terms, but these terms can be "bribes" or "payoffs" under formal social construction through *Taishinin*'s judicial behaviour as inevitability upon the contingency of circumstance (Diaz-Leon 2015, pp. 1138–1139).

The Meiji government's covert initiative to establish *Taishinin* as the ultimate appellate court in the European civil law tradition was not initially conceived with the objective of ensuring legal justice. A robust Japan necessitated a centralized political system with uniform, nationwide law enforcement. The Meiji government concluded that the implementation of a legal system analogous to that of the Western powers would enable the termination of the "unequal treaties" that had been signed by the bakufu, particularly with regard to extraterritoriality rights. As Hendry asserts, the comprehensive Western-inspired legal arrangement was meticulously orchestrated to appease the Western powers (Hendry 1995, pp. 216–219).

For this hidden purpose, the legislation for legal reform in the Meiji era was transplanted and then codified under government guidance instead of case laws resulting from accumulated judicial decisions as historical institutionalism. Consequently, a substantial discrepancy emerged between the formal legal principles codified in legal time and the actual judicial practices observed. Judges were at liberty to interpret the transplanted Western legal framework in accordance with traditional Japanese legal principles (Hooft 2002, pp. 17–18). It provided a dimension conducive to the incorporation of *dōri* with judicial behaviour, both in terms of attitude and in a continuous manner. The gradual accumulation of case laws resulting from Taishinin's judicial behaviour helped assimilate transplanted Western laws to the underlying premises of *dōri.* Maeda found that Japanese judicial behaviour tends to recognize unclear statutory provisions but clarifies them for legitimacy through legal interpretation by the court's exercise of discretionary judicial power (Maeda 1993, p. 40). That means the applicability of *dōri, giri, jōri* and situational mitigating or aggravating factors. The court's judicial behaviour of ideological manipulation of shame and morality as culpability can be regarded as cultural commitments to turn elements of informal social control into formal social control (Braithwaite 2006, p. 64).

In prewar Japan, *dōri* in judicial behaviour continued to incorporate with transplanted legal culture "hidden" in Germanic Penal Code as *wakonyōsai*. *Wakonyōsai* and Japanese body in a Western jacket are different expressions of similar phenomenon. *Dōri* should not be confused with *giri* (duty) in Japanese culture, though two concepts have overlapping area. *Dōri* has no embodiment of fixed set of norms or procedural rules for certainty of consistent articulation or application to specified types of court cases. *Dōri* is like Japanese common sense, ordinary reason

[39] On this see Carpenter (2003, pp. 52–54) and Akio (2010, p. 250, p. 252).

and a matter of natural justice as per prevailing moralistic social consensus instead of the strict adhesion to statutory provision (Dean 2002, p. 134). It is comparable with equity in common law jurisprudence in the sense that it is a historical outcome based on fairness or impartiality rather than legal technicalities. Haley treats *dōri* as a way to harmonize new laws with traditional norms and values by repeating the same judicial behaviour (Haley 1991, p. 43, p. 85). Judicial behaviour with *dōri* is like *recta ratio* (right reason) in European law. It depends on the court's judicial behaviour in understanding the social sense of right and wrong (Röhl 2005, p. 731). Western powers had not forced the Meiji government to abolish *dōri* in legal reform as a condition for cancelling the unequal treaties signed with the bakufu. The Meiji legal reform was a radical reorientation away from neo-Confucianism, traditional legal values and consciousness toward a transplanted Western legal culture of individual rights to property, family, marriage and citizenship in laws (Haley 1991, p. 69). *Dōri* interacts with particular social conditions, juridical facts, appeal ground and Taishinin's judicial behaviour in each corruption case. This is why no two corruption cases in prewar Japan were exactly identical. The moralistic flexible *dōri* in Japanese legal culture and judicial behaviour was thus like *wakon* (Japanese body).

3.17 Three-Fold Legal Reasoning in *Taishinin*'s Judicial Behaviour

Unlike *mens rea* (guilty mind) and *actus reus* (guilty act), the two broad elements of crime in common law jurisprudence, *Taishinin*'s judicial behaviour adopted Germanic three-fold legal reasoning process of *hanzai kōsei yōken* (constituent elements of crime), *ihō-sei* (illegality) and *sekininsei* (culpability). For conviction of a criminal offence and punishability, *Taishinin* had to rationalize its decision in this tripartite structure. All constituent elements of criminal behaviour should be identical to those prescribed in Penal Code and confirmed as illegal before the resultant culpability for punishment. Judges had to avoid taking only one step at the expense of the other two. This judicial behaviour is labelled as disjunctive. Individual penalties are supposed to be the synthetic denouement of the stereo typicality of constituent elements, illegality and culpability. For culpability in penalty, judges can rationalize it by moralistic responsibility, ideological preference, shameful stigma and social responsibility (Haley 1991, p. 69). Without rationalization for the clarity of a statutory provision through three-fold legal reasoning, the conviction and punishment are illegitimate.

Even after postwar judicial reform by American common law jurisprudence during the Occupation period, today's Japanese judiciary still follows this three-fold legal reasoning in the European civil law style for conviction and punishment. For example, in the Nagoya Central Post Office Case Incident under reference of *Keishū* (collection of precedent judgements) 31–3-182 dated 4 May 1977, the Grand Bench of

Japanese Supreme Court adopted an all-the-circumstances assessment with reference to Constitutional Law, *Yūbin-hō* (Postal Code), *Kōkyō kigyōtai-tō rōdō kankeihō* (Labor Relations Code for Public Corporations), *Rōdō kumiai-hō* (Trade Union Code) and finally Penal Code. The constituent elements and illegality in all these laws were examined one by one to assess defendant's constituent elements and the resultant illegality, while culpability was then rationalized for the judges' determination of punishment.

However, *Taishinin* in the five case studies in this book predominantly engaged in practices that align with more conventional methodologies, which are predicated on divergent ethical principles (Hendry 1995, pp. 216–219). The fundamental unwritten legal consciousness of moralistic *dōri* is, in fact, embedded in judicial behaviour for any civil and criminal legal proceedings (Tejani 2021, p. 735). *Taishinin* was strict and placed a greater emphasis on the equitable *dōri* for punishment than on the reintegration of individual offenders into mainstream society. The contemporary focus on individual well-being and quality of life in the study of free societies was neither a prevalent theme nor a foundation for *Taishinin*'s judicial behaviour in prewar Japan. This is why two authors of this book discover Taishinin's judicial behaviour of strict liability model. It is a valid assertion that the judicial interpretation of the Penal Code in prewar era was oriented towards the implementation of punitive measures, rather than prioritizing rehabilitation. Moreover, the Meiji Diet's legislative behaviour did not encompass the concept of rehabilitation, nor did it include subsequent social reintegration measures. Prior to the enactment of the Offender Prevention and Rehabilitation Act in 1949, which subsequently became the foundation for the present Offenders' Rehabilitation Act, the concept of "offender rehabilitation" remained unexplored in the annals of Japanese legal history. Judicial behaviour model for rehabilitation cannot be seen in Taishinin's judicial decision-making process.

3.18 Brief Remarks

Dōri represents an unwritten natural law-like legal consciousness and is regarded as the body of Japanese legal culture in the past 1500 years. According to the principles established by *Taishinin*, the judicial authorities were entrusted with the discretion to exercise *dōri*, a term denoting the authority to determine the acceptability of a given practice or ritual. In instances where such discretion was deemed necessary, the court was also empowered to impose sanctions.

The utilization of diverse methodologies in the examination of novel concepts pertaining to judicial behaviour is instrumental in fostering a more profound comprehension of the subject matter.[40] Before judicial behaviour analysis in the following from Chaps. 4 to 8, information on social conditions is provided as part of background information. This approach is borrowed from legal anthropology. Corruption in legal

[40] On this see Jain (2001).

anthropology is a multifaceted phenomenon interacting with situational social conditions. With the exception of the early work of James Scott, the study of corruption has been overlooked in anthropology.[41] The book, *Corruption in Legal Anthropology*, provides a comprehensive examination of the historical and cultural underpinnings of bureaucracy, with a focus on its corrupt interaction with the private economy in anthropological perspective (Rocca 1992, pp. 402–416).

In the domain of legal anthropology, social conditions are recognized as a salient variable that exerts a significant influence on the outcomes of legal proceedings. These social factors, which are often termed as determinants, play a crucial role in shaping the social outcomes of individual cases within the *Taishinin* legal system. The availability of social background was not consistent across all the judgements. The social condition in the present volume is the product of the collaborative efforts of two authors of this book, the purpose of whose contributions is to facilitate an understanding of *Taishinin*'s judicial behaviour as a complex social drama.[42] This supplementary information also assists readers in comprehending the significance of *Taishinin*'s courtroom demeanour and his social circle's composition within the context of the social drama (Bubandt 2006, p. 428). The authors express their aspiration that readers will find pleasure in this style inspired by legal anthropology. The subsequent chapter will address a significant corruption case that occurred after Great Kanto earthquake. Upon reading the analysis, readers are encouraged to consider the content in terms of the social conditions that are provided.

References

Akio, K. (2010) Public Service Ethics and Corruption in Japan. In Evan, M. B. et al. ed. *Public Administration in East Asia: Mainland China, Japan, South Korea, Taiwan*. CRC Press.

Arai, H. (1968) *Oritaku Shiba no Ki (Told Round a Brushwood Fire)* (12th ed.). Iwanami Shoten.

Arai, K. (1967) Mappō ni okeru Butsubatsu no Hō Minzoku: Nihon Chūsei Bukehō, Kishōmon no Baai (The Idea of Buddha's Punishment in the Latter Days from the View-point of Legal Folk-lore). *Indogaku Bukkyogaku Kenkyu (Journal of Indian and Buddhist Studies)*, Vol 16 (1), 293-297.

Arai, T. (2013) Meiji Zenki no Hangyaku ni Tsuite: Taigyaku-zai, Nairan-zai Kenkyū no Zentei toshite (High Treason in the Early Meiji Period). *Studies in political science and economics*, Vol. 49 (4), 1351-1372.

Aston, W. G. (2023) *Nihongi: chronicles from Japan from the earliest times to A.D. 697, translated from the original Chinese and Japanese by W.G. Aston*. Routledge.

Birmingham, R. L. (1970) Model of Criminal Process Game Theory and Law. *Cornell Law Review*, Vol. 56 (1), 57-73.

Bourdieu, P. (1977) *Outline of a Theory of Practice*. Cambridge University Press.

Braithwaite, J. (1989) *Crime, Shame and Reintegration*. Cambridge University Press.

Braithwaite, J. (2006) *Crime, Shame and Reintegration*. Cambridge University Press.

Brown, D. (2006) "*Shoku Nihongi*" Japanese Historical Text Initiative. University of California at Berkeley https://jhti.berkeley.edu/Shoku%20Nihongi.html. Accessed 31 August 2022.

[41] On this see Scott (1972).

[42] On this see Bourdieu (1977).

Britannica. *Natural Law*. https://www.britannica.com/topic/natural-law. Accessed 15 September 2025.

Britannica. *Nihonshoki*. https://www.britannica.com/topic/Nihon-shoki. Accessed 1 September 2025.

Bolz, H. F. (1980) Judicial Review in Japan. *Hastings International and Comparative Law Review*, Vol 4. (1), 87–142.

Bubandt, N. (2006) Sorcery, Corruption, and the Dangers of Democracy in Indonesia. *The Journal of the Royal Anthropological Institute*, Vol. 12 (2), 413–31.

Carpenter, S. (2003) *Special Corporations and the Bureaucracy: Why Japan Can't Reform*. Palgrave Macmillan.

Chua, L. J., Engel, D. M. (2019) Legal Consciousness Reconsidered. *Annual Review of Law and Social Science*, Vol. 15, 335-353.

Darnell, R. (1995) The Structuralism of Claude Lévi-Strauss. *Historiographia Linguistica*, Vol. 22 (1-2), 217–234.

Dean, M. (2002) *Japanese Legal System (2nd ed.)*. Cavendish Publishing Limited.

Diaz-Leon, E. (2015) What Is Social Construction? *European Journal of Philosophy*, No. 23, 1137–1152.

Enta, Y., Ogawa, I. (2011) Soshikiron de Yomitoku: Edo Jidai 8 (Organizational theory as decipher: Edo Period 8). *KEIEI SHIRIN (The Hosei Journal of Business)*, Vol. 48 (3), 87-101.

France, G. (2021) *Overview of lifestyle audits as an anti-corruption tool and country examples from Africa*. Transparency International.

Friedman, L. M. (1987) *The Legal System: A Social Science Perspective*. Russell Sage Foundation.

Fujioka, I. (1979). Wairo-zai no Ichi Kōsatsu: Kōmuin ni Taisuru Keiji Kisei no Junbiteki Kōsatsu (A study of bribery offense: An examination of Criminal Regulations for Public Officials). *Doshisha Law*, Vol. 31 (1), 40-57.

Galanter, M. (2005) *Lowering the Bar: Lawyer Jokes and Legal Culture*. University of Wisconsin Press.

Genryo, E. (1971) *Giri and Ninjō*. Chūōkōronsha.

Gloppen, S. (2014) Courts, Corruption and Judicial Independence. Tina, S., Aled, W. ed. *Corruption, grabbing and development: Real world challenges* (pp. 68–79). Edward Elgar Publishing.

Haley, J. O. (1991) *Authority Without Power: Law and the Japanese Paradox*. Oxford University Press.

Hall, J. W. (1955) *Tanuma Okitsugu (1719–1788): Forerunner of Modern Japan*. Harvard University Press.

Hamilton, C., Young, M. (2001) Historical Introduction to the Japanese Legal System. In Milhaupt, C. J., et al ed. *Japanese Law in Context – Readings in Society, the Economy, and Politics* (pp. 1-39). Harvard University Press.

Hasunuma, K. (2006) Ōmi-ryō no Seiteisha wa Dare ka: Tenchi-ki no Shiryō Hihan no Hihan (Who Enacted the Omi Order: A Criticism of Tenjiki's Criticism of Historical Materials). *Kobe University law review*, Vol. 56 (3). 1-28.

Hayashi, S. (1939) *Shōtoku Taishi Jūshichijō Kenpō (Prince Shotoku's Seventeen-Article Constitution)*. Gokoku Jokokai.

Hedinger, D. (2012) Globalization of legal cultures in the 19th century: Criminal trials, gender, and the public in Meiji Japan. *InterDisciplines Journal of History and Sociology*, Vol. 3 (2), 135-165.

Henderson, D. F. (1952) Some Aspects of Tokugawa Law. *Washington Law Review*, Vol. 27 (1), 85-109.

Hendry, J. (1995) *Japanese society*. Routledge.

Hirosaki City. *Nakatomi Hara*. https://www.city.hirosaki.aomori.jp/gaiyou/bunkazai/shi/shi55.html. Accessed 15 September 2025

Hōjō, H, Miyahira, S. (2009) Nihon Kindai Keihō no Seiritsu Katei (A Process of Enactment of Criminal Law in Modern Japan). *Ryūkei Hōgaku (Bulletin of Faculty of Law, Ryutsu Keizai University)*, Vol. 9 (1), pp. 13-57.

Hooft, W. M.V. (2002) *Japanese Contract and Anti-Trust Law: A Sociological and comparative study*. Routledge.

Igata, R. (1973) Kansei Kaikaku to Kyōto Machi-bugyōsho: Shuzō Seigenrei to Kuchitanba Sōdō (Kansei Reform and the Kyoto Municipal Magistrate's Office: Sake Brewery Restriction Ordinance and the Kuchitanba Riot). *Doshisha law review*, Vol. 24 (5), 1-34.

Ikeuchi, Y. (1962) Goseibai Shikimono Genpon no Kenkyū (A Study of the Original Text *Goseibaishikimoku*), *Shirin*, Vol. 45 (4). 485-511.

Jain, K. (2001) Corruption: a review. *Journal of Economic Surveys*, Vol. 15 (1), 71-121.

Karita, T. (1958) Giri no mondai (The problems of *giri*). *Kokubungaku Kenkyū (Japanese Literature Research)*, Vol. 17, 128-136.

Kawamura, K. (1982) *Hojo Tokuso-ke no Hensen (Changes in the Hōjō Tokusōke family)*. Rekishi kenkyūkai.

Keizaizashisha ed. (1897) *Kokushi Taikei Dai 2 Kan (Great National History Volume 2)*. Keizaizashisha.

Koaze, T. ed. (1910). *Daishinin Shin Keihō Hanrei Yōshi (Summaries of the Daishinin's new criminal code precedents)*. Ganshodo.

Kukita, K. (1980) Shōtoku Kaigen to Kōsatsu Seido – Shōtoku kara Kyōhō e (Shoutoku Kaigen and Kosatsu System: From Shotoku to Kyoho). *Meiji Daigaku Keiji Hakubutsukan Nenpō (Meiji University Criminal Museum Annual Report* No. 11, 49–66.

Langseth, P. (1999) *Prevention: An Effective Tool to Reduce Corruption*. Office of Drug Control and Crime Prevention, United Nations Office.

Levon, B. (2014) Evolution of legal consciousness from antiquity to modern age. *Law and Modern*, No. 2, 18- 24.

Lomnitz, L. (1971) Reciprocity of Favors in the Urban Middle Class of Chile. In George, D. ed. *Studies in Economic Anthropology* (pp. 93-106). American Anthropological Association.

Lomnitz, L. (1988) Informal Exchange Networks in Formal Systems: A Theoretical Model. *American Anthropologist*, Vol. 90 (1). 42-55.

Lomnitz, C. (1995) Ritual, Rumor and Corruption in the Constitution of Polity in Modern Mexico. *Journal of Latin American Anthropology*, No. 1, 20–47.

MacCormick, N. (1998) Norms, Institutions and Institutional Facts. *Law and Philosophy*, Vol. 17 (3), 301-345.

Maeda, M. (1993) *Keihō no Kiso (Basics of criminal law)*. Yūhikaku.

Masamune, A. (1930) *Nihonshoki: Genbun Gekan (Nihonshoki: Original text. Volume 2)*, Issue 22. Japan Classic Complete Works Publishing Association.

Mass, J. P. (1999) *Yoritomo and the Founding of the First Bakufu*. Stanford University Press.

Matsuzono, J. (2020) Muromachi Bakufu no Hōgainenn ni Kansuru Obōgaki (Memorandum on Legal Concepts of the Muromachi Shogunate). *Hitotsubashi Law*, Vol. 19 (1), 47-61.

Martinsson, J. (2021) Combatting institutional corruption: The policy-centered approach. *Crime Law Social Change*, Vol. 75, 267–280.

Meyers, H. (1950) Revisions of the Criminal Code of Japan During the Occupation. *Washington Law Review*, Vol. 25 (1), 104-134.

Ministry of Justice. (1959a) *Tokugawa Kinrei-kō Zenshū Dai 1 (Tokugawa Prohibition Examination Preliminary Collection No. 1)*. Sobunsha.

Ministry of Justice. (1959b) *Tokugawa Kinrei-kō Zenshū Dai 4 (Tokugawa Prohibition Examination Preliminary Collection No. 4)*. Sobunsha.

Ministry of Justice Research Division. (1932) *Shihō Shiryō. Dai 170-gō Tokugawa Kinreikō (Judicial Materials No. 170 Tokugawa Prohibition Considerations), Vol.* 1. Ministry of Justice.

Murphy, T. (2019) Natural Law and Natural Justice: A Thomistic Perspective. In Crowe, Lee, C. Y. ed. *Research Handbook on Natural Law Theory* (pp. 302–325). Edward Elgar.

Nadareishvili, V., Chkheidze, V. (2015) Legal culture and legal consciousness in terms of set and attitude. *European Scientific Journal*, Vol.2. 123-129.

Nakase, K. (1935) *Tokugawa Jidai no Wairoshi Kanken: Keizai Kurabu Kōen (Bribery History in the Tokugawa Era: Keizai Club Lecture), No. 80*. Tōyō keizai shuppan-bu.

Nakase, K. (1989) *Edo Jidai no Wairo Hishi (The secret history of bribery in the Edo period).* Tsukijishokan.

Naoki, K. (1999) Asuka Kiyomihara-ryō to Taihō-ryō Kansei o Chūshin toshite (Focusing on the *Asuka Kiyomihara* Code and the *Taiho* Code). *Shidai nihonshi (The historical journal of Japan, by Osaka City University)*, Vol. 2, 1-15.

National Institute of Japanese Literature. *Engishiki.* https://kokusho.nijl.ac.jp/biblio/100249538/1?ln=en. Accessed 15 September 2025.

Nielsen, L. B. (2000) Situating Legal Consciousness: Experiences and Attitudes of Ordinary Citizens about Law and Street Harassment. *Law and Society Review*, Vol. 34 (4), 1055-1090.

Nihon University. (1905) *Osadamegakihyakkajō, Nihon University 1938 Year 2nd Year Lecture Records*. Nihon University.

Nikaidō, Z. ed. (1563) *Kenmushikimoku.* Miyauchi Kiyohara ason utsushi.

Nishihara, H. (1967) Keihō Seiteishi ni Arawareta Meiji Ishin no Seikaku: Nihon no Kindaika ni Oyoboshita Gaikokuhō no Eikyō: Ura-men kara no Kōsatsu (The Character of the Meiji Restoration in the History of Criminal Law Enactment: The Influence of Foreign Laws on Japan's Modernization: Consideration from behind. *Hikaku Hōgaku (Comparative Law)*, Vol. 3 (1), 51-94.

Noda, Y. (1976). Anthony, H. A. trans. ed. *Introduction to Japanese Law.* University of Tokyo Press.

Ōhira, Y. (1996) Kinsei no Higōhōteki Soshō (Go): Kagosō, Kakekomisō o Sozai toshite (Early modern illegal litigation No. 5: Using palanquin lawsuits and rush-in lawsuits as materials). *Ritsumeikan Law*, Vol. 6 (250), 155–185.

Ōkubo, H. (1995) Tokugawa Bakufu Keihō ni okeru Sekininron Josetsu (Introduction to Responsibility in Tokugawa Shogunate Criminal Law). *Komazawa Daigaku Hōgaku Ronshū (Komazawa University Law Paper)*, Vol. 51, 43-70.

Ōfuchi S. (2021) Bakuhan Taisei ka ni okeru Kansei no Kaikō: Matsudaira Sadanobu to Jūnōshugiteki Keizai Seisaku (Kansei reforms under the shogunate system: Matsudaira Sadanobu and physiocratic economic policy). *Kokusai Kankei Kenkyū (Nihon University International Relations Studies)*, Vol. 41. 1-11.

Olson, M. (2002) *The Logic of Collective Action: Public Goods and the Theory of Groups (Twentieth printing).* Harvard University Press.

Ooms, H. (1996) *Tokugawa Village Practice: Class, Status, Power, Law.* University of California Press.

Persson, A. et al. (2013) Why Anticorruption Reforms Fail-Systemic Corruption as a Collective Action Problem. *Governance: An International Journal of Policy, Administration, and Institutions*, Vol. 26 (3), 449–471.

Posner, A., Grover, R. (2008) *How judges think.* Harvard University Press.

Rawls, J. (1999) Two Concepts of Rules. In *Rawls John: Collected Papers* (pp. 24–46). Harvard University Press.

Rocca, J. (1992) Corruption and Its Shadow: An Anthropological View of Corruption in China. *The China Quarterly*, No. 130, 402–416.

Röhl, W. (2005). *History of Law in Japan Since 1868.* Brill.

Rose-Ackerman, S. ed. (2006) *International Handbook on the Economics of Corruption.* Edward Elgar.

Rose-Ackerman, S. 2010. The Institutional Economics of Corruption. In Gjalt, d. G. et al. ed. *The Good Cause: Theoretical Perspectives on Corruption* (pp. 47–55). Verlag Barbara Budrich Publishers.

Sagers, J. H. (2006) *Origins of Japanese Wealth and Power: Reconciling Confucianism and Capitalism, 1830–1885.* Palgrave Macmillan.

Sato, Y. (2001) *Commercial Dispute Processing and Japan.* Kluwer Law International.

Scott, J. C. (1972) *Comparative Political Corruption.* Prentice-Hall.

Shirota, K. (2015) Tokugawa Bakufu Keihō ni okeru Keiji Sekinin no Honshitsu ni tsuite (On the Essence of Criminal Responsibility in the Tokugawa Shogunate Penal Code). *Nagoya Daigaku Hōsei Ronshū (Nagoya University Law and Politic)*, No. 264, 205–227.

Silbey, S. S. (2001) Legal Culture and Legal Consciousness. In Neil J. S., Paul B. B. ed. *International Encyclopedia of the Social and Behavioral Sciences* (pp. 8623-8629). Elsevier.
Stanford Encyclopedia of Philosophy. *The Natural Law Tradition in Ethics.* https://plato.stanford.edu/entries/natural-law-ethics/ Accessed 2 September 2022.
Stanford Encyclopedia of Philosophy. *Legal Interpretivism.* https://plato.stanford.edu/entries/law-interpretivist/. Accessed 7 September 2022.
Steenstrup, C. (1996) *A history of Law in Japan Until 1868. (2nd ed.).* E.J. Brill.
Takano, T. (1989) Kinchū narabi ni Kuge Shohatto ni kansuru Ichi Kōsatsu: Kuge no Kaku ni megutte (A Study on the Laws of the Court nobles: Concerning the family status of the court nobles). *Gakushūin Daigaku Shiryōkan Kiyō (Gakushuin University Archives Bulletin)*, No. 5. 1–24.
Tanaka, H. (1976) *The Japanese Legal System: Introductory Cases and Materials.* University of Tokyo Press.
Takayanagi, S., Ishii, R. ed. (1934a) *Ofuregaki Kanpō Shūsei (Collection of Imperial Letters Kanpo), No.1.* Iwanami Shoten.
Takayanagi, S., Ishii, R. ed. (1934b) *Ofuregaki Kanpō Shūsei (Collection of Imperial Letters Kanpo), No.15.* Iwanami Shoten.
Takeshita, K. (1992) Dōri to Hō no Shihai: Hikakuhō Shisōshiteki na Ichi Byōshō (Reason and the rule of law: A historical sketch of comparative law thought). *Kansai Daigaku Hōgaku Ronshū (Kansai University Law Papers)*, Vol. 41 (5-6), 1495-1534.
Takizawa, M. (2005) Hikakuhōgaku kara mita Nihonhō no Aidentiti (The Identity of Japanese Law from the Viewpoint of Comparative Law). *Waseda Daigaku Hikakuhō Kenkyūjo Sōsho (Waseda University Institute of Comparative Law Series)*, No. 32, 181–195.
Tejani, R. (2021) The life of transplant: Why law and economics has "succeeded" where legal anthropology. *Alabama Law Review*, Vol. 73 (4), 733-752.
Tezuka, Y. (1950) Kari Keiritsu no Ichi Kōsatsu (An examination of Provisional Criminal Law). *Keiō Gijuku Daigaku Hōgaku Kenkyū (Keio University Law Studies)*, Vol. 23 (12), 1-25.
Thompson, D. (1995) *Ethics in Congress: From Individual to Institutional Corruption.* Brookings Institution.
Tidey, S. (2018) A tale of two mayors: configurations of care and corruption in eastern Indonesian direct district head elections. *Current Anthropology*, No. 59 (suppl. 18), 117–127.
Toeba, T. (2019) The Impact of State-society relations on Anticorruption Agencies in Southern Africa. *Kyiv-Mohyla Law and Politics Journal*, No. 5, 165–192.
Transparency International. *What is grand corruption and how can we stop it.* https://www.transparency.org/en/news/what-is-grand-corruption-and-how-can-we-stop-it. Accessed 17 July 2022.
Treisman, D. (2003) Post-communist corruption. In Jan, F., Nauro, C. ed. *Political Economy of Transition and Development: Institutions, Politics, and Policies* (pp. 201-226). Springer.
Tsumaki, N., Aoyama, K. (1999) Ōsaka Machi Bugyōsho ni yoru Kanbun Hachinen Rei Kibun Kaishaku (Osaka Municipal Magistrate's Office's interpretation of scale in Kanbun 8th). *Nihon Kenchiku Gakkai Keikakukei Ronbunshū (Paper collection of Planning Section of Architectural Society of Japan)*, No. 524. 281–288.
Tucker, J. A. (2014) The Meanings of Words and Confucian Political Philosophy: A Study of M atsunaga Sekigo's Ethics. In Huang, C. C., Tucker, J. A. ed. *Dao Companion to Japanese Confucian Philosophy* (pp. 31-68). Springer.
Uematsu, A. (1920). *Kana NihonShoki*, Volume 2 (No. 17). Daidokan.
United Nations. (2004) *United Nations Convention against Corruption.* United Nations.
Venkatesan, R. (2015) Confronting corruption. *McKinsey Quarterly.* https://www.mckinsey.com/~/media/McKinsey/Featured%20Insights/Corporate%20Social%20Responsibility/Confronting%20corruption/Confronting%20corruption.pdf. Accessed 6 January 2023.
World Bank Institute. (2008). *Fighting Corruption through Collective Action: A Guide for Business.*
Yamakawashuppansha. (2016) *Nihonshi Shō Jiten: Kaitei Shinpan (A Short Dictionary of Japanese History: revised new edition).* Yamakawa Publishing Company.

Yamakawashuppansha. (2018) *Shin Nihonshi (New History of Japan)*. Yamakawa Publishing Company.

Yoshiwara, Y. (2017). Onore ni Hisomu: Mujun (Hidden in Self: Contradiction). *Kokushikan Tetsugaku (Kokushikan Philosophy)*. No. 21. 39–50.

Chapter 4
The Itabuneken and Hiratabuneken Compensation Case

4.1 Case Background

This judgement referenced as *Keishū* 13–419, dated 26 March 1934, concerns a significant corruption case that involved 19 appellants, who were represented by 55 lawyers. According to Article 55 of the prewar Penal Code, junior courts treated this case as *renzokuhan* trial, which was a trial of serial offender. This particular judgement addressed two criminal cases: *the Itabuneken and Hiratabuneken Compensation Case*, which is addressed in this chapter, and *the Keiseidensha (Keisei Electric Railway Company) Case*, which is addressed in the following chapter. In prewar Japan, it was legally permissible for court to deliver a single judgement encompassing two cases. Nevertheless, this constitutes a form of criminal injustice that hinders the comprehension of common people.

This is the most extensive and perplexing *Taishinin* judgement on corruption cases, spanning 50 pages of documentation. In this judgement of two cases, appellants and *Taishinin* presented their own versions of a long, complex chain of events and financial transactions that transpired over the course of several years. This suggests the absence of agreed juridical facts. A meticulous analysis and thorough review of the original judgement necessitate patience and effort. Readers may discern it is like the movie *Rashomon* directed by the late Kurosawa Akira. Each appellant gave different version of statement for the same event.

The phenomenon of corrupt public officials and stakeholders colluding in high-investment post-earthquake reconstruction projects is not an isolated occurrence limited to prewar Japan. A nation's degree of public sector corruption has been demonstrated to be positively and significantly correlated with the magnitude of destruction and loss of life caused by seismic events and natural disasters (Escaleras et al. 2007, p. 226). This is attributable to the substantial investment, the involvement of contractors and the possibility of public officials' rent-seeking. *The Itabuneken and Hiratabuneken Compensation Case* is not an exception to the rule. The Great

K. B. Wong and S. L. Fang, *Taishinin's Judicial Behaviour in Corruption Cases*,
https://doi.org/10.1007/978-981-95-5823-0_4

Kantō earthquake's correlation with grand corruption can be likened to the "act of God" for a corruption chance.

4.1.1 The Nihonbashi Fish Market

The Itabuneken and Hiratabuneken Compensation Case related to the old fish market in Nihonbashi, Tokyo. The history of government regulation for the central wholesale market of fresh fish can be traced back to the bakufu in 1603 (*Keichō* 8). Mercantilism in the late Edo era led to economic growth and wealthy stakeholders in the fresh fish business. The largest fish market in the Edo period was built around today's Nihonbashi Honcho 1-Chome and Nihonbashi Muromachi 1-Chome. The Japanese artist Utagawa Kuniyasu's famous *ukiyōe* of *Nihonbashi Sakanaichi Han'ei* (Prosperity of Nihonbashi Fish Market) depicts the bustling fish market crowed with people, stretching all the way to the bridge of Nihonbashi in the Edo period. In 1877, *Sakana Torinami Aomono Ichiba Oyobu Tonya Nakagai Eigyō Reiki Nami Zeisoku* (Rules for Business and Tax of Wholesaler and Broker of Fish, Chicken and Fish Business) was codified by the Meiji government for the designation of four wholesale fish markets, namely Nihonbashi, Shinba, Shibakanasugi and Senju. These Rules, promulgated in 1877, laid the foundation for today's Japanese fishing business. It changed the traditional discriminatory attitude against fishing businessmen by introducing new mercantilism (Metzler and Smits 2010, p. 5).

Itabuneken and hiratabuneken in the case refers to two important privileges in the Nihonbashi fish market. Usually, fish transported through the Nihonbashi River was traded and unloaded onto *hiratabune* (flat-bottomed boats) moored at the wharf. It was then displayed for sale on *itabune* (wooden planks) placed in front of the shops in the huts built along the riverbank. Therefore, *itabuneken* (the right to place the wooden planks) and *hiratabuneken* (the right to use the flat-bottomed boats) became propriety rights which could be traded, transferred, or leased and afterwards became extremely expensive and valuable intangible assets.[1]

In regard to urban development, the Meiji government had long planned to relocate the Nihonbashi fish market in Tokyo. Since 1889, when the *Tokyōshiku-kaiseijōrei* (Tokyo Urban Area Amendment Ordinance) was implemented to promote new mercantilism, there have been persistent proposals to eliminate it. However, these efforts had consistently met with failure. In 1919, the *Toshi-Keikakuhō* (City Planning Code) was codified to specify new building and street requirements, which were advantageous to city planning for mercantilism, including the development of the fish market. In March 1923, the *Chūōoroshiuichibahō* (Central Wholesale Market Code) was officially promulgated and plans for the removal of the fish market were underway. Six months after the enactment of this legislation, the Great Kantō earthquake occurred.

[1] See "the business in Nihonbashi fish market" at https://www.jtco.or.jp/column/readings/?act=detail&id=80. Accessed 30 September 2025.

4.1.2 The Great Kantō Earthquake and the Removal of the Market

The Great Kantō earthquake occurred on 1 September 1923, while Yamamoto Gonbee was organizing his cabinet after the death of Prime Minister Katō Tomosaburō on 24 August 1923. The earthquake was considered to result in the reported deaths or missing status of over 140,000 Tokyo residents. The estimated number of destroyed houses was approximately 300,000.[2] The citywide fire subsequent to the earthquake totally destroyed the Nihonbashi *uogashi* (quay), which was the central part of the fish market. On 2 September 1923, *Rinji-shinsai-kyūgo-jimukyoku* (Temporary Earthquake Relief Bureau) was formed to restore public order. As per the Emperor's Edict Number 418, dated 19 September 1923, *Teito-fukkou-shingikai-kansei* (Official System for Revival of Imperial Capital Reconstruction Council) was released to provide organized systematic post-earthquake relief.[3]

On 27 September 1923, which was 26 days after the earthquake, Japanese government promulgated *Teito-fukkōin-kansei* (Government Official System for Imperial Capital Reconstruction) in order to revive Tokyo and Yokohama through urban town planning and reconstruction. The Minister of Interior Gotō Shinpei took up this post additionally. *Tokubetsu-toshi-keikakuhō* (The Special City Planning Code) under Law number 53 in 1923 was also urgently passed for the revival of Tokyo as the imperial capital. On 1 December 1923, a portion of the fishmongers was temporarily relocated to Tsukiji, a district in the heart of downtown Tokyo that had previously served as a base for the Japanese Imperial Navy. On 25 February 1924, *Teito-fukkōin* (Imperial Capital Reconstruction Institute) was fully merged into the Ministry of Interior. Naoki Rintarō, who was in charge of the *Fukkōkyoku* (Reconstruction Bureau) in the Ministry of Interior, declared on 11 April 1924 to take this chance to improve the social turmoil and unsanitary conditions in the fire damaged Tokyo, which was divided into sixty-six areas for resettlement and redevelopment. The total expenditure for all reconstruction projects was estimated to be approximately 4.1 billion *yen* at the beginning. It was then reduced to 800 million *yen* and the final amount was 468 million *yen*.[4] All these constituted a golden opportunity for corruption (Komatsu 2011, p. 28, p. 30).

[2] See "Tokyo-Yokohama earthquake of 1923" at https://www.britannica.com/event/Tokyo-Yokohama-earthquake-of-1923. Accessed 15 September 2025.

[3] On this see Central Disaster Prevention Council (2008, pp. 66–78).

[4] On "Tokyo reconstruction plan" see "the first meeting record of Imperial Capital Reconstruction Institute" at https://www.timr.or.jp/degitalarchives_kantodaishinsai/OBZ-0190-01/OBZ-0190-01_0012.html -Accessed 13 October 2025; See "Tokyo reconstruction plan outline" at https://www.digital.archives.go.jp/das/image-j/M0000000000001756728 Accessed 15 September 2025.

4.1.3 The Lack of Disaster Relief Law

In most countries nowadays, earthquakes are considered a natural disaster and are typically covered by insurance policies. The impetus for this grand corruption case stemmed from the absence of a disaster relief law during the entire prewar Japan of the Showa era. The stakeholders of the Nihonbashi fish market were compelled to engage in a protracted negotiation with the government to ascertain the compensation amount following their relocation to another area for the government's land redevelopment project. The 1890 edition of the *Shōhō* (Commercial Code) incorporated provisions pertaining to earthquakes. However, subsequent amendments in 1899 led to the removal of these provisions (Hioki 2017, pp. 4–5). In the context of prewar Japan, those adversely affected by seismic events and subsequent conflagrations lacked alternative avenues for securing redress. A review of pertinent legislation reveals the absence of a statute explicitly delineating the legal obligations of the prewar government to provide compensation to citizens for the forfeiture of property rights in the context of natural disasters.

The first disaster relief law, *Saigai-kyūjo-hō* (Disaster Relief Code), was passed by the Japanese Diet in 1947 as Law Number 118,[5] while *Daikibo-jishintaisaku-tokubetsusochihō* (Large-Scale Earthquake Countermeasures Code) was passed in 1978 under Law Number 73.[6] In contrast to the prewar era, the Japanese government currently possessed two key attributes. Firstly, it possessed a robust re-insurance policy, which served to mitigate potential financial risks. Secondly, it had established clear legal obligations regarding the maximum compensation amount.[7] The absence of a codified methodology for calculating compensation and relief in prewar Japan engendered a loophole that permitted political corruption. Therefore, the stakeholders of the Nihonbashi fish market strategically utilized the Tokyo City Assembly members to optimize the allocation of public funds for their benefit. The local autonomy system established during the Meiji era conferred upon the City Assembly members unchecked discretionary power. This was due to the absence of a robust internal monitoring mechanism. Concurrently, the mass media, serving as a watchdog, demonstrated insufficient vigilance.

In the aftermath of the earthquake, fire disasters were not encompassed within the insurance policy's coverage. Consequently, the intricacies of subsequent land disputes and the deliberations concerning compensation amounts during reconstruction processes were addressed on an individual basis. In order to support the lives of those affected by the earthquake, the government issued an emergency Imperial Ordinance in September 1923 (*Taisho* 12), setting tax amounts and exemptions (income

[5] See the original text at https://laws.e-gov.go.jp/law/322AC0000000118. Accessed 15 October 2025.

[6] See the original text at https://laws.e-gov.go.jp/law/353AC0000000073. Accessed 15 October 2025.

[7] See "Outline of Japan's Earthquake Insurance System" at https://www.mof.go.jp/english/policy/financial_system/earthquake_insurance/outline_of_earthquake_insurance.html. Accessed 10 September 2025.

tax and business tax) for fiscal year 1923, as well as collection deferrals (land tax, income tax, business tax and inheritance tax) for fiscal year 1924.[8]

Taishinin judgement recorded that in 1923, certain landowners, including those operating the Nihonbashi fish market, declined to cooperate without receiving "satisfactory" compensation. This period of construction continued until the completion of all reconstruction projects in Tokyo as Imperial Capital in 1930. Consequently, the Nihonbashi fish market was transformed into a designated fire prevention area for contemporary buildings. The legislation stipulated the establishment of a railway network for the transportation of fish, thereby establishing the Tsukiji largest central wholesale fish market in Japan in terms of its size. Other important fish markets included Zakoba in Osaka, Zaimokucho, Yorozuyacho, Konyacho in Nagasaki and Yawatahama in Ehime.[9] Notwithstanding railway network, fishmongers remained reluctant to relocate from Nihonbashi to Tsukiji, citing concerns regarding the financial compensation offered. Therefore, Takamura Masutaro and Shinozaki Masaruji, who possessed the largest percentages of propriety rights of *itabune* and *hiratabune*, engaged in a conspiracy with the Tokyo City Assembly members, leveraging the removal of the fish market.

4.1.4 The Tokyo City Assembly and the Chance for Its Corruption

Since the Meiji period, the local autonomy system has entrusted the City Assembly with significant discretionary powers. This has led to the emergence of a corruption loophole, as the assembly has been granted considerable discretion in the execution of its duties. In prewar Japanese system, there were two levels of local public bodies: metropolis, circuit, urban prefecture, prefecture (*to, do, fu* and *ken*) and municipal (*shi, chō,* or *machi, mura*). The modern Tokyo has emerged from a historical context characterized by a dual administrative system comprising Tokyo-*fu* and Tokyo-*shi* (Nomura 1982, p. 189). In 1943, a novel administrative system for the Tokyo Metropolis was established through the unification of these two. In the context of prewar Tokyo, this *Taishinin* incident was indicative of two major forms of corruption: the first being a city-type grand corruption scandal, and the second being institutional corruption. The initiative encompassed a total of 19 Tokyo City Assembly members and a substantial allocation of public funds. In contrast to the price of 50 kilogrammes of rice, which exhibited fluctuations between 20 and 30 *yen* during the early 1930s (Hayami 1972, p. 22), the total financial sums referenced in this *Taishinin* judgement pertaining to bribery were substantial. The absence of a sense of social responsibility for the public interest in the redevelopment of Tokyo was evident in the

[8] See *the hundred-year history of Ōkurashō,* pp. 311–313.

[9] See "Tukiji Market: past, present and future" at https://www.jef.or.jp/journal/pdf/WUIJ.pdf. Accessed 15 September 2025.

behaviours of political factions in Tokyo City Assembly. These factions exhibited a selfish abuse of their voting power for private gain.

The government, under the authority of the Emperor as the primary administrator of public power, exhibited a deficiency in its oversight of its agents, specifically the City Assembly members, in this particular instance. City Assembly members were considered public officials. For the purposes of this study, it is essential to note that the accused were convicted of bribery offences under Articles 197 and 198 of the Penal Code. The accused were public officials acting as agents of the "principal" government, as defined by Article 7. Therefore, it is also possible to regard the Assembly members as citizens' agents within the electoral system. The exercise of the prerogatives by the electorate during the election process can be regarded as a form of empowerment. In accordance with this empowerment, the City Assembly members were granted a monopoly on unchecked decision-making authority regarding compensation amounts in local autonomy. No legal provision existed that obligated them to consult with the central government beforehand. A comparable legal technicality pertaining to corruption during post-earthquake reconstruction was also observed in the *Fukkōkyoku* (The Reconstruction Bureau) of the Japanese government, given the substantial amount of public funds involved. The removal of Nihonbashi fish market was covered under *Teito-fukkō-keikaku-hōan* (Imperial Capital Reconstruction Plan Bill) under the purview of *Fukkōkyoku* (Yamakoshi 2024, pp. 30–36). *Teito-fukkō-keikaku-hōan* had no rule for calculation of compensation amount to earthquake victims.

The discretionary decision-making power of local autonomy was not a novel concept before the Meiji era. Before the Meiji Restoration, the seigneurial class did not exercise direct authority over the peasants, either individually or collectively (Vlastos 1986, p. 10). The election of village heads or neighbourhood associations for local autonomy can be traced back to the Tokugawa era (Hayashida 1967, p. 52). In the nascent stages of the novel local government system during the Meiji Restoration, the Japanese electoral system was instituted by the *Gun-Ku-Chō-Son-Henseihō* (The Counties, Cities, Towns and Villages Organization Code) and the *Kuchousonkaihō* (Municipal Assembly Code) in April 1880. The determination of the election, reelection term of a session, the number of assembly members at different local levels, and the term of office of assembly members was instead determined by prefectural governors, as opposed to the central government in Tokyo (Kamiko 2010, p. 12). As demonstrated in the *Taishinin* case, elections for local autonomy had been found to be associated with bribery for lobbying, which is often concealed under the guise of political contributions to electoral campaign funds. The aforementioned act was a mere facade, serving as a pretext for the bribery of assembly members in exchange for their discretionary power in the matter.

4.2 Brief Facts in *Taishinin*'s Judgement

4.2.1 Compensation Case of no Rule for Compensation Amount

Taishinin's assessment of the Nihonbashi fish market yielded a precise measurement of its area, determined to be 20,000 *tsubo*, equivalent to approximately 66,000 square metres. The proprietors of *itabuneken* and *hiratabuneken* had been specially granted monopolies to sell fish in the market. The Tokyo mayor also granted the proprietors of the fish market the right to utilize an area limited to 20 *tsubo*. For the sake of ensuring public safety and managing river traffic, it had been obligatory for all proprietors to join a union. A total of 214 holders of *itabuneken* submitted compensation claims amounting to 7,090,000 *yen* each, while 13 holders of *hiratabuneken* submitted claims with a minimum value of 48,000 *yen* each. During the early Showa period of Japanese history, these figures were substantial, though they were open to negotiation. The amount of bargain fluctuated because neither an administrative formula nor a binding legal rule for calculation was available. The paucity of precedent court cases and the absence of insurance policies for disasters in the prewar Showa era complicated the valuation of such property rights.

The discretionary power of the Tokyo Assembly members to determine the compensation amount was subject to neither internal nor external constraints. There was no statutory ceiling of compensation amount. The City Assembly members had a free hand to provide assistance to stakeholders for maximum amount; nevertheless, they accepted bribes in exchange for exercising their discretionary power. In light of the mounting number of aggressive petitions from stakeholders for higher compensation amounts, the Tokyo Metropolitan Government endeavoured to reach a compromise. Nevertheless, these endeavours were ultimately unsuccessful. A review of historical data from the Tokyo *Shiyakusho* (City Office) in 1935 reveals that there was no information available regarding a compromised formula for calculating the amount in question.[10] The statutory limitation of Tokyo City Assembly members' discretion may have the potential to impede corruption; however, it may also be a demotivational factor to their productivity in public service (Kwon 2014, p. 766).

4.2.2 Fish Market Union and the Tokyo City Assembly

Takamura and Shinozaki expressed concerns that the relocation of the fish market to Tsukiji would result in their significant economic losses. Consequently, they sought to establish a political channel to maximize financial compensation from the Tokyo Metropolitan Government. On 30 March 1924, a coalition of individuals organized under the banner of the fish market union of fishmongers was established with the

[10] On this see Tokyo City Hall (1935, pp. 2–9).

objective of exerting pressure on the Tokyo Metropolitan Government to address their demands. The Tokyo City Assembly member Tsubono Fusaji stepped in and intervened as a mediator, pledging to convey their grievances to the senior leadership of the Tokyo Metropolitan Government.

On 12 February 1925, *Ichi Setsu Oroshibai Ichibashiyoujourei* (the Municipal Wholesale Market Use Ordinance) was tabled as an agenda item at the Tokyo City Assembly meeting in preparation for the closure of the market in Nihonbashi. On 24 March 1925, the City Assembly had resolution on the compensation amount, but it needed the mayor's endorsement as a matter of procedure. Within four days, on 28 March 1925, the mayor Nakamura Yoshikoto declared 1 September 1923 as the cut-off day for compensation amount, of which the ceiling was set at 1,000,000 *yen*. This ceiling amount of 1,000,000 *yen* without unclear guidelines and external monitory mechanism marked the commencement of the subsequent chain of events in this political corruption case.

On 30 September 1923, an ad hoc Compensation Committee of 19 City Assembly members was formed to re-screen the proposed compensation scheme. However, the terms of 8 City Assembly members, Segawa Mitsuyuki, Tsubono Fusaji, Ōno Keikichi, Komori Shichibee, Murayama Kensaku, Kurata Kinzaburō, Tanaka Kōzō and Saegusa Yonetarō expired in June 1926 before the scheduled completion of the whole re-screening process. While six City Assembly members in this Taishinin case, Komori, Tsubono, Gomeda, Ōno, Takigawa, Kurata and Murayama started their term in June 1922. After a short time gap in June 1926, they had been re-elected and had Tokyo City Assembly membership until 21 December 1928. Terms of other two co-accused Motegi Kyūhei and Oi Zenzo were from June 1926 to 21 December 1928.

In December 1926, Nishikubo Hiromichi succeed as the Tokyo mayor. He proposed to amend the cut-off day from 1 September 1923 to 29 January 1927 and the ceiling of compensation amount to be adjusted to 900,000 *yen*. These proposals were subject to re-approval of financial committee and the re-endorsement of Nishikubo. On 2 February 1927, 15 City Assembly members, including Gomeda and Oi, re-screened the amended compensation plan. The whole screening procedure finally completed in mid-March 1927 and represented to Nishikubo for reconsideration.

On 31 March 1927, Nishikubo screened and forwarded it back to the finance committee as an agenda item in City Assembly meeting scheduled on 18 April 1927. These 15 City Assembly members were then appointed to double up the duties of *Kōfu-kinshinshaiinkai* (Grant Examination Committee), which was a formalized name of the ad hoc finance committee composing of Koita Hisamankichi, Gomeda Jiro, Komori Nanabei, Ōno Keikichi, Takigawa Mitsuyuki, Oi Zenzo and Kurata Kinsaburo. Koita assumed a dual role, serving as both chairman and director. According to the decision made on 28 February 1928, those owners within the Nihonbashi Market were to be eligible for compensation. The Tokyo City Assembly passed a resolution on 30 March 1928, establishing the amended compensation amount at 700,000 *yen* and declaring it final. This decision was reached by a narrow margin of two votes. Consequently, the ad hoc Grant Examination Committee was immediately dissolved. This dissolution constituted one of the grounds for appeal, namely that an assembly member who was in private capacity after his or her appointment term should not be regarded as a constituent element in a bribery offence.

4.3 The Lack of Transparency and External Monitory Mechanism

The formal institutional framework of Japanese local autonomy was modelled after that of Germany around 1890. The Ministry of Interior had been entrusted with the responsibility of appointing prefectural mayors, while the populace exercised its democratic right by electing assembly members to govern local communities and establish local autonomy. In principle, this framework was designed to establish a system of checks and balances among the various interests involved (Saito and Yamada 2011, pp. 113–114). Local mayors functioned as the primary representatives of the central government. It is not possible to conclude from this procedural and organizational design that Meiji leaders had no foresight and commitment to ensure the integrity of bureaucrats and to prevent malpractice, malfeasance and bribery. Nevertheless, from a risk management perspective, there was a necessity for greater transparency and an external monitoring mechanism with regard to the exercise of discretionary power.

Moreover, the illicit use of campaign contributions to facilitate bribery was a recurring pattern in cases of political corruption. This case does not constitute an exception to the aforementioned rule. The Tokyo City Assembly members were elected by local residents in their respective electoral areas. In the event that a temporal interval occurred between the previous appointment and the subsequent appointment, it was necessary to determine whether a former City Assembly member retained the authority to carry out their official duties during this interim period. In principle, this former member reverted to the status of a typical Japanese national following the termination of their appointed term. It is imperative to ascertain whether this former member retained the capacity to serve as the agent for the power that had been delegated from the government in which Emperor was the principal at the time. This constituted the crux of the ongoing legal dispute surrounding *Taishinin*'s judicial behavior and the impending verdict.

4.4 Juridical Facts Against Appellants in *Taishinin*'s Judgement

In the context of *Taishinin* judgement, a juridical fact is defined as an occurrence that is formally acknowledged by the prevailing legal framework and is deemed to possess legal ramifications, thereby influencing the judicial behaviour of *Taishinin*. Throughout the existence of *Taishinin*, there was an inconsistency in the writing of judgements, with different styles being employed. A series of legal decisions were rendered, each addressing specific legal aspects of the case against the appellants. It is evident that the style has been adhered to in this judgement.

4.4.1 *Nakajima Moritoshi*

Nakajima's election as the head of the Tokyo Branch Office of the political party *Rikken Seiyūkai* (Association of Friends of Constitutional Government) was facilitated by the support and respect of the majority of its members. In the Tokyo City Assembly, he also served as a faction leader. The members of his faction engaged in a habitual *shintai*, or collective action, under his leadership. In recognition of the collaborative efforts and strategic alliance between him and Koita Hisamankich to garner the endorsement of the *Seiyūkai* faction within the Tokyo City Assembly to secure a favourable compensation amount, Takamura, one of the bribers, disbursed a total of 50,000 *yen* to the aforementioned individuals as *undō hōshū* (political campaign funds) in early March 1926. On 24 March 1928, a sum equivalent to 10,000 *yen* was formally transferred by Koita at his residence. Subsequently, four promissory notes, collectively amounting to 40,000 yen, were issued. In the *Taishinin* judgement, the court determined that Nakajima and Koita engaged in a conspiracy to accept a bribe, thereby establishing a joint agreement to engage in illicit activities. In the subsequent chapter, it is also noted that Nakajima was involved in the Keisei Electric Railway Company Case.

4.4.2 *Komori Shichibee*

Komori Shichibee's professional background includes serving as a Tokyo City Assembly member and a member of the Grant Examination Committee. Since 1925, Takamura had requested Komori to utilize his influence over his fellow Tokyo City Assembly members to advocate for an increased compensation amount, particularly during the resolution stage. In order to achieve this objective, Takamura provided Komori with a total of 1000 *yen* in cash and via a check outside of Komori's residence. This occurred in three instalments between mid-May and mid-September of 1926. The pretext for was contributions to his electoral campaign funds for Tokyo City Assembly membership. In June of 1927, Takamura provided him with an additional sum of 600 *yen* in support of his election to the House of Representatives. On 14 and 18 February 1928, Takamura provided Komori with a total of 500 *yen* on two separate occasions. This transaction occurred at the residence of Komori, and the funds were intended as a complement to his election campaign for the representative of the third electoral district of Tokyo-*fu*. *Taishinin* interpreted Komori's actions as constituting acceptance of bribes on each of these occasions.

4.4.3 Ōno Keikichi

Since March 1926, Takamura had obtained a pledge from Ōno Keikichi to advocate for enhanced compensation. Following the submission of the agenda item to the Tokyo City Assembly, Ōno endeavoured to secure the votes of the other members of the Grant Examination Committee. A sum of 5000 *yen* was issued in the name of his firm and addressed to another City Assembly member, Tsubono Fusoji. Ōno expressed a desire for Takamura to disregard it in exchange for immediate monetary compensation. On 10 April 1926, at Tsubono's residence, Takamura exchanged a promissory note for 5000 *yen* and a check for 4668.5 *yen*. Subsequently, the check was cashed by Zeniya Kinji, who is a director of Ichimuraza. The act in question constituted the acceptance of a bribe in relation to the official duties of Ōno as a member of the Tokyo City Assembly. On 17 May 1926, Takamura distributed an additional sum of 5000 *yen* to Kurata Kinzaburō and Ōno on the basis of a conspiracy with Kurata. In the subsequent year, specifically in May of 1927, Takamura proceeded to extend an additional sum of 1000 *yen* to the aforementioned firm, thereby augmenting the financial resources available to them. Kurata and Ōno collectively acknowledged receipt of a total sum of 6000 *yen* on these two occasions.

4.4.4 Koita Hisamankichi

Koita's role as chair of the Compensation Grant Committee of the Tokyo City Assembly is indicative of his significance within the political structure. Koita voiced his support for the 900,000-*yen* compensation plan proposed by mayor Nishikubo. This support was expressed in conjunction with the entrustment of Takamura and Shinozaki. In order to pass the compensation plan, Koita presented the demands of different interest groups upon screening and consideration of it in this Committee. In May of 1927, at the residence of Koita, Shinozaki extended a loan of 500 *yen*. *Taishinin* interpreted Koita's acceptance of the bribe as tacit consent. In mid-June of 1927, at the residence of Shinozaki, a total of 4000 *yen* was distributed to Koita, disbursed in three instalments. These actions constituted Koita's acceptance of a bribe.

Beginning in December of 1927, Takamura, Shinozaki and Aikawa endeavoured to persuade *Seiyūkai* members under the leadership of Nakajima, to acquiesce to the proposed compensation plan. To this end, they successfully persuaded Nakajima to conspire with other *Seiyūkai* members. In early March of 1928, Takamura, Shinozaki and Aikawa promised to remunerate Nakajima with 50,000 *yen* in recognition of his successful persuasion of *Seiyūkai* members. On 24 March 1928, Takamura and Koita paid Nakajima an additional 10,000 *yen* at Nakajima's residence. On 29 March 1928, Takamura presented four promissory notes at his office, each bearing a face value of 10,000 *yen*. The total sum of money disbursed on these two occasions amounted to

50,000 *yen*. In the judgement of *Taishinin*, it was stated that Koita and Nakajima had reached a mutual understanding regarding the acceptance of a bribe.

4.5 Linguistic Analysis of *Taishinin*'s Judicial Behaviour

Language is an integral component of judicial behaviour. *Hōgengogaku* (legal linguistics) is a prevailing methodology employed to comprehend the judicial mindset. The use of language in judicial proceedings serves as a component of judicial behaviour, with the objective of ensuring adherence to legal provisions. In addition to the legal terminology employed for identification, such as that utilized in criminal charges, the vernacular vocabulary is also significant.[11] A critical component of legal linguistics pertains to the existence of substantive fact and the manner in which judges perceive and articulate it in their own terms (Tsuji 2002, p. 106). The employment of active vernacular vocabulary and terms in legal discourse is indicative of more than mere rhetoric. It serves as an effective metric for assessing judicial behaviour as a component of the communicative-persuasive language process.[12] The employment of vocabulary or polysemous terms can offer insights into judicial behaviour in the context of a legal conundrum, facilitating a cognitive understanding of the subject matter.[13] An analysis of it in the legal arguments and judgement is a matter of language operation, which is akin to research on cognitive activity via language (Hotta 2005, pp. 440–441). A profile of *Taishinin*'s mindset in this case is provided below, citing the key terms and phrases in the *Taishinin* judgement.

4.5.1 *Sharei*

In this judgement, *Taishinin* frequently employed the term *sharei* in its juridical facts. *Sharei* had also been utilized repeatedly in other *Taishinin* judgements concerning corruption and bribery cases. This judicial behavioural pattern had profound implications. This term is often used in the context of financial transactions to convey a sense of gratitude. The Latin term *quid pro quo*, which is utilized in legal studies, signifies the principle of reciprocal exchange, whereby one action or event is met with another in a balanced and proportional manner. The gift is characterized by its unconditional nature, whereas the share is not. The absence of *quid pro quo* in a gifting act typically does not constitute bribery due to its unconditionality. The allocation of funds in exchange for *sharei* is considered a form of sharing, which is often utilized as a compensation for specific actions or contributions.

---

[11] On this see Davis (1985, pp. 354–356, p. 363).

[12] On this see Probert (1959, p. 35, pp. 43–44).

[13] On this see Rogers et al. (2008, p. 125, p. 127, p. 135).

From a cognitive perspective, *Taishinin*'s judicial behaviour, characterized by the utilization of *sharei*, signifies an underlying intent and consideration for *quid pro quo*, thereby indicating a conditional exchange of monetary compensation rather than an unconditional one. The term "condition in *sharei*" refers to the concept of exchanging *quid and quo* in a transaction, thereby establishing a mutually beneficial exchange between the parties involved (the *pro*). Accordingly, the financial resources allocated to this initiative were not designated as an unconditional contribution to the electoral campaign, as indicated by the unique identifier. Similarly, the financial resources allocated to the initiative identified by the unique identifier were not designated as an unconditional contribution to the electoral campaign. Ultimately, the concept of corruptibility had to be criminalized by *Taishinin*'s legal reasoning and factual finding in order to infer the criminal state of mind of both the briber and the bribee (Robertson et al. 2016, pp. 377–378). According to the attitudinal model of judicial behaviour, *Taishinin* justices were tasked with shaping the concept of *quid pro quo* and justifying its alignment with their personal morality and ideological inclinations as *dōri* for the purpose of criminalization.[14]

4.5.2 *Kanrei and Inzen-Shita-Seiryoku*

Part of the juridical facts was about bribery for Komori Shichibee under the cover of political patronage. It was clientelism built on Komori's personalized network of mutual trust and Nakajima's political factionalism in the Tokyo City Assembly (Bustikova and Corduneanu-Huci 2017, pp. 316–317). *Taishinin* used *kanrei* (past practice) and *inzen-shita-seiryoku* (obscure power) to depict political factionalism which was instrumental for the commission of corruption offence. Though *Kōshoku-Senkyohō* (Public Offices Election Code) was promulgated together with Meiji Constitution on the same day in February 1889, political party *Rikken Seiyūka* in this case was lately established on 15 September 1900. Without further elucidation, wordings *kanrei* and *inzen-shita-seiryoku* appear in this *Taishinin* judgement about electoral campaign, but no direct evidence to prove vote buying or undue influence on voting behaviour of Tokyo City Assembly members was provided.

In this *Taishinin* case, two mayors of Tokyo followed procedural justice to determine compensation amount. They made no attempt to counteract political party factionalism. In prewar Japan, even Japanese government existed transcendentally outside party politics. It was thus termed *chōzenshugi* (transcendentalism),[15] in which vote buying is a common political corruption phenomenon under the cover of political campaign funds. In this regard, *Taishinin* provides a clear example of it. Reishchauer wrote that vote buying is not widespread in Japan, as compared with many countries (Reishchauer 1977, p. 309), but Japanese political factionalism is still very common nowadays. The model of Japanese political party was formulated in the 1920s during

[14] On this see Hardy (1995, p. 410, p. 412, p. 413).

[15] On this see Matsuoka (1966, p. 35, p. 38).

the Taisho era. Funding for electoral campaigns were dominated by the individual candidates and their *koenkai* (personalized local support group) rather than by the political party. Party identification was comparatively weak because of lack of social cleavages for differentiation of parties. As political sub-organization, party faction at local level is indistinguishable from the personalized support group of the electoral candidate (Curtis 2004, pp. 3–4). Two bribers' act of lobbying through support group was possible but lobbying supported by monetary interest could constitute bribery.

Loyalty of political factionalism to follow the leadership of Nakajima was Nakajima's capital to accept bribe. It was described by *Taishinin* as *kanrei*:

> The defendant Nakajima Moritoshi is the branch head of Tokyo Branch of *Seiyūkai*. He has stunned influence on *Seiyūkai* members in Tokyo-*fu*, especially in the Tokyo City Assembly. The majority of *Seiyūkai* political party members respect him and habitually have a customary practice to adopt the same strategy.[16]

Taishinin did pay attention to and considered loyalty of *Seiyūkai* party factionalism in its judicial decision-making. Its comments on *sharei* and party faction leadership confirms it judicial behaviour of all-the-circumstances consideration of prewar Japan's political reality. Nakajima's status, leadership and power in the intraparty competition of political factions in the prewar Tokyo City Assembly were two bribers' *quid pro quo*. Without it, the bribery to Nakajima was very unlikely.

4.5.3 Nakajima's Carte Blanche Leadership

Taishinin remarked party faction members' collective action of *ishi o sonchō* (respect the will) to reinforce the negative meaning of *shintai suru o kanrei to nashi* (make it a custom to advance and retreat). *Taishinin*'s judicial behaviour to criminalize Nakajima by his leadership in party factionalism is clear. As mentioned, Nakajima's *quid pro quo* to bribers was out his intraparty reputation and networking power as fundamentals of his faction leadership. It related to the trust, norms of reciprocity and social networking ability of Nakajima. All these could exert undue influence or even "hijack" the political behaviour of *meue* (social superiors) over *meshita* (social inferiors). In Japanese political party faction, a *meshita* almost follows the *meue*'s leadership as a form of unrestricted "carte blanche leadership".[17]

According to such *Taishinin*'s descriptions, Nakajima had "carte blanche leadership" in a relatively well-organized political sub-group competing with other intraparty groups as power rivalry. As an asymmetrical exchanges of power resources, such factionalism was an institutionalized differentiation of vertical structure within a party (Köllner and Matthias 2005, pp. 9–13). The group of this kind is always disciplined with a comparatively solid consciousness of existence and stable personnel

[16] The original text in the judgements: 被告人中島守利は政友会東京支部長にして東京府下に於ける政友会所屬黨員を統制し隱然した勢力を有し殊に東京市會議員中正交會其の他政友会系所屬議員の大半は同人の意思を尊重し進退するを慣例と為し。

[17] On this see Ikeda and Richey (2005, p. 239, p. 242).

network based on mutual trust.[18] Such party faction usually had the group identity lasting until the end of political life.[19]

Taishinin's judicial behaviour, which included the expression of "the rituals of respecting the will and making it a custom to advance and retreat" for factionalism under Nakajima, indicates that *Taishinin*'s judicial behaviour was a strategic model characterized by a clear sense of purpose and intention. In the absence of substantiating evidence, *Taishinin*'s judicial behaviour can be interpreted as a strategic rationalization employed to refuse Nakajima's appeal. This strategic judicial behaviour was deemed reasonable in accordance with the principles of *dōri*, the concept within the framework of equitable jurisprudence. From a cognitive perspective, *Taishinin* demonstrated a negative stance toward Nakajima's self-centred, personalistic intra-party networks that were driven by the pursuit of private gain. This disposition was evident throughout the entirety of this *Taishinin* judgement.

A comparison of the political climate in contemporary Japan with that described in the *Taishinin* judgement reveals that Japanese politics today is still conservative. The concept of *kōenkai* functions as a conduit for the exchange of interests and power among factions within a political party (Yamada and Kabashima 1994, pp. 211–212). The contemporary relevance of the party faction concept persists in perpetuating instances of bribery. *Kōenkai*'s approach to political campaigning involves a nuanced strategy of monitoring and analysing irregularities, particularly in the context of factionalism, with the objective of ensuring the success of the campaign (Endō 2012, p. 11). It is an active, voluntary association that is linked to factional power. It is important to note that this seminal corruption case, which took place during the prewar period, caused significant upheaval within Japanese society. Notwithstanding the public's disapproval, Nakajima had been elected to the House of Representatives on three separate occasions since 1946.[20] *Taishinin*'s refusal to accept Nakajima's appeal was not indicative of discrediting his political party faction leadership or the trust of its voters. In the political landscape of Japan, the transfer of political party factions to subsequent generations of politicians is a notable phenomenon. In 2017, 25.8 per cent of the members of the Japanese House of Representatives were hereditary politicians.[21]

[18] On this see Hine (1982).

[19] On this see Beller and Belloni (1978).

[20] See "Nakajima Moritoshi" at https://jahis.law.nagoya-u.ac.jp/who/docs/who8-15687. Accessed 13 September 2025.

[21] See *Mainichi Japan* (28 October 2017) about "*Hereditary politicians' make up 25.8% of those elected in latest election*" at https://mainichi.jp/english/articles/20171028/p2a/00m/0na/001000c. Accessed 15 September 2025.

4.6 Appeal Grounds of Komori Shichibee

4.6.1 Komori's Additional Point on Judgement

In Komori's appeal grounds, he repeated his understanding of *Taishinin*'s juridical facts in full details. He then first accused junior courts' conviction was non-factual. He claimed the accusation against him was for wrongful conviction. First, he repeated the history of the Nihonbashi fish market, the removal of the market and the compensation plan for it. Different with the *Taishinin*'s version of juridical facts, besides the ownerships of *itabuneken* and *hiratabuneken* in the market, he also mentioned that there were two refrigerator owners, one of whom was Takamura. He also added the point of fishmongers' debtor-and-creditor relationship in the market, but this point was not significant for determination of bribery.

Komori continued to reiterate the resolution for the compensation was out of collective decision-making as it was screened and amended consistently by an ad hoc Grant Examination Committee of the Tokyo City Assembly. The resolution process was long and approved by consecutive mayors.

4.6.2 Komori's Character Evidence and Cultural Defence

Despite Komori's apparent reluctance to contest *Taishinin*'s interpretation of the legal facts, it is crucial to note that *Taishinin* categorically labelled all financial transactions as Komori's acquiescence to bribery, asserting that he had knowledge of the bribery in relation to his official duties. Komori's legal strategy entailed the execution of his own legal reasoning regarding the sequence of events, employing evidence of his moralistic character as a basis for challenging the conviction.

It is noteworthy that character evidence for the purpose of countering a conviction is seldom effective. This factor is often employed as a mitigating element in determining culpability, thereby facilitating more lenient sentences. Komori's decision to assert his moral and exemplary conduct as a legal means of securing his exoneration was a calculated risk. The concept of good character is inherently abstract and difficult to substantiate. This legal issue might be resolved by corroboration with witnesses' testimonies and concrete incidents to prove appellant's character, including the Tokyo City Assembly members who had personal knowledge of all relevant individuals in question. This testimony could encompass the opinions of other witnesses who also had specific knowledge of the appellant. If this was the case, Komori would possess the potential to "turn the table".

Komori accordingly advanced the argument that his actions were consistent with traditional Japanese cultural values. He sought to discredit junior courts' verdicts by labelling it as an unethical infringement on long-established Japanese principles of justice. Initially, he expounded on the extensive history and magnitude of the erstwhile market, thereby establishing a foundation for his subsequent moralistic arguments. It had been posited that the impetus behind the actions of the individual was rooted in a sense of moral rectitude. The objective of Komori's endeavours in Tokyo City Assembly was claimed to provide legal assistance to the fishmongers and ensure that they were duly compensated for their hereditary property rights.

Komori's first argument put *Taishinin* to confront moral dimension of anti-corruption law. He packed himself as a "well-conducted legal justice fighter[22]". He stigmatized the compensation amount was *kajiba-dorobō* (thief in fire disaster) taking the chance of fire disaster for embezzlement. While *Chūōoroshiuriichiba-hō* (Central Wholesale Market Code) was legislated, the Great Kantō earthquake and the fire disaster took place on 1 September 1923, creating an opportunity for *kajidoro* (fire thief) by compulsorily closure of old fish market and removal to Tsukiji. As a representative of Tokyo citizens in the City Assembly, it was a matter of course for Komori to actualize social justice by helping them seek fair compensation. *Itabuneken* and *hiratabuneken* had been hereditary property rights since the Tokugawa bakufu. The removal was injustice and exploitation of a traditional business of many generations' history. Komori accused that the compulsory removal was a deprivation of fishmongers' rights perpetually.

From a moralistic perspective on character evidence, Komori adroitly accused the confiscation of citizens' hereditary property rights without appropriate compensation as inequitable, although the removal might promote prosperity in Kyōbashi of Tokyo. It labelled it as an attack on Japanese *dōri*. Given his own residency in Kyōbashi, he was personally invested in the matter. The electorate's increased support for the candidate could be attributed, at least in part, to his decision to seek appropriate compensation. In light of the aforementioned context, the compensation issue was brought to the attention of the Tokyo City Assembly in 1924. Subsequently, he assumed a role as a member of the Grand Examination Committee in 1925, where he engaged in deliberations with the committee secretary, Ishibashi, regarding the compensation amount.

The screening and resolution process was suspended on 4 June 1926, due to the city assembly reelection. Following Takamura's receipt of information regarding the progression of the case in late April or early May of 1926, the ceiling compensation amount was revised, increasing it to 700,000 *yen*. Komori underscored that his actions were driven by a personal quest for justice, independent of any solicitation from Takamura. Accordingly, Komori's position was that junior courts had misunderstood and misinterpreted the sequence of events, leading to the erroneous conviction.

Secondly, Komori claimed to be a consultant to Takamura's business company and contributed to enhancing its profitability. In the spring of 1924, he counselled Takamura to procure a parcel of land measuring 200 *tsubo*. In a period of four to five days, the profitability of the venture amounted to 3000 *yen*. Takamura allocated a proportion of the accumulated financial gains to Komori, amounting to 300 *yen*. In 1926, the thoroughfare within Asakusa Park was characterized by insufficient width. In the name of Takamura's firm, they engaged in a collaborative effort to widen a road for

[22] The original text in the judgement is "社會正義の實行".

the convenience of pedestrians. Takamura's assistance proved instrumental in facilitating successful negotiations with government officials for the project. Following the success of this project, he submitted an application to extend the completion day of another construction project in the name of Takamura's firm. The Ministry of Police's refusal to grant an extension would have a deleterious effect on Takamura's reputation and result in a financial loss of between 50,000 and 60,000 *yen*. On behalf of Takamura, Komori successfully negotiated with the Ministry of Police for a six-month extension. Subsequently, Takamura bestowed upon him *hōshū sharei* (remuneration or reward) on several occasions. Two of them exhibited authentic affection for each other. It was a matter of course that Takamura was zealous to support Komori's election campaign by *jinchū mimai* (visiting soldiers at the front to provide comfort). The financial backing provided by Takamura for Komori's electoral campaign was initiated more than ten years after their initial introduction by a mutual acquaintance, Kosaka. Beyond their demonstrated commitment to public interests, no other compelling rationale was identified.

Komori's assertion that the financial transactions in question were not bribes but political donations for his electoral campaign is of particular interest. In anticipation of the Tokyo City Assembly election, scheduled for 4 June 4 1926, Takamura provided him with a sum of 500 *yen*, ostensibly for the purpose of electoral campaign funding. However, the 300-*yen* component of this sum was effectively a loan. In the evidence presented by the prosecutor to the junior court, Takamura's 300-*yen* check, written in format, was clearly addressed to another individual named Ogura Genjirō. Nonetheless, Komori regarded the lump sum *jinchū mimai*. It was not until eight months later, on 2 March 1927, that Komori settled the 300-yen loan by issuing a personal cheque to the Tokyo branch of Nagaoka Bank. The evidence at hand clearly indicated that the 300-*yen* coin had never been accepted. According to the fourth pretrial court report of the junior court, specifically paragraph 30,507 (d) in the first and second *kōhan chōsho* (court record), it is evident that the 300 yen had been returned to Takamura. The Tokyo Branch of Nagaoka Bank provided evidence that substantiated this claim. The cheque issued by Komori and addressed to the Takamura's firm of Takamura's was subsequently cashed. Consequently, the case nature should not be bribery. Junior courts misinterpreted the facts, leading to erroneous convictions. During the trial at the junior courts, Takamura erroneously confessed that Komori had received the money without returning it. Consequently, junior courts were found to have wrongfully convicted individuals.

On 20 June 1927, the election for members of House of Representatives was held. The name list of donators for Komori's *jinchū mimaikin* had clear records of all these financial transactions. For another House of Representatives election on 20 February 1928, which was eight months later, Takamura donated 200 *yen* instead of the recorded 500 *yen* to Komori. Takamura was all along zealous to support Komori's election campaign. On 18 February 1928, Imazu Gen'emon and Takamura attended Komori's home together. Takamura went there with this 200-*yen* cash in 1-*yen*, 5-*yen* and 10-*yen* coins wrapped in newspaper. Takamura told Komori to use it as 2-day travelling expenses during electoral campaign before 20 February 1928. The total amount of campaign funds donated by Takamura was 1600 *yen* instead of 1900 *yen*, because 300 *yen* had been returned. Komori emphasized that the prosecutor also endorsed the correctness of the amount of 1600 *yen*.

In January 1926, with Takamura's recommendation, the fish market management supported Komori to stand for electoral candidate in Kyōbashi district. Komori claimed he confidentially aimed to secure maximum number of votes with small amount of electoral funds. In late March 1926, Tsubono Fusaji stood for election as representative of the Nihonbashi district. The market union chairman Imazu Genemon also wanted to be a candidate for city assembly election. The fish market management intended to support Komori's electoral campaign. As Tsubono was then also an electoral candidate in Kyōbashi which overlapped with Nihonbashi, the competition made Komori lose 600 votes in the election and suffered from the blow of his fruitless expenditure on electoral campaign funds.

To relieve Komori's distress from this blow, Takamura therefore provided logistic support of the aforesaid financial donations of 1600 *yen* for his electoral campaigns in 1927 and 1928. The campaign funds were for one City Assembly election and two House of Representatives elections. Komori reiterated that the transactions were limited to pure electoral *kizōenjo* (donation and aid). To him, it was very surprising that such donation and aid intertwined with this corruption case. The whole chain of events was based on their mutual acquittance for more than ten years and Komori's consultant service to Takamura's firm. In return for it, Takamura facilitated and supported him as a matter of so-called *iwayuru shinyū* (so-called close friendship) instead of corrupt remuneration. As a well-known fact, expenses for election campaign tended to exceed the ceiling of statutory budgetary limit. In case of insufficient electoral budget, assistance from friends and relatives was common. The receipt of financial assistance from companies and friends was not curious and impurity.

As a city assembly member, Komori claimed it was unnecessary for him to consider *hōshū sharei*. He simply did his utmost for what he believed to be justice. Komori had no relationship with Takamura's interest whatsoever in *itabuneken and hiratabuneken* ownership. The proposal for compensation in 1925 was endorsed unanimously in city assembly. This unanimous endorsement was *jihaji* (self-initiated). All these could be seen in the official record of city assembly. Takamura's financial support for Komori was apparently *kiyoshizai* (clean pure money). The term *kiyoshizai* was used as a counterattack to the terms of *hōshū* and *sharei*.

To fight for appropriate compensation amount in this case was emphasized as purely Komori's own initiative out of his sense of city assembly responsibility. There was no Takamura's entrustment in this regard. Komori then criticized junior courts mistakenly criminalized his acts as receipt of *hōshū* for the aforesaid efforts. Such misconception was against Komori's belief that *itabuneken and hiratabuneken* should have equitable compensation amount. His behaviour to act on behalf of fishmongers was out of his belief in justice. Takamura had thrice financially supported his election campaign funds with donations instead of bribery for lobbying and intention to secure better compensation amount.

4.6.3 Analysis of Komori's Appeal Grounds

In his extensive appeal strategy, Komori incorporated the concept of cultural defence, which was integrated with his existing moralistic character defence, with the objective of exerting an attitudinal influence on *Taishinin*'s judicial behaviour. Komori's appeal ground was characterized by an integration of attitudinalism with a strong sense of traditional Japanese values, particularly *jinchū mimaikin*. At the outset, he articulated his primary contention, asserting a misinterpretation and misunderstanding of the case facts. He went on to accuse junior courts of the most egregious criminal injustice: the wrongful conviction of an innocent individual. Throughout the appeal ground, Komori strategically avoided mentioning that Takamura was the primary stakeholder of *itabuneken* and *hiratabuneken*. In order to achieve exoneration, Komori endeavoured to sever the link between the financial obligations of a City Assembly member and conceptual *quid pro quo* in all financial transactions. He prepared himself as a proponent of social justice.

The most significant vulnerability identified in Komori's case is the absence of a substantiated rationale to support the reasonableness of substantial financial transactions. It was determined that Takamura's financial resources were a result of their friendship and assistance during the election campaign. This finding indicated that these financial resources were considered legitimate *jinchū mimai*.

The term *jinchū mimai* is of Japanese cultural origin and was used to denote acts of offering comfort and provisions to individuals engaged in combat. Komori employed this cultural defence on multiple occasions. The concept of bribery encompasses the notion of reciprocal exchange, often characterized by *quid pro quo*. However, within the context of certain cultural practices, this exchange may be viewed through a different lens, with cultural defence mechanisms serving as a rationalizing factor. The financial transactions between Takamura and Komori were characterized as *jinchū mimaikin*, denoting both business and friendship. Komori employed the cultural term *jōzai* (clean finance) to negate corrupt *quid pro quo* transactions. In the context of Japanese religious tradition, *jōzai* is defined as a form of financial donation characterized by its unconditional nature, typically directed towards Buddhist temples or charitable organizations. The practice of requesting donations to cover the expenses of memorial services can be traced back to the 1061 inscription of the phrase "take donation for the expenses of memorial service" in the *Kōtodoku Nagon Ganmonshū* (Donagon's Prayer Collection).

Komori employed this cultural analogy to persuade *Taishinin*. Komori's strategy of cultural defence and character evidence was exerting influence on *Taishinin*'s attitudinal judicial behaviour. In order for evidence to be considered admissible, it must be demonstrated that there is corroboration with the facts of the case. However, character evidence is considered indirect evidence that is used to reconstitute the facts of the case and assess culpability.[23] Komori's approach was characterized by the presentation of subjective reputation evidence and oral evidence, which lacked the comprehensive social consensus that would be expected in such cases.

---

[23] On this see Sasakura (2018, p. 172, p. 173, p. 179).

In the context of shame culture, the most noteworthy expressions in Komori's appeal were, "in heaven and on earth, he was convinced that there was nothing to be ashamed of".[24] He reiterated that his relationship with Takamura was not *mizukusai aidagara* (a relationship in odorous water). His role was characterized as that of a representative of the citizenry, with the objective of facilitating the realization of social justice. This approach bears a resemblance to the traditional Japanese jurisprudential concept of *tendō* in *hirihōkenten*, which is a kind of ultimate equitable natural justice against bias. The level is higher than *dōri*. Referral to Japanese shame culture was employed to exert a persuasive effect on *Taishinin*'s judicial behaviour. Individuals who exhibited moral integrity and adherence to the law demonstrated a reduced propensity to engage in criminal activity. This objective is the most common one in the realm of character evidence.

Komori's two appeal grounds—*jinchū mimai* and character evidence—were not substantiated to the extent that they could be considered irrefutable. The term *jinchū mimai* remains a prevalent *modus operandi* in contemporary political corruption. The prewar Japan lacked a legal framework that regulated political contributions for the purpose of lobbying. The attitudinal model of the judicial behaviour of judges is the key determining factor in the criminalization of such actions until 1947, in which the *Seijishikinkiseihō* (Political Funds Control Act) was passed as part of a broader postwar law reform initiative. In this judgement, the customary gifting practice of *ochūgen* (midyear gift-giving) also appeared intermittently. The customary practice of *jinchū mimai*, which encompasses gift-giving and bribery, is characterized by a lack of clarity regarding the distinction between these concepts. In the subsequent chapters, the subject of Japanese gifting practice is elucidated with reference to *Taishinin*'s judicial behaviour.

4.7 *Taishinin*'s Judicial Behaviour in Respect of Komori's Appeal

This is a case of *Taishinin*'s strict attitudinal model of judicial behaviour versus Komori's appeal grounds of cultural defence and character evidence. In his extensive submission, Komori presented his version of the case facts, character evidence and cultural defence. This was done to support his grounds of social justice. He was righteous to assist fishermen in obtaining fair compensation and financing, without the presence of any corrupt *quid pro quo* activities. Judicial behaviour of attitudinalism is defined as the judges' attitudes in response to the stimuli they receive. The focus of this analysis is not on the dictates of the law, but rather on the attitudes and cultural preferences of the judges (Cameron and Kornhauser 2015, p. 2). Nonetheless, *Taishinin* disregarded Komori's character evidence, as evidenced by its judicial conduct, through the doctrine of strict liability. This doctrine renders the possibility of quashing Komori's conviction, as asserted by the junior courts,

[24] The original text in the judgement: 俯仰天地にして恥つるところなしと確信して。

unfeasible. The court's jurisdiction encompasses the determination of the defendant's actions, independent of their personal characteristics or background. Judicial behaviour that disregards the probative value of character evidence is not an uncommon occurrence.[25]

As delineated in the preceding chapter, the three-stage model of judicial behaviour for criminalization comprises constituent elements, illegality and culpability. The scope of coverage may extend to persuasive legal arguments, judicial activism and the question of whether the legal principles are adhered to or if judicial behaviour is constrained by self-restraint to adhere to precedent rulings.[26] *Taishinin*'s judicial behaviour in this judgement exhibited a self-referential quality, characterized by a simultaneous acknowledgement and challenge of its own principles. Although *Taishinin*'s court judgement acknowledged the consideration of intention, it paradoxically asserted that appropriate intention or behaviour in good faith was, de facto, not within the purview of *Taishinin*'s deliberations. *Taishinin*'s position was unambiguous: even if Komori's actions were technically correct, his acceptance of financial shares constituted bribery.[27]

In the context of the *Itabuneken and Hiratabuneken Compensation Case*, *Taishinin*'s primary concern pertained to the role of Komori's actions in securing approval for compensation, a request that had been in fact made by Takamura. The central issue was to ascertain whether the acceptance of monetary compensation was directly associated with Komori's efforts. In the context of *Taishinin*'s judicial behaviour model, characterized by its emphasis on strict liability, the concepts of intention, character evidence and cultural defence hold no significance. *Taishinin* did not engage in the process of legal reasoning with regard to the claims of character and Japanese culture made by Komori. *Taishinin*'s primary focus was on the formula of public official plus acceptance of interest as constituent elements only. According to Article 7 of the Penal Code, a public official is defined as a national or local government official, a member of an assembly or committee, or any other employee engaged in the performance of public duties in accordance with the established laws and regulations. According to Article 7, Komori's status as a public official could not be refuted.

In this particular instance, the authors of this book have designated *Taishinin*'s judicial behaviour as falling under the rubric of the "strict liability model of judicial behavior". As Komori asserted his integrity and the righteousness of his actions, *Taishinin* offered a unique remark in its judgement, stating, "Irrespective of the justification of the measures employed". The finding indicates that in instances where a

[25] On this see Ross (2003, p. 2, p. 12, p. 17, p. 21, p. 35).

[26] On this see Hume (2018, pp. 71–90).

[27] The original text in the judgement: 盡力することが正當なるとするも謝礼として金錢を收受したること。

public official's actions are deemed to have been motivated by a desire for recompense, a conviction may be upheld despite the presence of other exculpatory factors. The concept of strict liability can be likened to that of illegally parking a car.[28]

As elucidated in Chap. 3, the evolution of anti-corruption legislation in Japan demonstrates that, in order to cultivate stable social relations, the nation's anti-corruption laws have historically been rigorously enforced from the pinnacle of the social hierarchy. It is akin to a command system. A precise and exact parallel can be drawn between the judicial behaviour of strict liability as exhibited by *Taishinin* and its behaviour. The strict liability judicial behaviour model has been demonstrated to assist in the discipline of public officials and the deterrence of corrupt intentions. In this particular instance, *Taishinin* manifested characteristics of a public administration institution engaged in criminal justice policymaking, diverging from the strategic or historical institutionalist model of judicial behaviour. In this judgement, Taishinin wrote its judicial behaviour of strict liability model very clearly. Whether what the appellant did was appropriate or not was out of the ambit of its legal reasoning. His act itself constituted acceptance of bribery.[29]

4.8 Strict Liability in Germanic Law

Legal pluralism is defined as the interaction of multiple legal systems within a particular type of law in a society.[30] In the context of legal transplantation during the Meiji Restoration, the judicial behaviour associated with legal pluralism, as embodied by the strict liability model, did not give rise to any discernible conflicts with the prevailing Japanese tradition of enforcing anti-corruption laws as a form of social control. The initial phase of legal pluralism was marked by the gradual evolution of primitive law into state law, as well as the establishment of a clear distinction between law and custom.[31]

It can be posited that *Taishinin*'s strict liability model represents a stage in the evolution of legal pluralism. In the context of Japanese legal terminology, the concept of strict liability offence is denoted by the term *genkaku sekinin tsumi*. This legal construct bears certain resemblances to the concept of *verbotsirrtum* in Germanic jurisprudence, though it does not fully align with the precise nuances of the latter. In

[28] The original text in the judgement: 公務員が其の職務に関して謝礼を受くる以上其の職務上執りたる措置が正當なると否とを問ばず収賄罪を構成するものなれば板船権平田船權に付補償を與ぶる議案の通過に盡力することが正當なるとするも被告人小森が高村増太郎等の請託に基き板船権等補償案の通過に盡力し其の謝礼として金錢を收受したること……収賄罪の責を免るべがらず。

[29] The original text in the judgement: 措置が正當なると否とを問ばず…収賄罪の責を免るべがらず。

[30] On this see Benda-Beckmann and Tuner (2018).

[31] On this see Merry (1988, p. 870, pp. 875–876).

the Japanese context, *verbotsirrtum* is interpreted as *kinshi no sakugo*, which translates to "forbidden error" and is derived from "*kōsei yōken no sakugo*", meaning "forbidden constituent element". In the context of Germanic law, the judicial behaviour exhibited by *Taishinin* is characterized as *tabestandsirrtum*, a term denoting a judicial approach that prioritizes social ethics as the fundamental consideration in legal decision-making. The bribery offence, as delineated in Articles 197 and 198 of the Penal Code, pertains to the *tekihōsei* (legality) of *shokumukōi* (behaviour of official duty). In the context of Germanic jurisprudence, the concept of *tekihōsei* functioned as the counterpart to *rechtmäßigkeit*.[32] In this particular instance of *Taishinin*, readers are presented with an opportunity to observe the judicial phenomenon known as "Japanese body in a Germanic jacket".

4.9 Brief Remarks

The principal conclusion of this chapter, as advanced by the two authors of this book, relates to the conceptual framework of *Taishinin*'s judicial behaviour, which is characterized by a strict liability model. This finding provides a tool that can be applied to conduct a more thorough review of *Taishinin*'s judicial behaviour in the following four chapters. It is challenging to assert that judicial behaviour of this nature is equitable.

From the perspective of fairness in fair society studies, which is inextricably linked to the fundamental concept of justice, the prewar local autonomy of the Tokyo government demonstrated a commitment to democratic representative politics through the electoral process. The issue at hand did not constitute an infringement on the property rights of stakeholders as a matter of legal justice. Rather, it entailed the administration of compensation in accordance with the rule of law and the individual's propriety rights of the parties involved. It is evident that no effort has been made to compromise the well-being of fishmongers by providing them with an inequitable amount of compensation without prior agreement.

The establishment of a robust political coalition for collective bargaining at the Nihonbashi fish market ensured that all stakeholders possessed equal and liberty rights regarding the acceptance, rejection, or counterproposal of compensation amounts to the government. These interactions were characterized by mutual consent and respect, forming the foundation for the development of these relationships. The Tokyo government's commitment to individual's propriety rights under the law constituted an essential underpinning for personal freedoms, even in today's democracy. The relocation of the fish market to Tsukiji, facilitated by enhanced facilities and a modern transportation network, had been demonstrated to enhance the quality of life and well-being of both fishmongers and consumers. This development signifies a substantial advancement in the realm of fair society studies. The fairness of the Tokyo government was unfortunately subject to abuse. The Tokyo City Assembly

[32] On this see Naka (1964, p. 619, p 621, pp 629–630).

members who engaged in corrupt practices, in conjunction with two capitalists, had taken advantage of the Tokyo government's commitment, thereby squeezing for more public funds. It is evident that the pervasive bureaucratic corruption in Japan is characterized by a lack of accountability and transparency, primarily due to the absence of an effective and efficient external monitoring mechanism.

The multifaceted versions of the legal facts in this judgement bear resemblance to the renowned film of *Rashomon*. However, the absence of compelling material evidence prevented a definitive resolution. The appellant endeavoured to utilize this procedural ambiguity to secure an acquittal by means of character evidence and cultural defence. It was determined that *Taishinin* employed a strict liability model of judicial behaviour to address this dilemma straightforwardly. The strict liability model itself exhibited no inherent discriminatory tendencies against the two capitalists of the largest number of junk ownership and the corrupt Tokyo City Assembly members. The task of enumerating and refuting discrepancies in the various versions of the chain of events in this intricate and voluminous legal case, known as "legal *Rashomon*", proved to be a formidable challenge. Obtaining corroborating evidence against character evidence proved to be a challenging endeavour. Despite its apparent difficulty, it was challenging to establish a unifying consensus on moral principles across the legal and cultural domains. The strict liability model proposed by *Taishinin* is characterized by its straightforwardness, simplicity, directness and comprehensibility from the vantage point of judicial effectiveness and efficiency. The same model reappears in the subsequent *Keisei Electric Railway Company Case* and other three judgement analysis.

A systematic account of all *Taishinin*'s judicial behaviour models must, at the very least, inquire into the mechanism of discretion and the constraints imposed on the judiciary. Such an account must also inquire into the structure and organizational role of the court, the effect of its role in the judicial hierarchy, and whether it is independent of the other administrative arms in prewar Japan for policymaking. It has been demonstrated that all of the aforementioned elements are pertinent to its judicial behaviour in the context of factors exogenous to *Taishinin* and endogenous factors determined by those within the organization, as detailed in Chap. 9.

References

Beller, D. C., Belloni, F. P. (1978) Party and faction: modes of political competition. In Beller, D. C., Belloni, F. P. ed. *Faction Politics: Political Parties and Factionalism in Comparative Perspective* (pp. 417–470). ABC-Clio.

Benda-Beckmann, K, V., Turner, B. (2018). Legal pluralism, social theory, and the state. *The Journal of Legal Pluralism and Unofficial Law*, 50(3), 255–274.

Britannica. *Tokyo-Yokohama earthquake of 1923*. https://www.britannica.com/event/Tokyo-Yokohama-earthquake-of-1923. Accessed 15 September 2025.

Bustikova, L, Corduneanu-Huci, C. 2017. Patronage, Trust, and State Capacity: The Historical Trajectories of Clientelism. *World Politics*, Vol. 69 (2), 277–326.

Cameron, C. M., Kornhauser, L. A. (2015) Rational Choice Attitudinalism? A Review of Epstein, Landes and Posner's The Behavior of Federal Judges: A Theoretical and Empirical Study of Rational Choice. New York University Law and Economics Working Papers, 412.

Central Disaster Prevention Council. (2008) *1923 Kantō Daishinsai Hōkokusho: Dai 2 Hen (1923 Great Kanto Earthquake Report: Volume 2)*. Japan System Development Laboratory.

Curtis, G. (2004) *Japanese Political Parties: Ideals and Reality*. Research Institute of Economy, Trade and Industry.

Davis, W. E. (1985) Language and the justice system: Problems and Issues. *The Justice System Journal*, Vol. 10 (3), 353–364.

Endō, A. (2012). Kōenkai Dōin to Nihon no Yūkensha: Yoron Chōsa Mōdo Kan Hikaku (Supporter Association Mobilization and Japanese Voters: A Comparison Between Opinion Poll Model). *Waseda Seiji Kōhō Kenkyū (Waseda Politics and Public Law Research)*. Vol. 100. 1–14.

Escaleras, M. et al. (2007) Public Sector Corruption and Major Earthquakes: A Potentially Deadly Interaction. *Public Choice*, Vol. 132 (1/2), 209–230.

Hardy, P. D. (1995) The Emerging Role of the Quid Pro Quo Requirement in Public Corruption: Prosecutions Under the Hobbs Act. *University of Michigan Journal of Legal Reform*, Vol. 28 (2), 409–457.

Hayami, Y. (1972) Rice Policy in Japan's Economic Development. *American Journal of Agricultural Economics*, Vol. 54 (1), 19–31.

Hayashida, K. (1967) Development of Election Law in Japan. *Legal and Political Studies*. Vol. 34 (1), 51–104.

Hine, D. (1982) Factionalism in West European Parties: A Framework for Analysis. *West European Politics*, Vol. 5, 36–53.

Hioki, S. (2017) Jishin Hoken no Rekishi to Kongo no Kadai ni tsuite (The history of earthquake insurance and future challenges). *The Finance*, Vol 52 (2), 2–7. https://dl.ndl.go.jp/view/download/digidepo_11380950_po_201702c.pdf?contentNo=1&alternativeNo=. Accessed 27 July 2022.

Hotta, S. (2005). Hōgengogaku to Kagakusei (Forensic linguistics and scienc). *Ritsumeikan Hōgaku (Ritsumeikan Legal Studies)*, Vol. 300 (2&3), 439–452.

Hume, R. J. (2018) *Judicial Behavior and Policymaking*. Rowman & Littlefield Publishers.

Ikeda, K., Richey, S. E. (2005) Japanese Network Capital: The Impact of Social Networks on Japanese Political Participation. *Political Behavior*, Vol. 27 (3), 239–260.

Imperial Capital Reconstruction Institute. (1924) *The first meeting record of Imperial Capital Reconstruction Institute*. https://www.timr.or.jp/degitalarchives_kantodaishinsai/OBZ-0190-01/OBZ-0190-01_0012.html. Accessed 13 October 2025.

Japan Economic Foundation. (2006) *Tukiji Market: past, present and future*. https://www.jef.or.jp/journal/pdf/WUIJ.pdf. Accessed 15 September 2025.

Jinjikoshinroku database. *Nakajima Moritoshi*. https://jahis.law.nagoya-u.ac.jp/who/docs/who8-15687. Accessed 13 September 2025.

JTCO. *Edo no Uogashi (Riverside fish market in Edo)*. https://www.jtco.or.jp/column/readings/?act=detail&id=80. Accessed 30 September 2025.

Kamiko, A. (2010). *Historical Development of Japanese Local Governance Vol. 1: The Start of Modern Local Government (1868–1880)*. Institute for Comparative Studies in Local Governance, National Graduate Institute for Policy Studies and Council of Local Authorities for International Relations.

Kayagi, M., Itō, H. (2008) Tōkyō no Kindai ni okeru Bōka Chiku no Hensen to Shinsai Fukkō-ki no Kyōdō Kenchiku ni kansuru Kenkyū (Research on the transition of fire prevention districts in modern Tokyo and joint buildings in the post-earthquake reconstruction period). *Nihon Toshi Keikaku Gakkai Toshi Keikaku Ronbunshū (The City Planning Institute of Japan: City Planning Papers)*, Vol. 43 (2), 11–18.

Komatsu, A. (2011) Kantō Daishinsai-tō Fukkō to Toshi Keikaku-hō (Reconstruction after the Great Kanto Earthquake and the City Planning Act). *Urban Study*, No. 53, 26–35.

Köllner, P. , Matthias, B. (2005) *Factionalism in Political Parties: An Analytical Framework for Comparative Studies*. German Overseas Institute (DÜI).

Kwon, I. (2014) Motivation, Discretion, and Corruption. *Journal of Public Administration Research and Theory*, Vol. 24, 765–794.

Mainichi Japan. (28 October 2017) *Hereditary politicians' make up 25.8% of those elected in latest election*.https://mainichi.jp/english/articles/20171028/p2a/00m/0na/001000c.

Matsuoka, H. (1966) Rikken Seiyūkai no Sōritsu (Establishment of Rikken Seiyukai). *Tōyō Hōgaku (Tōyō Legal Studies)*, Vol. 10 (1), 35–70.

Metzler, M., Smits, G. (2010) Introduction: The Autonomy of Market Activity and the Emergence of Keizai Thought. In Gramlich-Oka, B., Smits, B. G. ed. *Economic Thought in Early Modern Japan* (pp. 1–20). Brill.

Merry, S. E. (1988) Legal Pluralism. *Law & Society Review*, Vol. 22 (5), 869–896.

Naka, Y. (1964) Genkaku Sekinin-setsu to Seigen Sekinin-setsu: Kōsei Yōken oyobi Koi no Kinō (Strict liability theory and limited liability theory: Constituent Element Requirements and Intentional Functionality). *Kansai Daigaku Hōgaku Ronshū (Kansai University Law Papers)*, Vol. 13 (4–6), 617–640.

Nomura, S. (1982). Problems of Local Administration: The Case of the Tokyo Metropolitan Government. *International Review of Administrative Sciences*. Vol. 48 (2), 187–197.

Probert, W. (1959) Law and Persuasion: The Language-Behavior of Lawyers. *University of Pennsylvania Law Review*, Vol. 108 (1), 35–58.

Reishchauer, E. (1977) *The Japanese*. Belknap Press.

Robertson, C et al. (2016) The Appearance and the Reality of Quid Pro Quo Corruption: An Empirical Investigation. *Journal of Legal Analysis*, Vol. 8 (2), 375–438.

Rogers, R. et al. (2008) The Language of Miranda Warnings in American Jurisdictions: A Replication and Vocabulary Analysis. *Law and Human Behavior*, Vol. 32 (2), 124–136.

Ross, J. (2003) He Looks Guilty: Reforming Good Character Evidence to Undercut The Presumption of Guilt. *University of Pittsburgh Law Review*, Vol. 65 (2), 1–82.

Saito, J., Yamada, K. (2011) Local government in Japan. In Alisa, G. ed. *Routledge Handbook of Japanese Politics* (pp. 103–114). Routledge.

Sasakura, H. (2018) "Shōko no kanrensei" o meguru mō hitotsu no "tsumazuki no moto": "shōko no kanrensei" ni kansuru Hirano Ryūichi hakushi no setsumei ni tsuite (Prevailing misconceptions about the relevance requirement for evidence: going back to basics by a rough reading of Ryuichi Hirano's 1958 landmark treatise). *Keiō Hōgaku (Keiō Legal Studies)*, No. 41, 169–191.

Yamakoshi, N. (2024) Kantō Daishinsai 100-nen · Teito Fukkō no Risō to Genjitsu: Shinsai Fukkō o Meguru Seifu, Ki Shū Ryōin no Kangaekata no Sōi (The 100th Anniversary of the Great Kanto Earthquake: The Ideal and Reality of the Imperial Capital's Reconstruction — Differing Views on Post-Disaster Recovery Between the Government and the Houses of Peers and Representatives). *Economic Prism*, No. 233, 1–43.

Tokyo City Hall. (1935) *Itafune Ken ni Kansuru Setsumeisho (Explanatory documents for Itabuneken)*. Tokyo City Hall.

Tsuji, Y. (2002) Hō to Gengo: Gengo Ninshiki to Meta Kōzō (Law and Language: Linguistic Recognition and Meta structure). *Hannan Ronshū (Hannan Anthology)*, Vol. 37 (4), 105–119.

Vlastos, S. (1986) *Peasant Protests and Uprisings in Tokugawa Japan*. University of California Press.

Yamada, M., Kabashima, I. (1994) Kōenkai to Nihon no Seiji (Supporters' Associations and Japanese Politics). *Nenpō Seijigaku (Annals Political Science)*, Vol. 45, 211–231.

Chapter 5
The Keisei Electric Railway Company Case

5.1 Case Background

The Keisei Electric Railway Company Case (hereinafter the Keisei case) in this chapter, and *the Itabuneken and Hiratabuneken Compensation Case* (henceforth the compensation case) in last chapter are under the same court case reference of *Keishū* 13–419, dated 26 March 1934. The consolidation of two cases within a single judgement was predicated on the legislation enumerated in Article 55 of the prewar Penal Code. *Taishinin* was obligated to deliberate on two cases concurrently, yet they delivered a single judgement legally. The question of whether the matter was one of criminal injustice was subject to debate, but the legitimacy of the claim was endorsed by Article 55.

5.1.1 Background of Keisei Electric Railway Company Limited

The Skyliner, operated by Keisei Electric Railway Company Limited, offers an airport express service between Ueno in downtown Tokyo and Narita Airport today. However, a railway firm with a similar name was involved in this grand corruption case in the 1920s. The corruption case under consideration pertains to a private railway line that connects Katsushika and Asakusa in Tokyo. In the prewar Showa era, Asakusa was a prosperous downtown. However, it was completely destroyed by the Great Kantō earthquake in 1923. The Asakusa Station of *Tōbutetsudō* (Tōbu Railway) was destroyed in a complete fire. The proposed expansion of Keisei's railway network had the potential to not only augment its market share in the economically vibrant heart of Tokyo but also generating substantial profits from its subsidiaries in sectors such as electricity supply, real estate development, bus transportation services, cement production, tourism, recreation, entertainment and

K. B. Wong and S. L. Fang, *Taishinin's Judicial Behaviour in Corruption Cases*,
https://doi.org/10.1007/978-981-95-5823-0_5

the provision of essential commodities to residents along the railway line. Additionally, gravel obtained from tunnel construction is a valuable resource. The proposed project by the Keisei Company includes the construction of a tunnel that would facilitate direct connectivity between the regions of Ueno and Narita. The quantity of gravel was sufficient for the construction of a large real estate project. At that time, it was common for private railway firms to possess subsidiary businesses of this nature. The integration of the railway line with lucrative businesses in the entire area was thereby accomplished, resulting in the establishment of a unified railway network.

Following the seismic event, analogous strategies of gradual market infiltration were adopted by other private railway firms, resulting in heightened competition for railway licences. For example, *Tōkyū Dentetsu Kabushikigaisha* (Tōkyū Electric Railway Company Limited), which was formerly known as *Musashidenkitetsudō* (Musashi Electric Railway), opened the amusement park *Tamagawaen* in 1925 and the Tōkyū Department Store in Shibuya in 1934. In addition, numerous private railway companies competed for prime locations to establish department stores, including the Matsuzakaya Department Store at subway station of Ueno Hirokoji, the Mitsukoshi Department at Mitsukoshimae and the Takashimaya Department Store at Nihonbashi. Railway transportation constituted a relatively modest segment of the overall profitability of the enterprise, with subsidiary businesses generating a greater proportion of the financial gains. For instance, in 1941, the percentage of annual income of major private railway firms from electricity supply and transportation was 29.4 per cent and 10 per cent, respectively.[1] The provision of electricity proved to be a lucrative venture in at least seven cities: Toyama, Yokohama, Nagoya, Kumamoto, Sapporo, Kagoshima and Wakamatsu. These cities had close connections with railway companies.[2]

The intense competition among these private railway companies resulted in the targeting of bureaucrats from *Tetsudōshō* (Ministry of Railway) by bribery attempts. In prewar period, Japan witnessed five prominent incidents of grand bribery involving private railway companies. These incidents, which have been characterized as *goshitetsu gigokujiken* (literally, five private railway suspicious incidents) in the annals of Japanese history, exemplifying the pervasive corruption that plagued the era. In addition to The Keisei Company, the other five were Hokkaido Railway, Ise Electric Railway, Higashi-Osaka Electric Railway, Nara Electric Railway, Hakata Bay Railway Steamship. After acceptance of bribe, all these five railway lines were approved by Minister of Railways Ogawa Heikichi during the Tanaka Giichi Cabinet.[3] The primary rationale pertained to these railway networks was remarkably elevated levels of profitability and effectively established a semi-monopoly over district development.

---

[1] On this see Tamekuni et al. (1995, pp. 195–202, p. 206).

[2] On this see Nishino (2014, p. 2); also see Ishida (2019, pp. 129–130).

[3] See "Five Private Railways Scandals" at https://kotobank.jp/word/%E4%BA%94%. Accessed 10 October 2025.

The *quid quo pro* of bribery in this case was the approval for extension of Keisei's railway lines, the history of which can be traced to its establishment on 28 November 1903. On 28 May 1907, it was granted its first railway licence for a railway service between Oshiage and Narita. After the appointment of Honda Teijirō as the first managing director, it set up its headquarters in today's Yaesu in Tokyo as a *Kabushiki-gaisha* (joint-stock company) in June 1909, with an initial paid-up capital of 1500,000 *yen*. In October 1909, its headquarters was removed to Asakusa.[4]

Similar to the legal *Rashomon* style of *Taishinin* judgement in Chap. 4, the juridical facts in this *Taishinin* judgement are also confusing. The number of co-accused's networking, relations among many Tokyo City Assembly members in the political party faction, and the style of presenting complex bribery transactions in non-chronological order create difficulties to understand the data in this judgement.

5.2 Juridical Facts in *Taishinin* Judgement

5.2.1 The Conspiracy to Bribe the Tokyo City Assembly Members

The Keisei Company is a prominent provider of railway transportation services between Tokyo, Chiba and Narita. The primary business of its main subsidiary was the provision of electricity to areas situated along the railway line. The proposed new Tokyo subway and railway network, which was to be owned by a competitor, was linked between Ochanomizu and Ryogoku. This could have a negative impact on the interests of the Keisei Line. Since April 1915, the company had sought authorization from the Ministry of Interior and the Ministry of Railway to extend its railway lines. Nevertheless, the Tokyo City Assembly demonstrated an unwavering reluctance to approve the measure.

To actualize this long-term plan, on 13 October 1927, the Keisei Company submitted a proposal to modify the initial route of its railway line according to *Kidōhō* (Rail Tracks Code). The company reached out to the two Ministries to inquire about the feasibility of constructing a subsidiary line that would connect Katsushika and Asakusa. On 31 October 1927, the Tokyo mayor, through the Director of Civil Engineering of Tokyo-fu, solicited opinions from relevant stakeholders regarding a proposal to grant a new railway permit. On 25 May 1928, the mayor reached a decision to discontinue the implementation of the aforementioned plan. He subsequently submitted his decision to the Tokyo City Assembly for consultation. In the judgement of *Taishinin*, *Keiseidenkikido Unoriirian* (Keisei Electric Railroad Introductory Plan) was the agenda item that was formally presented at the Tokyo City

---

[4] See "Keisei Electric Railway's History" at https://www.keisei.co.jp/keisei/keisei_museum/history/. Accessed 2 October 2025.

Assembly meeting. Concurrently, a committee of 15 Tokyo City Assembly members was established to oversee the plan.

On 26 May 1928, in view of the past experience in difficulty to secure approval of the plan by the Tokyo City Assembly, the Director of the Keisei Company Honda Teijirō, two assistance directors Goto Kuniya and Yoshida Hideya, agreed to make use of the undue influence of two politicians, who were the branch consultants to the political party of *Rikken Minseitō*, Miki Bukichi and the director of Tokyo branch of *Seiyūkai* Nakajima Moritoshi. Through Miki and Nakajima, Honda, Goto and Yoshida conspired to influence the voting behaviour of the Tokyo City Assembly by lobbying. Honda Teijirō himself was also an in-service member of the House of Representatives. He could make use of his network of *Rikken Minseitō* members to persuade Miki, while Goto could rely on the Director General of *Hōseikyokuchō* (Legislative Bureau) Maeda Yonezo to convince Nakajima to help. *Taishinin* remarked that the conspiracy was a well-organized crime with an explicit division of labour.

According to Goto, prior networking with Miki and Nakajima should be secured as a basic step to ensure a lobbying channel. Shōriki Matsutarō, the director of the newspaper *Yomurai Shinbun*, had a close friendship with both Miki and Nakajima. In late May 1928, Goto approached Shōriki, and Shōriki found it difficult to decline Goto's request because of their close friendship, then decided to participate in this conspiracy. Goto then acted as the coordinator for all lobbying efforts by offering bribery of *sharei* or *hōshū* to the City Assembly members. After that, Goto informed Honda of the progress in detail. They agreed to give political campaign rewards to Miki and Nakajima for *kaiosamuhi* (expenses for acquisition) of the Assembly members. *Taishinin, prima facie,* treated all these activities as *zōshūwai* (bribery offences), according to the judgement.

As a faction leader in the House of Representatives and a consultant to the Tokyo branch of *Minseitō,* Miki was influential to other party members in both party factions of *Kakushinkai* and *Nihachikai*, also in the House of Representatives. In case of city affairs, members of these two factions followed Miki's advice. They also had a dominant percentage of the Tokyo City Assembly members. In late May 1928, as per the advice of Honda and Shōriki, efforts were made to exert undue influence on the voting behaviour of these two party factions. Miki was asked to act as a go-between to persuade them to vote in favour of the Keisei Electric Railroad Introductory Plan upon resolution at the Tokyo City Assembly. Miki accepted this *seitaku* (entrustment) and promised to make efforts for it. Since early June 1928, Miki had repeatedly convinced the City Assembly members, Ōno Keikichi, Sokura Kaichi and Takigawa Mitsuyuki to vote for approval of the plan. On 4 June 1928, at a restaurant, Shōriki gave 30,000 *yen* to Miki as campaign funds for lobbying.

Since 28 May 1928, Honda Teijirō had been appointed the chairman of the committee for railway line, of which the active committee members included Komori Shichibee, Ōno Keikichi, Sokura Kaichi, Kurata Kinzaburō and Tsukaichi Kaneko. After screening and discussions in several meetings, on 10 July 1928, the Tokyo City Assembly disapproved *the Keisei Electric Railroad Introductory Plan.* On 12 July 2018, Miki secured the majority of *Kakushinkai* members to resume the same plan as a future agenda. The members of political faction *Nihachikai* in the committee, Ōno and Sokura, also agreed. The majority vote for this plan should be a "sure win".

In the Assembly meeting on 13 July 1928, the disapproval dated 10 July 1928 was successfully reversed. With 43 votes for and 35 votes against, the plan was finally given the green light. The original stance of *Kakushinkai* was to vote against it, but they changed their decisive vote after receiving Shōriki's money through Miki, which happened on 14 July 1928, at a restaurant that Shōriki gave 50,000 *yen* to Miki. *Taishinin* stigmatized Miki for understanding the corrupt co-intention of Shōriki, Honda and Goto upon his acceptance.

On the same day, Mike met Ōno, Sokura and Komori in a restaurant and gave 2000 *yen* to each of them for *ochūgen* (midyear gift-giving). Miki appropriated the 50,000 *yen* received from Shōriki to other City Assembly members as *sharei* for their votes in favour of the plan. 1000 *yen* was given to Oi Zenzo on 15 July 1928. Later he gave 1000 *yen* to Ōno. Five days later, he gave Hirabayashi 1000 *yen*. Therefore, Miki's chain of acts of giving money to members in his political party faction constituted the offence of giving bribe, but he had not lodged appeal against junior courts' conviction of this offence.

5.2.2 Juridical Facts Against Three Appellants

Katayama was a member of *Seiyūkai* in the Tokyo City Assembly. On 12 July 1928, he formally accepted the entrustment of Yano Genkichi, who was operating as an agent under Nakajima's directive to secure votes in favour of the Keisei Company's plan. On 17 July 1928, Yano Genkichi donated 1000 *yen* to Katayama for *ochūgen*. Katayama was aware that the payment was a bribe but nevertheless accepted it. This acceptance was associated with Katayama's official obligation to the Tokyo City Assembly.

Ōno Keikichi was a member of the Tokyo City Assembly and a cadet of *Nihachikai* in *Minseitō*. Upon receipt of the communication from Miki, in which he expressed his entrustment for the resolution of the matter in favour of the plan, Ōno and Sokura assumed the role of intermediaries. Their objective was to secure and gather the support of other Assembly members in their respective political factions. The resolution was then passed by an anonymous vote, constituting an official duty of the Assembly member. As previously indicated, on 14 July 1928, for *ochūgen*, Miki transferred 2000 *yen* to Ōno, whose actions were indicative of bribe acceptance.

A thorough examination of the legal findings against Nakajima Moritoshi reveals a presentation of facts that was both extensive and haphazard. As a co-accused in the case, Nakajima received the entrustment of Shōriki and the bureaucrat of the Legislative Bureau, Maeda Yonezo, in late May and early June of 1928, respectively. Two of them delegated the responsibility to Nakajima to guarantee that *Seiyūkai* members would cast favourable votes for the extension of Keisei's railway network. On 4 June 1928, Shōriki provided Nakajima with 10,000 *yen* under the pretext of electoral campaign funds. In point of fact, he was leveraging Nakajima to exert influence over the voting behaviour of other Assembly members, who were Yano, Motegi, Kurata and Tsukaichi Kaneko affiliated to *Seikokai.*

As previously stated in this *Taishinin* judgement, the initial committee decision of 10 July 1928 was disapproval of the plan. However, Nakajima's significant influence over his party faction members, in conjunction with the supplementary support provided by the political factions *Seikokai* and *Chushokai*, resulted in a reversal of the prevailing disapproval during the meeting held on 13 July 1928, as evidenced by a majority vote. In consideration of this achievement, Shōriki, Goto and Honda engaged in a conspiracy to provide *sharei* to the relevant Assembly members in order to comprehend the contributions of their efforts. In this particular instance, Nakajima utilized the 10,000 *yen* that had been previously received from Shōriki, resulting in a total bribe amount of 53,700 *yen.* Nakajima, in conjunction with Yano and Motegi, collectively appropriated a sum total of 63,700 *yen* to their respective faction members as a form of remuneration in acknowledgement of their favourable votes.

In the judgement, *Taishinin* specifically emphasized that Nakajima conspired with Yano and Motegi as go-betweens to appropriate bribes to other faction members in the Assembly. On 13 July 1928, in the lobby of the Tokyo-fu Government Building, Motegi gave 1000 *yen* to Yoshii Hamaiirō. Then Yoshii distributed 300 *yen* to Tanaka Kōzō. Four days later, Nakajima appropriated 1000 *yen* from Katayama Kyuzo for *ochūgen.* On 18 July 1928, Nakajima met Kaneko Tōichi and gave him 1500 *yen.* On the same day, at a company in Kyōbashi, Nakajima gave Oi Zenzo 500 *yen* for *ochūgen.* Two days later, Nakajima gave1000 *yen* to a *Chushokai* member, Kondo Tatsuji. Then Kondo appropriated 300 *yen* to another member, Obata Toshiobun. On 22 July 1928, Nakajima's faction member fellow, Yano Genkichi gave Kojima Kozo 300 *yen* under the excuse of *ochūgen* at Kojima's home in Asakusa. On the same day, at Nihonbashi, Yano gave Hosoya Tetsutaro 500 *yen* and 300 *yen* for Tsubono Fusaji under the same *ochūgen* pretext. In late July 1928, Yano gave Gokita Jirō 300 *yen* for *ochūgen.* In early August 1928, Nakajima used *ochūgen* as a pretext to give 1000 *yen* to Matsui Kintachi. On 21 August 1928, Yano gave 2500 *yen* which received from Nakjiama to Kurata at a restaurant in Asakusa.

5.3 Appeal Grounds of Katayama Hisashi

On behalf of Katayama, two lawyers claimed that the prosecutor's accusation was inequitable under *fukokufuri no gensoku* (the legal principle of no adjudication without prosecution). Such accusations were aimed at pressuring Katayama to confess. In the *Yoshinseikyuusho* (application for pretrial) submitted by the prosecutor on 25 August 1928, for the Compensation Case, in which Katayama was accused of conspiring with Okazaki Keijirō for the 17,000-*yen* bribe from the big *itabuneken* owner, Takamura Gentaro. On 1 November 1928, the prosecutor Matsusakai issued *a renzokuhan-tsūchisho* (Consecutive Criminal Offense Notice) by adding this Keisei case for joint prosecution, thereby combining the two cases into one as *renzokuhanichizai* (a continuous serial crime). The ruling of *yoshin* (pretrial) unfairly determined that it met the legal requirements for prosecution. It was not justice to integrate two cases for one trial at the court of first instance of the Tokyo District Court.

Katayama's lawyers accused the notice *renzokuhan-tsūchisho* of not being an independent indictment with independent brief facts. The Keisei case was unreasonably combined with the brief facts of the compensation case as one *kōso-jijitsu* (facts for public prosecution) for court hearings. Such a combination was for the convenience of public prosecution on the basis of personal *iken* (opinion) and the public prosecutor's *kibō* (hope) to have the upper hand in litigation. This was different from the original concept of *renzokuhanichizai,* which disallowed other irrelevant chains of events to be added for new prosecution, as per *the Taishinin* ruling in 1904. Therefore, this *renzokuhan-tsūchisho* was neither a new indictment nor a new independent public prosecution.

Katayama was not a suspect in the *kihon jijitsu* (fundamental facts) of the compensation case, but he was currently involved as a serial offender under *renzokuhanichizai*. Without continuous criminal acts, prosecutors should not mistakenly grant approval to combine two cases as one at the pretrial stage. The "continuity" of the Keisei case connecting the compensation case was unfounded.

The appellants' lawyers argued that it was like a tree being cut all *edaha* (branches and leaves); there was no *renzokuhan* (serial offence) as the trunk of the tree. The "trunk" was cut out from *shinpan-han'i* (scope of trial), and the other part was naturally *shimetsu* (died or extinct). In the view of the absence of a material time factor in the sequence of events connecting two brief facts, the prosecution should be waived. Katayama should be found not guilty. In the absence of a *renzokukankei* (relationship of continuation), a *renzokuhan-tsūchisho* could not be substantiated. Thus, the prosecutor had neither the legal authority to accuse Katayama nor the legal authority to add new criminal elements to the compensation case. The prosecutor wrongly made it like a *hentai-teki-kiso* (transformational prosecution).

Katayama's lawyers had no legal argument on the "constituent element" of the crime in the prosecutor's *renzokuhan* but raised objection to the prosecutor's power to issue the notice of *renzokuhan-tsūchisho*. Lawyers advocated that the structural injustice of *renzokuhan* should be solved and clarified through legislative behaviour. *Renzokuhan-tsūchisho* should be limited to a notice document only. The nature of this notice was incorrectly transformed by prosecutor into a new indictment. The whole process was like a *yūreiteki* (phantom) to initiate inequitable prosecution. Both *tsūchisho* and *kisojō* (indictments) were exercises of *kokuka-no-ishi* (state power over citizens and subjects). Lawyers reiterated that the facts indicated were simply for the objective of prosecuting one continuous crime and one guilty conviction, because such notice was actually used in lieu of one indictment. The notice was not supposed to be abused as a new, independent indictment for one legal proceeding. Therefore, the court hearing for the Keisei case should be conducted separately. Without such separation, both two cases were mistakenly regarded as one incident for a judicial decision-making process.

5.4 *Taishinin*'s Grounds for Refusal

Taishinin's judicial behaviour in rejecting the appeal exhibited a conservative and pro-prosecutor posture, suggesting an absence of any intent to challenge the legislative intent of the Diet over lawmaking. *Taishinin* established that in instances where facts were deemed to constitute serial crime, the prosecutor was only obligated to provide *renzokuhan-tsūchisho* of facts for the purpose of prosecution. Furthermore, *Taishinin* was vested with the paramount judicial authority to determine the correlation between the events in *renzokuhan-tsūchisho*, thereby establishing a comprehensive understanding of the interconnected nature of these chains of events. In the capacity of the prosecutor, *Taishinin* reaffirmed that the prosecutor's objective was not to introduce new evidence or to instigate new legal proceedings. It was the contention of *Taishinin* that the prosecutor had not circumvented the recently implemented prosecution procedure by employing *renzokukan-tsūchisho*.

The appellant petitioned for the prosecutor's issuance of the notice *renzokukan-tsūchisho*, which combined the two cases for the purpose of prosecution under the following legal condition: The relationship in question is one that is characterized by its uninterrupted nature. Taishinin held that the prosecutor was legally empowered to take such action by means of notice *renzokukan-tsūchisho* for unitary legal *kōka* (effectiveness) through legal proceedings against Katayama. Notwithstanding the aforementioned combination, the case facts of the Keisei Company alone sufficed for prosecution and judicial decision to find the offender guilty. *Taishinin* reiterated the court's authority to pronounce the appellant not guilty in the initial case while concurrently finding him guilty of a separate offence in the remaining components of the notice *renzokukan-tsūchisho*.[5]

5.5 Analysis of *Taishinin*'s Judicial Behaviour to Refuse Katayama's Appeal

5.5.1 *The Unwillingness to Clarify Legal Ambiguity*

Taishinin's judicial behaviour was characterized by rigidity and conservatism, as evidenced by its reluctance to resolve legal ambiguities by confirming legislative intent with the Diet. *Taishinin* posited that it could exhibit justice, the purpose of which would be to identify relevant facts for different offences from both the Keisei case and the compensation case. Therefore, the determination of the case hinged on impartiality of *Taishinin*'s judicial behaviour to assess each appellant's individual criminality from the complex chains of events of two cases, particularly with regard to

[5] The original text in the judgement: 本件に於て豫審判事が前に起訴せらしたる所謂板船權補償案事件の公訴事実を免訴すべきものと認めたるに拘らず通知を受けたる所謂京成乗入案事件の事実に付有罪と認め公判に付する決定をためしたるは洵に相當にして。

the traditional equitable *dōri* applied with an event-by-event approach. It is unfortunate that the information on *Taishinin*'s state of mind upon its exercising discretionary power in identifying each event was not provided in this *Taishinin*'s judgement.

Second, the main appeal ground of Katayama was the prosecutor's breach of the legal principle of *fukokufuri no gensoku* (the principle of no adjudication without prosecution) by *renzokuhan*. To refuse this appeal ground, *Taishinin* rationalized *renzokuhan* as a lawful exercise of the prosecutor's authority without *ultra virus* (an act without legal authority). *Taishinin* subjectively believed that the prosecutor intended to combine the two cases as one solely for legal *kōka* (effectiveness). Nonetheless, the term *kōka* was not explained or justified further. *Taishinin* had not further explained the reason for such belief. To err is human, prosecutor might also have recklessness or negligence. How could *Taishinin* view internally to the mind of prosecutor? What kind of *kōka* was expected by prosecutor? These are not available between the lines of this *Taishinin* judgement.

Third, the criminal law term *renzokuhan* is misleading. Other than the same charge of bribery, the two chains of events were totally irrelevant, let alone continuity or connectivity of chains of events in brief facts. The continuity of serial offence in one case as *renzokuhan* was thus *prima facie* non-available, irrational and a matter of procedural injustice. *Renzokuhan* was legislated and maintained for the prosecutor's administrative convenience and court proceedings instead of criminal justice. It had a grey area to extend the time for criminal investigation and search to delay court hearing. The most obvious procedural injustice against the legal consciousness of *dōri* was that a suspect might be investigated and searched for an irrelevant case. Such judicial behaviour did not match the traditional Japanese legal consciousness of the equitable reasonableness of *dōri,* which functioned as the core of judicial behaviour of socially accepted legitimacy and hegemony to soften the rigidity of the statute. Even so, there was no statutory provision that could render *renzokuhan* unconstitutional or illegal, let alone *ultra virus*. The puzzle is why *Taishinin*'s judicial behaviour was conservative and pro-prosecutor, notwithstanding the unreasonable combination of procedural injustice. The main reason is likely *Taisninin*'s reluctance to criticize the legislative intent of the Diet in state polity.

Fourth, *Taishinin*'s judicial behaviour of sticking to the statute reflected the legislative limitation of Taishinin's discretion in judicial behaviour of judicial activism. *Taishinin* were unwilling to engage in judicial behaviour *contra legem*, which meant that *Taishinin* would rule the prosecutor's *renzokuhan* as "contrary to law or a legal obligation under a principle of equity". Taishinin had no power for judicial review of Article 55 of prewar Penal Code. In prewar Japan, Japanese courts rarely ruled *contra legem* (contrary to the clear, literal meaning of the text). The codification of Article 55 in the prewar Penal Code was drafted by *Hōseikyoku* for the Diet. *Hōseikyoku* was established after the cabinet system was launched 1885. Leaders in the early Meiji period took this legislative procedure from the *Daijōkan* system (Grand Council of State). Ito Hirobfmi, Inoue Kaoru and Yamagata Aritomo took this office and converted it into an indispensable control tower for bureaucracy. In the vertical structure of state polity, *Taishinin* was not assumed to challenge law issued in the Emperor's name.

Fifth, Katayama's lawyers rightly lodged an appeal on the ground that the addition of the compensation case was a breach of the legal principle of *fukokufuri-no-gensoku*. Some Japanese legal scholars in prewar Japan had also contentiously criticized *renzokuhan*, arguing that it infringed on the *fukokufuri-no-gensoku* and potentially breached the *ichijibusairi* (prohibition against double jeopardy, *ne bis in idem* in legal terms) (Yoshida 1977, p. 69). In the perspective of fair society studies, the menace of double jeopardy is against psychological well-being of individuals and social well-being of a society. An accused person might be punished twice for the same offence in two incidents, at least suffering from delay of justice by prolonged court hearing. When Japan had legal transplant of Germanic Penal Code in 1907, it was a selection of 264 articles out of the 730 articles for Emperor's issue. *Renzokuhan* was introduced into the Penal Code in 1907 against the background of unconsciousness of potential conflict with traditional Japanese *dōri*. This legislative behaviour was *contra legem*, which means contrary to a legal obligation based on equity. It is against rule of positive law. It was therefore not surprising that upon the Tentative Draft of the Revised Penal Code in 1926, Japan needed to amend some articles of Penal Code for "the morals and good customs and manners proper to Japan" in order to fit Japanese body better.[6]

Sixthly, though legislation is the prerogative of the Diet, *Taishinin*'s judicial behaviour could soften statutory rigidity by a lenient legal interpretation. The paradox is that *renzokuhan* was not unconstitutional. The Meiji Constitution did not have provision which prohibited combination of two criminal cases for prosecutor's convenience. In Meiji Constitution, Article 23 stipulated that no Japanese subject shall be arrested, detained, tried or punished, unless according to law, which was considered as *zaikeihōtei-shugi* in Japanese term and *nulla poena sine lege* in common law jurisdiction. *Prima facie*, *Taishinin*'s judicial behaviour of sticking to literal interpretation of Article 55 had not touched this bottom line, even if it might potentially lead to additional punishment in irrelevant case facts. It depended on whether court was on the alert against possibility of procedural injustice leading to double jeopardy. Article 39 of postwar Japanese Constitution clearly prohibits possibility of double jeopardy, but it is unfounded in the Meiji Constitution. Literally, prosecutor was neither illegitimate nor *ultra virus* as per *renzokuhan* stipulated in Article 55 of prewar Penal Code. Article 55 legitimatized several chains of events infringing same criminal offence to be combined as one for adjudication. The ceiling of combination was not limited to two cases as per literal interpretation. *Renzokuhan* in the currently deleted Article 55 was "when several consecutive acts fall under the same crime, they shall be punished as a single crime".[7] In this connection, *renzoku shitaru* means similar offence of several acts consecutively. And *sūko no kōi* implied the legality to treat several behaviours infringing same article of Penal Code as one offence. The ambiguity is that Article 55 did not specify whether it should be "acts in the *same* sequence of events" or "acts in *separate* chains of events". It gave discretionary power

[6] On this see Ida (2014, pp. 139-140); also see Uematsu (1964, pp. 1-4).

[7] The original text is "連続シタル数個ノ行為ニシテ同一ノ罪名ニ触ルルトキハ一罪トシテ之ヲ処断ス".

for *Taishinin*'s judicial behaviour to determine it. The traditional legal consciousness of equitable *dōri* could be applied on a case-by-case basis to soften statutory rigidity. However, *Taishinin* had not done so for this case.

5.5.1.1 Article 312 (1) of Postwar Criminal Procedure Code

Current Japanese Criminal Procedure Code codified under Act No. 131 in 1948 has a new Article 312 (1) for joint trial in lieu of the rescinded Article 55 of prewar Penal Code. It states that the court must allow the prosecution to add, withdraw or change a court in the indictment on condition of no effect on the unity of facts.[8]

In Chap. 2, ideology in the attitudinal model articulated by Segal and Spaeth is the core of their judicial behaviour theory.[9] Strategic model argues that strategy may be formulated by judicial behaviour to achieve a judge's preferred policy outcome. Both models cannot fully explain *Taishinin*'s conservative judicial behaviour of unwillingness to exercise discretion to soften statutory rigidity in this case. In the perspective of historical institutional model of judicial behaviour, *Taishinin* was a legal institution in a state political system of no power of judicial review. Without judicial review power, *Taishinin*'s conservative judicial behaviour resultant from being constrained by legislation in state polity is understandable. If judges literally stick to statutes without challenge to it, then legislature can continue to constrain judicial behaviour. Judicial behaviour can be substantively constrained by codification of statute (Moyer 2012, p. 297). Statutory constraints thereby keep judges' judicial behaviour in check without time limitation. When statutory constraint increases, judges' discretionary power under their ideological preference decreases.[10] Judicial behaviour and legislative behaviour for statutory constraints are like an ongoing "interaction" about codification and interpretation of statutory language to resolve a factual legal question (Widiss 2020, p. 51). In case judges have absolute freedom of judicial behaviour to exercise discretionary power and apply it with their ideological preferences as court rulings, then the development of judge-made-law can substantially be reflected by its judicial behaviour.

5.5.2 Historical Institutional Model of Judicial Behaviour in State Polity

In the historical institutional model of judicial behaviour, the Japanese judiciary was subject to the authority of the Ministry of Justice prior to Pacific War. As Nishigawa has previously indicated, the Minister of Justice in the state polity functioned as

[8] See "Criminal Procedure Code" at https://elaws.e-gov.go.jp/document?lawid=323AC0000000131. Accessed 2 March 2023.

[9] On this see Segal and Spaeth (2008 and 1993).

[10] On this see Randazzo etal. (2011, pp. 779–780, p. 782, pp. 786–787).

a control tower for bureaucrats rather than serving as the sole authority within the criminal justice system.[11] The judicial behaviour of *Taishinin*, which entailed the strategic employment of *dōri* in its legal interpretation to contest the fairness of legislation and prosecutorial decisions, was effectively curtailed. In the event that a court declared a statute to be in violation of its principles, the statute in question was typically characterized as having been struck down or rendered void. Judicial behaviour of this nature would be regarded as an overt challenge to the Minister of Justice.

According to the Japanese legal scholar Wagatsuma Sakae, the Japanese constitutional questions in prewar era were subject to the Japanese Privy Council's consultation. However, in reality, this kind of consultation or clarification was almost non-existent (Wagatsuma 1937, p. 288). Eliminating this statutory constraint was not possible through clarification of the legislative intent surrounding *renzokuhan*. This finding aligns with the observations presented in Chap. 3, which revealed that Japanese law had historically been implemented by the upper class as a means of maintaining social stability. In traditional Japanese judicial behaviour, law enforcement was the domain for it. The court's decision did not contest the validity or authority of the legislation, nor did it overrule the previous ruling by providing further clarification on the legislative intent or declaring it unconstitutional. Similar conservative judicial behaviour of *Taishinin* can be found in its precedent under reference *Keijihanketsuroku* 22–1774 dated 5 November 1916. It was a case about the legitimacy of Akita Prefectural Police's excessive criminal punishment order for administrative purpose. Its judgement only stated that as a result of *Taishinin*'s examination, there were no previous judgement which deemed the order to be illegal or invalid.[12] *Taishinin* conservatively followed judicial precedent, instead of examination of police power on a case-by-case basis as *dōri* and the possibility to have judicial activism. Legislative intent was not mentioned for clarification on the legitimacy of police power. In 1931, *Taishinin* repeated the same conservative judicial behaviour in Kagoshima Prefectural Police's criminal punishment order case under reference *Keijihanreishū* 10–445 dated 12 October 1931.

Japanese High Court's last application of Article 55 was its refusal of appeal delivered on 16 March 1948 under reference *Keishū* 2-3-220 and case number Showa 22 (re) 235. Article 55 was in fact more relevant to criminal procedural justice than substantive justice. It could put the accused under the possibility of groundless accusation upon combination of two or more irrelevant cases. Procedural fairness (or procedural justice of similar concept) is also relevant to the perceived fairness of judicial behaviour. Deference to judicial decision can thereby be more penetrative to other law-related aspects.[13]

---

[11] On this see Nishigawa (2000).

[12] The original text in the judgement: 審査の結果命令の違法又は無効を判定した例はなかった。

[13] On this see Tyler (2003, pp. 283–284, p. 290, p. 350).

5.5.3 *Article 81 of Postwar Japanese Constitution*

As long as the requirements of "no law, no crime and no punishment" in Article 23 of Meiji Constitution were met, *Taishinin* had legitimacy for its judicial behaviour in a strict liability model.[14]

Clarification on legislative intent was not deterministic in strict liability model. Legal tradition of *hōrei-shinsaken* (right of judicial review) and *contra legem* in prewar Japan judiciary were found non-existence prior to today's Article 81 of Japanese Constitution. If Japanese judges wanted to exercise discretionary power for new ruling against public prosecutor, timing was important (Bolton and Thrower 2020, p. 26, p. 29). Article 55 of prewar Penal Code existed until it was rescinded in 1947 in view of the inequity confirmed during postwar law reform. Postwar judicial review power facilitates strategic model of judicial behaviour to challenge legislative behaviour of Diet. In contradistinction to constraints of *Taishinin*'s judicial behaviour in state polity, postwar Supreme Court of Japan has the judicial behaviour to strike down or rendered a statutory provision to be void under new legal ideology. Usually, it is done as a strategy to accomplish a goal. This is common in the strategic model of judicial behaviour.

5.6 Ōno Keikichi's First Appeal Ground

5.6.1 *The Lack of Corrupt Consideration in Promise*

Ōno Keikichi was a member of the City Assembly who had been involved in both the Keisei case and the compensation case. The appellant's primary contention was that no specific sum of money had been committed to the bribery in question. Furthermore, the acceptance of the funds occurred subsequent to the resolution of the matter within the Assembly. This financial transaction was claimed to have no association with the official duty of Tokyo City Assembly.

Ōno's first appeal ground was based on his acceptance of funds after the final resolution of the Keisei Company's plan on 13 July 1928. Thereafter, the whole Keisei case and the compensation case had been completed without further resolution in the Tokyo City Assembly. Ōno emphasized that since then, the Assembly had ceased its power in respect of these two cases. The Assembly members had also fully disconnected from their official duties in this regard. Accordingly, even if a City Assembly member might have accepted interest subsequently, there was no relationship between his acceptance and his official duty whatsoever. Without connectivity with official duty, an Assembly member had no capacity to actualize previous promise relating to it, if any. The rationale was no evidence could identify and prove connection between constituent elements of corrupt interest and official

[14] On this see Matsuo (1969, pp. 655–660).

duty. As per this logic, Ōno's receipt of 2000 *yen* from Miki on 14 July 1928 should not be deemed bribery. Junior courts had not written to show it had considered "amount of bribe promise". No evidence had been provided to prove the concrete amount of money which could constitute a promise of bribe to Ōno. Notwithstanding the aforesaid demerits in junior courts' legal reasoning, junior courts punished him on the basis of acceptance of bribery offence relating to official duty.

5.6.2 Analysis of Taishinin's Judicial Behaviour for Refusal

In response to Ōno's appeal ground against the junior court's no consideration of "amount of money in promise", *Taishinin* ruled that money accepted after the final resolution of Keisei case was deemed acceptance of bribe. Junior courts had neither explained nor defined the constituent element of "promise" in the "promise of bribe" in their judgement. It did not mean the junior courts had not considered it before judicial decision-making. As long as a civil servant received a *sharei* in connection with his official duties, such receipt was a criminal offence of acceptance of bribe.

Taishinin's judicial behaviour was so strict that it ruled unnecessary to question whether the receipt was before or after the execution of the official duties.[15] The appellant's acceptance of bribe after completion of official duty did not need a prior concrete promise for it. On 13 July 1928, Ōno contributed efforts in persuading the Tokyo City Assembly members to grant approval for the Keisei's plan and received Miki's money on 14 July 1928. *Taishinin* criminalized the money as *sharie* of corruptibility in relation to Ōno's official duty.

5.6.3 Strict Liability Model and Judicial "Black Hole"

Taishinin's equitable handling of Ōno's relationship with official duty in the Keisei case, as the evidence indicated that the resolution on 13 July 1928 was not definitive. Nonetheless, it is an established fact that the judgements of junior courts did not address the question of prior promises regarding the offer of *sharei*. However, *Taishinin* stated that the absence of court ruling did not imply that the junior court's decision was illegitimate. *Taishinin* refused to concur with appellant's ground that the court had not considered the constituent element of the bribery offence. Nevertheless, *Taishinin* offered no further compelling evidence to substantiate this assertion. On the basis of the available evidence, Ōno's accusations against the junior courts are both reasonable and accurate. The junior courts had failed to provide any information regarding the identification of the financial amount in the prior promise of *sharei*. *Taishinin* disagreed with Ōno's assertion that the acceptance of *sharei* on 14 July

---

[15] The original text in the judgement: 公務員が其の職務に関し謝礼を収受する以上受賄罪を構成するものにして其の収受が職務執行の前たると後たるとは之を問ふを要せず。

1928 could be considered as unrelated to official duty in the absence of any prior promise. At the pinnacle of the judicial hierarchy, *Taishinin* asserted that the absence of formal confirmation of amount promised as *kōseiyōken* (constituent elements) in junior courts' judgements did not imply a complete oversight of these elements by the junior courts without consideration.

This *Taishinin* ruling did not disclose the process by which junior courts arrived at a conviction in the absence of concrete evidence regarding the "promise". It was a "judicial black hole" of junior courts' judicial behaviours. The pursuit of justice should not only be executed with impartiality but also be evident and indisputable to all observers. In the course of the present judgement, *Tasihinin* made no mention of indirect or circumstantial evidence, which would have served to substantiate the promised financial amount. The document in question merely designated the 2000-*yen* coin from Miki on 14 July 1928 as *sharei*, in acknowledgement of Ōno's influence on the voting behaviour of the Assembly members on 13 July 1928. Details of promise were still non-available in judgement.

Notably, the judgement omitted any mention of Ōno's alleged culpable mental state. *Taishinin* elaborated that even without promise, the act of acceptance of *sharie* sufficed for *Taishinin* to criminalize Ōno. It was not disregarding constituent element.[16] Miki's act of bestowing monetary gifts upon Ōno was deemed questionable, particularly in light of Miki's notable influence on the voting patterns of political party factions within *Kakushinkai* and *Nihachikai*. Nevertheless, dubious character does not constitute criminal behaviour or criminal intent. It is evident that the briber and bribee did not make any prior promise. The conviction of acceptance of bribe on the basis of acts without referral to criminal intent is a typical judicial behaviour of strict liability model. In case Taishinin's judical decision was based on circumstantial evidence, it could mention it in court judgement.

The judicial behaviour of strategic model, the strict liability model, the historical institutionalist model and the attitudinal model are not mutually exclusive. From the perspective of the strategic model of judicial behaviour, Taishinin's strict liability model in this case can be regarded as both ideology and strategy to control dysfunctional bureaucrats in the state polity. This is in accordance with traditional legislative intent in Japanese anti-corruption law as detailed in Chap. 3, in which the term *mahinahi* is explained. *Mahinahi* pertains to bribery implications in *Nihonshoki* exclusively encompasses gifts. From the standpoint of the historical institutionalist model, *Taishinin*'s judicial behaviour in the strict liability model conformed to traditional Japanese judicial behaviour. In principle, even a single *yen* could be considered a bribe from a legal standpoint. The criminality in question pertains to the funds intended to serve as a form of remuneration for the efforts made by a bureaucrat in the course of his official duties.

The judicial behaviour that is informed by the strict liability model has implications for the calculation of the cost of crime. This cost encompasses the probability

[16] The original text in the judgement: 原判決が第二の(十七)の事実を認定し事前に豫め謝礼供與の約束ありしたることを判示せずして......瀆職罪の構成要件を無視したるの違法あるものに非ず。

of apprehension and conviction, as well as the imposition of strict heavy punishment (Becker 1993, pp. 234–237). It is posited that *Taishinin*'s judicial behaviour functions as a form of deterrence that is rooted in strict liability. Articles 197 and 198 of the Penal Code were designated as "general clauses", which permitted expansive legal reasoning. The strict liability model for social deterrence is not limited to *Taishinin*'s judicial behaviour in prewar Japan. Similar judicial behaviour has also been identified in the Austrian Supreme Court's judicial behaviour during the early 1950s.[17]

5.7 Ōno Keikichi's Second Appeal Ground

5.7.1 *Time Gap Between Two Appointments*

In alignment with the appeal ground of Katayama Hisashi, Ōno's strategy in his second appeal ground was also predicated on denial and disconnection between the two cases. A critical distinction between the legal circumstances of Katayama and Ōno is the involvement of Ōno in both cases.

Ōno emphasized that the prosecution should have terminated the legal proceedings against him. In the prosecutor's request for pretrial by combining Keisei case and compensation case with *renzokuhan* on 11 August 1928, Ōno, in his capacity as a member of the Tokyo City Assembly, raised the issue of his term of appointment in the ad hoc Grant Examination Committee of the compensation case. This Committee was ended on 4 June 1926 for term break. Concurrently, he experienced a loss of his authority to determine the compensation amount for it thereafter. Following his reelection to the Assembly, he raised the issue of compensation once more during the Assembly's new proceedings on 31 March 1927. On 18 April 1927, he was reappointed to the same committee. One year later, on 30 June 1928, the final decision regarding the revised compensation amount was to be made. During the screening process prior to resolution, the Nihonbashi fish market union leader, Takamura Masutaro, repeatedly sought Ōno's assistance to secure favourable decisions from the Assembly members.

According to *Taishinin*'s judgement, Takamura had previously and consistently remunerated Ōno in the same compensation amount issue. On 10 April 1926, in the vicinity of Kyōbashi, a transaction occurred, involving Ōno and a discounted *yakusokutegata* (promissory note) of reduction in value. The document in question was a promissory note. This financial instrument in question was issued in the name of Tsubono Fusaji and had a value of 4660 *yen*. In mid-May 1926, Takamura engaged in a conspiracy with Kurata to provide Ōno with an additional 5000 *yen* in cash. In May or June of 1927, Takamura engaged in a conspiracy with Kurata, resulting in the provision of an additional 1000 *yen* cash to Ōno.

[17] On this see Alexander (2018, pp. 531–538).

In consideration of the sequence of events that transpired, the prosecutor sought to combine the Keisei case and the compensation case in the pretrial on 29 September 1928. The pretrial was conducted on 29 September 1928. While serving on the committee responsible for evaluating the application submitted by the Keisei Company, Ōno received a sum of 2000 *yen* from Miki. The prosecutor classified such behaviours as an offence under *tokushokuzai* (crime of corruption), constituting *renzokuichizai* (continuous serial crime) in his notice of *renzokuhan*.

In a manner analogous to Katayama's strategy, Ōno also lodged accusations against the junior courts, asserting that they had erroneously interpreted this case as falling under the purview of Article 55 of the Penal Code for adjudication as a single crime. The legal issues in the Keisei case were distinct from those in the compensation case. A close examination reveals no fundamental commonalities between these two cases. The crux of Ōno's assertion pertains to the absence of continuous membership in the Tokyo City Assembly from June 1922 to December 1928, a period characterized by an interruption in the short-term break which took place in June 1926. The following Taishinin's legal reasoning addresses the applicability of the prosecutor's *renzokukan*. Therefore, Ōno's claim was groundless.

With reference to *Shisei* (Municipal Organization Number 19) in Law in Meiji 44 No. 68, Ōno explained that city assembly membership was simply an honorary post of an appointment term of four years. The calculation of term was from the day of being elected. Being elected in one election was not equivalent to permanent city assembly membership. The expiry of one appointment term had to be renewed by another appointment term acquired through new election. In view of the time gap between the expiry of old appointment term and reappointment consequential on a new election, courts' legal reasoning to treat two separate appointments as one continuous appointment was illogical. In the time gap between two appointment terms of city assembly membership, Ōno lost his public official status and power.

Ōno reiterated that the constituent element of *renzokuhan* was one criminal offence involving several criminal acts. Its meaning should apparently be continuous criminal acts without interruption. In case of any change of intention, it should not be regarded as *renzokuhan*. It was not merely the *gaikei* (exteriors) of several behaviours were continuous, but such behaviours should also be activated by one identical intention for repetition of similar offences subjectively. Notwithstanding juridical facts of *tokushokuzai* (corruption) against Ōno, objectively the "continuity" bridging the behaviour in his first term of city assembly membership and his second term of it had been broken. Subjectively, it should not be said that all behaviours in *renzokuhan* were activated by two identical intentions. Ōno's acts of acceptance in *Keisei Electric Railway Company Case* took place during the lengthy three-year period covering 1926, 1927 and 1928. No matter in what perspective, it should not be regarded as continuous *renzokuhan* in view of the lengthy time gap and term break, which quashed the continuity in the chain of Ōno's acts, especially the factor of term break. This prosecution of two cases as one was therefore illegal. *Renzokuhan-tsūchisho* was abused for an indictment criminalizing several behaviours as one offence. Junior courts' acceptance of *renzokuhan* for one simultaneous trial constituted an infringement against law.

In contradistinction to Katayama's appeal ground based on accusation against breach of *fukokufuri-no-gensoku*, Ōno's second appeal ground aimed at no constituent element of *renzokuhan* which was "one criminal offense involving several acts[18]". If acts in the whole chain of events were not continuous, then *renzokuhan* could not be established as one constituent element legitimately under Article 55. The hidden agenda behind Ōno's appeal strategy was seeking protection under "no law, no crime" in Article 23 of Meiji Constitution. In other words, junior courts acted unconstitutionally and illegally.

5.7.2 Taishinin's Refusal to Ōno's Second Ground

Taishinin refused Ōno's second appeal ground, criticizing Ōno was wrong to say that his act of acceptance in the first term of City Assembly membership and similar act in the second term had no suitability for the applicability of *renzokuhan*. While the early act of acceptance of bribe had *yosō* (prior thought) for the later act of acceptance of bribe, it meant continuous intention to commit crime. Even if two acts had not taken place in the same appointment term, it could be adjudicated as *renzokuhan*. Notwithstanding lengthy time gap among Ōno's acts between March 1926 and 14 July 1928, *Taishinin* held junior courts were legally correct to treat these acts as having similar continuous criminal intention. Accordingly, *Taishinin* ruled that *renzokuhan* was appropriately applied. The prosecutor's *renzokuhan-tsūchisho* was thus legal.

5.7.3 Analysis of Taishinin's Second Refusal

The contemporary notion of criminality encompasses the convergence of criminal acts and the presence of culpable intent. This is similar to *mens rea* and *actus reus* in common law jurisdiction. *Taishinin*'s refusal to accept Ōno's second appeal was based on the notion of "continuous" intention, otherwise known as *yosō* (prior thought), which pertains to bridging acts of accepting a bribe in two distinct cases. Taishinin effectively eliminated the intervening factor of the time gap.

Yosō was like the prior intention with foreseeability for the chain of subsequent events or consequences. *Taishinin* thereby rationalized acts of acceptance in two cases as ongoing and continuous in order to meet constituent element of *renzokuhan*. In other words, *yosō* under similar intention bridged time gaps among different acts for contemporaneity.[19] It is noteworthy that *Taishinin* had not applied *yosō* to rebut Katayama's appeal ground against *renzokuhan*. *Taishinin* reserved its rebuttal to pinpoint Ōno's appeal strategy.

---

[18] The original text is "同一罪名に觸るる數個の行為".

[19] The original text is "單一意思の發動".

The term "continuous crime commission" is typically employed to denote a series of ongoing violations within a specific chain of events, as opposed to the completion of a single criminal act (Nissel 2004, pp. 664–665). A secondary appeal by Ōno's legal counsel also suggested a violation of his right to a fair trial for justice. A close examination of the Keisei case and the compensation case reveals that they were not connected and did not continue in the same sequence of events. The applicability of Article 55 of the Penal Code was, at first glance, highly questionable.

In accordance with *Taishinin*'s ruling on Ōno's second appeal ground, Ōno's act of acceptance of bribe in the compensation case occurred in May 1927. Four months later, on 13 October 1927, the Keisei Company commenced the process of modifying the original railway network under the auspices of the *Kidō-hō* (Railway Act). This initiative followed an earlier incident involving bribery. Ōno had been determined that the acceptance was finalized in May of 1927. Accordingly, the criminal act was not an ongoing, continuous situation that persisted until the Keisei case.

A judicious judicial decision-making process was necessary to address the matter in a satisfactory manner. Although *dōri* was traditionally employed as an equitable legal consciousness to mitigate the rigidity of statutes, *Taishinin*'s judicial behaviour did not align with this approach in the present case. In order to resolve this dilemma, it is incumbent upon the legislature to elucidate the legislative intent of the statute and to provide the term *renzokuhan* for the purpose of judicial reference. This is a matter of significant importance in the context of legislative behaviour (Bell 2000, p. 2–3). As previously mentioned in this chapter, *Taishinin* was unable to request Diet to elucidate legislative intent. Meiji Constitution did not explicitly mandate it as an obligation for the legislature.

Taishinin's judicial behaviour with regard to Ōno's second appeal is consistent with the historical institutionalist paradigm. This paradigm compels judges to adhere to historical landmark rulings through the process of judicial decision-making, which is informed by prior legal factors. While *stare decisis* (to stand by things decided) as binding landmark ruling was non-available, it generally entailed the definition of legal problems, the formulation of alternatives and the establishment of policy for implementation.[20] In this context, *Taishinin* adopted the perspective of Ōno and made subjective inferences. Ōno exhibited both continuous foresight and intention, qualities that align with the concept of *yosō* in two instances. A dispassionate examination reveals that, apart from the nature of corruption offences, two cases exhibited no discernible connectivity. It is imperative to ascertain how *Taishinin* was able to objectively verify that Ōno possessed such *yosō*. *Taishinin*'s judgement did not provide additional clarification regarding the legal reasoning employed in this regard. *Taishinin*'s approach is objective foreseeability in legal studies. *Taishinin* should have been convinced that Ōno acted as a reasonable person who could have foreseeability or ability to predict the occurrence of the end outcome. *Taishinin*'s judgement had not mentioned how Ōno could have the capacities to foresee or reasonable prediction that criminality of corruption in compensation case would continue to the Keisei case. *Yosō* relates to Ōno's ability to predict or foresee potential consequences of

[20] On this see Mather (1995).

connection between his different chain of events in two different cases and terms. In the context of *renzokuhan,* it plays a crucial role in establishing constituent element.

5.8 *Legalitätsprinzip* in Germanic Law

The ambiguous legislative intent for *renzokuhan* in Article 55 of the Penal Code represented an atypical outcome of legal transplantation from Germanic law as a "Western jacket on Japanese body", as opposed to an evolutionary outcome of indigenous Japanese legal culture, which is outlined in Chap. 3. The literal statutory constraints enumerated in Article 55 impeded the applicability of equitable *dōri* under the strict liability model of judicial behaviour. *Dōri* was, *prima facie,* in favour of *Ōno.* Causation of this legislative phenomenon can be traced back to the transposition of Japanese law from European countries. However, the primary concern at the time was the establishment of a novel social and legal order by the Meiji oligarchs, as well as the social relations inherent within a vertical state polity. Due to the absence of a similar congruent evolution in Germanic legal systems, a disconnection emerged between the transplanted Germanic statutes and the actualities of Japanese culture and daily life in urban and rural areas (Goodman 2003, p. 28).

Taishinin adhered to the literal meaning of Article 55 in order to facilitate its strict liability model of judicial behaviour. The *kisohōteishugi* (mandatory prosecution principle) is a legal concept that is integral to the Japanese legal system. The following assertion is made with the understanding that it is the original legislative intent behind *renzokuhan* in Germanic law, not Japanese law. The literal interpretation of statutory provisions was regarded as a judicial behaviour subject to statutory constraints rather than equitable considerations with *dōri. Kisohōteishugi* is derived from the German legal term *Legalitätsprinzip,* which signifies the principle that a prosecutor is obligated to initiate legal proceedings in instances where there is sufficient evidence to substantiate a criminal offence and the applicable criminal procedural framework is in place. In essence, the prosecutor's role entails the diligent and meticulous prosecution of each case. This is predicated on the assumption that there exists sufficient *prima facie* evidence to support a prosecution in accordance with the literal interpretation of *renzokukan.*[21]

Without literal vagueness to render Article 55 unenforceable, *Taishinin*'s judicial behaviour in respect of *renzokuhan* was legal vis-a-vis the original legislative intent of *legalitätsprinzip* in Germanic law. As stated in Chap. 2, *Taishinin*'s judicial behaviour can also be influenced by other political stakeholders and by the structural institutional settings in state polity. Judges may strategically individualize dynamics for decisional setting (Perino 2006, pp. 497–498). In the perspective of strategic model of judicial behaviour, *Taishinin*'s legal reasoning for criminalization by *yosō* could achieve a goal consistent with prosecution policy of the Ministry of Justice,

[21] On this see Uchida (1965, p. 21, p. 24, p. 27).

which was for maintenance of strict discipline and integrity of bureaucrats. This consideration was more important than criminal justice.

5.9 Appeal Ground of Nakajima Moritoshi

5.9.1 No Conspiracy

Nakajima Moritoshi appealed on the ground that junior courts' verdicts were illegitimate because it was based on neither evidence nor legal ground to convict him as *kyōhansha* (accomplice). He claimed he had been wrongly convicted of having accepted *sharei* for his assistance to the Keisei Company and mistakenly criminalized him of conspiracy with Yano Genkichi and Motegi Kyūhei. Wrongful conviction is the most serious judicial error and accusation. The truth was that through Motegi, he gave 1000 *yen* to Yoshii Amajirō and Tanaka Kōzō. Yoshii then additionally gave Tanaka 300 *yen.* Nakajima's act of giving money to Yoshii and Tanaka was wrongfully convicted of giving bribe. He accused that no evidence had been adduced to prove he had *kyōbō* (conspiracy) or bribery in this chain of events.

The punchline of Nakajima's appeal ground was that he gave the 1000 *yen* to two recipients through the hand of Motegi but he had neither face-to-face oral nor written communication with them. Without communication, *kyōbō* could not be established. He actually had no knowledge of who would be a *kyōbōsha* (co-conspirator) through the acceptance of his money.

5.9.2 Taishinin's Ground of Refusal

Many laymen of law assume that evidence must be tangible. However, statement of credibility beyond reasonable doubt could be legally considered evidence. With *Taishinin*'s strict liability model of judicial behaviour in corruption cases, conviction was possible in a persuasive and coherent case without direct evidence. In this judgement, *Taishinin* even did not mention any reference to evidence substantiating Nakajima's *quid pro quo* intention.

Taishinin's ruling was characterized by its brevity and directness. At the time that Nakajima handed Motegi the 1000 *yen*, he had been informed of the following: The allocation of financial resources to the City Assembly members was imperative. It was evident that the accomplices Motegi, Yoshii and Tanaka should be held accountable for their actions in their capacity as Assembly members. The aforementioned evidence is sufficient to substantiate the authenticity of Nakajima's conspiracy, as outlined in paragraph 2 (3) of the junior court's judgement.[22]

[22] The original text in the judgement: 被告人中島は千圓を交付する際其の結局市會議員の何人に交付せらるるかを知らさりしとするも共犯者たる茂木か吉井田中に對し同人等の市

Taishinin concluded that Nakajima was informed of the Assembly members to whom the money should be given. This information met the constituent element of conspiracy of two or more persons to commit a crime, as defined by the relevant legal statutes. In opposition to Nakajima's assertion of ignorance regarding the two recipients, *Taishinin*'s judicial behaviour in rejecting the appeal aligns with the principles of the strict liability model. In the judgement, *Taishinin* made three references to the act of providing financial compensation to two public officials, Yoshii and Tanaka, through an intermediary. The absence of any reference to evidence substantiating the *quid pro quo* intention and the method by which *Taishinin* ensured that Nakajima was apprised of the identities of two recipients is a notable omission in the documentation. The issue of whether *quid pro quo* was related to their official duty and within the scope of their knowledge was omitted in the court judgement.

5.9.3 Similar Precedent Strict Judicial Behaviour of Taishinin

The judicial behaviour of *Taishinin* has thrice been analyzed by strict liability model in this longest judgement on prewar corruption case. In this part, *Taishinin* exhibited a marked conservatism, reminiscent of a prior ruling issued on 3 March 1896, referenced *Keiroku* (collection of precedent judgements) 2–3-10, *kyōbō-kyōdō-seihan* (co-conspirators) could be established objectively from the acts of offenders. The presence of direct evidence is not a prerequisite for conviction. Evidence indicating prior communication was not a prerequisite for the conviction of co-conspirator.[23] In another *Taishinin* case in the Taisho era, as referenced *Keishū* 1–233, dated 18 April 1922, the individual who perpetrated a criminal act on behalf of another individual was also classified as a joint principal offender. The term *anmoku-no-kyōbō* is a Japanese idiom that translates to "implied conspiracy".[24] An additional reference can be found in another ruling of *Taishinin*, which is documented under reference *Keishū* 5–584 and dated 23 December 1926. In this seminal case, the court determined that individuals who printed their share certificates at the behest of others were deemed co-principals, given the forgery of the stock certificate intended for the purpose of exercising. In the absence of a conspiracy to engage in the counterfeiting of stock, individuals involved in such activities should nevertheless be regarded as primary offenders in the context of securities counterfeiting. In the Taisho case, the joint principal was identified as *hanzai-no-hatsuisha* (initiator of the crime) which subsequently led to a series of events subsequently. In the context of Japanese legal

會議員たる職務に関したる行為に付其の責に任せさるへからさることもち論なれは敍上證據は原判決第二の(三)乙の事実を証明するに足るものして。

[23] On this see Shimomura (1975, pp. 48-82); The original text in the judgement: 共ニ謀リテ事ヲ行フ以上ハ何人カ局ニ当ルモ其行為ハ共謀者一躰ノ行為ニナラス。

[24] The original text in the judgement: 二人以上共同して犯罪を実行したるものは皆正犯する
。

terminology, this phenomenon is characterized as *hanzai-no-hatsuisha* (犯罪の発意者, initiator of crime).[25]

Nakajima was convicted under prewar Article 60 of Penal Code listed on page 421 of this *Taishinin* judgement. He also used the term *kyōbō* (conspiracy)in his appeal ground. Article 60 of prewar Penal Code stipulated those two or more persons who commits a crime jointly are principal offenders. Without oral or written communication with the recipients as a constituent element, Nakajima believed that *kyōbō* could not be established. Article 60 in prewar Penal Code also had legal ambiguity. Postwar Article 60 is therefore specifically clarifying it as *kyōdōseihan* (co-principals), which is two or more persons who commit a crime *in joint action* are *all* principals. In case of evidence for proving joint action, all parties in it should have similar culpability for the crime jointly committed. Postwar Article 60 is more reasonable and equitable than that in prewar Penal Code.

5.10 *Taishinin* is Stricter Than Today's Supreme Court of Japan

The Japanese term *bōgi* (conspiracy) is defined by multiple connotations. One of these connotations is "conspiracy", and it is also associated with the concept of communication. In the context of a complicity or conspiracy case, *Taishinin*'s judicial behaviour was characterized by a high degree of strictness, to the extent that communication among co-conspirators was deemed to be unnecessary. The question of whether the absence of communication of intention, as a constituent element in a conspiracy, was equitable must be addressed.

An examination of *Taishinin*'s judicial conduct reveals a potential incongruity with the conventional legal perspective known as *dōri*. This discrepancy prompts a critical inquiry into the rigour and strictness of *Taishinin*'s legal practices, and whether they deviate from the established norms of *dōri*. The judicial behaviour of judges can be characterized as either liberal, conservative, strict, rigid, equitable, or unequitable. In the legal context of conspiracy, the judicial behaviour of the postwar Supreme Court of Japan, as outlined in the subsequent paragraph, is characterized by a comprehensive consideration of all pertinent factors. This approach is regarded as both reasonable and equitable in comparison with the judicial behaviour exhibited by *Taishinin* in this particular case.

In the context of Article 60 of the prewar Penal Code, *Ishi-no-renraku* (communication of intentions) pertains to an individual who has committed a crime in conjunction with two or more persons, otherwise referred to as the "joint party" under Article 207 of the aforementioned Code. The Supreme Court of Japan has determined that

[25] On this see Matsubara (2011, p. 1489); The original text in the judgement: 暗黙の共謀も判例上認められてきた例えば、行使の目的をもって株券を偽造するものであることを知りながら、他人の依頼に応じてその株券を印刷するものは、偽造行使の謀議をしなくても、有価証券偽造罪の正犯である。

both Articles refer to scenarios where there should be communication of intention between two or more offenders. It is imperative to note that the Supreme Court's judgement under consideration makes explicit the necessity of effective communication of intention, according to *Saiban-shū (Keiji)* of 24 January 1959, Number 7–109.[26]

Despite concurring with *Taishinin*'s assertion in the Nakajima case that Nakajima was aware of the identities of the two recipients of his 1000 *yen*, it remained challenging to reach a conclusive determination that Nakajima's awareness of the recipients and his actions of transferring funds through an intermediary are tantamount to overt communication of his intent. This was further compounded by the evidentiary challenges in substantiating such a claim to the extent that it met the standard of beyond a reasonable doubt. The allocation of 1000 yen can be attributed to a variety of factors. This is distinct from the clear common objective in *anmoku-no-kyōbō* (implied conspiracy). Communication can also be conceptualized as abstract, manifesting in the form of conduct, gesture or the production of visual representations such as drawings. In the judgement, *Taishinin* did not specify any methods of communication.

One month later, in another case under reference *Keishū* 3–2-113, Supreme Court of Japan further overruled against *Taishinin*'s judicial behaviour of strict liability model by recognition of *kyōdōhankō-no-ninshiki* (co-commission of crime). To convict of conspiracy, Supreme Court of Japan ruled that it was necessary to prove co-offenders' recognition of co-commission of crime. Constituent element of conspiracy should include a *recognition of joint crimes* among several people. Merely being aware of crime commission by someone else cannot be labelled as co-conspirator.[27]

The labour dispute case of Nerima Incident took place in Nerima Ward, Tokyo on 26 December 1951, in which a police officer was murdered. On 28 May 1958, the Grand Bench of Supreme Court delivered a landmark ruling under reference *Keishū* 12–8-1718 that in order to establish the conspiracy among co-principals, two or more persons to commit a specific crime should have mutual unity under a common will, took mutual advantage from actions of each other and conspired to carry out one's will. Accordingly, the fact that the crime was committed must be acknowledged. It is unnecessary to deliver judgements to offenders one by one specifically.[28]

According to these rulings of postwar Supreme Court of Japan in the aforesaid three cases, *Taishinin*'s judicial behaviour of strict liability model in the current judgement was apparently not equitable *dōri* and far stricter. The benefit of doubt

---

[26] The original text in the judgement: 意思の連絡という用語によるもの。刑法第六〇条に、二人以上共同して犯罪を実行したものとある共同又は同法第二〇七条にいわゆる共同者とあるのは、すべて二人以上の者の間に意思の連絡のある場合をさすものである。

[27] The original text in the judgement: 共謀とは数人相互の間に共同犯行の認識があることを云うのであって、単に他人の犯行を認識しているだけで、その者が共謀者であると云うことはできない。

[28] The original text in the judgement: 共謀の判示は、謀議の行われた日時、場所またはその内容の詳細、すなわち実行の方法、各人の行為の分担役割等についてまで、いちいち具体的に判示することを要しない。

was allocated to the prosecution. However, when readers consider *Taishinin*'s role, as outlined in Chap. 9 of this book, a different impression may occur.

5.11 Brief Remarks

The fourth and fifth chapter examine *Taishinin*'s strict liability model in addressing instances of political corruption for three times in this longest *Taishinin* judgement on corruption. The analysis delves into the intricate interplay between political party factions, electoral funding mechanisms and the discretionary powers wielded by city assembly members in the absence of an external monitoring system. Additionally, it explores the post-earthquake reconstruction efforts in Tokyo, highlighting the role of the city assembly in shaping the urban landscape in the aftermath of a major disaster. The egalitarian political factions were accused of misappropriating a significant portion of public funds allocated for the compensation and approval of the railway network. In the context of the aforementioned series of events, *Taishinin*'s approach to judicial management exhibited characteristics more aligned with the formulation of judicial policy than with the principles of criminal justice.

In the compensation case and Keisei case under joint consideration in one judgement of *Keishū* 13–419, dated 26 March 1934, it was determined that economic power and a significant market share were concentrated or even monopolized by main stakeholders in the fish market and small number of capitalists in railway service sectors. This phenomenon led to a pervasive motivation to engage in bribery, with the aim of securing financial interests and ensuring long-term profitability. It is more probable that substantial investments in political bribery, manifesting through lobbying activities and campaign contributions, will be made under such motivations.[29]

In this lengthy *Taishinin* judgement of two cases, the corruption of political factions occurred within a network of close interpersonal relations and commitments that were embedded in a social structure characterized by mutual trust and loyalty to political faction leaders. In political party faction, members were more well-organized in vertical structure. Under the cover of political hypocrisy of *jinchū mimai* and customary gifting practice, factionalism under Nakajima at the tip of this vertical structure was a form of dysfunctional personalism. This case reflects that expensive internal party competition among factions was a significantly motivation for illicit campaign contributions (Golden and Chang 2001, pp. 595–596). Bribery was usually covered as political campaign funds for it. Before the promulgation of Political Funds Control Code in 1948, Japanese courts had no special legal provisions to control political donation of funds. Taishinin's strictness can be regarded as a judicial necessity in this regard.

In Keisei case, *Taishinin* made no comment on the cultural defence by traditional norm of *jinchū mimai* but straightforwardly criminalized it as *modus operandi* of bribery. This strict liability model was like a command for social administration.

[29] On this see Teachout (2018, p. 112, pp. 119–121).

Even with Political Funds Control Code now, donations for political party faction and corruption are still commonly intertwined. *Taishinin*'s strictness as an administrative means against corruption was understandable. Taishinin's strict judicial behaviour had equitable side-effect of plugging the loophole of absence of statute. The legal and policy implication out of different judicial behaviour models deviate differently (Slocum 2017, p. 16). In the course of extensive examination of two cases, *Taishinin* repeatedly invoked the principle of short statutory interpretation. In the context of the strict liability model, a succinct legal statement was sufficient grounds for *Taishinin*'s rejection of the appeal. This decision was made under the premise that the court in question was the final appellate authority, and it was not subject to any subsequent judicial challenge.

In the absence of comprehensive information, a cursory statutory interpretation might be perceived as inadequate rationale for judicial decision-making. This is in opposition to the Japanese interpretation of *kōhei-kaishaku* (equitable interpretation).[30] Legal interpretation attaining a justified and rational goal as rationale for verdict is associated with mitigation of risk of social discontent (Dybowski 2018, p. 30–31). In the context of Japanese jurisprudence, the legal term *ratio legis* can be rendered as *hanketsu-riyū* (reasons for judgement). This term refers to offering a comprehensive understanding of the legal rationale underlying a particular decision or ruling. In certain instances, *Taishinin*'s judicial behaviour, characterized by its rigidity and inflexibility, does not readily yield a clear *ratio legis*.

Taishinin occupied the uppermost echelon of the pyramidal judicial structure, representing the final court in the hierarchy. The *mokutekironteki-kaishaku* (teleological interpretation) is defined as the function of judicial decision-making in light of the strategic goals of statutory provisions or the overall intent to be achieved through judicial behaviour. In addition to their primary function, the final courts are also responsible for formulating judicial policy, with the overarching objective of contributing to the governance and public policy of the state (Reid 1988, pp. 509–512). Policy is a multifaceted concept, one that can be interpreted in various ways. In this particular instance, the focus is on the implications of *Taishinin*'s judicial policy (Rosenfeld 2019, p. 38). The judicial apparatus was characterized by its own set of appointment practices, an institutional design and a sense of obligation among judges (Matsui 2011, p. 1376). In addition, there is a need to consider stable, valued and recurring patterns of judicial behaviour (Huntington 1968, p. 12). In the context of prewar judicial policy for corruption control, *Taishinin* exhibited a distinctive objective: the implementation of rigorous disciplinary oversight of public officials, with the aim of safeguarding its hegemonic dominance. This strategic objective, veiled within the context of judicial behaviour, transcends the realm of mere equilibrium for the purpose of rational decision-making. The intricacies of this phenomenon are elucidated in comprehensive detail in Chap. 9.

[30] On this see Ishibe (2010, p. 6, p. 10, p. 12).

References

Alexander, L. B. (2018) Is There a Case for Strict Liability? *Criminal Law and Philosophy*, Vol. 12, (3), 531–538.

Becker, G. (1993) Nobel Lecture: The Economic way of Thinking About Behavior. *Journal of Political Economy*, Vol. 10, 234–267.

Bell, B. W. (2000) The Public Justification Approach to Statutory Interpretation. *Rutgers Law School (Newark) Faculty Papers*, Working Paper 5.

Bolton et al. (2020) Legislative Constraints, Ideological Conflict, and the Timing of Executive Unilateralism. *Legislative Studies Quarterly*, Vol. 47 (1), 3–36.

DIGITALIO. *Five Private Railways Scandals*. https://kotobank.jp/word/%E4%BA%94%. Accessed 10 October 2025.

Dybowski, M. (2018) Articulating Ratio Legis and Practical Reasoning. In Verena, K., Maciej, ed. *Ratio Legis: Philosophical and Theoretical Perspectives* (pp. 19–28). Springer.

Golden, M. A., Chang, E. C. C. (2001) Competitive Corruption: Factional Conflict and Political Malfeasance in Postwar Italian Christian Democracy. *World Politics*, Vol. 53 (4), 588–622.

Goodman, C. F. (2003) *The Rule of Law in Japan, A Comparative Analysis*. Kluwer Law International.

Huntington, S. P. (1968) *Political Order in Changing Societies*. Yale University Press.

Ida, M. (2014) Gaikokuhōgaku no keiju to iu kanten kara mita Nihon no keihō to keihōgaku (Japanese criminal law and criminal law studies from the perspective of inheriting foreign law study). In Institute of Comparative Law, Waseda University ed. *Nihonhō no naka no gaikokuhō: Kihonhō no hikakuhōteki kōsatsu (Foreign Law in Japanese Law: A Comparative Legal Examination of Basic Law)* (pp. 139–161). Institute of Comparative Law, Waseda University.

Ishibe, M. (2010) Hōkaishaku hōhō no hikakushi (A Comparative History of Law Interpretation Methods). *Nanzan Daigaku Yōroppa Kenkyū Sentā Hō (Nanzan University European Studies Center Bulletin)*, Vol. 16, 1–14.

Ishida, T. (2019) Sekai de shinkō suru toshika no keikō to toshi kaihatsu senryaku sono 4: Nihon no ensen toshi kaihatsu jirei (Urbanization Trends and Urban Development Strategies in the World Part 4: Examples of urban development along railway lines in Japan). *Report of the Policy Research Institute of Land, Infrastructure, Transport and Tourism*, Vol.71, 128–143.

Keisei Electric Railway Co.,Ltd. *Keisei Electric Railway's History*.
https://www.keisei.co.jp/keisei/keisei_museum/history/. Accesssed 2 October 2025.

Mather, L. (1995) The Fired Football Coach (Or, How Trial Courts Make Policy). In Epstein, L. ed. *Contemplating Courts* (pp. 230–267). Congressional Quarterly Inc.

Matsubara, Y. (2011) Kyōbō kyōdō seihan no genzai (Current status of co-principals in conspiracy). *Hōsō jihō (Lawyers Association Journal)*, Vol. 63 (7), 1488-1491.

Matsui, S. (2011) Why is the Japanese Supreme Court so Conservative? *Washington University Law Review*, Vol.88 (6), 1375–1423.

Matsuo, S. (1969) Dai-kyo-shō Heigōzai : Dai-gojūgo-jō (Chapter 9 Consolidation Crimes: Article 55). In Dandō S. ed. *Chūshaku keihō (Commentary Criminal Law), 2-II*. (pp. 655–660). Yūhikaku .

Moyer, L. P. (2012) The Role of Case Complexity in Judicial Decision Making. *Law and Policy*, Vol. 34 (3), 291–312.

Nishigawa, S. (2000) Senzenki Hōseikyoku Kenkyū Josetsu (Introduction to Prewar Legislative Bureau Research). *Seikei Ronso (Collection of Articles of Politics and Economics)*, Vol. 69 (2&3), 139–170.

Nishino, T. (2014) Senzen ni okeru shiei denki jigyō no tenkai to tokusei (Development and Characteristics of Municipal Electricity Business in the Prewar Period). *Chi'iki Seisaku Kenkyū (Regional Policy Research)*, Association for Regional Policy Studies, Takasaki City University of Economics, Vol. 16 (2), 1–19.

Nissel, A. (2004) Continuing Crimes in the Rome Statute. *Michigan Journal of International Law*, Vol. 25 (3), 653–689.

Perino, M. A. (2006) Law, Ideology, and Strategy in Judicial Decisonmaking: Evidence: from Securities Fraud Actions. *Journal of Empirical Legal Studies*, Vol. 3 (3), 497–524.

Randazzo, K. A. et al. (2011) State Supreme Courts and the Effects of Statutory Constraint: A Test of the Model of Contingent Discretion. *Political Research Quarterly*, Vol. 64 (4), 779–789.

Reid, T. V. (1988) Judicial Policy-Making and Implementation: An Empirical Examination. *The Western Political Quarterly*, Vol. 41 (3), 509–527.

Rosenfeld, M. (2019) Judicial Politics versus Ordinary Politics : Is the Constitutional Judge Caught in the Middle? In Landfried ed. *Judicial Power: How Constitutional Courts Affect Political Transformations* (pp. 36–65). Cambridge University Press.

Segal, J. A., Spaeth, H. J. (1993) The Supreme Court and the Attitudinal Model. Cambridge University Press.

Segal, J. A. (2008) Judicial Behavior. In Gregory, A. C. et al. ed. The Oxford Handbook of Law and Politics (pp. 19–33). Oxford University Press.

Shimomura, Y. (1975) *Kyōbō kyōdō seihan to kyōhan riron (Conspiracy Co-principles and Complicity Theor)*. Gakuyōshobō.

Slocum, B. G. (2017) *The Nature of Legal Interpretation: What Jurists Can Learn about Legal Interpretation from Linguistics and Philosophy*. University of Chicago Press.

Tamekuni, T. et al. (1995) Senzen ni okeru Keisei Denki Kidō no keiei shisaku to chiiki to no kakawari ni tsuite no ichi kōsatsu (A Study of Management Policies of Keisei Electric Tramway in the Prewar Period and its Relationship with Local Communities). *Dobokushi kenkyū (Civil Engineering History Research)*, Vol. 15, 195–206.

The Yomiuri Shimbun Company History Compilation Office ed. (1955). *Yomiuri Shimbun Hachijū-nen-shi (Yomiuri Shimbun 80-Year History)*. Yomiuri Shimbun.

Teachout, Z. (2018) The Problem of Monopolies & Corporate Public Corruption. *Dædalus: the Journal of the American Academy of Arts & Sciences*, Vol. 147 (3), 111–126.

Tyler, T. R. (2003) Procedural Justice, Legitimacy, and the Effective Rule of Law. In Tonry, M. ed. *Crime and justice: A review of research* (Vol. 30, pp. 283–357). University of Chicago Press.

Uematsu, T. (1964). "Trends of the revision of the Penal Code in Japan. *Hototsubashi Journal of Law and Politics*, Vol. 3, 1–15.

Uchida, I. (1965) tsu ni okeru kiso hōtei shugi (Prosecution Statutory Principle in Germany). *Waseda Hōgaku*, Vol. 40 (2), 21–45.

Wagatsuma, S. (1937) *Iwanami Hōritsugaku Shō Jiten (Iwanami small dictionary of law)*. Iwanami Shoten.

Widiss, D. (2020) How Courts Do and Don't: Respond to Statutory Overrides. *Judicature*, Vol. 104 (1), 51–58.

Yoshida T. (1977) Keihō o kiru (Break Criminal Law). *Tōyō hōgaku (Tōyō Legal Studies)*, Vol. 20 (2), 67–77.

Chapter 6
Banquet Bribe, Social Trust and Hybrid Judicial Behaviour

6.1 Case Background

Contrary to the pervasive political corruption that characterized the preceding two chapters, the corruption prevalent in the education sector has the potential to erode social trust in the education system and even state political system, exacerbate existing inequalities and impede the intellectual development of future social leaders. Education is the process of acquiring knowledge and skills that will enable the next generation to contribute to the societal well-being.

This chapter explores the phenomenon of corruption within the education sector, with a particular focus on the issue of unfairness in the procurement of textbooks. This practice has the potential to distort market competition, distort supply chain and lead to adverse outcomes for stakeholders' interests involved. The recovery of money in publishers' bribery can be achieved through an increase in textbook prices. It is imperative to acknowledge that students must incur a greater financial expenditure to obtain knowledge capital. Nepotism and favouritism have the potential to result in textbook supplies of inferior quality.

To ensure hegemonic governance, social values and integrity in the education sector, *Taishinin* introduced the moralistic element of social trust to its judicial behaviour in this judgement. Contrary to the preceding chapters, the present chapter does not concern grand political corruption case of large amount of financial interest. The case under consideration pertains to a matter of minor corruption, specifically pertaining to the provision of culinary entertainment by textbook suppliers to two junior high school teachers. The corrupt *quid pro quo* pertains to the allocation of book quotas and the selection of bookstores by two junior high schools in Fukuoka. This petty corruption case under consideration involves five appellants, as referenced in *Keishū* 9–413 dated 6 August 1931. In the context of the exchange between *mikaku-no-zōtō* (gift of taste) and *quid pro quo*, *Taishinin* is defined within the legal parameters established by these two concepts. According to the judgement, two teachers engaged in acceptance of bribery, consuming culinary entertainment in

K. B. Wong and S. L. Fang, *Taishinin's Judicial Behaviour in Corruption Cases*,
https://doi.org/10.1007/978-981-95-5823-0_6

restaurants without the intention of taking the food away for resale. In the context of the attitudinal model of judicial behaviour, *Taishinin*'s approach entails the moralistic conceptualization of the breach of social trust as a factor that serves to exacerbate culpability.

6.1.1 Textbook System in Prewar Japan

The causation of this corruption was embedded in the structure of prewar Japanese textbook supply chain system. School textbook is nothing new in Japanese history. The pedagogical value of textbooks for assurance of quality learning and teaching had long been recognized in Japan. The earliest extant textbook of this kind can be traced back to *ōrai-mono* at the end of the Heian period. *Ōrai-mono* was initially the collection of letters exchanged between the intellectuals and *meikō-ōrai.* It was undertaken by a nobleman known as Fujiwara no Akihira. Subsequently, the utilization of *ōrai-mono* as textbooks became pervasive. In the context of *terakoya* (private educational institutions that emerged during the Edo period), *ōrai-mono* also served as textbooks for formal schooling. The textbook system of ō*rai-mono* provided freedom of education for a large number of subjects of applied learning without censorship, such as *jukugo* (idiom), *shōsoku* (information communication), *kun'iku* (discipline training), *jitsugyō* (business knowledge about agriculture, industry and commerce), history and geography. The subject of *zatsu* (miscellaneous subject) even included professional training of fortune-telling and calendars. Before the Meiji era, a state-sanctioned textbook system was non-existent. A nationwide syllabus and standardized technical knowledge training programme to limit educational freedom were not in place. Emphasis on local geographical education and identity was allowed without fear of superiority of regionalism over nationalism during the Edo period. Although the limitations set on overseas travels declined textbook publications on foreign geographies as a nationwide policy,[1] increasing education opportunities and academic freedom stimulated the market growth of *ōrai-mono* to have seven thousand varieties. Female educationalists also enjoyed such freedom to author their own textbooks for literature and even fine art (Isome 2008, pp. 171–173).

In the 1870s, women could express opinions by publication though it was mainly in regional small newspapers (Suzuki 2019, p. 20). Upon the Meiji Restoration, the new government issued *Gakusei* (School System Order) in 1872, which continued this freedom of textbook publication policy and extended to the use of translated versions of Western textbooks. Even enlightenment books about Western culture and science were allowed. In 1874, the Ministry of Education reported record-breaking 3,109,430 copies of school textbooks were being used by elementary and junior high students in most regions of Japan. A bank named *Tōkyō Waribiki Ginkō* (Tokyo Discount Bank) was intentionally set up to boost this boom of freedom for textbook

[1] On this see Yoshiwara (1969, pp. 19–26).

publication.[2] While textbook became a standardized instrument for mass instruction and students' knowledge capital in labour market, it served the objective of instilling national pride and patriotism.[3]

Today's Japanese Ministry of Education, Culture and Technology has been no stranger to diplomatic controversy over its censorship of textbook in support of national identity and pride. The current Japanese textbook screening and authorization system dates back to prewar state polity when such official narratives as the Imperial Rescript on Education was emphasized for Japanese identity formation (Nozaki and Inokuchi 2000, p. 97). In 1880, the Ministry of Education set up its own section to investigate the adequacy of textbooks at prefectural level and notify them of prohibition of textbook content of infringement against Meiji nationalist policy. In 1883, free textbook system was changed to system of governmental approval. Since 1886, the *kentei-seido* (official certification system) had been implemented. The equilibrium of supply and demand in this substantial and remunerative market does not align with the conventional buyer's or seller's market paradigm. This is contingent upon the discretionary authority of the Ministry of Education's certification. The context of this textbook saga became increasingly intertwined with political and economic factors. The system had transitioned from a fully market-based competitive environment to a bureaucratic system characterized by rent-seeking opportunities for bureaucrats.[4]

6.1.2 Precedent Nationwide Corruption in Education Sector

It is possible that even Japanese may not be aware of this fact that the introduction of the *Kokutei-kyōkasho* (state-designated textbook) system in 1903 was a response to a nationwide scandal involving the corruption of textbook publishers, which had occurred in 1902. The mastermind behind the operation was a textbook publication firm, *Kinkōdō*. In 1875, Hara Ryozaburo established *Kinkōdō* as a publication firm in Yokohama. The following year, he relocated the firm to Nihonbashi in downtown Tokyo. In 1892, Hara undertook a reorganization of the company, establishing *Kinkōdō* Book Company Limited. This enterprise would go on to become the largest publication firm in the Meiji era, with 500,000 *yen* in paid-up capital.[5] The annual profit was between 170,000 *yen* and 180,000 *yen*, achieved through the networking of bureaucrats and the utilization of new typography for printing textbooks and magazines. In the context of an oligopolistic textbook market, the company in question competes with the market leader, which is identified as *Kunimitsusha*. In the aftermath of the Ministry of Education's textbook content revision, two publishing companies

[2] On this see Inaoka (1985, pp. 78–79, pp. 118–121).

[3] On this see Ingrao (2009, p. 180, p. 182).

[4] On more details about the textbook system in prewar Japan, see Nakamura (1992).

[5] On this see Inaoka (2019).

engaged in a competitive race to swiftly release revised editions, aiming to capture a larger share of the market.[6]

In 1902, more than 200 suspects, including governors, school principals, inspectors and teachers, were detained from all over Japan for this textbook corruption (Inaoka 1987, pp. 139–140). Police conducted research at publication firms *Kinkōdō,Shueisha, Fukyūsha* and arrested education inspectors in Mie, Ishikawa, Shizuoka and Gunma. 20,000,000 copies of elementary school textbooks were involved, and 9,900,000 copies of high school textbook were also counted.[7] Finally, 157 suspects were charged, and the range was over 30 prefectures. As same as the *modus operandi* in other *Taishinin* cases, this case made use of hosted hospitality amounted to a total of 5,483 *sen* and entertainment provided by 493 geishas (Chiba 1977, p. 32). *Kinkōdō* was the biggest among the bookstores. Its business came to a standstill after being convicted of bribery. Afterwards, Fujiwara Sakichi, a former staff of *Kinkōdō* in Yokohama, set up a bookstore under the name of *Kinkōdō* afterwards in Sendai in 1910. With its own publication department, a bookstore of the name *Sendai-kinkōdō* is operative today.[8] Staff of the same company name also provided culinary entertainments to teachers in this case.

The first grand textbook corruption scandal in Meiji era led to a public outcry demanding a nationally designated textbook system, which coincided with the rise of nationalism in state politics. This period, during which private publishers were permitted to produce textbooks under the auspices of the Ministry of Education's elementary school book review board system, had reached its final conclusion. In 1903, the Minister of Education, Kikuchi Dairoku, decided to carry out *kokutei-kyōkasho* system for national designation of textbooks whose copyright would be owned by the Ministry. A national designation system was established for all elementary school textbooks. In 1904, a specialized firm *Kabushikigaisha Kokutei Kyōkasho Kyōdō Hanbaijo* (National Textbook Joint Sales Office Company Limited) was set up. With its low profitability policy, consumers' total amount of annual expenses on elementary school textbook had been largely reduced from 4,517,450 *yen* to 1,997, 256 *yen*,[9] which proved that previous textbook contracts of private firms were over-priced. Before *kokutei-kyōkasho* system for elementary school textbook was extended to schools for teacher training and high schools in 1943, the lucrative junior high school textbook market had intensive competition because of a comparative free government policy.[10] The subsequent shift of intensive competition among elementary textbook suppliers to the more lucrative junior high school textbook market segment led to product diversification. This system was not a cartel. Bribery to school teachers at management level became a marketing strategy. Their provision of early accurate information on textbook demand could ensure no overproduction

[6] See Inaoka (1981, p. 125, pp. 129–130, p. 144).

[7] See Higano (1990, p. 17, pp. 26–30).

[8] On this see Namimoto (2012a, b).

[9] Chiba (1977, p. 33).

[10] See Higano (1990, pp. 35–36).

in a publication firm's supply chain. The availability of market information was important to both publication firm and retailing bookstore.

6.1.3 Oligarchic Junior High School Textbook Market

Under the prewar system, junior high school education was five-year. The content of junior high school textbooks had to be conformed to the Ministry of Education's *Chūgakkō-kyōju-yōmoku* (Middle School Teaching Guideline) issued in 1902, 1911, 1931 and 1942 (Takahashi and Tetsuo 2012, pp. 72–74). Though it was not law, it was official standardized administrative guidelines for textbook publication and teaching (Yano 2012, p. 8). Some decision-makers in *Chūgakkō-kyōju-yōmoku* were nationalists. Multiple private sector publishers had to draft textbooks according to their guidelines, which had at least two important facets in state polity: instrumental rationality and value through its impact on teaching and learning, and symbolic political function on school operation.

In preparation for *Chūgakkō-kyōju-yōmoku,* a conference of school principals was held in November 1900 in which subjects for professional education were determined to be part of the general education in high school education.[11] The first *Chūgakkō-kyōju-yōmoku* in 1902 extensively covered the twelve subjects of *shūshin* (disciplinary training), Japanese and Chinese, foreign language, history, geography, mathematics, *hakubutsu* (natural history), physics and chemistry, legal system and economics, drawings, music and gymnastics. In 1899, there were 191 schools and 69,179 students. Within ten years, the number increased to 305 schools and 118,133 students in 1909 (Yagi 2008, p. 49). While one junior high school student had to purchase at least 12 textbooks in one academic year, the huge amount of book sales revenue was a temptation to publishers.

Each textbook publisher in the new system made applications for junior high school textbooks individually. In addition to the standards stipulated in *Chūgakkō-kyōju-yōmoku,* the Ministry of Education determined whether or not *kentei-gōkaku-hon* (books that passed the examination) to be granted for use in junior high school (Ogasawara 2020, p. 45). The Ministry of Education owned intellectual property rights of primary school textbook, and oligarchic textbook publishers owned the copyright of junior high school textbook for lucrative profitability. The competition among textbook suppliers for market share led to bribery as a strategy in this oligarchic textbook market. The research findings of Alexeev and Song, Diaby and Sylwester confirm that the number of competing publication firms in oligarchic textbook market was positively and significantly associated with bribe payments to corrupt officials.[12] Against this historical background and development of prewar textbook system, readers can easily understand why junior high school textbook

---

[11] On this see Nishihara (2017, p. 8, pp. 14–15).

[12] On this see Alexeev and Song (2013); also see Diaby and Sylwester (2015).

market instead of elementary school textbook was the scene of bribery in this *Taishinin* judgement.

6.1.4 Penal Code and Hospitality

The prewar Penal Code did not stipulate what reasonable value, minimum fiscal value or threshold to legally "qualify" as a gift, hospitality or culinary entertainment statutorily. For gifts, there is an obligation to give, an obligation to receive and an obligation to reciprocate in Japan. Gift may also be a sign of respect, generosity, friendliness and reciprocity to repay debt of *on* (favour) to anyone the giver is indebted. Exchanging gifts is not only a formality, but also a kind of lively social life (Seigle 2016, pp. 26–27). It can easily become a cover for bribe. However, hospitality and culinary entertainment are not physical but the provision of entertainment, food and/or drink for consumption can foster business relationships and goodwill. In Japan, entertainment connected with geisha performance may also be provided simultaneously together with banquet. The practice of offering a banquet as a bribe has been a historically subtle and cultural aspect in the Japanese context of corruption.

Banquet bribe is subtle and cultural with a long Japanese history of corruption. During the Muromachi period, banquet entertainment was an act that symbolized a profound gesture of hospitality and respect. Money was presented to the shogunate on such special celebrations occasions as *reisen*. The financial compensation provided in exchange for the act of extending an invitation to the other party to attend the banquet celebration. It was a common Japanese hospitality to invite the other party to a banquet, and the money given in exchange for inviting the other party to the banquet was also called *shukoryo. Reisen, shukoryo* and bribes easily became practically indistinguishable. Culinary entertainment may or may not constitute a corrupt advantage as *quid quo pro.* An abstract benchmark to gauge the possibility of corruptibility in a culinary entertainment is whether it goes beyond social etiquette and has defilement of work. The pronunciation of *oshoku* means corruption and implies *shoku o yogosu* (defilement of work),[13] but same pronunciation can also refer food (お食). The kanji 食 is a combination of人 (*hito*, person) and 良 (*yoi*, good). In linguistic discourse, food is intended by Japanese to make a person better, not for banquet bribe.

6.2 Juridical Facts in *Taishinin* Judgement

There were two bribees in this case, who were *kyōyu* (teacher) and *kyōtō* (principle or vice principle) in two junior high schools in Fukuoka. Shimizu Masanori was a teacher in Shūyūkan Junior High School, which is today's Fukuoka Prefectural

[13] On this see Tanaka (1994).

Shūyūkan High School. The history of this famous school can be traced to the clan family under Kuroda Nagamasa (1656–1623), who was the first lord in this clan domain with emphasis on education.[14] The second bribee Ito Tsurumatsu was the vice-principal of *Chikushi-chūgakkō* (Chikushi Junior High School), which is a Buddhist legal entity of its own education system from kindergarten to graduate school now in Fukuoka Prefecture. In 1907, it was founded as a private junior high school for girls.[15] The abbreviated term *Chikushi-chūgakkō* was used in *Taishinin* judgement.

Taishinin judgement gives no hint that two junior high schools had either systemic or institutional corruption of other teachers' involvement. This case should thus be regarded as sporadic petty corruption case. According to this *Taishinin* judgement, both Ito and Shimizu doubled up the post of *kyōmu-buchō* (or *kyōmu shunin,* section head for education affairs), but they had vague job description of *issai-shokumu-bunshō* (co-handling all divisions of official duties). As *kyōyu* and *kyōtō*, Shimizu and Ito used to take their school principal's verbal instruction for duties, including the power to designate bookstores for their students' textbook suppliers and the appropriation of textbook quotas for each supplier. In respect of it, two of them accepted the bribery of *shushoku-no-kyōen* (luxury feasts) from Muroi, Yamamoto and Higuchi with *han'i keizoku* (continuous criminal intent). Two bribees were convicted of acceptance of bribe under Article 198(1) of the Penal Code.

The two bribers, Muroi Muneo and Yamamoto Yoshita were the director and branch manager of *Kinseidō* bookstore in Fukuoka, respectively. Another appellant Higuchi Jinzaburō was responsible for marketing section of the bookstore *Sekibunkanshoten*. All three of them were convicted of giving bribe under Article 197 (1) of the Penal Code.

For a total of four times from 19 January 1929 to 5 February 1930, at a restaurant in Fukuoka, Muroi of *Kinseidō* treated Shimizu and Ito meals of a total value of 70 *yen* 38 *zen* for each one. On 3 January 1930, at another restaurant, he treated each of them meal of 12 *yen* 46 *zen.* Within a period of eleven months from 9 March 1929 to 2 February 1930, he hosted meal to Ito for five times, amounting to a total of 64 *yen* 64 *zen.* Between 3 April 1929 and 18 May 1929, he provided two meals of the total amount of 31 *yen* 67 *zen* to Shimizu.

Through his staff Yamamoto Yoshita to act on behalf of him, Muroi provided meal to bribee teachers Shimizu and Ito on 19 March 1929. The value was 18 *yen* 46 *zen* for each. On 9 February, 19 April 1929 and 11 January 1930, Yamamoto treated Ito three meals of a total amount of 41 *yen* 98 *zen.* From 11 February 1929 to 9 January 1930, he also treated Shimizu meals for a total of eight times, amounting to 104 *yen* 48 *zen.*

The appellant briber Higuchi Jinzaburō of *Sekibunkanshoten* provided food entertainment to Shimizu for a total of 30 *yen* 98 *zen* by three times on 7 January 1928, 11 January 1929 and 15 January 1930. Between 26 January 1928 and 11 February 1929, he entertained Ito four meals totalling 70 *yen* 28 *zen.* On 30 January 1929, 23

[14] On Kuroda family's scholarship enterprise see Ogawara (2017).

[15] On *Chikushi-chūgakkō*'s history see Kawamura (2011).

April 1929 and 25 January 1930, he provided Shimizu and Ito meals amounting to 25 *yen* 93 *zen* for each.

6.3 Appeal Grounds of the Bribers and Bribees

6.3.1 Hostile Witness Statements Against Appeal Ground

The appeal lodged by the legal representatives of the two accused bribe recipients and three accused bribe givers centred on *shokumugongen* (scope of statutory power in official duty). The two bribee teachers Shimizu and Ito asserted that they lacked the statutory authority to potentially compromise the interests of publication firms. The conviction of the Junior Courts was predicated exclusively on misinterpretations of the school principal's verbal statements, rather than on concrete corroboration of these statements with legal and material evidence. Two individuals did not deny their receipt of culinary entertainments. However, they were not officially tasked with the responsibility of determining the designation of student textbooks or establishing the requisite textbook quota for bookstores. Based on Article 4 of *Shokuin-kōritsu-gakkō-shokuinsei* (Regulations for Public School System), the regional government official only empowered to order school principals to handle school affairs and staff supervision. The two bribees could neither be ordered nor delegated statutory power for textbook designation under this system.

Against this appeal ground of two bribees, two school principals gave hostile witness statements. Shirasaka Eihoko, the principal of Shūyūkan Junior High School, confirmed that he was authorized by the Article 4 for school administration. As per Regulation number 33 of *Fukuokaken chūgakkōsoku* (Regulations for Junior High School of Fukuoka Prefecture), *kyōmu-buchō* or *kyōmu shunin* was appointed to have school administration as *shokumugongen* under Article 6 of *bunshō-kitei* (Regulations for Division of Duties). This Article 6 empowered him as principal to designate textbooks for assurance of uniformity of teaching material. The end of Article 6 vaguely mentioned "other performance of school affairs to be ordered by principal" but the nature and definition for "other performance" were unspecified.

Ikuta Totaro, the Principal of Chikushi Junior High School, gave similar hostile witness statement that the appointment of Ito as *kyōmu-shunin* meant empowerment to Ito for comprehensively handling all affairs relevant to *kyōmu*. Ikuta added hostile witness statement against Ito that the scope of official duty apparently covered designation of textbook supplier and apportionment of quota for teaching convenience of uniformity.

6.3.2 Being Followers of Procedure Without Power

Facing two principals' hostile witness statements, appellants' lawyer argued that as per the appellants' statements, anyone could follow procedure for performing such duty in this legal dispute. The *toriatsukai-furi* (handling behaviour) in designation was a matter of *keishiki-tetsudzuki* (procedural formality) under *junjo-tetsudzuki* (orderly procedure or sequence). Teachers merely followed procedures without any guilty intention. Two principals had freedom to give witness statements, but such statements were subject to Taishinin's jurisdiction-specific insights.

Appellants reiterated that even if court ignored the nonavailability of information as evidence for corroboration with appeal ground, *Taishinin* had to consider availability of statutory provision to confirm constituent element. Designation of textbook quota for bookstore could not be found in any statutory provision. Objectively speaking, such legislation was in fact non-existent. Without citation of statutory provision, it was merely personal opinion and meaningless evidence instead of proof for official duty statutorily. Conviction or criminality should be clearly based on *saishoho-jō-meihaku* (clarity in evidence law). The current statutes, decree and the legal interpretation for case facts needed further *shokumuchōsa* (investigation for or clarification on duty). This clarification process of *Taishinin* should not be unduly influenced by two principals' hostile witness statements which were essentially personal opinions of no probative value. The crucial factor was whether the quota and designation of bookstore for textbook supply belonged to the statutory official duty of Shimizu and Ito. Without statutory provision, junior courts' convictions of them on the basis of two principals' statements were illegal and infringements against *saishoho* (law of evidence).

Furthermore, the act itself will not make a person guilty unless the intent and until is also guilty simultaneously. Appellants thus tried to exculpate their guilty intention on the ground that teachers were simply followers of procedural formalities for designation of textbook supplier and quota setting. They took no initiative to do so. Two appellants accused junior courts' negligence to have statutory citation to corroborate bribee teachers' acts with two principals' statements.

6.3.3 Analysis of Appeal Grounds

The appellants identified a lack of substantiation for the confirmation of constituent element in the context of official duties. The aforementioned elements served to reinforce the emphasis placed by two appellants' legal counsel on the issue of wrongful convictions in junior courts, which were solely based on the personal opinions of two principals. In the absence of any constituent element of official duty, the convictions in this case were deemed unconstitutional due to the violation of *nullum crimen sine lege*, a principle articulated in Article 23 of the Meiji Constitution. This constitutional provision stipulated that no Japanese subject shall be subjected to arrest, detention, trial or punishment without the presence of a law that explicitly authorizes such action. In the context of the Japanese state political system, the populace was granted rights and privileges exclusively as subjects of the Emperor. These rights were bestowed upon them by the "will of the Emperor" to promulgate statutes (George 1990, pp. 72–73). Neither Diet nor the Emperor had promulgated any law that covered two teachers' acts in this case as official duties. The question of the statutory authority for conviction remained unresolved.

6.4 *Taishinin*'s Moralistic Ground for Refusal of Appeal

Taishinin held that the main official duties of public junior high school teachers related to students' education, and school principals had power to manage teachers. The proper way to handle students' textbook demand was closely relevant to education. From the junior courts' judgements, it was easy to *suichi* (infer) whether they had additionally taken principals' delegation of powers for such duty. It was not a matter of *tanjun* (pure or mere) *hōreikaishaku* (statutory interpretation) but de facto of what had happened. According to two principals' hostile witness statements, two appellants' official duties were de facto under delegation. Textbook order and designation of bookstore were thus belonging to the official duty of Shimizu and Ito. Appellants were groundless to argue illegality of junior courts' convictions.

Taishinin reiterated that the junior courts had no judicial error leading to wrongful conviction. It rationalized the correctness of conviction by *higai-hōeki* (victimized legal interest) in corruption offence. As the culinary entertainments related to the scope of their official duty, convicting these five appellants of the bribery offences was appropriate. The *hōeki* (legal interest) of the bribery offence was to ensure the proper *kōsei-shikkō* (fair execution or performance) of civil servants' duty and the *kikensei* (potential danger) to victimize it. *Hōeki* also existed in civil servants' *jijitsujō* (de facto) manipulation and *toriatsukai* (operation). The nature of proper execution of official duty was a matter of *seishitsukankei* (relationship with nature) in the power of official duty which should be considered in terms of *jissainaiyō* (actual content of practice) of official duty. The *jissainaiyō* in this case covered selection of textbooks, amount of price and payment for it, total number of textbook copies involved and necessity of time management for books purchased.

The aforesaid was the victimized legal interest of bribery offence in this case. In *hōri* (jurisprudence or legal doctrine), the potential danger to the scope of official duty could be regarded as victimized legal interest in bribery. To the victimized *hōeki* in this education corruption case, it was the *shitei waritou* (designated apportionment or quota) which belonged to two teachers' official duty.

Taishinin ruled that two teachers had de facto power of official duty. In case all these were all along *jūrai-jissai-toriatsukai* (de facto substantially handling) of two bribee teachers, two of them had de facto power for it as official duty could be substantiated. A considerable factor was whether the offer and acceptance of culinary entertainment constituted *rieki-juju* (offer and acceptance of interest) inflicting actual harm on proper execution of their official duties or constitute *kikensei* (potential danger). Shimizu and Ito had *yochi* (room or discretion) to *shinshaku* (determine) all these by their *tegokoro* (discretion) to designate bookstore. In case *kyōmu-shunin* had *hanto-rieki-no-juju* (act of offer and acceptance of interest while the process was in progress and incomplete), would it be impossible to *sayū* (exert influence)? *Taishinin* reiterated that this potential danger was not *sōzō* (imagination).

Taishinin then had attitudinal model of judicial behaviour to infer criminality objectively. Though textbooks had been examined by the Minister of Education for a standardized price, would the market leader's pricing policy be unfair to consumers after acquisition of a large market share? *Taishinin*'s third consideration was the quantity of textbook copies to be ordered by Shimizu and Ito. In the judgement, *Taishinin* cast doubt on whether the giving and accepting interest would help briber bookstores sell more copies than the original number of copies demanded by students at the beginning?

On the basis of the aforesaid three considerations, *Taishinin* believed that the impacts of appellants' discretion to determine textbook supply existed. *Taishinin*'s fourth consideration was provision of marketing and fiscal advantages to bookstores. Students' purchase in cash quickened cash flow of bookstores. Students' parents and siblings were considered better consumption power. In bookstores, they might buy textbooks on students' behalf and do shopping for stationery and other necessities at the beginning of a new semester. In the textbook supply chain, late delivery, fire, burglary or other uncertainties might happen to delay publication and supply. *Taishinin* thus took early acquisition of textbook order and correct quota as the bookstores' self-evident *kyōsōteki-dai-mokuteki* (main objective of competition) in a textbook market under fierce competition.

Taishinin commented that bookstore owner's market management was different from that of the wholesaler and publisher. Actual allotment of quota was significant for time management of cash flow. In respect of the variety, quality, contents, pricing, quantity, time of availability of textbook, neither law nor executive order was available for formal legal control. Grey area for two teachers' exercise of discretionary power did exist. *Taishinin* clearly wrote: "In the perspective of statutory application or the act of giving and receipt of interests, the scope of official duty power should absolutely give no room for such discretion. Corruption was the *higai-hōeki* of official duty".[16]

Taishinin's main refusal ground of breach of social trust was a landmark in its judicial behaviour of attitudinal model. *Taishinin* expressed its moralistic standpoint very clearly in terms of Japanese cultural value that fair execution of official duty should be ensured for the maintenance of *shakai-shinrai* (social trust) in the impartiality of civil servants' execution of it. As mentioned in junior courts' judgements, the two bribee teachers had culinary entertainment from three briber appellants in relation to their official duties. Even no harm had been inflicted on all students'

[16] The original text in the judgement: 法令上實際上或るの利益の授受に依り絕對に左右斟酌を為すべき餘地なきことを職務權限なりとするは瀆職罪に於ける被害法益の存せさる職務權限なりと歸する。

acquisition of textbooks at a fair price according to the scheduled time management, damage had been inflicted on the social trust in the impartiality of two junior high school teachers' official duty performance and the *higai-hōeki*.[17]

6.5 Analysis of *Taishinin*'s Judicial Behaviour

Taishinin confirmed two teachers' constituent element of official duty by expansive legal reasoning based on relevance to education. According to jurisprudential logic in it, any teacher's act of relevance to the umbrella term "education" could become official duty, of which the judicial behaviour is very similar to "public peace and order" in the police corruption cases in Chaps. 7 and 8 of this book. With all-the-circumstances consideration to assess competitive advantages of bookstores secured by banquet bribe, teachers' acts in education sector were rationalized from *jijitsujō* (de facto) official duty to become *de jure* official duty. *Jijitsujō* (de facto) means an act in reality or in fact which is not enumerated by legislation. The existence of de facto power delegated from principals for education means that the acceptance of its existence was a matter of fact. Though two teachers' de facto power was not a matter of statutory authorization, Taishinin ruled it as *de jure* that was officially recognized by law through Taishinin's court ruling. In view of the *quid pro quo* of banquet bribe was based on *Taishinin*'s moralistic inference of corroboration with evidence, it was more balance of probabilities than proof beyond reasonable doubt.

The moralistic label of breach of social trust (*shakai-shinrai*) was a serious immorality in Japan but not a criminal offence. People's beliefs, values, norms and emotions can be intertwined to determine the extent of trust in a particular case (Fetchenhauer, et al. 2017, p. 139–140). *Taishinin* criminalized it by victimized legal interest (*higai-hōeki*) of the Penal Code. It means the whole Japanese society was monitoring the damage to social solidarity caused by such breach. Such monitor is essential to the checks on deviance of government officials (Misztal 1998, p. 198). *Taishinin*'s judicial behaviour in this education sector corruption case is analysed as follows.

To *Taishinin*, competition in textbook market was like law of the jungle. *Taishinin* firmly supported the appropriateness of junior courts' convictions with "well-founded culpability of bribery". As a matter of objective fact, acquisition of unfair competitive advantages might happen through banquet bribe. Fairness or unfairness was a question depending on the potential danger posed to harm official duty of civil servants as *higai-hōeki*. *Taishinin* adopted "all-the-circumstances" expansive legal reasoning to determine that justice or injustice was a relative objective fact depending on whether

---

[17] The original text in the judgement: 法が收賄罪を處罰する所以は公務員の職務執行の公正を保持せんとするに止らず職務の公正に對する社會の信頼をも確保せんとするに在れは被告人政則及鶴松が原判示の如ぐ其の職務に関し他の被告人等より賄賂を收受したるに於ては縱令之が為に各生徒が正當の代價を以て一定の日時迄に所要の教科書を整ふるを得るとに何等の障害を與へさりしとするも中學教務主任の職務上の公正に對し社會の信頼を傷ふこと多大にして所論の如ぐ何等の被害法益なきものと謂ふへがらず。

bookstores' competitive advantages existed, including certainty of textbook types, price, payment, quantity, time management and marketing stationery.

Taishinin assumed all these were *quid pro quo* hidden in culinary entertainments. Though the assumptions of *Taishinin* were speculative in view of no corroboration with evidence, it was equitable *dōri* in *Taishinin*'s legal reasoning to reasonably infer market competition and bribers' intention to offer food entertainment for thirty-four times within two years. *Taishinin*'s judicial behaviour in legal reasoning was attitudinally like a "social Darwinist" with the law of the jungle in its legal mindset. *Taishinin* wrote that one bookstore's competitive advantage was to the disadvantage of another market competitor. *Taishinin* linked the acquisition of such advantage with the proper or improper execution of a civil servant's official duty. The essence of the relationship between guilty intention of bookstore and civil servants' official duty was thereby concretized.

Taishinin additionally considered whether potential danger to victimize *hōeki* was existing and its relationship with official duty performance. *Taishinin* accordingly reinforced its confirmation of teachers' official duty. *Taishinin*'s totality consideration for refusal of appeal substantiated its claim in its judgement that it had no judicial error in junior courts' identification of material facts.

6.5.1 Judicial Behaviour of Inference

This is a case of petty corruption under the impact of market competition. The use of the term *suichi* (inference) evinces *Taishinin* judicial behaviour of expansive legal reasoning for judicial decision-making, which is based upon the phrase "relevance to education" to determine and rationalize the appropriate outcome of statutory duty in this specific court case. Terms or phrases are usually taken from statutes or a precedent case for applicability to specific case facts (Zeleznikow and Hunter 1995, pp. 142–144). Based on two principals' hostile witness statements of no corroboration with material evidence, *Taishinin* further inferred "competitive advantages" of bookstores and its relation with the umbrella term "official duty" to criminalize hosted meals as "banquet bribe". Taishinin's attitudinal model of judicial behaviour was reflected by its ruling of "breach of social trust" substantiated by two teachers' de facto exercise of discretionary power delegated from principals. In order to rationalize *Taishinin*'s decision on refusal of appeals, *Taishinin* additionally applied *higai-hōeki* for culpability. In the perspective of legal linguistics, *Taishinin*'s negative attitudinal model of judicial behaviour was so obvious that the term *shushoku-no-kyōen* (luxury feasts) was used to denote food entertainment in this case. This term was not for normal *bonafide* hospitality. Bookstore staffs likely had corrupt *quid pro quo* to gain competitive advantages by banquet bribe. Without evidence for corroboration, the culpability and illegality were like legal standard of balance of probabilities in civil law instead of beyond reasonable doubt in criminal law. *Taishinin*'s judicial behaviour in this landmark ruling is basically like strict liability.

6.5.2 Label of Shushoku-No-Kyōen and Standard of Proof

Language discourse henceforth helps gauge the state of consciousness behind *Taishinin*'s judicial behaviour. *Taishinin* did not mention its standard for its label of *shushoku-no-kyōen* to the food entertainments. It was true that two teachers accepted culinary entertainments but there was possibility of hospitality out of friendship or a matter of social gathering. However, whether it was luxury was subject to argument if we compare the price of meal with commodity price.

The 34-time culinary entertainments with total value of 471 *yen* 26 *zen* took place over a longtime span between February 1928 and February 1930. The frequency was averagely 1.4 times per month. The average amount for meal was only 13.85 *yen* on each occasion, which was far cheaper than 22 yen for ten eggs in 1931. *Taishinin* usage of *shushoku* (wine and food) with the additional label of *kyōen* (luxury feasts) as aggravating factor was subject to argument. In *Taishinin* judgement, the term *shushoku-no-kyōen* (luxury feasts of wine and food) was repeatedly used. We have to take note that deflation started in the late 1920s in Japan and lasted until the recovery period after 1932 (Hatase 2002, p. 144). To make the worse, global economic depression aggravated the two-year Showa Depression of 1930–31.[18] The price of ten eggs was 22 *yen* but the average monthly salary of a male teacher was surprisingly low at 75 *yen* in 1931 *vis-a-vis* 86 *yen* in 1926. In the same year, the tuition fee of Keio University was 140 *yen* (Yamamoto 2013, p. 96). The total food entertainment amount of *471* yen 26 *zen* within two years was not low, but the average meal only costed 13.85 for each. Whether the amount of 13.85 *yen* was per head or the total amount of an appellant and one bookstore staff on each occasion was not mentioned in the judgement.

In the toolkit of judicial behaviour studies, linguistic discourse is a common tool. In cultural linguistics, the term *kyōen* was different from another Japanese term *enseki* (banquet) for ordinary banquet. *Dairishiki* was a book about traditional Japanese court rituals written in 833. The conceptual origin of the term *kyōen* can be traced from it. *Kyōen* was the Emperor's most luxury feast in social ritual to treat his subordinates.[19] It reflects *Taishinin*'s attitudinal mode of judicial behaviour of moralistic contempt against teachers' act of having accepted banquet bribe. The price of banquet was not that significant. The crucial consideration was the act of acceptance. Moreover, whether the two bribee teachers misinterpreted the hosted meals as normal social gathering should not be discarded in view of the commodity price mentioned before. Two teachers' appeals based on *dōki-koto-ji-naki* (no criminal intention) was neither unreasonable nor groundless. In addition to attitudinal model, *Taishinin* also adopted judicial behaviour of strict liability model. Guilty intention was out of consideration.

Appellants used the term *shinshō* to describe the judicial behaviour of court's inference based on two principals' statements. *Shinshō* refers to legal principle of *jiyū-shinshō-shugi*, which means libertarianism of free evaluation of evidence or

[18] On this see Shizume (2009).

[19] On more details of "*kyōen*"see Kurabayashi (1965).

the principle of judge's freedom of discretion as to the probative value of evidence and its evidentiality to prove. It implies judges' cognitive consistency or state of consciousness as to the existence or non-existence of a fact (Nishidai 2010, pp. 11–12). Attitudinal model of judicial behaviour with referral to morality belongs to this kind.

In other words, it empowers judge's freedom of judicial behaviour. *Shinshō* denotes subjective judicial behaviour of perceptions and convictions pending to be proven in litigation. *Jiyū-shinshō-shugi* in Japan was a legal transplant from the Germanic law term *Grundsatz der freien Beweiswürdigung* of the meaning of free weighing of evidence. This is in contrast to *hōtei-shōko-shugi* (doctrine of statutory evidence) which originates from Germanic *Prinzip der gesetzlichen Beweisregeln* for stipulation of the need of admissibility of evidence or the evaluation of probative strength by law. It thereby imposes evidential constraints on judges' freedom of legal reasoning. Case facts and defendant's culpability in criminal case should be proven firm authenticity of truth beyond reasonable doubt.[20]

For *muzai-suitei-hōri* (presumption of innocence) and legal justice, a conviction should not be solely based on the testimony or statement, unless corroborating evidence is provided. *Jiyū-shinshō-shugi* is currently a judicial behaviour statutorily empowered by Article 247 of the Civil Procedure Code. It states that in reaching a judgement on civil litigation, the court decides whether to find allegations of fact to be true based on its freedom of personal conviction, in light of the entire oral arguments and the results of the examination of evidence. This standard is lower than "proof beyond reasonable doubt" in criminal litigation. Appellants' use of the term *shinshō* connoted that court freely interpreted statements as evidence for fact-finding and subsequent conviction (Nishidai 2013, p. 61).

In this case, the demarcations of de facto power of official duty and the competitive advantages to bookstores were solely depending on *Taishinin*'s inference based on two principals' statements and the number of meals. *Suichi* (infer) was written in this *Taishinin* judgement but evidence of verifiability and observability for the concrete proof of *quid pro quo* had not been mentioned. Unsubstantiated information can mislead legal reasoning.[21] Without production of evidence for corroboration with statements, appellants could not exercise their *shōkoshirabe-seikyūken* (right to request evidence) for self-defence as a legal right. If the prosecutor's evidence was available, they might ask for the right of application for examination of evidence. These procedural justice concepts were transplanted from the Germanic counterpart of *Beweisermittlungsrecht* (Kumon 2006, pp. 43–45).

[20] On this see Fujimoto (2016, p. 86); also see Masuda (1992, pp. 5–7).

[21] See Florou (2019, p. 423, pp. 440–441).

6.5.3 *Hōeki as "Japanese Body in the Germanic Jacket" of Rechtsgut*

The terms *higai-hōeki* and *hōeki* were written by *Taishinin* judges in this judgement, which stated social trust was the main legal interest to be protected. In original Germanic legal term, *hōeki* is *Rechtsgut* or *Rechtsgutslehre,* which is the doctrine of legal protection or doctrine of protected legal interests. For legal interest, criminal law not only protects such personal legal interest as life and liberty, but also communal legal interest. Collective security is a common type. Criminal law thereby has legitimacy for law binding obedience and ultimate effectiveness of enforcement. The criteria for the determination of legal interest as social good to be protected should be clear. If not, it has no legitimacy. *Taishinin* therefore had to ponder on what constituted legal interest in this banquet bribery case, or what a statute was codified for protection of rationalization for and legitimacy of verdict (Stuckenberg 2013, p. 35–37). The legal reasoning of this kind combines clarification on legislative intent with statutory interpretation of statutory terms under textualism, intentionalism from statutory text and legislative history, or purposivism to interpret statutes at the service of social good (Healy 1999, pp. 232–235).

It is noteworthy that *Taishinin*'s attitudinal judicial behaviour moralistically ruled "breach of social trust" as victimized legal interest. It then became one of the most important rulings in Japanese legal culture. If criminal law cannot protect legal interest, it should be rescinded or amended as per the opinions of Japanese legal scholars. Criminal law should be codified to help citizens understand different types of legal interests which may be subject to victimization, because criminal law is for the protection against it (Oda 2018, pp. 2–5). Broadly speaking, protection of legal interest is commonly about the maintenance of ethical behaviour and social order. An example is control of drug crime for national health under *jinkakuteki-hōeki-ron* (theory of personal legal interests) in Japanese legal studies. In interwar years, it extended to *kokka-hōshi* (sacrifice and service for state) in state polity.[22]

Page 421 of this *Taishinin* judgement stated that the *hōeki* of bribery offence was assurance of impartiality in civil servants' proper performance of official duty and prevention against the possibility of infringement against it. For this strategic goal of hybridity with judicial behaviour in attitudinal model, it was correct to criminalize appellants for social deterrence. The question was whether this judicial behaviour of *Taishinin* was too strict of no suitability to equitable *dōri* in this case of ordinary meal entertainment. In 1931, the average monthly expense of a salaryman and worker was 82.46 yen and 73.08 yen respectively (Kase 2015, p. 58). As abovementioned, a 13.85yen meal might be a bit high but not excessively luxury meal *shushoku-no-kyōen. Prima facie*, teacher's acceptance of ordinary meal from a stakeholder in education sector is a matter of *rieki-sōhan* (role conflict or conflict of interest) for internal disciplinary enquiries. It should be correct to say that *Taishinin*'s attitudinal judicial behaviour sets a very high standard to ensure the goal of social trust in

[22] See Kamon (2007, p. 36, pp. 38–39), Kim (2007, p. 31), Kawabata (1998, p. 189).

government's bureaucrats and hegemony. *Rieki-sōhan* is the act that benefits one party and detriment to another party, but issue of interest conflict arises between parties with a preexisting relationship or role.

Rieki-sōhan had been a common concept in Meiji civil law but not criminalized in Penal Code. In prewar Japanese law, *rieki-sōhan* can be found in Article of 57, 826 and 851 of *Minpō* (Civil Code, Law number 89 codified in 1896), Article of 75, 265 and 309 of *Shōhō* (Commercial Code, Law No. 48 of 1907), Article 30 of *Yūgengaishahō* (Limited Company Law, Law No. 74 of 1938) and Article 89 of *Tanpo-fushasaishin-takuhō* (Secured Bond Trust Law, Law No. 52 of 1903). The two junior high schools in this *Taishinin* case apparently did not have the consciousness of *rieki-sōhan*. Otherwise, it should have been mentioned in the judgement. In today's education sector, some Japanese education institutions, such as Tohoku University, even have special committees to review and screen management practices to prevent *rieki-sōhan*.[23]

6.6 Implications of *Taishinin*'s Judicial Behaviour in This Case

6.6.1 Strategic Goal for Social Education

An act can be evaluated from a legal standpoint in either a subjective or objective perspective. In this case, the pivotal element pertained to the absence of a sense of conflict of interest among the teachers who had been accepting culinary entertainments for a prolonged duration. It is conceivable that even the interest of one *zen* in prewar Japan could be criminalized as a bribery offence under the rubric of breach of social trust. In the event that *Taishinin*'s judicial behaviour could rationalize its ruling according to circumstantial evidence, this would be a possibility. In this context, *Taishinin*'s judicial behaviour can be characterized as the utilization of two teachers' minor mistake of continuous greed to deter society and ensure the establishment of social trust in the impartiality of civil servants' execution of their official duties. This approach was undertaken to safeguard legal interests and thereby facilitated hegemonic education and governance. According to the provisions outlined in the prewar Penal Code, the judicial behaviour of *Taishinin* was permitted to proceed for this strategic goal without the imposition of a minimum bribery threshold.

The subjective nature of *Taishinin*'s hybrid attitudinal model and strict liability model of judicial behaviour in this case is a subject of debate. The following is a discussion of the contributions of the influential Japanese jurist Ono Seiichirō. The term *kōseiyōkenron* is a Japanese term that is often translated as "constituent element theory". From an objective standpoint, Taishinin's judicial decision should

[23] See Tohoku University Intellectual Property Office for Research Promotion (2005, pp. 11–13).

be dismissed for subjectivism. The question of whether *Taishinin*'s attitudinal application of social trust as national morality necessitates the objective consideration of the offender's personality, as proposed by Ono's theory of justice, remains a subject of scholarly discourse. In Ono's objectivism, two teachers might have good integrity and accepted such culinary entertainments as a matter of courtesy or social ritual. In comparison with Ono's legal theory, *Taishinin*'s judicial behaviour in this case was subjectivism in the sense of protecting the strategic goal of victimized legal interest.[24]

6.6.2 *Taishinin's Shakai Was State Polity*

In order to deter other similar unethical behaviour which might inflict damage on the hegemony of state polity, *Taishinin* criminalized banquet bribe by legal interest with the expression of the breach of *shakai-shinrai* (social trust). In this judgement, *Taishinin* twice mentioned the importance of *shakai-shinrai* as a determinant in legal interest. Nevertheless, one puzzle remains. What kind of society was represented by *Taishinin* to punish two teachers for breach of their trust? Ethnocentrism to interpret *Taishinin*'s linguistic term *shakai* (society) with the Western concept of civil society can be misleading.

Shakai in Japanese language was not society in the Western sense, but a place where people from different regions gathered together for religious ceremony of *tochi-no-kami* (land God) (Naitō 1893, p. 972.). The conceptual framework of society in Japan is resultant from a long evolutionary process under Buddhism. Common social terms of Buddhist origins are *hito-no-wa* (People's close connecting to each other), *seken* (the world), *ningen-kai* (world of humans), *jinkai* (human world), *hito-no-yo* (human world), *ukiyo* (fleeting world), *shaba* (corrupt world), *shigan* (This bank "in this world"), *kōko* (all corners of the secular world) and *tenka* (world) (Kōra 2011, pp. 42–43). *Hito-no-wa* is from "*hito no wa ga hito no wa ni* (a circle of people becomes a harmony of people)" of *Jōdoshū* (Jōdo sect). The term *ukiyo* is found in *Ise Monogatari* written in the Heian period, but the meaning is not today's society in the Western sociology sense.

During Tokugawa bakufu, Kaibara Ekiken wrote *Wazokudōjikun* in 1710, which was the first textbook designed for early child education in order to socialize them into Japanese society. Scrutiny of this book revealed nothing about *shakai* in Western sense. The nearest term was *seken* but it treated villages as society (Kōno 2015, p. 40). In 1852, Fukuzawa Yukichi introduced the Western society in his book *Political Economy, for Use in Schools, and for Private Instruction,* which was published by William and Robert Chambers in London and Edinburgh. Tsuda Mamichi, enlightenment thinker in early Meiji era, used a very Confucianist term *aiseiyō-no-michi*

[24] See Yada (2015, p. 123, pp. 128–130).

for description of European division of labour or profession in Western society,[25] instead of the term *shakai* of two *kanji*.

The most noteworthy is *yochishiryaku*, which was an official geography textbook of four volumes written by Uchida Masao for the Ministry of Education. The content of volume one of it was Japanized for state polity by association of Emperor *Jinmu* with unbroken imperial line. Religious sects were at the service of Emperor's rule in Japanese society (Uchida 1870, pp. 66–67). In Meiji era, the term *shakai-kyōiku* (social education) was invented in *kanji* to express the means to manipulate *shakai* for a stable social relation in state polity.[26]

In *Nihon-kyōiku-saku* (Japanese Education Policy) and *Nihon-kyōiku-ron* (Japanese Education Theory) edited by Mori Arinori from 1874 to 1875, the Western concept of society, community and public were translated by various overlapping terms including *shakai*, *zen-shakai* (whole society), *kuni* (state), *shakai-gundō* (social group), *kōritsu* (public) (Hisaki 1991, pp. 4–5). It was consistent with the concept of publicness of society that a society was characterized by ties of reciprocity and mutuality, voluntary association and exchange relationships, while rational behaviours predominate.[27] The introduction of Japanese terms of publicness does not mean that Japanese society is a society in Western sense.

In the legal perspective of the Meiji Constitution, this publicness of society took place in a society headed by the Emperor. The elements of state polity penetrated into the Japanese term *shakai* and converted the aforesaid Buddhist implications of society. In *Nihon-kyōiku-rei* (Japanese Education Decree) dated 14 May 1878, education was regarded as a means to enhance *shakai-keishō* (social prosperity) for state. *Nihon-kyōiku-rei* was issued to enhance Japanese *shakai* to be an Imperial Japanese Empire headed by Emperor above *bankoku* (all countries) in the universe..[28] *Shakai* in *Taishinin*'s attitudinal judicial behaviour implied state polity, which was neither a civil society nor today's concept of fair society.[29]

6.6.3 Breach of State Polity's Trust in Teacher

While prewar Japanese society was state polity instead of a society in Western sense, *Taishinin*'s ruling of breach of social trust means breach of state polity's trust in two teachers' conduct and discipline. The notion of *shakai-shinrai* (social trust) in the judgement refers to a contributing factor to social cohesion as organic solidarity. The ongoing existence of a society is contingent upon the presence of cooperation and consensus among its members concerning established values and customary

[25] On this see Kimura (2013, pp. 267–283).

[26] On this see Satō (2009, pp. 129–138).

[27] On this see Turner (2006, p. 592; also see Luhmann 2012, p. 40).

[28] See Watanabe (2010, pp. 260–270).

[29] The original text in Nihon Kyōikurei: 教育ノ途漸ク闢ケ奎文ノ景象ヲ社会二現シシハ固ヨリ気運ノ然ラシムル所ト雖モ。

practices.[30] The implications of *shinrai* in *shakai-shinrai* as an aggravating factor for culpability extend beyond the scope of the English term "trust". The violation of trust is considered to be ethically reprehensible; however, *Taishinin* established a legal framework that explicitly sanctioned such actions by court ruling.

The translation of *shinrai* as "trust" in English only provides half of the meaning. In Japanese, *shinrai* is not a single concept but a combination of two concepts. The act of *shin* (trust or believe) is followed by another act of *rai* (reliance). *Shin* is an independent act before the act of *rai*. Once *shin* is established, *rai* can be acted on it without reservation. In this Japanese literal sense, *rai* is reliance with neither disbelief nor hint of suspicion. As revealed in Chap. 3, one of the functions to impose top-down anti-corruption law in the history of Japan was to ensure official's conduct and discipline under upper social hierarchy's *shin* for the subsequent *rai*. Japanese moralistic emphasis on *shin* has a long tradition of informal social control function. *Taishinin* simply integrated it into case law.

Unlike the history of British contract law which had been the most mature in common law jurisdiction, contract law had not been popular in prewar Japan. *Shinrai* functioned like unwritten moralistic law and reinforced as social fabric of social relations even after legal transplantation during the Meiji Restoration. *Nihonshoki* in 720 recorded that in April 604, the social expectation was that each person should behave *makoto* (honest trust) which was a behavioural standard of *kotowari* (righteousness).[31] In *Ujishūimonogatari* (Ujishūi Relic Story) written in the Kamakura era for collections of Buddhist narratives,[32] in Chap. 10, it mentioned the importance of moralistic virtue of "*makotoni tanomoshikute arishi minari* (to be really reliable and well dressed)" in Japanese society.[33] *Shinrai-kankei* (relationship based on trust) made traditional rural villages like a *kyōdōtai* (commune) of interdependence.[34]

Shinrai in Japanese social psychology is a complex of culture values and publicness in society for cooperation and coexistence (Kitayama 1999, pp. 60–65). Breach of social trust is accordingly damaging a social fabric. *Taishinin*'s judicial behaviour of attitudinal model is a reflection of it. In the macro perspective of society, trust, as a social fabric, enables individuals to take risks in dealing with others, solve problem by collective action, or behave in ways that seem different from standard definitions of self-interest (Levi 1998, pp. 77–78). It consists reasonable expectation on the part of large number of social groups' common interests. This expectation arises as a regular, honest and cooperative behaviour on the basis of commonly norm shared (Fukuyama 1995, p. 26). Trust in society is relevant to public perceptions of legitimacy, especial whether the public thinks law enforcement is just, fair, sensible and rooted in legal authority. These are keys to legal compliance (Kleinfeld and Dancig-Rosenberg 2022, p. 820). Social trust contributes to better predictability and

---

[30] See Giddens et al. (2019, p. 54, p. 72).

[31] The Original text in *Nihonshoki*: 信は是れ義の本なり事毎に信有るべし。

[32] On this see Kobayashi (1973).

[33] See Masamune (1929); The original text in *Ujishūimonogatari*: まことに頼もしくてありし身なり。

[34] See Yamagishi and Komiyama (1995, p. 11, p. 34, p. 37).

reliability of interactions, social cohesion through groupism relationship and collaboration through mutual respect and solidarity. Social consensus is instrumental to transform conflict to harmony.[35] *Taishinin*'s judicial behaviour of criminalization by "breach of social trust" is a reflection of important traditional Japanese social relations of *shinrai-kankei* (social relationship based on trust) in prewar society under state political system, in which the Emperor was at the tip of its vertical structure.

As an informal social control in Japan, the most common cultural values for evaluation of trust are *giri* and *ninjo*. Japanese cultural emphasis on social trust can be seen in the example of popular traditional Japanese ballad drama *jōruri*. In *Jitōtennō-utagunpō* (Emperor Jito's Song Military Law) of *jōruri* written by Chikamatsu Monzaemon in 1713, *giri* for loyalty and honesty to the Emperor was strongly glorified by "*tanomoshiku giri o haritaru azusayumi* (reliable *giri* is like a pushing a bow)".[36]*Giri* in *shinrai* is a hidden core value in voluntary act to comply with morality. It is subject to social pressure to conform and fulfil through shame culture (Nagano 2000, p. 58). *Giri* can be defined as a sense of collective responsibility and a sense of moral obligation, as well as a sense of empathy and compassion. Trust is among these factors.

In prewar Japan, a person who had breached *shinrai* in society was therefore regarded as detrimental to the harmony and unity in state polity under *giri* (Akatsuka 1971, p. 80). *Giri* thus had a hybrid sense of *masayoshi* (justice) and *dōgi* (moral righteousness) (Masaharu 1985, pp. 49–51). As a unity of cohesion, *kyōkan* (resonance) of a mutual trustworthiness among Japanese was formed under *giri* as an informal social control of moralistic binding force (Nakamura 1990, p. 28). *Giri* embodies moralistic burden of obligation or duty on the basis of trustworthiness with strong loyalty, personal trust, promise as something like "contractual obligation", against which the temptation of bribery makes a bribee to breach trust and hard to keep moralistic integrity of *giri* or *ninjo*. Japanese proverb of "*bushi wa kuwanedo kō yō eda* (even a samurai has no food, he pretends to have finished a meal by a toothpick in his mouth)" reflects the importance of integrity and dignity against temptation under unfavourable conditions (Tsuchimoto 2004, pp. 26–27).

The earliest record of *ninjo* can be traced back to *Shokunihonki*. It records as human feelings that in May 716 (*Reigi* 2), "*hōkon ninjo yayausu, ryō oso* (Now *ninjo* is a bit swallow. Buddha declines)".[37] Japanese sociologist Arugaki Zaemon straightforwardly classifies *giri* as public affairs in daily social relations life *vis-à-vis ninjo* within the scope of private affairs.[38] No single English noun is exactly equivalent to *giri* and *ninjo*. *Giri* and *ninjo* can integrate with traditional equitable *dori* in court's attitudinal judicial behaviour for Penal Code enforcement on a case-by-case basis.

---

[35] See Bradbury et al. (2013, p. 120, p. 122, p. 125).

[36] See Chikamatsu (1922, p. 325); The original text in *Jitō tennō utagun pō*: 頼もしく義理を張りたる梓弓。

[37] On this see National Diet Library 2011; The original text in *Shokunihonki:* 方今人情稍薄釈教陵遅。

[38] On this see Arugaki (1967).

Under the principal-agent theory, both school principals and teachers in prewar Japanese society had *shinrai* of being entrusted with power delegated by Emperor through Article 10 of the Meiji Constitution and various Imperial Decrees for education, instead of a private legal entity for business profitability. Teachers had been delegated official duty to advance national fortune of Japan (Mori 2004, p. 286). Teachers therefore had to display and set themselves for *chūjitsu-kōi* (loyalty and integrity in good faith). Social trust is a social capital for mutual linkage among citizens and enabling them to pursue agreed objectives more effectively and efficiently (Jasinski 2011, pp. 47–48). It involved collective moralistic values which could provide social cohesiveness (Uslaner 2002, p. 18). Ryūzaki finds that *shinrai* and *giri* are still active values impacting judicial behaviour of Japanese courts nowadays.[39]

6.7 Breach of State Polity's Trust in Teacher's Special Role

In the context of the principal-agent theory of corruption, it is imperative to ascertain the entity that delegated the official duty power to the two teachers in question. According to Article 10 of the Meiji Constitution, the Emperor was responsible for determining the organization of the various branches of administration and establishing the salaries of all civil and military officers. He had the authority to appoint and dismiss these individuals as he saw fit.[40]The Emperor periodically distributed *chokurei* to ensure the integrity of the officials, who were entrusted with the management and discipline of public funds.[41]

According to the provisions of Article 10 of Meiji Constitution, all civil servants, including educators, functioned as agents of the Emperor, holding power that had been delegated to them by the Emperor. The concept of educational sovereignty, in which the authority over education is retained by the state, was not applicable in this context. Instead, principals and teachers in schools were regarded as "entrusted" agents of the Emperor in the realm of education. In prewar society, the Emperor was the originator of all forms of power for the education sector's personnel (Namimoto 2012a, b, p. 13). This power relationship constituted the reason why social trust in it was so important. The education sector has been distinguished from ordinary workers in that it has been entrusted with a distinct mission and social role since the Meiji era.

Upon visiting the normal school in Saitama Prefecture in December 1885 in the official capacity of Minister of Education, Mori Arinori emphasized that there should be many ways to advance the national fortune of Japan, but the main strength was relying on this normal school (Mori 2004, p. 286). Teachers had been reminded of

---

[39] See Ryūzaki (1988, p. 53, p. 58, p. 65).

[40] See the Constitution of the Empire of Japan, at https://www.ndl.go.jp/constitution/e/etc/c02.html. Accessed 11 August 2022.

[41] See Education Law Study Group (1949, p. 13).

the importance of strong sense of discipline and simple life for Japan's national fortunate.[42] Teachers had to display moralistic exemplary behaviour of *son'nō-aikokuron* (theory of respect for Emperor and patriotism) (Ogawa 1936, p. 241). As per *Shihan-gakkō-rei* (Normal School Order under *Chokurei*) number 15 in 1886, Emperor instructed teachers to equip students with a temperament of obedience, "trustworthiness", love and dignity. "Trustworthiness" was a core social value in education sector as per Emperor's instruction.[43]

As Emperor's supreme order, Articles 1 and 2 of *Shōgakkō-rei* (Elementary School Order) in *Chokurei* number 215 dated 6 October 1890 stipulated that school principals and teachers should comply with Emperor's command in his *Kyōiku-chokugo* (Imperial Rescript on Education).[44] It concerned education and performance of teacher duties according to legal instructions. School principals had responsibility to organize school affairs and supervise teachers under them.[45] School principals had vicarious liability to Emperor for supervision of teachers as per Emperor's Imperial Rescript on Education. While this *Taishinin* judgement was delivered in 1931, all teachers had duty to teach *chūkun-aikoku* (loyalty to the Emperor and patriotism) and *kokutai-no-songen* (national dignity) in *Shihan-gakkō-kitei*, which was issued in the same year.[46] The impact of it lasted until 1937. The Ministry of Education reinforced this Imperial Rescript by the issue of *kokutai-no-hongi* (the true meaning of the state polity) for teacher's mission, emphasizing divine empire, indebtedness to Emperor and loyalty. The country called Japan as one big family nation, in which Emperor was the father, and the subjects were like babies.[47] In *Kokumin-gakkō-rei* (National School Order) dated 8 March 1943, Article 1 explicitly stated the purpose of national schools was to provide basic education for citizens in accordance with the *sumeragikuni* (empire) way.[48]

The culpability of an ordinary citizen's breach of social trust might not be regarded as breach of social trust, but two teachers in this *Taishinin* case were. Teacher was a respectful appointment for the role of socialization duty by education service in state polity. For example, on 27 December 1927, Emperor Hirohito signed *Chokurei* number 65 to appoint *kyōyu* for a senior girl high school in *Karafuto* at state polity service. In the perspective of prewar administrative law, Minobe Tatsukichi, the most famous scholar in this field, believed that public officials should have a public law

[42] See Hattori 1940, p. 662; The original text in Mori Arimori's speech: 国運を進むるの方法許多あるべしと雖、十中八九は此師範学校の力に依らずんばあらず。

[43] The original text in *Shihan-gakkō-rei*: 但生徒ヲシテ順良信愛威重ノ気質ヲ備ヘシムルコトニ注目スヘキモノトス。

[44] The original text in *Shōgakkō-rei*: 第1条、小学校長及教員ハ教育ニ関スル 勅語ノ旨趣ヲ奉体シ法律命令ノ指定ニ従ヒ其職務ニ服スヘシ;第2条、学校長ハ校務ヲ整理シ所属教員ヲ監督スヘシ。

[45] See Ministry of Finance Printing Bureau (1891, p. 189).

[46] See Takahashi (2018, p. 6); Also see Itsumi (1977, pp. 12–13).

[47] See Ministry of Education (1937, pp. 9–49).

[48] See Ministry of Finance Printing Bureau (1943, p. 232); The original text in *Kokumin-gakkō-rei*: 國民學校ハ皇國ノ道ニ則リテ初等普通教育ヲ施シ國民ノ基礎的錬成ヲ為スヲ以テ目的トス。

duty to be loyal and faithful to the state and to serve an unlimited amount (Minobe 1941, p. 695). In 1899, Emperor issued *Shiritsu-gakkō-rei* (Private School Order) under Imperial Rescript number 359. Article 1 of it stipulated supervision of private schools under local governor. To Minobe, the compulsory education for Japan's next generation was at the service of state polity (Minobe 1940, p. 525). The legal control of teachers and education in both private and public sector for this goal was clear.[49] Teacher had been entrusted the duty by Emperor to educate and socialize youngsters to serve state polity, not democracy or equality in fair society.[50] Divergent interpretations of a deviant behaviour may emerge for different distinct strategic objectives in public administration during different political periods.[51] *Taishinin*'s moralistic rulings of breach of social trust served as a public administration strategy, particularly with regard to the discipline, conduct, sensitivity to shame culture and integrity of teachers and other civil servants. Taishinin formulated a judicial policy of public administration nature on behalf of the government. In Chap. 2 of this book, the pioneers of judicial behaviour studies had already found that judiciary posited in power matrix. Court was not only at the service of legal justice.

6.8 Impacts of *Taishinin*'s Judicial Behaviour and Banquet Bribe Remain

The repercussions of this *Taishinin* ruling, which established a precedent in the realm of *shakai-no-shinrai*, continue to resonate in postwar Japan. The Japanese government publishes *Hanzai-hakusho* (White Paper on Crime) on an annual basis. The 1996 edition of the publication still applied the conceptual framework of this landmark *Taishinin* ruling of "breach of social trust". Japanese government deemed an individual who had committed bribery had caused harm to the *kokumin-no-shinrai* (trust of the nationals) in the *kōmu-no-kōsei* (fairness or impartiality of the civil service).[52] Under the shadow of Taishinin's judicial behaviour, the mindset of postwar Japanese government continued to regard *shinrai* in government as its social capital.[53]

Notwithstanding *Taishinin*'s attitudinal and strict liability model of judicial behaviour for the strategic goal of deterrence and social control, textbook corruption continues in Japan nowadays. Japanese textbook firms' *modus operandi* of bribery by hosted hospitality is not fully eliminated. For example, in 2016, the industry group

[49] Haruyama (2019), p. 156.

[50] The Original text in Minobe's work: 国家に対し忠実に無定量の勤務に服すべき公法上の義務を負ふもの。

[51] On this see O'Sullivan (2017, pp. 27–29, p. 114); also see Powell (2013, p. 12).

[52] On this see Legal Research Institute 1996.

[53] See Ministry of Internal Affairs and Communications (2009, p. 111).

Kyōkasho-kyōkai (Textbook Publishers Association of Japan) formulated a voluntary *Kyōkasho-hakkōsha-kōdō-kihan* (Code of Conduct for Textbook Publishers)[54] regarding the sales activities of each publisher. The provision of money and goods to educators was prohibited. Hosted meal is not exempted. Notwithstanding code of conduct for voluntary compliance, it is not easy to eradicate the culture of hosted meal that makes the most of old human relationships. In September 2022, the textbook company Dainippon Tosho Company provided 38,000-*yen* food entertainment to the Superintendent of Education and three civil servants of Gokachō, Ibaraki Prefecture. Textbook Publishers Association of Japan merely apologized and expressed regret to Japanese society. Asahi Shimbun Company.[55] However, it did not end luxury food entertainment in education sector. On 25 January 2023, Osaka District Court convicted the principal of a city secondary school for his acceptance of banquet bribe.[56] This case first surfaced in Fujiidera City by a whistle blower in late 2022. Employees of school textbook publisher Dainippon Tosho Company gave banquet bribe to a school principal in the city's textbook selection committee. A culinary entertainment of 38,000 *yen* nowadays is lavish *kyōen* luxury feast according to today's standard.[57]

6.9 Brief Remarks

In Chaps. 4 and 5, the bribers and bribees involved in the Keisei case and the compensation case are designated as tigers. In this chapter, two teachers are small flies in a case of bookstores' seeking favouritism in textbook procurement through hosted meals. *Taishinin*'s actions ultimately led to the demise of both the tigers and the flies. Its judgement was not substantiated by evidence for corroboration that the two teachers had been informed of the guilty intention of the bookstores, which was the corrupt *quid pro quo* of banquet bribery. Therefore, the Appellants' appeal grounds were not unreasonable. It is important to acknowledge the notion that the benefit

[54] See *Kyōkasho-hakkōsha-kōdō-kihan* (Code of Conduct for Textbook Publishers) formulated by Kyōkasho Kyōkai (Textbook Publishers Association of Japan) at http://www.textbook.or.jp/about-us/data/code220203.pdf. Accessed 11 April 2023.

[55] On details see "Dainippon Tosho, a textbook company, entertained the superintendent of education in Goka Town, Ibaraki Prefecture (Asahi Shimbun 30 September 2022)" at https://www.asahi.com/articles/ASQ9Z6FF9Q9ZUTIL008.html#:~:text=%E5%90%8C%E7%A4%BE%E3%81%AB%E3%82%88%E3%82%8B%E3%81%A8%E3%80%81%E6%94%AF%E7%A4%BE%E9%95%B7,%E5%9C%9F%E7%94%A3%E3%81%A8%E3%81%97%E3%81%A6%E6%B8%A1%E3%81%97%E3%81%9F%E3%81%A8%E3%81%84%E3%81%86%E3%80%82. Accessed 13 April 2023.

[56] On details see "The report points out that the textbook selection corruption bribery also entertained two city board members (Asahi Shimbun 23 January 2023)" at https://www.asahi.com/articles/ASR1X4JYHR1WPTIL00N.html. Accessed 5 May 2023.

[57] On details see "Editorial 27 March 2023: Japan needs more transparency in selection of public school textbooks (Mainichi Shimbun 27 March 2023)"at https://mainichi.jp/articles/20230327/ddm/005/070/008000c. Accessed 6 May 2023.

of doubt was attributed to *Taishinin*'s approach to judicial discretion. In the context of net-widening effects, its judicial behaviour aligns with the strict liability model, which stands in opposition to the well-established principle articulated by William Blackstone in the domain of common law jurisdiction. Blackstone's principle asserts that the release of ten guilty individuals is preferable to the punishment of an innocent person.

Through analysis of this judgement, it is evident that a single model of judicial behaviour is inadequate in explaining the full range of judicial behaviours. It is possible that a single judgement may exhibit a hybridity of two or more judicial behaviour models. *Taishinin*'s judicial behaviour in this judgement can be characterized as a hybrid model, encompassing elements of strategic model, an attitudinal model and a strict liability model. *Taishinin*'s attitudinal judicial behaviour against breach of social trust was rational in view of infringement against *giri*.[58] Hybrid judicial behaviour of attitudinal model and strict liability model can consolidate and reinforce the maintenance of social trust as a strategy for social cohesion, which is determined by reputation effects driving social cooperation and a general belief that law enforcement can keep social stability.[59] This strategic goal is advantageous to the legitimacy and hegemony of governance, political effectiveness and a lower administrative cost. Both legislature and judiciary are instrumental for it.[60] This hybridity is intricately interwoven with historical institutionalism in state political system, the ideological inclinations of judges, political considerations, personal values, attitudes and traits. Breach of social trust is in fact breach of state political trust in two teachers' role for socialization and cultural assimilation of Japan's next generation.

Taishinin's judicial behaviour is analogous to the "Japanese body" in the "Western jacket of the transplanted Germanic Penal Code". The "body of cultural motivated" criminalization by breach of social trust is still not overruled by today's Supreme Court of Japan. According to the "Western jacket" of Articles 197 and 198 of the contemporary Japanese Penal Code, this landmark ruling is still valid and binding on every person in the area under Japan's judicial sovereignty.

In the following two chapters, readers will read how *Taishinin*'s judicial behaviour addressed the intricate nexus of police corruption, sexual bribery and the moral implications of commercial sexual activities. From the perspective of fair society studies, codification of legislation and law enforcement should advocate justice, freedom and equality as the three pillars for sustainability of collective and individual wellbeing in fair society development. However, the next two chapters may expound that *Taishinin*'s judicial behaviour did not contribute in such way. Its judicial behaviour surprisingly legitimatized the development of supply chain of sex workers to sex industry in prewar Japan.

[58] On this see Terasawa (2002, p. 118, p. 123).

[59] On this see Bergh et al. (2021, pp. 9–10, pp. 24–25).

[60] On this see Bevir (2007, p. 175, pp. 408–409, p 922, p. 993); Also see Hui (2018, pp. 5–8).

References

Akatsuka, Y. (1971) *Giri to Ninjō: Nihonjin no Kōdō Genri o Saguru (Giri and Ninjō: Exploring the Principles of Japanese Behavior)*. Shodensha.

Alexeev, M., Song, Y. (2013) Corruption and product market competition: an empirical investigation. *Journal of Development Economics*, Vol. 103 (C), 154–166.

Arugaki, Z. (1967) Ōyake to Watashi: Giri to Ninjō (Public and Private: Obligation and Humanity). In *Kizaemon Ariga Works Vol. IV Architectural System and Modernization*. Miraisha.

Asahi Shimbun Company. (2022) *Dainippon Tosho, a textbook company, entertained the superintendent of education in Goka Town, Ibaraki Prefecture*. https://www.asahi.com/articles/ASQ9Z6FF9Q9ZUTIL008.html#:~:text=%E5%90%8C%E7%A4%BE%E3%81%AB%E3%82%88%E3%82%8B%E3%81%A8%E3%80%81%E6%94%AF%E7%A4%BE%E9%95%B7,%E5%9C%9F%E7%94%A3%E3%81%A8%E3%81%97%E3%81%A6%E6%B8%A1%E3%81%97%E3%81%9F%E3%81%A8%E3%81%84%E3%81%86%E3%80%82 – Accessed 13 April 2023.

Asahi Shimbun Company. (2023) *The report points out that the textbook selection corruption bribery also entertained two city board members*. https://www.asahi.com/articles/ASR1X4JYHR1WPTIL00N.html Accessed 5 May 2023.

Bergh, A. et al. (2021) Social and Legal Trust. In Vallier, K., Weber, M. ed. *Social Trust*. Routledge.

Bevir., M. (2007) *Encyclopedia of Governance*. Sage Publications.

Bradbury, J.A. et al. (2013) Trust and Public Participation in Risk Policy Issues. In Cvetkovich, G., Lofstedt, R. E. ed. *Social Trust and the Management of Risk*. Routledge.

Chiba, C. (1977) Kyōkasho Gyōsei ni Kansuru Ichi Kōsatsu : Meiji-ki no Kyōkasho Giongoku Jiken no Shiji suru Mono (A Consideration on the Textbook Administration: A Meaning of the Textbook Scandal in the Meiji Period). *Bulletin of Tokyo Kasei University*, Vol. (17), 29-36.

Chikushi J. n.d. *School history*. https://www.chikushi.ac.jp/history/ Accessed 13 April 2023.

Chikamatsu, M. (1922) *Dai Chikamatsu Zenshū: Kaisetsu Chūshaku. Dai 5-kan (The Complete Works of Ochikamatsu : Commentary and Commentary. Volume 5)*. Ochikamatsu Complete Works Publishing Society.

Chr Michelsen Institute. n.d. *Education sector corruption: How to assess I and ways to address it*. https://www.u4.no/publications/education-sector-corruption-how-to-assess-it-and-ways-to-address-it/shortversion. Accessed 13 April 2023.

Classical Waka. n.d. *Ise Monogatari*. https://wakastream.jp/article/10000239WbxQ. Accessed 19 August 2022.

Diaby, A., Sylwester, K. (2015) Corruption and Market Competition: Evidence from Post-Communist Countries. *World Development*, Vol. 66 (C), 487–499.

e-Gov.n.d. Criminal Procedure Code. https://elaws.e-gov.go.jp/document?lawid=323AC0000000131. Accessed 14 August 2022

Education Law Study Group. (1949) *Kyōiku Kōmuin Tokurei Hō: Kaisetsu to Shiryō (Special Law for Educational Public Servants: Commentary and Materials)*. Jiji Press.

Encyclopedia Britannica. n.d. *Gemeinschaft and Gesellschaft*. https://www.britannica.com/topic/Gemeinschaft-and-Gesellschaft. Accessed 16 August 2022.

Encyclopedia of Japan (Nipponica) n.d. *textbook*. https://kotobank.jp/word/%E6%95%99%E7%A7%91%E6%9B%B8-52503 Accessed 5 May 2023.

Fetchenhauer, D. et al. (2017) The Mysteries of Trust: Trusting Too Little and Too Much at the Same Time. In Paul, A.M. et al. ed. *Trust in Social Dilemmas*. Oxford University Press.

Florou, A. (2019) Adverse Inferences and Penalty Default Rules in International Investment Arbitration: A Policy: Approach to the Production of Evidence. *Journal of International Dispute Settlement*, Vol. 10 (3), 423-442.

Fujimoto, K. (2016) Keiji Shōko Hōshi Kenkyū no Gendaiteki Igi to Kadai: Kettō Saiban kara no Keizoku to Danzetsu (Contemporary Significance and Issues of Criminal Evidence Law History Research: Continuation and Discontinuation from Duel Trials). *Hitotsubashi Hōgaku (Hitotsubashi Legal Studies)*, Vol. 15 (1), 86-97.

Fukuyama, F. (1995) Trust: *The social virtues and the creation of prosperity.* Free Press.
George, B. J. Jr. (1990) Rights of the Criminally Accused. *Law and Contemporary Problems,* Vol. 53 (2), 71-107.
Giddens, A. et al. (2019) *Essentials of sociology.* W. W. Norton & Company, Incorporation.
Haruyama, K. (2019) Kyōin no Hōteki Mibun ni Kansuru Ichi Kōsatsu: Kenpijō no Kōmuin Gainen to no Kankei ni oiteA Study on the Legal Status of Teachers: In Relation to the Constitutional Concept of "Public Servant). *Senshu Law Journal,* Vol. 15, 151-176.
Hattori, K. (1940) Nara-ken Shihan Gakkō Zaigaku Tōji no Kaikoroku: Meiji 25-nen Sotsugyō (Nostalgia for being a student at Nara Prefectural Normal School: Graduated in 1892). *50 Years History of Nara Prefectural Normal School.* Nara Myōshinsha.
Hatase, M. (2002) Devaluation and Exports in Interwar Japan: The Effects of Sharp Depreciation of the Yen in the Early 1930s. *Monetary and Economic Studies,* Vol. 20 (3), 143-180.
Healy, M. P. (1999) Legislative Intent and Statutory Interpretation in England and the United States: An Assessment of the Impact of Pepper v. Hart. *Stanford Journal of International Law,* Vol. 35 (2), 231-254.
Heibonsha. n.d. *Doctrine of Statutory Evidence* in World Encyclopedia (2nd Edition) https://kotobank.jp/word/%E6%B3%95%E5%AE%9A%E8%A8%BC%E6%8B%A0%E4%B8%BB%E7%BE%A9-132326. Accessed 10 May 2023.
Higano, Tokuhisa. (1990) Kyōkasho Shinsa Jiken: Kotei Kyōkasho e no Michi (Textbook Examination Case: Road to National Textbook). *Hakūei Joshi Tandai Ronshū (Hakūei Women's Junior College journal),* Vol. 14 (2), 15–38.
Hisaki, Y. (1991) Shakai Kyōiku Sogen (Origin of social education), *Kyōiku Gakubu Ronshū, Bukkyō Daigaku Gakkai (Faculty of Education Journal, Buddhist University Society),* Vol. 3, 1–20.
Hui, E. S. (2018) *Hegemonic Transformation: The State, Laws, and Labor Relations in Post-Socialist China.* Palgrave Macmillan.
Inaoka, M. (1981) Kinkōdō "Shashi" no Hōhō ni Tsuite (About the method of Kinkodo company history). *Shuppan Kenkyū (Journal of the Japan Society of Publishing Studies),* Vol. 12, 124-148.
Inaoka, M. (1985) Meiji Zenki Kyōkasho Shuppan no Jittai to Sono Ichi (The Reality and Position of Textbook Publishing in the Early Meiji Era). *Shuppan Kenkyū (Journal of the Japan Society of Publishing Studies),* Vol. 16, 72-125.
Inaoka M. (1987) Hara Ryōsaburō: Den no Shinwa to Shōzō (Hara Ryōsaburō: Legendary Myths and True Images). *Shuppan Kenkyū (Journal of the Japan Society of Publishing Studies),* Vol. 18, 128-143.
Inaoka M. (2019) *Meiji Shuppanshi-jō no Kinkōdō: Shashi no nai Shuppansha "Shi" no Kokoromi(Kinkōdō in the history of Meiji Publishing: An attempt at a publishing company "history" without a corporate history).* Kōseisha.
Ingrao, C. (2009) Weapons of Mass Instruction: Schoolbooks and Democratization in Multiethnic Central Europe. *Journal of Educational Media, Memory, and Society,* Vol. 1 (1), 180–189.
Isome, T. (2008) Isome Tsuna no Ōraimono (It's the first time or Ōrai-mono). *Geibun Kenkyu,* Keio University Arts and Literature Society, No. 95. 170–176.
Itsumi, K. (1977) 1931 "Shihan Gakkō Kisoku" Kaisei ni Tsuite 1931 Revision of the Normal School Regulations). *Hokkaidō Daigaku Kyōiku Gakubu Kiyō (Bulletin of the Faculty of Education, Hokkaido University),* Vol. 30, 1-44.
Jasinski, M. P. (2011) *Social Trust, Anarchy, and International Conflict.* Palgrave and Macmillan.
Kase, K. (2015) *Senkanki Nihon no Kakei Shōhi (Household Consumption in Interwar Japan).* Institute of Social Science, University of Tokyo.
Kawamura, K. (2011) *Chikushi Jogakuen to Tomo ni Yonjū-nen (Forty Years with Chikushi Girls'Academy).* Chikushi Jogakuen High School.
Kōno, M. (2015) Seken to Shakai wa Nihon to Seiyō o Hikaku dekiru Kijun darō ka (Are the world and society a standard by which Japan and the West can be compared). *Aichi Daigaku Bungaku Ronsō (Aichi University Literature Collection),* Vol. 1 (151), 35–68.
Kamon, Y. (2007) Hōekiron no Gendaiteki Igi (The Modern Significance of the Theory of Legal Interest). *Keihō Zasshi (Criminal Law Journal),* Vol. 47 (1), 36-48.

Kawabata, H. (1998) Nihon no Keihō oyobi Keihō Riron no Hatten (Development of Japanese Criminal Law and Criminal Law Theory). *Hōritsu Ronsō (Legal Papers)*, Vol. 70 (4), 177-201.

Kim, S. G. (2007) Jinkakuteki Hōekiron to Daivājon no Kanōsei (Personal Legal Interest Theory and the Possibility of Diversion). *Keihō Zasshi (Criminal Law Journal)*, Vol. 47 (1), 24-35.

Kimura, N. (2013) Shakai Izen to Shakai Igo: Meiji-ki Nihon ni okeru Shakai Gainen to Shakaiteki Sōzō no Hensei (Pre-Society and Post-Society: Organization of Social Concepts and Social Imagination in Meiji-era Japan). *Nihon Bunka Kenkyū Sentā Kaigi Happyō-yō Shiryō (Conference presentation material, Japanese Culture Research Center)*, Vol. 44, 267-283.

Kitayama, S. (1999) Shakai Shinrigaku no Shimei to Shinrai no Kōzō no Igi: Gēmu Riron to Bunka Shinrigaku (Mission of Social Psychology and the Significance of Trust Structures': Game Theory and Cultural Psychology). *Kyōto Daigaku Sōgō Ningen Gakubu Shakai Shinrigaku Kenkyū (Department of Social Psychology, Faculty of Integrated Human Studies, Kyoto University)*, Vol. 15 (1), 60- 65.

Kleinfeld, J., Hadar, D. R. (2022) Social Trust in Criminal Justice: A Metric. *Notre Dame Law Review,* Vol. 98 (2), 815-883.

Kobayashi, T. (1973) *Complete Works of Japanese Classical Literature (28): Uji Shui Monogatari.* Shōgakukan.

Kōra, K. (2011) Shakai Yōgohō no Hensan (2): Meiroku Zasshi no Baai (Changes in Social Terminology (2): The Case of Meiroku Magazine). *Ryūkyū Daigaku Kyōiku Gakubu Kiyō (Bulletin of Faculty of Education, University of the Ryukyus)*, Vol. 79, 41-59.

Kumon, T. (2006) Muzai Suitei Hōri no Saisei: Shōmei Hōsoku toshite no Kinō (Reproduction of the Presumption of Innocence Doctrine: Its Function as a Law of Proof). *Criminal Law Magazine*, Vol. 45 (20, 42-56.

Kurabayashi, M. (1965) *Kyōen no Kenkyū (A study of Kyōen).* Ōfūsha.

Kyōkasho Kyōkai. (2016) *Kyōkasho Hakkōsha Kōdō Kihan (Code of Conduct for Textbook Publishers).* http://www.textbook.or.jp/about-us/data/code220203.pdf. Accessed 11 April 2023.

Legal Information Institute, Cornell University. n.d. *Corroborating evidence.* https://www.law.cornell.edu/wex/corroborating_evidence. Accessed 5 May 2023.

Legal Research Institute. (1996). *Hanzai Hakusho (Crime White Paper).* Legal Research Institute.

Levi, M. (1998) A State of Trust. In Braithwaite, V, Levi, M. ed. *Trust and Governance* (pp. 77-101). Russell Sage Foundation.

Luhmann, N. (2012) Rhodes, B. trans. *Theory of Society Volume 1.* Stanford University Press.

Masaharu T. (1985) Giri Ninjō Kō (Thoughts on Giri-Ninjo). *Hitotsubashi Kenkyū (Hitotsubashi Research)*, Vol. 9 (4), 43-71.

Masamune, A. (1929) *Ujishūimonogatari.* Japan Classic Complete Works Publishing Association.

Masuda, Y. (1992) Keiji Tetsuzuki ni okeru Saibankan no Kakushin to Shōmeido: Sōgō Shukansetsu e no Josō (Judge's Conviction and Degree of Proof in Criminal Proceedings: A Run-up to the Intersubjective Theory). *Hōritsu Ronsō (Legal Papers)*, Vol. 64 (5-6), 1-72.

Ministry of Education. (1937) *Kokutai no Hongi (The True Meaning of the State Polity).* Ministry of Education.

Ministry of Education, Culture, Sports, Science and Technology. n.d 1. *Establishment of the National Textbook System.* https://www.google.com/search?q=japanese+to+english+translation&rlz=1C1VDKB_zh-HKHK938HK938&oq=&aqs=chrome.5.35i39i362l3j46i39i199i362i465l2j35i39i362l3.51180392j0j15&sourceid=chrome&ie=UTF-8. Accessed 5 May 2023.

Ministry of Education, Culture, Sports, Science and Technology (文部科学省). n.d 2. T*he concept of legal conflicts of interest.* https://www.mext.go.jp/b_menu/shingi/gijyutu/gijyutu8/toushin/attach/1366593.htm. Last accessed 10 May 2023.

Ministry of Education, Culture, Sports, Science and Technology. n.d.3. *(iv) promulgation of an education order.* https://www.mext.go.jp/b_menu/hakusho/html/others/detail/1317583.htm. Accessed 18 August 2022.

Ministry of Education, Culture, Sports, Science and Technology. n.d.4. *Normal School Edict No. 13 of April 10, 1884.* https://www.mext.go.jp/b_menu/hakusho/html/others/detail/1318073.htm. Accessed 12 August 2022.

Ministry of Education, Culture, Sports, Science and Technology. n.d.5 *Private School Order Imperial Decree No. 359 of 3 August 1907.* https://www.mext.go.jp/b_menu/hakusho/html/others/detail/1317973.htm. Accessed 1 August 2022.

Minobe, T. (1941) *Nihon Gyōsei-hō Jōkan Dai 3-han (Japanese Administrative Law Volume 1, 3rd ed.).* Yuhikaku.

Minobe, T. (1940) *Nihon Gyōsei-hō Jōkan (Japanese Administrative Law Volume 2).* Yuhikaku.

Misztal, B. (1998) *Trust in Modern Societies: The Search for the Bases of Social Order.* Polity Press.

Nagano, A. (2000) Giri wa Nihon Bunka ni Koyū no mono ka (Is giri an inherent part of Japanese culture). *Tōyō Daigaku Shakaigakubu Kiyō (Bulletin of the Faculty of Sociology, Toyo University),* Vol. 38 (1), 55-74.

Naitō, C. 1893. *Kinshiroku Lecture Note (Complete Book of Chinese Literature; Vol. 16).* Hakubunkan.

Nakamura, K. (1992) *Kyoukasho no Shakaishi : Meiji Ishin kara Haisen made (Social History in Textbooks: From the Meiji Restoration to Defeat in World War II).* Iwanami Shinsho.

Namimoto, K. (2012) Nihon ni okeru Gakkō Un'ei to Kyōiku Katei Hōsei no Mondaiten (Problems of School Management and Curriculum Legislation in Japan). *Risshō Daigaku Shinrigaku Kenkyūjo Kiyō (Bulletin of Rissho University Institute of Psychology),* No. 10, 9–29.

Namimoto, K. (2012) Nihon ni okeru Kyōkasho Sainaku Seido no Rekishiteki Hensen (Historical Changes in Japan's Textbook Adoption System). *Risshō Daigaku Shinrigaku Kenkyūjo Kiyō (Bulletin of Rissho University Institute of Psychology),* No. 3, 33–48.

National Diet Library. n.d. *Chronicles of Japan.* https://dl.ndl.go.jp/info:ndljp/pid/1288454. Accessed 16 August 2022.

National Diet Library. 2011. *Shokunihonki.* https://dl.ndl.go.jp/info:ndljp/pid/772184. Accessed 12 August 2022.

National Institute for Educational Policy Research Educational Library. n.d. *Oraimono Digital Archive.* https://www.nier.go.jp/library/darchives/orai.html. Accessed 5 May 2023.

Nishidai, M. (2010) Jiyū Shinshō Shugi to Shōmei (libertarianism and proof). *Akita Daigaku Kyōiku Bunka Gakubu Kenkyū Kiyō (Akita University Faculty of Education and Human Studies),* Vol. 65, 11-18.

Nishidai, M. (2013) Minji Soshō ni okeru Shōmeido (Degree of proof in civil litigation). *Akita Daigaku Kyōiku Bunka Gakubu Kenkyū Kiyō (Akita University Faculty of Education and Human Studies),* Vol. 68, 61-67.

Nishihara, M. (2017) Meiji Sanjūgo-nen Chūgakkō Kyōju Yōmoku no Seikaku Nature of The 1902 Middle School English Teaching Guideline). *Toyama Kōtō Senmon Gakkō Kiyō (Toyama National College Bulletin,* No. 4, 7–16.

Nomura Securities Company Limited. n.d. *Conflict of interest.* https://www.nomura.co.jp/terms/japan/ri/a01855.html#:~:text=%E4%B8%80%E8%88%AC%E7%9A%84%E3%81%AB%E3%81%AF%E3%80%81%E3%81%82%E3%82%8B,%E5%88%A9%E7%9B%8A%E7%9B%B8%E5%8F%8D%E5%8F%96%E5%BC%95%E3%81%A8%E3%81%97%E3%81%A6%E3%81%84%E3%82%8B%E3%80%82. Accessed 15 August 2022.

Mori, Y. (2004). Kaminuma, H. ed. *Shinshū Mori Arinori Zenshū Bekkan 2 (Newly edited Mori Yure's complete works: Separate volume 2).* Bunsendo Shoten.

Nakamura, M. (1990) Giri to Kyōkan: Kin-Gendai Nihon Shakai ni okeru Ningen Kankei-kan no Ichi Isō (Giri and "Empathy: A phase of human relations in modern Japanese society). *Sociologos,* Vol. 14, 19-35.

Nozaki, Y., Inokuchi, H. (2000) Japanese Education, Nationalism, and Ienaga Saburo's Textbook Lawsuits. In Hein, L., Selden, M. ed. *Censoring History: Citizenship and Memory in Japan, Germany, and the United States* (pp. 96-126). M. E. Sharpe.

Ministry of Finance. Kanpō (*Official Gazette*): 8 March 1943. Ministry of Finance Printing Bureau

Oda, N. (2018) Hōeki Shingai-setsu ni Tsuite (About legal interest infringement theory). *Kōbe Hōgaku Nenpō (Kobe Law School Annual Report),* Vol. 31, 1-35.

Ogawa K. (1936) Omoeba Natsukashi Zaigaku Tōji: Meiji 25-nen 7-gatsu Sotsugyō (Nostalgic when I was in school: Graduated in July 1892). *Hokkaido Sapporo Normal School 50 Years History*. Hokkaido Sapporo Normal School.

Ogawara, M. (2017) *Kyū Hanshuke no Ikuei Jigyō ni Kansuru Ichikōsatsu: Kyū Fukuoka-han, Kuroda-ke o Chūshin ni (A study on scholarship enterprise of old feudal lord: specially focusing on Kuroda family of old Fukuoka domain)*. Academic Promotion Fund Research Results Report.

Ogasawara, T. (2020) Senzen-ki Chūtō Gakkō Kokugoka Kyōkasho ni Kansuru Kenkyū: Kyōkasho Ichiranhyō no Sakusei to Mokuji Dēta no Toriatsukai o Chūshin ni (A study on Pre WWII-Japanese Language Textbooks of Secondary School: Focusing on how to make a textbook list and how to handle table of contents data). *Chiigaku Ronshū: Tottori Daigaku Chiigakubu Kiyō(Regional studies : Tottori University journal of the Faculty of Regional Sciences)*, Vol. 16 (3), 43–60.

Open Educational Contents Archive of Tokyo Gakugei University. n.d. *Overview and Classification of Ōrai-mono*. https://d-archive.u-gakugei.ac.jp/collection/orai/description-0. Accessed 5 May 2023

O'S. (2017) *Universal Jurisdiction in International Criminal Law: The Debate and the Battle for Hegemony*. Routledge.

Planning Division, Minister's Secretariat, Ministry of Internal Affairs and Communications. (2009) *Gyōsei no Shinraisei Kakuho, Kōjō Hōsaku ni Kansuru Chōsa Kenkyū Hōkokusho (Research Report on Measures to Secure and Improve Government Reliability)*. Planning Division, Minister's Secretariat, Ministry of Internal Affairs and Communications.

Powell, J. L. (2013) *The social analysis of emotion and trust*. Nova Science Publishers, Inc.

President online. (2014) *Tomomi Fujiwara: Important teachings of Shuyukan High School, predecessor of Kuroda Domain School*. https://president.jp/articles/-/13679?page=1. Accessed 12 August 2022.

Ryuzaki, K. (1988) *Giri Ninjō to Saiban (Giri Ninjō and Judgment)*. Chikuma.

Satō, S. (2009) Shakai Kyōiku wa, Naze "Shakai Kyōiku" to Meimei sareta no ka Sono 1: Meiji 10-nendai no Shakai Kyōikuron Kenkyū no Kentō o Tōshite (Why was social education named "social education"? Part 1: Through the study of social education theory research in the 1870s). *Hirosaki Daigaku Kyōiku Gakubu Kiyō (Bulletin of the Faculty of Education, Hirosaki University*, No. 101, 129–138.

Seigle, C. S. (2016) Tokugawa Shogun and Gifts. Department of East Asian Languages and Civilizations. University of Pennsylvania. Paper 10.http://repository.upenn.edu/ealc/10_ Accessed 1 September 2025.

Shizume, M. (2009) The Japanese Economy during the Interwar Period: Instability in the Financial System and the Impact of the World Depression. *Bank of Japan Review May 2009*. Bank of Japan.

Stuckenberg, C. (2013) The Constitutional Deficiencies of the German Rechtsgutslehre. *Oñati Socio-Legal Series*, Vol. 3 (1), 31-41.

Suzuki, M. C. (2019) *Gendered Power Educated Women of the Meiji Empress Court*. University of Michigan Press.

Takahashi, H. (2018) Shōwa Senzen Senchū-ki ni okeru Shihan Gakkō no Kyōshoku Karikyuramu (Teaching Curriculum at Normal Schools in the Showa Prewar and Middle War period). *Yokohama Shiritsu Daigaku Ronsō: Shakai Kagaku Keiretsu Yokohama City University Journal: Social Science Series)*, Vol. 69 (1), 1–40.

Takahashi, K., Tetsuo, I. (2012) Senzen no Kyūsei Chūgakkō ni okeru Shinka no Shidō ni Kansuru Kenkyū (Evolution Was Taught in Japanese Secondary Schools before World War II). *Seibutsu Kyōiku (Japanese Journal of Biology Education)*. Vol. 54 (2), 68-83.

Tanaka, K. (1994) Chūsei Kōki ni okeru Reisēn, Reimotsu no Juju ni tsuite: Muromachi Bakufu, Betsubugyō, Tōji Gohō nado o megutte (On the Exchange of Gratuities and Gifts in the Late Middle Ages: Focusing on the Muromachi Shogunate, Special Magistrates, and the Five Directions of Tōji Temple). *The Journal of Economics*, Vol. 35 (4), p107-132.

Terasawa, M. (2002) *Nihonjin no Seishin Kōzō: Dentō to Genzai (Japanese Mental Structure: Tradition and Present).* Koyoshobo.

The Asahi Shimbun Company. (2021) *Is hospitality a crime of bribery? Legally out...* https://www.asahi.com/articles/ASP2T1C5KP2SUTIL00N.html – Accessed 14 April 2023.

The Mainichi. (2023) *Editorial 27 March 2023: Japan needs more transparency in selection of public school textbooks.* https://mainichi.jp/articles/20230327/ddm/005/070/008000c – Accessed 6 May 2023.

Tohoku University Intellectual Property Office for Research Promotion. (2005) *Conflicts of Interest: A Case Study on Dealing with Conflicts of Responsibility - A Report on the Results of a Model Program for Building 21st Century Industry-Academia-Government Collaboration Techniques.* http://www.bureau.tohoku.ac.jp/coi/report/pdf/h16houkoku.pdf – Accessed 15 August 2022

Tokushima Teachers Union. n.d. *Read the teacher as a doctrine.* http://tokutu.mond.jp/2020/03/12/%E6%95%99%E8%AB%AD%E3%82%92%E6%95%99%E8%AB%96%E3%81%A8%E8%AA%AD%E3%82%93%E3%81%A7%E3%81%97%E3%81%BE%E3%81%A3%E3%81%9F/ - Accessed 13 April 2023.

Tsuchimoto, T. (2004) Nihon ni okeru Zōshūwai no Tokuisei to Hōteki Kisei (Peculiarities and Legal Regulations of Bribery in Japan. *Hōritsu Bunka (Law Culture)*, Vol. 16, 22-27.

Turner, B. S. ed. (2006) *The Cambridge Dictionary of Sociology.* Cambridge University Press.

Uchida, M. (1870) *Yochishi Ryaku Kan 1 (Concise Geography Vol.1).* Ministry of Education.

Uslaner, E. M. (2002) *The Moral Foundations of Trust.* Cambridge University Press.

Watanabe, H. (2010) Nihon Seiji Shisōshi: Jūshichi - Jūkyū Seiki (History of Japanese Political Thought: 17th-19th Centuries). Tokyo University Press.

Yada Y. (2015) Ono Seiichirō no Jikkō Kōi-ron to Seihan · Kōhan-ron: Jikkō Kōi Gainen no Gakusetsushiteki Kōsatsu to Kansetsu Seihan-ron (Ono Seiichiro's Execution Act Theory and Prison/Complicity Theory: Theory of Execution Act Concept Historical Consideration and Indirect Prison Theory). Kokushikan Hōgaku (Kokushikan Legal Studies), Vol.48, 123

Yagi, Y. (2008) Chūgakkō Kyōju Yōmoku Kaisei 1931, Shōwa 6: ni okeru Kyōka Naiyō Kettei no Haikei: Gendaibun no Teichaku ni Tomonau Koten Gainen no Keisei (Background of the decision on subject content and revision of junior high school teaching guidelines of 1931, Showa 6: With the establishment of "modern literature" alongside the formation of the "Classicals" concept) *Kokugoka Kyōiku (National Language Science Education)*, Vol. 65, 43–50.

Yamagishi, T., Komiyama, N. (1995) Shinrai no Imi to Kōzō: Shinrai to Komittomento Kankei ni Kansuru Rironteki Jisshōteki Kenkyū (The Meaning and Structure of Trust A Theoretical and Empirical Study on Trust and Commitment). *Kabushiki Kaisha Genshiryoku Anzen Shisutemu Kenkyūjo (Institute of Nuclear Safety System, Incorporation*, Journal 2, 1-59.

Yamamoto, M. (2013) *Nihon Kindai Kyōin Yōseishi Kenkyū: 2013-nendo Yamamoto Zemi Kyōdō Kenkyū Hōkokusho (Research on the History of Modern Teacher Education in Japan: Yamamoto Seminar Joint Research Report 2013).* Keiō Gijuku Daigaku Bungakubu Kyōikugaku Senkō Yamamoto Kenkyūkai (Keio University Faculty of Letters Department of Education Yamamoto Study Group).

Yano, H. (2012) Kyōkasho o Kenkyū suru to iu Koto: Kyōkasho Bunseki no Wakugumi to Hōhō (Research on textbooks: Framework and method of textbook analysis). *Ongaku Kyōiku Jissen Jānaru (Journal of Musical Education Practice)*, Vol. 9 (2), 6-13.

Yoshiwara, Y. (1969) Kinsei no Terakoya ni okeru Ōraimono ni yoru Kyōdo Chiri Kyōiku ni tsuite (Local Geographical Education Using TrChaditions at a Terakoya in the Early Modern Period). *Shin Chiri (New Geography).* Vol. 69 (4). 19-30.

Zeleznikow, J., Dan, H. (1995) Deductive, inductive and analogical reasoning in legal decision support systems. *Law, Computers and Artificial Intelligence*, Vol. 4 (2), 141-159.

Chapter 7
Police Corruption and Sex Industry in Tokyo

7.1 Case Background

A police officer in the administrative division of prewar Tokyo Metropolitan Police had extensive discretionary law enforcement power for public order. This case concerns the judicial behaviour of *Taishinin* to determine whether the mediation efforts of police officers in their private capacity constituted official duty. It is noted that these efforts contributed to the maintenance of public order and in the red-light district in downtown Tokyo. The *modus operandi* for bribery can vary, much like the patterns of a kaleidoscope but the most common form of bribery is always gift-giving. The judicial behaviour of strict liability model, as implemented by *Taishinin*, functioned as a legal panacea in this police corruption case, serving to delineate between the concepts of gift and bribe. This chapter explores the intertwined themes of the prewar sex industry, *ochūge* (customary midyear gift-giving) and police officers' private endeavours. The judgement is under the reference of *Keishū* 12–55 of 1933.

7.2 Legitimate Sex Industry in Japan

Sex industry is regarded as a necessary evil, or *hitsuyō-aku* in Japanese, for fundamental human desire. The Japanese sex industry and red-light district, which emerged as a consequence of a protracted historical evolution, are notable examples of this phenomenon. In the Japanese context, the designation for an establishment providing sexual entertainment is *yūkaku*, which literally means a place that engages in sex "custom". This term is used in a more polite manner when contrasted with *baishunyado*,

K. B. Wong and S. L. Fang, *Taishinin's Judicial Behaviour in Corruption Cases*,
https://doi.org/10.1007/978-981-95-5823-0_7

which implies brothels or vice establishments that provide venues for prostitution. It is noteworthy that the latter term is predominantly utilized by Japanese mass media.[1]

Sex industry was nothing new in Japan. The origin of the term *yūjo* for courtesan in Japanese history can be traced in the Japanese classic *Manyōshū* in about 700. In the perspective of folklore, both Nakayama and Yanagida believe that the origin of *yūjo* was from religious ceremony of Shintō.[2] In *Manyōshū*, the term *yūjo* or *yūkōjofu* had nothing to do with prostitution. In the *waka* (Japanese classical poetry in short sentence style) of *Manyōshū*, the term *yūkōjofu* referring to the wondering woman performing songs and dances for the requiem and summoning of souls for religious ceremony, was used for the first time in Japan. *Satomiko* performed for the same purpose in the village temple.

In the history of Japanese sex industry, there were other terms for sex-related adult entertainment and red-light district. For example, *kanrakugai* (entertainment district), *akasenkuiki* (red-light district), *okabasho* (generic term for private brothels), *seirō* (brothel), *kashizashiki* (rental room) and *yūri* (a certain area where prostitutes are allowed to operate in groups); *girō* (brothel), *yūjoya* (courtesan house), *shōka* (a house where a prostitute is placed to take guests), *jorōkoya* (prostitute's hut), *jorōya* (a house whose business is to keep prostitutes and entertain guests) are also common terms for brothels inside such areas. These districts where contain people who earn their living in sex industry are jargoned with *karyūkai*, *kagai* or *hamamachi*, which literally mean "flower town" or "flower street". The term *karyū* is borrowed from a poetry of Chinese poet Li Bai.[3]

From the viewpoint of the immigration history, Takigawa Masajirō advocates *yūjo* were originally the Korean *Paekcho* immigrants, who were considered discriminated people on the Korean Peninsula.[4] *Asobime* (a woman who mediates entertainment such as a drinking party by orchestra, song and dance and also prostitutes) is another term implying *yūjo*. *Shōfu* explicitly refers to a woman who obtains money by providing sexual services. Other terms such as *meshimorion'na* (a private prostitute who existed in post towns in the Edo period), *kugutsume* (a woman who used puppet to sing but she also provided sex entertainment), *baijo* (a discriminatory and derogatory term against prostitute) and *keisei* (a term means beauty as well as courtesan) have the similar meaning. *Baishunpu*, *baishōfu* and *inbaifu* have common meaning of sexual worker, and *shūgyō* means scourge. There is a discriminatory term *shūgyōfu*, which refers to a lady who made a living by prostitution which is regarded as scourge.

Japanese sex industry was historically a licenced legitimate industry of self-discipline and a sense of public order before the Meiji era. Shōji Jinzaemon was the founder of the largest licenced red-light district *Yoshiwara Yūkaku* in Edo. In 1612, he sought bakufu's legal permission for brothel as *keiseimachi* (an area for licenced prostitution) in today's Chūōku, Nihonbashi Ningyōchō in Tokyo. In March

---

[1] On this see Mainichishinbun (2021).

[2] On this see Nakayama (2012) and Yanagida (1990).

[3] The original text in Li Bai's poetry *Liu Yelang presented Judge Xin* (流夜郎贈辛判官): 昔在長安醉花柳五侯七貴同杯酒。

[4] On this see Takigawa (1969).

1617, sex industry licence was granted through the Tokugawa legal order *Keiseimachi Hiōsetsuke Sōrōsetsu Okakitsuke*, which had explicit regulation limiting sex industry to the designated area as *Keiseimachi* (Takaki 2018, pp. 2–4). There were certain rules such as that customers could not stay longer than one day and one night, or no other business could have establishment in the designated area.[5] As mentioned before, under the public administration policy of the Tokugawa bakufu, sex industry in Edo era relied on self-discipline for public order. For example, gambling was prohibited in red-light district. The court judgements in this period confirmed that *burakumin*'s (people at the bottom of Japanese caste system) visit to red-light district was a criminal offence in consistent with government's policy for caste system (Takaki 2018, pp. 4–5). *Hanka-chō* (collection of criminal judgements) of *Nagasakibugyō-sho* (Nagasaki Magistrate's Court), which was court of first instance in Nagasaki during Edo era, collecting judgements of discriminatory judicial behaviour against *burakumin*'s right for sexual service.[6] In 1656, the red-light district in Tokyo moved to *Shinyoshiwara*, where is today's Senzoku and Taitōku in Tokyo. At its peak, it had 3,000 sex workers.[7] Customers for sex-related entertainment were shifted from the upper class to the mass sex industry market of ordinary citizens in Edo (Takaki 2016, pp. 132–133). The pursuit of sexual satisfaction could never be obsolete.

At the dawn of the Meiji era, sex industry was a huge legitimate business. As sex entertainment was regarded as a necessary evil for fundamental human desire, *Taishinin*'s judicial behaviour was affected by this mindset in a prewar landmark contract law ruling.

7.3 *Taishinin* Ruling Legitimatizing Supply Chain of Sex Worker

Taishinin's ruling in *Minji Hanketsuroku* (civil judgement record) numbered 6–2-1900–83 stated that if the contract was for the objective of restraining the body of a person who intended to give up the freedom of her body for prostitution, it should be regarded as an independent contract.[8] *Hōritsu Shinbun* (law newspaper) dated 20 February 1916 also recorded a landmark *Taishinin* ruling in respect of legality of income from prostitution for debt settlement instead of treating it as illicit funds.[9]

---

[5] The original text in legal order of *Keiseimachi Hiōsetsuke Sōrōsetsu Okakitsuke*: 傾城屋商売不可致… 傾城買遊び候者、一日一夜より長留不可致事。

[6] See Miyamoto (1984, pp. 19–29).

[7] On this see National Diet Library (2014).

[8] The Original text in the judgement: 貸座敷ヲ以テ営業トナス者ト娼妓ヲ以テ稼業ト為スモノ丶間ニ於ケル金銭貸借上ノ契約ニ関シ娼妓ヲ稼業ト為スモノカ身体ノ自由ヲ譲与スル意思即チ身体ヲ拘束スルヲ目的トスル契約トハ各自独立スル契約と見做シ。

[9] The original text of law report in *Hōritsu Shinbun*: 娼妓営業の収入を以て債務の弁済に充つることの適法なる(中略)一方が娼妓稼業を為し其収益を以て債務弁済の手段とし一方が之を計算の対価として一定の金員を貸与することは法令の認許する範囲内の行動にして公序良俗に反するものにあらず。

Taishinin's attitudinal judicial behaviour was not against immoral sex entertainment but in favour of it indirectly by assurance of supply chain in sex industry. It stated that as a means of repayment of debts, one party can lend a certain amount of money as consideration in the contract for the debtor prostitute. *Taishinin* set legal condition that it should be "acts within the scope permitted by laws and regulations and are not contrary to public order and morals". Prewar Japan had a malpractice of selling or pawning oneself or a family member to solve monetary problem. Long before this *Taishinin* ruling, the indenture and loan contract for working in a Nagasaki brothel as *kamuro* (underage prostitute) had legally existed since Edo era.[10]

Theoretically, the abovementioned landmark *Taishinin* rulings infringed the Meiji Emperor's *Dorei-kaihōrei* (Emancipation Decree), under which emancipation and freedom should also be granted regardless of gender and social stratification. This Decree criminalized human trafficking but the aforesaid two *Taishinin* rulings prevented personal freedom of movement to be granted to sex worker *yūjo* in *yūkaku.* A contract in breach of *Dorei-kaihōrei* could not be enforced but these rulings was paradoxically upheld by *Taishinin*'s favourable attitudinal judicial behaviour with binding legal force lasted until postwar Japan. *Yūkaku* was then developed into a licenced sex industry in area under public management of government by community policing.

The two contract law rulings were controversial in legal studies. The rulings intertwining debt repayment and prostitution with protection of contract should thus be void accordingly. Sex-related industry with "special restaurant business license" all along could follow these *Taishinin* rulings to legitimatize prostitution by loan settlement (Hirakawa 2018, pp. 16–18). Article 90 of the Civil Code in 1898 stipulated that a *juridical act* which is against public policy is void.[11] *Taishinin*'s judicial behaviour in this regard merely accepted the social reality without treating the objective of contract as contrary to public order or good morals stipulated in Article 90 of prewar Civil Code.[12] As a result of change of social conditions, Article 90 was amended in 2017 to "any legal act contrary to public order or good morals shall be invalid".[13] The legislative restraint of "objective" was deleted to give more freedom for court's judicial behaviour to apply equitable *dōri.* This legal amendment has achieved the connection between postwar social conditions and judicial behaviour.[14] The criminalization of prostitution was delayed until the codification of *Baishun-bōshihō* (Anti-Prostitution Code) in 1956. However, there are still 162 such "special restaurant business licenses" being used by the members of today's *Tobitashinji Ryōri*

[10] On this see Matsui (2014, pp. 173–174; pp. 180–182).

[11] On this see Ministry of Justice (2023).

[12] The Original text of prewar Civil Code: 公ノ秩序又ハ善良ノ風俗ニ反スル事項ヲ目的トスル法律行為ハ無効トス。

[13] The original text in Civil Law amended in 2017: 公の秩序又は善良な風俗に反する法律行為は、無効とする。

[14] On the original text see e-Gov(the Civil Law, No.89 in *Meiji* 29)at https://laws.e-gov.go.jp/law/129AC0000000089#Mp-Pa_1-Ch_5-Se_1-At_90. Accessed 2 October 2025.

Kumiai (Tobita Shinchi Restaurant Association) as the interest group for legal sex entertainment in Osaka.[15]

7.3.1 Community Policing to Ensure Public Order for Sex Business

The prewar administrative police played a key role in the development of sex industry. Precisely, they legally aided the sex industry management directly. In 1885, the Ministry of Interior published *Keimuyōsho* (Police Guidebook), the name *fūzoku-keisatsu* (custom police) was formally adopted as a special type of police.[16] One of the main duties for *fūzoku-keisatsu* was monitoring the sex industry and keeping the prostitutes register. *Fūzoku-keisatsu* demonstrated adherence to *Taishinin*'s civil law rulings concerning the contractual obligation. These rulings exhibited congruence with the prevailing tradition of a lenient legal culture, which endorsed the legitimacy of the sex industry as an adult entertainment medium. During prewar Japan, the prewar administrative police-maintained oversight of brothel proprietors and sex workers, who continued to engage in the development of the oldest trade in human history through private contractual relationships. The legal framework in place ensured a stable supply chain of sex workers.[17] The administrative police were endowed with extensive discretionary authority over public order. However, mediation for disputes arising from private contracts and competition among brothel owners was not encompassed within the scope of their responsibilities (Uchida 1982, p. 31).

Taishinin's attitudinal judicial behaviour toward sex workers and the development of the sex industry was consistent with the traditional policy of the Tokugawa bakufu. *Taishinin*'s judicial behaviour was in alignment with the policies established by the Ministry of Justice of the Meiji Government. Obinata and Hayakawa's research indicates that the Ministry of Justice of the Meiji Government demonstrated a preference for the adoption of acquiescence as its judicial policy, with the objective of ensuring the survival of the sex industry.[18]

In the context of this *Taishinin* case, the legal question of whether mediation constituted an element of official police duty was the pivotal point of contention. The efficacy of mediation by police officer is contingent upon the cultivation of positive community relations, which in turn fosters the willingness of disputing parties to reach a mutually acceptable resolution. On 2 October 1900, the Ministry of Interior issued *Shōgi-torishimari-kisoku* (Prostitution Control Regulations) as the Ministry Order number 44, of which Article 3 required the brothels to furnish *shogi-meibo-no-tōroku* (written application for registration of prostitution list) to the nearest

[15] On this see Inoue (2021).

[16] See *Keimuyōsho* (1885, p. 357).

[17] On this see Yoshimi (2019, pp. 1–14).

[18] On this see Obinata (1992) and Hayakawa (1998).

police station (Masugi 2009, pp. 239–241). According to *Taishinin* contract law ruling, a sex worker's income to fulfil contract obligation of debt settlement could be legitimate. Police could not treat the pimps in the licenced brothels as criminals living on the earnings of prostitute. On the contrary, police indirectly aided and abetted the pimps in the sex industry by the maintenance of public order and enforcement of contractual obligations. This licenced public prostitution system thus relied on police management in the form of control and monitor, and the community policing keeping relations between police and *rōshu* (owners of brothels) was essential. This culture of community relations promoted the sex industry prosperity and police efforts for conflict resolutions (Tran 2017, p. 39). The sex industry gradually became a wealthy nationwide interest group of capabilities to provide tangible and intangible interest to police in prewar Japan. In this connection, would readers of this book agree that prewar Japanese police aiding and abetting pimps' immoral act of living on the earnings of prostitutes.

In a gradual process, sex business unions were established with the objective of coordinating with law enforcement entities and engaging in negotiations with the government regarding its policies pertaining to the sex industry. The first one was *Tōkyō Geigiya Dōmeikai* (Tokyo Geisha Association) established with 15 members in 1902. In 1927, it expanded into a nationwide union including 201 sub-unions. In 1926, the total number of the members under the union of *Zenkoku-ryōrigyō-kumiai* was 5763. The main objective was bargaining for tax rate reduction with the government and helping solve conflicts among union members.[19]

Under the blessing of *Taishinin*'s judicial behaviour and community policing, stakeholders in the sex industry had high profitability but problems also arose. A newspaper in 1911 reported that community policing in red-light districts was abnormally lenient in the monitor of brothels. In one brothel, about 10 percentage of the prostitutes were found to be teenagers between 14 and 17 (Motomori 2013, p. 153). Although the spirit of *Dorei-kaihōrei* (Emancipation Decree) implied that a sexual worker had equality and freedom to take up or refuse this job, its intention was apparently not for the support of such freedom of immorality and sex industry development, let alone underage girls. Police corruption likely involved in underaged prostitution.

After the Great Kantō earthquake in 1923, population in Tokyo increased very rapidly. The earthquake burned a lot of licenced brothels and led to large number of unlicensed brothels. In 1924, the Jūnisō (the western part of today's Shinjuku Ward) in Yodobashi was an entertainment area of *nigyōchi*, a type of red-light districts where sex workers and restaurants were permitted to operate together for sexual service, near today's Kabukicho. Although Kabukicho is famous for its adult entertainment today, it was almost unknown in prewar Japan.

Other than *nigyōchi*, some areas in Tokyo were more leniently under permission for *sangyōchi* to provide sex service under the cover of *geigiya* (geisha house), *machiai* (greeting room) and restaurants. The railway extension to Nishikoyama, Ikebukuro, Nakano and Shinbashi in 1928 helped the development of the imperial capital, as well as the adult entertainment areas. The sex industry developed rapidly

[19] On this see Terasawa (2018), p. 33, p. 35, pp. 41–42.

alongside with the reconstruction of Tokyo (Nishimura et al. 2008, pp. 303–304). The founder of first *sangyōchi* was Akimoto Tetsugorō, who got the first *sangyōchi* licence in a small town of today's Bunkyōku, and he was considers as a pioneer of sex entertainment business and the founder of *Tokushu-ianshisetsu-kyōkai* (Recreation and Amusement Association). During the Occupation period, Akimoto's contribution to Japanese sex industry was his role of managing the sex entertainment specially provided to the American troops.

In 1928, dancing halls entered the mass sex entertainment market in cities. The Metropolitan Police Bureau's *Butōba-torishimari-kisei* (Dancing Hall Control Rules) in 1928 respected dancing halls as part of the entertainment market but intentionally did not fully plug the loophole for sex service (Nojima 1984, p. 62). Even café became a popular venue for unlicenced prostitutes to solicit customers (Murata 2007, pp. 48–49). In 1930, senior administrative police officers openly advocated the legalization of prostitution in the view of the impossibility for total elimination (Yoshitsugu 1930, p. 35). In early 1930s, the main target of police enforcement was the elimination of unlicensed private prostitution in cities to maintain the licenced sex industry under the police petrol. A total number of 2310 unlicenced prostitutes were arrested by the Metropolitan Police Bureau from January 1929 to the end of 1934 (Terasawa 2014, p. 118). *Tokush-inshokuten-eigyō-torishimari-kisei* (Special Restaurant Business Regulation) was formulated in 1933 for the suppression of this wave of unlicenced prostitution and stricter prevention of social hygiene disease. This regulation was not intended to criminalize prostitution or abruptly alter the prevailing policy within the sex industry (Nagai 1996, pp. 211–212).

In this *Taishinin* case, two *rōshu* (owners of brothels) had open violent conflicts, who were members of the same-sex business union in *nigyōchi* of today's Shinjuku. Administrative policemen had favouritism of not arresting *rōshu* for their assault occasioning bodily harm in *nigyōchi* openly. The union tried to pacify themselves by mediation but in vain. Administrative police of Metropolitan Police Bureau therefore stepped in for mediation in their own "private capacity". They exercised their discretionary power and police status to pressurize two conflictual parties to "cease fire" and compromise. The mediation all along had not been listed as a formal police duty, but police officer might make use of his police status to exert influence on sex businessmen to participate in mediation.

7.4 Juridical Facts in *Taishinin* Judgement

This *Taishinin* case pertains to the midyear customary practice of bestowing gifts upon administrative police officers. This practice is referred to as *ochūgen*. The judgement offers no indication of any corrupt consideration *quid pro quo* prior to or *ex post facto* guilty intention to the gift-giving act in the legal question. It mentions that gifts in this case were for the appreciation of the police mediation to pacify violent conflicts among the brothels. *Taishinin* deliberately omitted the given names of certain union staff members. It is reasonable to hypothesize that *Taishinin* exhibited a degree of confidentiality in its judicial behaviour. It seems that *Taishinin* had some respect for privacy.

7.4.1 Ochūgen as a Customary Midyear Gifting Practice

Kenjo set up a sex business union for 60 geisha restaurants in Jūnisō, Tokyo on 12 May 1930, and he acted as one of the directors in geisha union. Yoshida Sei and Wasuke were also union directors owning geisha restaurants in the same district, fighting against each other violently due to the fierce market competition to solicit customers since November 1927. They both showed no willingness to compromise. Assault occasioning actual bodily harm cases happened frequently. It constituted menace to the public order and public peace in downtown Tokyo.

Miyata Kisaku was a *keishi* (police superintendent) of Tokyo Metropolitan Police Bureau in charge of Yodobashi Police Station. He had official duty for crime prevention and to deal with open violent conflict for assurance of *fūki-eisei* (public morals and hygiene). He was assumed to have capacity to perform *chōtei-chinbu* (mediation and dispute settlement) for Yoshida and Wasuke's conflicts. With his mediation efforts since mid-April 1930, the conflictual geisha houses were disbanded. Peaceful agreement on the formation of a new *Jūnisō nigyō* union was concluded on 12 May 1930.

In order to appreciate the efforts of Miyata and his subordinate patrol policeman Uekō Shi for the conflict settlement and lenient treatment of Jūnisō nigyō union members, on 12 July 1930, Kenjo, Yoshida Sei, Wasuke and several Jūnisō nigyō union members came to Yodobashi Police Station to greet the police inspector, Iwasa Hachizou and Miyata's subordinate police constables at the Jūnisō Police Kiosk. Kenjo had discussion and *bōgi* (conspiracy) with them on financial *sharei* as a token of gratitude. *Taishinin* judgement recorded that Kenjo and Wasuke had the following acts of bribery with continuous guilty intention:

> On 13 July 1930, at the hostel for the officer in charge of Yodobashi Police Station, Kenjo and Wasuke gave 300 *yen* to Miyata as *sharei* on *ochūgen* in appreciation of Miyata's mediation efforts. On the same day, at Haramachi, Tokyo, police inspector Iwasa Hachizou refused the acceptance and returned the 100-*yen* gift on *ochūgen,* which was claimed as the gift for the appreciation of his efforts of official duty. The police patrol constable Suzuki and other police constables at the Jūnisō Police Kiosk also returned 50-*yen sharei* to Kenjo and Wasuke. Police constable Yuhara and several subordinates under him at Tsunohazu Police Kiosk returned 30-*yen sharei,* which was given under the cover of gift of *ochūgen.* On 14 July 1930, at Tama, Tokyo, the geisha house owner Yoshida Sei gifted 100 *yen* to the police officer Uekō Shi as *ochūgen.* Yoshida, Kenjo and Wasuke had the acts of giving bribe to Miyata and Uekō Shi and offered bribe to the policemen at Jūnisō Police Kiosk and Tsunohazu Police Kiosk.

7.5 Yoshida Sei's Appeal Grounds

The appellant union director Yoshida Sei claimed that bribery should be a civil servant's acceptance of inappropriate interest in relation to the official duty of two administrative police officers Miyata and Uekō, who contributed their utmost as "*shokumu igai watashi-jin no shikaku*[20]" (in private capacity outside the ambit of official duty). The junior courts had "*hōritsu no geshaku o gori*[21]" (misinterpretation of law).

Yoshida and Kenjo gave 450 *yen* and 100 *yen* to the policemen Miyata and Uekō respectively as *sharei* on *ochūgen*. Yoshida claimed his motive was appreciation of two policemen's mediation for conflict resolution and lenient treatment of the new union in Jūnisō district. It was for maintenance of public morality and hygiene. Their offer of a total of 150 *yen* to police constables at two police kiosks for the same reason was incomplete inchoate act because of policemen's refusal of acceptance. Yoshida emphasized that two administrative policemen mediated in their private capacity which was outside the ambit of statutory official duty.

Yoshida did not argue on whether the maintenance of the public morality and hygiene was specific official police duty. He relied on the administrative police officers' private capacity outside official duty as the punchline of his appeal ground. He emphasized that these two policemen made private efforts for the mediation to pacify the violent conflicts in the red-light district *nigyōchi*, which was the focus of his argument. The demarcation of official duty of these two administrative policemen confirmed that mediating conflicts was conducted privately without connectivity with official duty. It is true that *gyōsei-keisatsu* (administrative police) had neither power nor official duty for mediation.

In historical perspective, the logic of Yoshida's appeal ground was not groundless or unreasonable. In the early Meiji era, *Dajokan* was established as a supreme government office with power to issue *Dajokan-tasshi* as laws and ordinances in 1875. *Dajokan-tasshi* (大政官達し) Number 29 was specifically for *gyōsei-keisatsu-kisoku* (Administrative Police Regulations) in police system (Suzuki 2018, p. 289). During the Meiji era, Japan followed the European Civil Law system to set up national police under the Minister of Interior. *Keishi-sōkan* (superintendent general) was senior official at the prefectural level. As national agency, *Keishichō* (Metropolitan Police Bureau) was set up in Tokyo and *keisatsubu* (police departments) were in prefectures.[22] *Gyōsei-keisatsu* in the structure of police organization all along had no mediation power. In prewar Japan, mediation had been a specific statutory power authorized by law, but police was outside the scope of statutory authorization.

Under *Gyōsei-shikkōhō* (Administrative Execution Code) dated 2 June 1900 (*Meiji* 33, Law No. 84), the administrative police had official duty to enforce this Code. Administrative Execution Code listed the scope of official duties as follows:

---

[20] The original text in the judgement: 職務以外私人ノ資格。

[21] The original text in the judgement:法律ノ解釋ヲ誤リ。

[22] On this see National Police Agency (2004), p. 68.

Arrest and Provisional Retention (Article 1)
House invasion (Article 2)
Compulsory Diagnosis, Compulsory Treatment and Restrictions on Residence (Article 3)
Restrictions on use of land objects (Article 4)
Execution by proxy, punishment by execution, direct coercion (Article 5)
Compulsory collection of fees, etc. (Article 6)
Property belonging to the national treasury (Article 7)[23]

The above-tabulated concise official duty list underscores the potential for discretionary power held by administrative police to be exploited for private gain, particularly with regard to compulsory sanction and immediate enforcement as outlined in Article 5. The legislative intent was predicated on the assumption that Japanese nationals possessed the obligation to assist law enforcement in attaining the objective of public order in social relations through the implementation of community policing initiatives.[24] However, all articles in *Gyōsei-shikkōhō* had not included *chōtei-assen* (mediation and arbitration) as official duty. Therefore, it was not incorrect for Yoshida to argue on it. In the perspective of the Meiji Constitution, *Gyōsei-shikkōhō* reinforced the relationship between Japanese subjects under the Emperor in state polity (Shimada 2012, p. 111). On 27 May 1948, *Gyōsei-shikkōhō* was rescinded as part of the postwar law reform.[25]

In *Chian-keisatsuhō* (Security Police Code) codified on 10 March 1900 under Law number 36 and *Chian-ijihō* (Peace Preservation Code) passed on 22 April 1925 under Law number 46, Japanese policemen were empowered to have thought control over Japanese nationals and the limitation on the freedom of speech, press, expression, assembly and association for the public order. These two codes were rescinded in 1945, on which scrutiny also confirmed that no legal provision empowering police to make mediation as a part of their official duty.

Under *nullum crimen sine lege* (no law, no crime and no punishment), police officers had no legal mediation power statutorily. The prewar Japanese legislation provided police power to arrest criminal offenders, but neither authorized nor required administrative policemen to act as mediators according to the legislation. And the background was that the sex industry was not considered criminal but a legal and licenced business under the police monitor in prewar Japan.

7.6 *Taishinin*'s Two Grounds of Refusal

Taishinin's two rulings for refusal of appeal, from the perspective of crime prevention, were unambiguous. First, *gyōseikeisatsu-no-mokuteki* (the objective of administrative police) was to ensure the smooth functioning of society by addressing issues

[23] On the original text see National Diet Library Digital Collections (2011a, p. 1).

[24] On this see Sudo (2007, p. 251 and p. 271).

[25] On this see National Diet Library (2019, p. 480).

that fall outside the purview of other law enforcement agencies. The responsibility of safeguarding the public interest and maintaining peace and order was undertaken. In the event that there was a risk of crime commission, it fell within the scope of their duties to strive for the maintenance of public order. It was imperative that measures be taken for the prevention of crime before its occurrence. It is imperative that such preventive measures be implemented in anticipation of directives from superior authorities. Accordingly, the maintenance of public order was considered an integral component of their professional obligations.[26] *Taishinin* employed the term *gyōseikeisatsu-no-mokuteki* (the objective of administrative police) as an overarching concept to describe the process of criminalization. According to *Taishinin*'s judicial behaviour, any police work that was relevant to the maintenance of public order and public peace was considered official duty.

Secondly, in the event that a police officer is able to fulfil their duties related to crime prevention and the maintenance of peace and order, they should respond to it in an opportunistic manner according to the objective of administrative police. These findings are consistent with the duties of an administrative police officer, who is responsible for administrative affairs.[27] In instances where law enforcement officials perceive a potential for criminal activity, they are obligated to take proactive measures to forestall such occurrences. *Taishinin*'s discourse did not include a direct mention of the concept of mediation. However, *Taishinin* employed the umbrella term *gyōseikeisatsu-no-mokuteki* in a very broad sense, using it to imply a responsibility for the police to engage in crime prevention through mediation. The question of whether mediation constituted a specific statutory duty was not posed directly.

Taishinin's ruling established that the monetary contributions allocated for *ochūgen* were *sharei*, allocating funds for appreciating administrative officers' efforts in mediating and regulating public order and hygiene within the newly established Jūnisō union. In view of confirmation of the relation between funds and objective of administrative police, constituent element of bribery offence was established.

[26] The original text in the judgement:行政警察の目的は人民の兇害を予防し安寧秩序を保全するに在り此の行政警察の事務を管掌する警察署又は此の一般警察事務に關する補助機關たる巡査は苟も安寧秩序を紊し又は犯罪行為等を為す虞ある場合に自を又は其の上司の命に依り予め之を防止すべき方策を講し因て以て治安の維持に努むるは其の職務の範圍に屬するもの。

[27] The original text in the judgement:犯罪の予防安寧秩序の保全に關する警察官吏の職責を全ぶし得さる場合に於て機に臨み變に應し...犯罪の未然に防止し安寧秩序を保全する...行政警察の目的に合致し...行政警察の事務を管掌する警察官吏の職務に屬するもの。

7.7 Analysis of *Taishinin*'s Refusal of Appeal

7.7.1 Criminalization of Customary Gift-Giving Practice

In this judgement, *Taishinin* articulated a definitive ruling that neither gifting nor private capacity was permissible. The legal reasoning employed was of an expansive nature, encompassing the umbrella term of objective of police *gyōseikeisatsu-no-mokuteki*. The police officers' actions related to *an'nei-chitsujo* (peace and order) was the official responsibility of a *kanri* (a government official). The judgement did not provide any guidelines for the criminalization of misconduct by a civil servant in their private capacity outside of office hours. *Taishinin*'s strategic judicial behaviour was characterized by the rationalization of the objective of police as its ultimate goal. Its extensively legal reasoning underscored the paramount importance of crime prevention and maintenance of peace and order to law enforcement officials. This fundamental responsibility of police officers was reiterated to underscore its constant and unwavering commitment to public safety and order. It was determined that a full statutory listing of official police duties was not required under *an'nei-chitsujo* (peace and order).

The sequence of *Taishinin*'s judicial behaviour exhibited a tendency to first assess official duty, followed by an overall circumstances assessment, together with an attitudinal value judgement and/or strategy for judicial activism, if applicable (Fujioka 1979, p. 42). In accordance with the prevailing judicial practices associated with the *Taishinin* strict liability model, the mitigating factor that would absolve culpability for bribery was not considered in this judgement.

Taishinin's judicial behaviour is akin to a court that exhibits a variety of characteristics under different circumstances. Judicial activism is a term used to describe the strategic implementation of new rulings by courts to achieve a specific objective. Activist judicial behaviour is known to establish novel, radical precedents that wield binding legal force, a phenomenon referred to within the legal context as *stare decisis*. This stands in contrast to the conventional judicial approach of restraint, which emphasizes a more circumscribed and deferential judicial function (Yildiz 2020, p. 75). The judicial behaviours of restrictive, extensive, or expansive legal reasoning are frequently employed for judicial activism, especially when the literal meaning of a legal provision does not precisely correspond to the intended meaning of the legislature (Canale and Giovanni 2018, p. 67). In this case, *Taishinin* employed a strategy of judicial activism to make use of the objective of administrative police to criminalize the mediation of police officers in private capacity and reject Yoshida's appeal. However, no explicit legal provision could be cited to confirm that mediation fell within the purview of police power according to legislation.

In the perspective of strategic judicial behaviour, *Taishinin* mentioned Miyata was an administrative police officer in charge of the police station who should take *fūki* (public morals) and *eisei* (hygiene) as official duty. As per Article 1 of *Gyōsei-keisatsu-kisoku*, the mission of the administrative police was to prevent people's violent behaviour and preserve peace.[28] The term *fūki-eisei* is one of the many objectives of administrative police (Suzuki 2018, p. 289). In Article 3 of *Gyōsei-keisatsu-kisoku*, assurance of people's health, control of pornographic indecent and immoral behaviour and criminal investigation were further added as objectives, but *chōtei-chinbu* (mediation and dispute settlement) was not covered.[29]

As a behaviour of judicial activism, *Taishinin* introduced another umbrella term *an'nei-chitsujo* (peace and order) in this judgement. In order to emphasize it as the official police duty, *chōtei-chinbu* was rationalized as a means to attain the goal of *an'nei-chitsujo. Taishinin* thereby judicially activated and rationalized the linkage of *an'nei chitsujo* with *chōtei-chinbu* as administrative police officer's official duty. Even so, *Taishinin* made no direct comment on and analysis of appellant's claim of mediation in private capacity after official duty hours.

In theory, a policeman was not assumed to be on 24-hour round-the-clock duty except under a special order. Without statutory orders or authorization, appellant's mediation efforts should not be counted a constituent element of the official duty under Article 198(1) of the prewar Penal Code, and the conviction was against "no law, no crime and no punishment" in Article 23 of Meiji Constitution. Without any evidence stated in the judgement for corroboration, *Taishinin*'s claim of lenient *fūki-eisei* treatment of brothels was neither fully substantiated nor evidence based. It seems that *Taishinin* had a presumption that Yoshida gave *sharei* for the police favouritism of lenient treatment. The judicial behaviour aimed to rationalize this presumption as its strategic goal.

As to the mitigating factor for culpability, as usual, *Taishinin*'s judicial behaviour of strict liability model paid no attention to police officer Mitaya's mediation as a contribution to public order. The circumstantial evidence indicated that Mitaya did it out of his own initiative for social good and public order without superior's authorization or prior approval. He had no intention and reasonable foreseeability to exchange his initiate with financial interest beforehand or after resumption of public peace and public order. *Taishinin*'s judicial activism strategically intertwined objective of police with strict liability.

Attitudinally, *Taishinin*'s judgement recorded a total of 550 *yen* was gifted to administrative police officers as *sharei* on *ochūgen*. As mentioned before, *sharei* is the most frequently used term in the judgements on bribery cases. Literally, *sharei* should be pure appreciation for others' efforts and an expression of gratitude. It may also be a one-off gifting act of intention to acknowledge, or seek, a favour from superiors or business connections by gifting act (Sugimoto 2010, p. 238). *Sharei* on the occasion of *ochūgen* or *oseibo* (both are gifting for holidays) can easily become a bribery transaction. Under the "package" of customary midyear gift-giving *ochūgen* or *oseibo*, a gift of corrupt consideration *quid pro quo* may be morally justifiable by local population, depending on what actors in a culture honestly believe what they are.

---

[28] The original text of *Gyōsei-keisatsu-kisoku* mentioned in the judgement: 行政警察ノ趣意タル民ノ凶害ヲ予防シ安寧ヲ保全スルニアリ。

[29] On this see Ministry of Foreign Affairs (1884, pp. 459–460).

As recorded in this *Taishinin* judgement, some police officers in two police kiosks refused to accept *sharei*, which meant that they refused to establish human relationships with the geisha house owners. Otherwise, the debt would be owed when the gift or *sharei* was accepted until a return gift was given after an appropriate amount of time. A relationship could thereby be set up (Shimokawa 2011, p. 18). The relationship established by gifting act is more obvious in Japanese rural society, where gift is defined in reciprocal terms. Gift-giving itself is a matter of *giri*, which requires reciprocation as moral obligation (Befu 1968, p. 450). Reciprocation is a relationship in an endless cycle built on the memory of what a person has promised upon his receipt of a gift or *sharei*. Man has thereafter become a moral being who has to keep one's moral duty of reciprocation (Kanematsu 2022, p. 239). This is the tricky ambiguous aspect of *sharei* and gifting act in Japanese bribery offence. Gifting and *sharei* should be unconditional, but it may not the case in view of the hidden cultural agenda of building social relationships for reciprocation.

The judgement made no mention of the extent of the personal reciprocal relationship between the bribees and the bribers. In *Taishinin*'s strict liability model of judicial behaviour, this confirmation was omitted following the confirmation of a gift of linkage with official duty at the constituent element stage. *Taishinin* provided no commentary on whether the amount of money was modest or lavish. Even if *bone fide* gift or *sharei* on *ochūgen* in appreciation of police mediation efforts in good faith, conviction of bribery was unavoidable under *Taishinin*'s judicial behaviour of strict liability model.

This *Taishinin* judgement conveys a clear message to Japanese society that a gift should be a token of goodwill with no suspected strings of *quid pro quo* attached, even transparent straightforward honest gratitude for nonauthorized job might be punishable. In order to maintain the integrity of bureaucrats, the judicial system could impose strict criminal penalties on the practice of customary gift-giving, as it is understood to constitute a corrupt reciprocal relationship. Notwithstanding the absence of any prior assurance of a gift before the start of mediation, the subsequent acceptance connected to the completed mediation was deemed improper in view of official duty under police objective. In this particular instance, *Taishinin* exhibited a commendable degree of judicial propriety, which means *Taishinin* conducted itself in a manner that is above suspicion in order to initiate judicial behaviour *proprio motu* (by its own motion) to demarcate bribe from gift.

7.7.2 Taishinin's Judicial Behaviour Consistent with that in Edo Era

The blurred thin line between customary gift-giving practice and *sharei* or bribe had been a legal issue long before the establishment of *Taishinin*. This was evident in the court judgements of *hyōjōsho* which was the highest court of Tokugawa bakufu during the Edo period. The term *hyōjōsho* originally denoted the location where the councils of the Kamakura Shogunate and Muromachi Shogunate convened. In the year 1635, the Tokugawa government founded the bakufu *hyōjōshom,* which was of the status similar to *Taishinin* as the Edo Shogunate's highest judicial body. In Japanese culture, gifts are typically more symbolic than material, with a far more significant symbolic value than a material value. It was difficult for *hōjōsho* to differentiate between bribery and *sharei*, due to the moral duty of reciprocation inherent in Japanese gifting culture.

In the judgements on bribery in *Oshiokireiruishū* (Collection of Judicial Precedents on Criminal Cases), it is evident that the *hōjōsho* under Tokugawa government had rendered its decision. As same as *Taishinin*'s judicial of strict liability model, the distinction between bribery and gifting was ambiguous. The notion of intention was rarely confirmed very substantially.[30] In order to deter the abuse of genuine gratitude by *sharei* and gift-giving act from bribery, *hōjōsho* also implemented a judicial behaviour model of strict liability. This model imposed a significant cost on individuals engaging in lavish gift-giving, thereby discouraging such practices, and contributing to a more ethical social condition as judicial environment.[31] The aforementioned elements had similarity with *Taishinin*'s judicial behaviour of strict liability model. The two authors designated such rigorous judicial behaviour of *hyōjōsho* as the "Japanese body" in view of its long-standing existence prior to the legal transplantation of Germanic jurisprudence in the Meiji era. In this connection, *Taishinin*'s judicial behaviour is old wine in new bottle.

7.7.3 *Judicial Behaviour of Cognitive Consistency*

The term "cognitive consistency" refers to the tendency of individuals' internal attitudes and thoughts to align with their external actions. The internal thoughts of an individual may encompass a variety of elements, including reflections on personal beliefs, internal logic and words that are conceptualized but infrequently articulated. It has been demonstrated that this phenomenon guides people's judgement and the interpretation of the environmental factors as a summary evaluation of an object of thought. Furthermore, it has been established that linguistic discourse assumes a person who speaks out of his own knowledge system represented in the mindset.[32] Linguistic discourse analysis helps understand *Taishinin*'s judicial behaviour of cognitive consistency with the Meiji Constitution.

It is important to note that constitution law fell outside the scope of *Taishinin*'s jurisprudence. In this judgement, the most evident cognitive consistency was the extensive, all-encompassing interpretation of *annei-chitsujo* (public peace and order), which was a broad and vague term that had been precisely borrowed from Article 9 of the Meiji Constitution. Despite the inability of *Taishinin* to issue an explicit ruling on

---

[30] The original text of *Oshiokireiruishū* mentioned in the judgement: 七、賄賂之部:賄賂謝礼金等差出候類・賄賂謝礼金等之所持いたし候類。

[31] On this see Shirota (2018, pp. 102–117).

[32] On this see Gawronski and Brannon (2019, pp. 92–96).

the Meiji Constitution, a binding judicial policy was formulated by incorporating the constitutional obligation of *annei-chitsujo* into the duties of police officials. An examination of *Taishinin*'s judicial behaviour reveals a consistent cognitive consistency of *annei-chitsujo.*

The Meiji Constitution is a pivotal document that elucidates the strategic objectives of the *Taishinin.* It is evident that the *Taishinin*'s primary objectives encompass the maintenance of police integrity, the implementation of continuous crime prevention measures and the establishment of social control mechanisms. Moreover, the document underscores the *Taishinin*'s commitment to aligning their actions with the expectations of the public.[33] *Taishinin*'s cognitive consistency was reflected by terms and notion in conformity with Article 9, which stipulated that *annei-chitsujo* was intended to promote the well-being of Japanese subjects and to serve the interests of the monarch (*shinmin*). The Emperor possesses the authority to promulgate, or cause to be promulgated, the ordinances necessary for the execution of the laws, or for the maintenance of public peace and order.[34]

In this judgement, *Taishinin* thrice described the police officers as *keisatsu-kanri* (police bureaucrat). *Kanri* (bureaucrat) was of special status in prewar Japan. *Jinjiin* (National Personnel Authority) treated all Japanese bureaucrats as *ten'nō-no-kanri* (Emperor's official). *Taishinin*'s term for *chii* (status) of *keisatsu-kanri* had cognitive similarity with *mibun-sekinin* (status responsibility) in the legal culture of the Tokugawa bakufu though not identical. This is not surprising because bribery offence itself is based on the status of bureaucrat. Otherwise, it is a transaction in private law sector. As per Articles 10 and 19 of the Meiji Constitution, the Emperor granted the *chii* of *kanri* according to qualifications prescribed in statutes. *Kanrifukumukiritsu* (Government Official Service Discipline) was issued by the Emperor Meiji under the Imperial Decree No. 39 in 1887, which stipulated a person of the *chii* of *kanri* should be loyal and diligent toward the Emperor and the Emperor's government and should perform their respective duties in accordance with the legal orders and law. Since *Shokunihongi* in 797, the bureaucrats' loyalty had long been glorified as *dōri* of righteousness. *Kanrifukumukiritsu* simply reinforced it to ensure the Emperor's governance under Article 1 of the Meiji Constitution. The Empire of Japan shall be reigned over and governed by a line of the Emperors unbroken for ages eternal. Corruption of bureaucrats is apparently a breach of *dōri* of righteousness for it.

This cognitive consistency in Japanese legal culture continued in postwar Japan. According to the judgement of *Keishū* 7–10-1971 dated 27 October 1953, the Supreme Court of Japan ruled that a civil servant's official duty should be determined in accordance with his *chii*, and the scope of official duty should be determined by the objective of a statute as a whole.[35] Therefore, *Taishinin*'s judicial behaviour

[33] On this see Samuels (2000).

[34] The original text in Article 9 of the Meiji Constitution:天皇ハ法律ヲ執行スル為ニ又ハ公共ノ安寧秩序ヲ保持シ及臣民ノ幸福ヲ増進スル為ニ必要ナル命令ヲ発シ又ハ発セシム但シ命令ヲ以テ法律ヲ変更スルコトヲ得ス。

[35] The original text in the Supreme Court judgement: 日本法における「職務」とは、「公務員がその地位に伴い公務として取り扱うべき一切の執務」である…職務行為の範囲は、法令全体の趣旨により決せられることになり。

regarding to *kanri*'s *chii* and *annei-chitsujo* as the objective was somehow inherited by courts in the postwar era. Judicial behaviour was repeating itself, so to speak.

7.8 Police Mediation Was *Ultra Vires*

The administrative police only had the power to perform duties within the boundaries set down by the law. Otherwise, his performance was *ultra vires* or excess of jurisdiction, which was an act beyond the statutory power. Therefore, police mediation in private capacity was based on their relationship built up by the neighbourhood policing or community policing.[36] High-power distance between the police and the ordinary citizens can influence the policing duty and interaction with the society (Tran 2017, p. 57). This power distance and community relation facilitated two police officers' mediation efforts without being empowered by the Tokyo Metropolitan Police Bureau. They had to do it in private capacity. No other capacity was available.

In *Taishinin* judgement, the term *chinbu* (sooth or pacify) is combined with *chōtei* (mediation) for *chinbuchōtei*. The origin of the term *chinbu* is from the record of *Shokunihonki* in October 709,[37] which means to quell the unrest. The culture of quelling the unrest for public peace and order had long existed in Japan for more than one thousand years.[38] The two police officers' mediation act for public order and public peace was not new in prewar Japan. Compromise between two conflictual parties implies a prior condition and intention to give up something in exchange for a win–win solution. Merit should thus be given to two police officers' rightful exercise of discretionary power for the objective of *annei-chitsujo* in Article 9 of Meiji Constitution through mediation. Scrutiny of prewar mediation legislation confirms that prewar policemen had not been specifically authorized by law to act as mediators. Although there were eight *chōteihō* (mediation code) in the prewar Japanese legal history, none had authorized police officer the mediation power. The eight mediation codes as legal means for alternative conflict resolution are as follows:

1. *Shakuchi-shakka-chōteihō* (Land Lease and Rented House Mediation Code) 1922
2. *Kosaku-chōteihō* (Tenant Medication Code) 1924
3. *Shōji-chōteihō* (Commercial Mediation Code) 1926
4. *Rōdōsōgi-chōteihō* (Labor Dispute Mediation Code) 1926
5. *Kinsensaimurinji-chōteihō* (Monetary Debt Extraordinary Mediation Code) 1932
6. *Jinji-chōteihō* (Personnel Mediation Code) 1939
7. *Kōgyōhō* (*Kōgai-chōteikitei*) (Damage Mediation Regulations, Mining Code) 1939
8. *Senjiminjitokubetsuhō-no-minjitokubetsu-chōteikitei* (Chap. 4 for mediation, Civil special mediation provisions of the Wartime Civil Special Code) 1942

[36] On this see Leishman (2007, pp. 196–202).

[37] The original text in *Shokunihonki*: 雖加鎮撫未能安堵。

[38] On this see *Rokkokushi Volume 3 Continued Nihongi*, edited by Saeki (1929).

The first three mediation codes were for co-ordination and harmonious social relations among farmers, labourers, landlords and tenants of no role for police (Yamanaka 1994, pp. 248–249). For example, Article 2 of *Shōji-chōteihō* stipulated parties in dispute could approach court for mediation service. Article 5 stipulated the court had duty to offer mediation service, not the police.[39] The disputing brothel owners in this *Taishinin* case thus could seek assistance of a court, not police station, to act as mediator for their business dispute. Similar example can also be found in civil special mediation provisions under Article 14 of *Senjiminjitokubetsuhō* in 1942.[40] Both Article 2 of *Shōji-chōteihō* and Article 14 of *Senjiminjitokubetsuhō* had the similarity that the nearest court had jurisdictional power for mediation. The process of the mediation was not judicial proceedings for a verdict. The court, acting as the mediator, could professionally and statutorily help the two owners in this case find the common ground and deal with unrealistic expectations. The large number of specific mediation codes of comprehensive coverage proves that Kawashima Takeyoshi was correct that prewar Japanese society did not like litigiousness but preferred private compromise and settlement for dispute.[41] The key factor of mediation was not the coercive power of police but the conflictual party's intention to accept or reject the mediator's proposal. In a narrow sense, mediation needs relevant parties to give mutual understanding, conciliation and concession under the assistance of a state institution for solution of a civil case, not a criminal case (Ishikawa and Kajimura 1993, p. 3). This is different from the traditional top-down model of Japanese Police's criminal law enforcement.

The prewar organizational structure and power of police lasted until postwar Police Law in 1954, which covered the organizations and structures of police at national and prefectural level. Police Duties Execution Code codified in 1948 redefined and re-specified the power and duties of police officers. The Regulation for the Operation of the Community Police in 1969 regulates police operation at the community level by police kiosk. Both Police Duties Execution Code and Regulation for the Operation of the Community Police formalize today's relationship between community and police as community policing, not the process of mediation. After these law reforms, mediation is still not part of today's official duty of police statutorily.[42] If a Japanese police officer wants to act as a mediator to settle dispute nowadays, he/she has no choice expect voluntary mediation service in private capacity.

---

[39] The original text in *Shōjichōteihō*: 第二条:民事に関して紛争を生じたときは、当事者は、裁判所に調停の申立をすることができる。(管轄)第五条，裁判所は、調停委員会で調停を行う。但し、相当であると認めるときは、裁判官だけでこれを行うことができる。

[40] On this see Umezawa (1943, pp. 68–70, pp. 87–90).

[41] On this see Kawashima (1967).

[42] See Miyata (2012).

7.9 Brief Remarks

According to Minobe Tatsukichi's *Ten'nōkikansetsu* (Emperor's Organization Theory) and *kokutaimeichō* (national physique), *kanri* was explicit agent or bureaucrat of the Emperor.[43] With the status of *kanri*, bureaucrats were in charge of national affairs, shoulder ethical obligations and responsibility for *futeiryō* (indeterminate quantity) of national affairs within a certain range. The scope of their official duty could not be fully definable.[44] The scope of official duty itself might be on unexpected ad hoc basis and contingent on the circumstantial factors which were not predetermined (Rubin and Feeley 2003, p. 619). *Taishinin*'s flexible judicial behaviour to determine the scope of official duty for criminalization is thus not unreasonable.

This case is inconsistent with Nye's definition of corruption, which has gained significant traction in academic discourse, characterizes corruption as the behaviour of a public official who deviates from the formal duties of their office. Such behaviours may be driven by a variety of motivations, including personal interests, familial relationships, participation in private social groups, financial gain or the desire to enhance status. Corruption may be caused by a violation of the established regulations that pertain to the exercise of private-regarding influence (Nye 1967, p. 419).

In contradistinction to Nye's definition, the police officers' mediation in this case was not a deviation from formal duties. Without guilty intention beforehand, two police officers' *ex post facto* acceptance of *sharei* abused their "unwritten" duty of public order and peace for private gain. According to the relevant legislation, the mediation process was considered to be *ultra vires*. The endeavours undertaken to appease the violent conflicts among geisha houses in the red-light district of Tokyo were devoid of any private-regarding influences or other motivations that would be enumerated in Nye's definition. The criminality was the *ex post facto* gift on *ochūgen* being labelled as bribery with judicial behaviour of attitudinal model and strict liability model for a strategic goal, which was to ensure purity of power delegated from Emperor and bureaucrats' conduct and discipline at his majestic service. *Taishinin* demonstrated a forward-looking and far-sighted perspective in this judgement by cognitive consistency with Meiji Constitution in order to rationalize its ruling in state political system.

In next chapter, an examination is conducted into a corruption case related to a police constable who engaged in acceptance of sexual bribery in Osaka. The consistency in *Taishinin*'s implementation of the strict liability model might be found more evident by examining the judgement in next chapter. It involved sex industry in Kansai.

---

[43] See Minobe (1936).

[44] On this see Minobe (1929, p. 217, p. 220, p. 223).

References

Befu, H. (1968) Gift-Giving in a Modernizing Japan. *Monumenta Nipponica*, Vol. 23 (3/4), 445–456.

Canale, D., Giovanni, T. (2018) Analogical reasoning and extensive interpretation. In Kapten, H., Van der Velden, B. ed. *Analogy and Exemplary Reasoning in Legal Discourse.* Amsterdam University Press.

Fujioka, I. (1979) Wairozai no Ichi Kōsatsu : Kōmuin ni Taisuru Keiji Kisei no Junbi-teki Kōsatsu (A Study of Bribery Crimes: Criminal Regulations for "Public Officials" Preliminary Considerations. *Dōshisha Hōgaku (Doshisha Legal Studies)*, Vol. 31 (1), 40–57.

Gawronski, B., Brannon, S. M. (2019). What is cognitive consistency, and why does it matter? In Harmon-Jones, E. ed. *Cognitive dissonance: Reexamining a pivotal theory in psychology (2nd ed.)* (pp. 91–116). American Psychological Association.

Goodrich, P. (1984) *Legal discourse: studies in linguistics, rhetoric and legal analysis.* Unpublished doctoral dissertation. School of Law, University of Edinburgh.

Hayakawa, K. (1998) *Kindai Tennōsei Kokka to Jendā — Seirituki no Hitotsu no Rojikku (The Modern Emperor System and Gender: A Logic of the Establishment Period).* Aoki Shoten.

Hirakawa, T. (2018) Kinsen Shakkashibo ni Miru Tokushu Inshokuten de Hataraku Shakufu no Seikatsu (Life of a barmaid working at a special restaurant as seen in the money lease book. *Seinan Gakuin Daigaku Daigakuin Kenkyū Ronshū (Seinan Gakuin University Graduate School Review)*, No. 7, 11–23.

Home Ministry Police Affairs Bureau. (1885). *Keimuyōsho. Hakubunsha.* https://dl.ndl.go.jp/pid/791032/1/1 Accessed 27 February 2026.

Inoue, R. (2021) Saigo no Iromachi: Tobita No.1 (Final Color Street: Tobita. No.1). *Bunshun Online.* https://bunshun.jp/articles/-/42656. Accessed 7 August 2022.

International Research Center for Japanese Studies. n.d. *Thoughts on the Tokugawa Prohibition* http://ys.nichibun.ac.jp/KojiruienSearch/docs/jinbu_2/jinb_2_0872_2328.html. Accessed 6 August 2022.

Ishikawa, A., Kajimura, F. (1993) *Chūkai Minji Chōtei Hō: Minji Chōtei Kisoku Kaitei (Commentary on Civil Conciliation Law: Civil Conciliation Rules: revised).* Seirin Shoin.

Japan Intellectual Property Arbitration Center. n.d. *What is mediation.* https://www.ip-adr.gr.jp/business/mediation/about/. Accessed 8 August 2022

Kanematsu, N. (2022) Zōyoron to Kōkan Genri: Suijō ni Kansuru Ichikōsatsu (The Gift Theory and the Exchange Principle: A Consideration on Transfer). *Kyoto Sangyo Daigaku Nihon Bunka Kenkyūjo Kiyō (Bulletin of Kyoto Sangyo University Institute for Japanese Studies)*, No. 27, 233–273.

Kawashima, T. (1967) *Nihonjin no Hō Ishiki (Japanese Legal Awareness).* Iwanami Shinsho.

Keizai Zasshi. (1897) *Kokushi Taikei Dai-ni-kan: Shoku Nihongi (Systematically Compiled National History Volume 2: Continued Nihongi).* Keizai Zasshisha.

Leishman, F. (2007) Koban: Neighbourhood Policing in Contemporary Japan. *Policing: A Journal of Policy and Practice*, Vol. 1 (2), 196–202.

Mainichishinbun. (2021) *Katsute no Baishun-yado ni Namamameshii Konseki: Yokohama Koganechō de Shinjin Keikan ga Manabu Kako (Vivid Traces of a Former Brothel: A New Cop Learns the Past in Koganecho, Yokohama)* https://mainichi.jp/articles/20211008/k00/00m/040/392000c. Accessed 6 August 2022.

Masugi, Y. (2009) Jinshin Baibai Haijo Hōshin ni Miru Kindai Kōshō Seido no Yōsō (Aspects of the Modern Licensed Prostitution System as Seen in the "Elimination of Trafficking in Persons" Policy). *Ritsumeikan Daigaku Jinmon Kagaku Kenkyūjo Kiyō (Ritsumeikan University Research Institute for Humanities Bulletin).* No. 93, 237–268.

Matsui, Y. (2014) The Debt-Servitude of Prostitutes in Japan during the Edo Period, 1600–1868. In Campbell, G, Stanziani, A ed. *Bonded Labour and Debt in the Indian Ocean World* (pp. 173–186). Pickering and Chatto.

Minobe, T. (1929) *Gyōsei Hō Satsuyō Jō-kan, Dai 1-han (Essentials of Administrative Law, Volume 1, 2nd Edition).* Yuhikaku.

Minobe, T. (1936) *Gyōsei Hō Satsuyō Jō-kan, Dai 2-han (Essentials of Administrative Law, Volume 2, 2nd Edition).* Yuhikaku.

Miyamoto, Y. (1984) Maruyama Yūjo no Seikatsu: Nagasaki Bugyōsho Hanketsu Kiroku Hankachō o Chūshin to shite (The Life of Maruyama Courtesans--Focusing on the "Nagasaki Magistrate's Office Verdict Records and Criminal Register"). *Komazawa Shigaku (Journal of historical studies)*, Vol. 3, 19-46.

Miyata, S. (2012) *Jissen Keisatsuhō (Pratical Police Law).* Shinzansha Series.

Motomori, E. (2013) Jiyū Ishi naki Seiteki na Shintai: Senzenki Nihon no Kōshōsei Mondai ni okeru (Kodomo) Ron no Ketsujo (Sexual Bodies Without Free Will: The Lack of "Children" Theory in Prewar Japan's Licensed Prostitution Issues). *Meiji Gakuin Daigaku Shakaigaku, Shakai Fukushigaku Kenkyū(Sociology and Social Welfare Research, Meiji Gakuin University)*, No.139, 143–181.

Murata, M. (2007) Kindai Nihon ni okeru Kafē no Hensent (The Transformation of Cafés in Modern Japan), *Shisō (History Window)*, No. 64, 45–53.

Nagai, Y. (1996) Seiyoku no Basho: Fūzoku Eigyō Torishimari no Senryaku (Places of Sexual Desire: Strategies for Cracking Down on Adult Entertainment Businesses). *Gendai Seimeiron Kenkyū (Gendai Life Theory Research)*, Vol. 9, 207-215.

Nakayama, T. (2012) *Nihon Miko-shi (A history of Japanese shrine maidens).* Kokusho Publishing Association.

National Diet Library Digital Collections. (2011a) *Kanpō (Official Gazette), No. 5073 dated 2 Jun 1900.* https://dl.ndl.go.jp/info:ndljp/pid/2948367/1 Accessed 7 August 2022.

National Diet Library. *New Yoshiwara.* https://www.ndl.go.jp/landmarks/sights/shinyoshiwara/ Accessed 6 August 2022.

National Diet Library. (2019) *Kanpō (Official Gazette), Extra dated 27 May 1948.* https://kokkai.ndl.go.jp/simple/dispPDF?minId=100205254X05019480526 Accessed 7 August 2022.

National Police Agency. (2004) *Heisei Jū-roku-nen Keisatsu Hakusho (Police White Paper 2004).* National Police Agency.

Nishimura, A. et al. (2008) Kindai Tōkyō ni okeru Kagai no Seiritsu (Establishment of Hanamachi in Modern Tokyo). *Keikan Dezain Kenkyū Enkōshū (Collection of lectures on landscape design)*, No. 4, 300–307,

Nojima, M. (1984) Shakō Dansu no Shakai-shi Nōto 1: Senzen no Nihon ni okeru Shakō Dansu no Tenkai (Notes on the Social History of Ballroom Dance 1: Development of Ballroom Dance in Prewar Japan). *Seikatsu Kagaku Kenkyū (Bulletin of Living Science)*, No. 6, 58–68.

Nye, J. (1967) Corruption and political development: a cost-benefit analysis. *American Political Science Review*, Vol. 6 (2), 417-427.

Obinata, S. (1992) *Nihon Kindai Kokka no Seiritsu to Keisatsu (The Formation of the Modern Japanese State and the Police).* Azekura Shobo.

Police Division, Home Ministry. (1885) *Keimu Yōsho (Police Guidebook).* Hakubunsha.

Rubin, E. L., Feeley, M. M. (2003) Judicial policy-making and litigation against the government. *Journal of Constitutional Law*, Vol. 3 (3), 617-664.

Saeki, Y. ed. (1929) *Rokkokushi Volume 3 Continued Nihongi.* Asahi Shimbun Company.

Samuels, J. E. (2000) *The Measurement of Police Integrity.* https://www.ojp. gov/pdffiles1/nij/181465.pdf. Accessed 8 August 2022.

Shimada, S. (2012) Meiji Kenpō-ka ni okeru Gyōsei Shikkō-hō no Sho-mondai (Issues of the Administrative Execution Law under the Meiji Constitution). *Tsūshin Kyōiku-bu Ronshū (Correspondence Education Department Journal)*, No. 15, 110–131.

Shimokawa, M. (2011) Rekishigaku ni okeru Zōyo, Kōkan no Kenkyū Shikaku: Nihon Chūseishi o Jirei toshite (Research Perspectives on "Gift" and "Exchange" in History–Based on the Case of Japanese Medieval History). *Komazawa Joshi Daigaku Kenkyū Kiyō (Komazawa Women's University Research Bulletin)*, No. 18, 17–33.

Shirota, S. (2018) Tokugawa Bakufu Keihō ni okeru Zōshūwai-zai (Bribery in the Tokugawa Shogunate). *Meijō Hōgaku (Meijō Law Studies)*, Vol. 68(2), 96-144.

Sudo, Y. (2007) Chokusetsu Kyōsei ni Kansuru Ichi-Kōsatsu (A Consideration on Direct Coercion). *Ritsumeikan Hōgaku (Ritsumeikan Law)*, No. 312 (2), 251–279.

Sugimoto, Y. (2010) *Japanese Society*. Cambridge University Press.

Suzuki, Y. (2018) Meiji Ishin to Kindai Keisatsu Seido (Meiji Restoration and Modern Police System). *Keisatsu Seisaku (Police Policy)*. Vol. 20, 263-303.

Takaki, M. (2016) Yoshiwara Yūkaku ni okeru Kyaku to Kyaku (Relationships of visitors to Yoshiwara). *Jōmin Bunka (Ordinary People's Culture)*, No. 39. 128–149.

Takaki, M. (2018) Yoshiwara Yūkaku ni okeru Kyaku no Torishimari (Crackdown on customers at Yoshiwara Yukaku). *Seijō Bungei (The Seijo University Arts and Literature Quarterly)*, No. 243, 1–26.

Takigawa, M. (1969) *Yūgijo, Yūjo, Kugutsuma: Eguchi, Kanzaki no Yūri*. Shibundo.

Terasawa, Y. (2014) 1930-nendai no Cafē ni miru Seifūzoku Sangyō-kai: Dōyō no Uragawa ni aru Jokyū no Rōdō Jittai (Sex industry seen in cafes in the 1930s: Reality of working women wages behind the upheaval). *Ritsumeikan Daigaku Jinmon Kagaku Kenkyūjo Kiyō (Ritsumeikan University Research Institute for Humanities Bulletin)*, No. 103, 113–140.

Terasawa, Y. (2018) Senzen Nihon ni okeru Zenkoku Geigi-ya Dōmei-kai no Setsuritsu to Kakudai: Sangyō Jihō, Kagai Shinbun o Chūshin (Establishment and Expansion of the National Geisha Association in Prewar Japan: Focusing on Sangyojiho and Hanamachi Shimbun). *Ritsumeikan Bungaku (Ritsumeikan Literature)*, No. 657, 32–45.

Tran, K. (2017) How Japan's Cultural Norms Affect Policing: A Side-By-Side Comparison with the United States. *Themis: Research Journal of Justice Studies and Forensic Science*, Vol. 5 (3), 37–62.

Uchida, M). (1982) Meiji Zenki ni okeru Gyōsei Keisatsu-teki Torishimari Hōrei no Keisei (Formation of Laws and Regulations for Administrative Police Control in the Early Meiji Era). *Waseda Hōgakkai-shi (Journal of Waseda Law Society)*, Vol. 33, 29–59.

Umezawa, T. (1943) *Senji Keiji Minji Tokubetsu-hō Gikai: Narabi ni Saibansho Kōsei-hō Senji Tokurei Senji Ryōji Saiban no Tokurei ni Kansuru Hōritsu (Explanation of Special Law on Wartime Criminal and Civil Cases: Law Concerning Parallel Courts Constructing Wartime Exceptions for Wartime Consular Trials)*. Nihon Hogakushoin.

Yamanaka, E. (1994) Nihon Kindai Hōron Josetsu: Nihon Kindai Hō no Rekishi to Hō Bunka (Introduction to Japanese Modern Law: History and Legal Culture of Japanese Modern Law). *Otemon Keizai Keiei Kenkyū (Otemon Economic and Management Review*, No. 1, 240–254.

Yanagida, K. (1990) *Yanagita Kunio Zenshū 11: Imōto no Chikara / Miko Kō / Kebōzu Kō Hoka (Yanagita Kunio Complete Works 11: Sister's Power/Consideration of Priestess/Consideration of Mobozu, etc.)*. Chikuma Shobo.

Yildiz, E. (2020) A Court with Many Faces: Judicial Characters and Modes of Norm Development in the European Court of Human Rights. *The European Journal of International Law*, Vol. 31 (1), 73–99.

Yoshimi, Y. (2019) *Baishun suru Teikoku (Empire of Prostitution)*. Tokyo: Iwanami Shoten.

Yoshitsugu, K.1930. *Fūzoku Keisatsu: Keisatsu Kōwashū (Sex Police: Lectures by the Police)*. Keisatsu Kyōkai.

Chapter 8
Sexual Bribe, Culinary Entertainment and Police Corruption in Osaka

8.1 Case Background

Two police divisions co-existed in prewar Japanese state polity, namely administrative police and judicial police. In the last chapter, *Taishinin*'s judicial behaviour of the hybrid models of judicial behaviour was applied to criminalize senior administrative police officers' *ex post facto* acceptance of midyear gift *ochūge*, notwithstanding bribee police officers' contribution by mediation in private capacity to settle violent conflicts in the red-light district of Tokyo. In this chapter, a junior judicial police constable accepted culinary and sex entertainment provided by the sex industry in Osaka. Like its counterpart in Kanto region, some areas in Osaka had long history of being a sexual entertainment centres of the Kansai region well before the twentieth century.

In corruption cases, monetary connection is important, but other factors, such as damage to social relationships, should also be considered. In situations where there is a close relationship or strong social connection with the person offering the bribe, the bribee might make decisions of favouritism and leniency for the briber.[1] Even though there are many ways that police corruption can happen, we mainly focus on how *Taishinin*'s judicial behaviour to deal with it.

One of the appellants in this *Taishinin* judgement under reference *Keishū* 16–961 dated 16 June 1937 was a judicial police constable, Hikata Rikio who had friendly and close relationship with the brothel owners in the red-light district in Ebisu of Osaka, where he intermittently accepted sex and culinary entertainment. As a junior judicial police constable, he statutorily did not have official duty for public order and law enforcement in the red-light district. He thus lodged appeal on this ground. Another appellant, Nakano Masatarō was the chairman in the trade union of brothels under the cover of specially licensed restaurants in Ebisu. It was a nationwide public

[1] On this see Zheng et al. (2021, pp. 855–856 and p. 866).

K. B. Wong and S. L. Fang, *Taishinin's Judicial Behaviour in Corruption Cases*,
https://doi.org/10.1007/978-981-95-5823-0_8

administration strategy to eliminate street-based freelancer sex workers and to reduce disturbance to their neighbourhood. Kanto and Kansai made no difference.

8.2 *Yūkaku* in Osaka and Other Areas

The previous chapter primarily chronicles the evolution of the sex industry in the Kanto region, with a particular emphasis on the city of Tokyo. This chapter shifts its focus to the development of the subject in Kansai and other areas, especially in Osaka. *Tobita Yūkaku*, also known as *Tobita Shinchi*, is famous for its 162 brothels under the cover of specially licenced restaurants nowadays. It is located in Nishinari Ward of Osaka near the Imaike Station. In May 2017, the NHK television programme, *Tanken Bakumon* had an episode that introduced the history and background of the sex industry in *Tobita Shinchi.* The *kanji* 廓or郭 (*kaku*) in 遊廓 or 遊郭 (*yūkaku)* is read as *kuruwa*, representing the surrounding enclosure or the area within the enclosure. In Osaka, the early development of *yūkaku* was not in today's Tobita but mainly in Shinmachi, Horie, Nanchi and Kitashinchi. As a late comer, *Namba Shinchi* became the most famous one in the early 1900s. In 1912, a fire totally destroyed the *yūkaku* in *Namba Shinchi*. Four years later, an area of approximate 22,600 *tsubo* in Abeno was developed to replace *Namba Shinchi* as *hanamachi* (red-light district) with specially licenced restaurants of *kashizashiki* (rental room, a type of sex industry). This development was the initial of today's *Tobita Yūkaku*.[2] *Yaritebaba* was the barker in each licenced restaurant to solicit customers. In addition to supervising sex workers, *yaritebaba* was the frontline staff of professionalism in this competitive sex entertainment market, especially the assessment of customer satisfaction and the quality control of individual service.

In the movie of *In the Realm of the Senses* about the famous sex worker Abe Sada, the prosperity of the sex industry in Tobita could be sensed. According to the record of the pretrial statement for court, from January 1927, Abe made a debt contract with the *yūkaku* named *Misonro* for a 2,000-*yen* loan, thereby legalized her live-in prostitute career as *Taishinin*'s contract law ruling protected the freedom of contracts for debt settlement,[3] which was elucidated in last chapter. Abe's destiny was consequential on *Taishinin*'s judicial behaviour of granting legitimacy to supply chain of sex workers by debt settlement contract. *Taishinin*'s attitudinal judicial behaviour directly gave a way to earn livelihood to poor females who were suffering from gender injustice. It rationalized sex workers supply, sustainability and the market growth of the sex industry nationwide. Sex entertainment became an accepted social reality but needed strict control of social hygiene. In prewar Tobita, the number of *kashizashiki* was 220 with about 2,700 sexual workers, mainly from the villages in Kyushu and Shikoku.

[2] See Kasai, T and Kasai, J (2017, pp. 188–194).

[3] On this see Maesaka (1998).

During the rush hour in the afternoon to the midnight, the service charge was 5 *yen* 25 *zen*.[4]

Sex industry and entertainment attitudinally were thus not regarded as immorality but a social reality of desire and human instinct. In general, men were comparatively free to have it and women were restricted (Morrison 1998, pp. 472–474). It is a logical government policy to have social management of it as an industry for tax collection rather than strict prohibition (Garon 1997, p. 6). Frühstück's research shows that Japan before the war was more focused on maintaining the racial purity of the nation through the management of public health and the sexual development of young children, rather than on addressing social injustices (Frühstück 2000, pp. 336–339). There had been no drastic change of legislation and court ruling in respect of sex industry before codification of Anti-Prostitution Code in 1956.

8.3 "American Jacket" of the Abolishment of Licenced Prostitution

Sex industry in the Edo era had been under formal social control and management but no elimination. *Taishinin* continued this legal legacy in its judicial behaviour. Same approach can also be seen in postwar law reform. The prewar licence system for prostitution illegitimatized by Anti-Corruption Code in 1956 was neither initiated by Japanese government nor postwar *Taishinin* ruling. In a meeting with Prime Minister Shidehara on 11 October 1945, General MacArthur expressed "Five Major Reform Directives" in which gender justice and equality were emphasized for future law reform. It was a "jacket of law" compulsorily imposed by the order of General Headquarters (GHQ) on the Japanese "body".[5] The impacts of it were not limited on sex industry in Tokyo in last chapter or Osaka in this chapter, but the whole Japan. It has implications of equality and freedom in today's fair society studies.

On 12 January 1946, the Metropolitan Police Department issued a notice to the chiefs of the police stations, concerning the maintenance of social morals by prohibiting prostitution legalized under the system of specially licenced restaurants.[6] On 21 January 1946, GHQ formally filed a memorandum of "Concerning the Abolishment of Legal Prostitution in Japan". GHQ thereby forcibly abolished the licenced prostitution. As a matter of social management, prostitution exclusively for the U.S. soldiers remained permissible and lasted for a relatively short period of seven months.[7] It is noteworthy that *Tobita Shinchi* continues its survival until now.[8]

[4] On this see Nippon Yuransha (1930, pp. 342–350).

[5] On the "Five Major Reform Directives" see https://www.ndl.go.jp/constitution/e/shiryo/01/033/033_001l.html. Accessed 24 October 2025.

[6] On this see Fujino (2014, pp. 42-46).

[7] On this see Maeda (2001, p. 41 and p. 46).

[8] On this see Nishimoto (2016).

8.4 Juridical Facts in *Taishinin* Judgement

Another appellant Nakano Masatarō had been the chairman of the specially licenced restaurant union in Ebisu of Osaka since May 1932. Another appellant Hikata Rikio was a *shihō-keisatsu* (judicial police constable) working at the *bōhan-gakari* (Crime Prevention Unit) of Ebisu Police Station from September 1932 to October 1935.

According to the juridical facts of the judgement, as Nakano intended to secure leniency of police treatment and tip-offs of police control of the specially licenced restaurant owners in his union, he provided sex and food entertainment to Hikata. In late 1933, at a *kashizashiki* in *Namba Shinchi*, he provided *shushoku* (wine and sex) entertainment valued at 5 *yen* to Hikata. On 11 January 1934, he provided same *shushoku* amounted to a total of 22 *yen* in Naniwa. One month later, at the same *kashizashiki* in *Namba Shinchi*, 14-*yen shushoku* was further provided on 19 February 1934. One year later, on 25 January 1935, at another restaurant in the same district, he entertained Hikata with *shushoku* that valued 2 *yen* 79 *zen*. *Taishinin* remarked that this chain of events constituted giving bribe in relation to Hikata's official duty.

Hige Hideo was not an appellant but mentioned in this judgement. In addition to acceptance of wine and sex entertainment from Nakano, Hikata accepted the similar entertainment from Hige, who acted as a consultant in the union. From June 1933, Hige doubled up the post of consultant to mahjong club union there. In order to secure convenience and lenient police control of union members, Hige provided the following *yūkyō-settai* (entertainment of sexual implications) to Hikata, who accepted with the knowledge of Hige's intention:

In June 1933, Hige provided 6-*yen yūkyō settai* to Hitaka at *Tobita Yūkaku*; At a *kashizashiki* in *Namba Shinchi*, he provided wine and sex entertainment of 8 *yen* 33 *zen* on 28 December 1933, 8 *yen* in September 1934; In December 1934, he gave 4-*yen* entertainment at a *kashizashiki* in *Tobita Yūkaku* again; On 19 January 1935, at a *kashizashiki* in *Namba Shinchi*, Hikata received the similar entertainment of 15 *yen* 75 *zen* from Hige.

Matsuda Kazuo was a mahjong club owner in Ebisu. For lenient police control and convenience, Matsuda provided the following hospitality and sex entertainment to Hikata:

On 18 September 1934, at a restaurant in Namba, *shushoku* valued at 12 *yen* 65 *zen*; on 24 October 1934, at a restaurant in Osaka, food and drink feast of 15 *yen* 59 *zen*; in December 1934, at a *kashizashiki* in Namba, wine and sexual entertainment of 8 *yen*; in February 1935, at a *kashizashiki* in Tobita, *yūkyō settai* of 5 *yen.*

Taishinin wrote in the judgement that Hikata's acceptance of all these sex and culinary entertainments constituted his acceptance of bribes in relation to his official duties of judicial police constable. *Taishinin* did evaluate evidential proof for corroboration with the case facts presented by the prosecutor, though its main focus was on the appeal grounds.

8.5 Appeal Grounds Against Junior Courts' Misidentification of Facts

The grounds of appeal are long but very reasonable and lucid. Two appellants claimed that Hikata's duty was limited to monitoring the execution of arrest in criminal cases. The sex entertainment provided by Nakano was claimed to be normal hospitality. The two bribers had no expectation for *ben'eki-no-kitai* (convenience and advantage). Bribery offence was about *taika* (a favour, finance or advantage granted in return for something) as *quid pro quo* and prohibition of contamination of the *shinsei* (holiness or purity) of official duty. Prosecutor could not adduce evidential proof to establish the corrupt relationship between *yūkyō-settai* (entertainment of sexual implications) and Hikata's official duty.

With reference to cross examination records in the second and third pretrial, Nakano emphasized that the case nature was sheer *kokoroyasu* (frank) *kōsai* (companionship). As a would-be union chairman, it was normal to have social receptions in preparation for future communication with Ebisu Police Station on the behalf of his union. This incentive should not be distorted as guilty intention to commit corruption offence. Accordingly, the relationship between the receptions and Hikata's official duty could not be substantiated.

In order to claim no intention to bribe, Nakano stated that he had no foreseeability as to what action to be taken by Hikata upon his performance of official police duty. Nakano, therefore, had no sense of what convenience and advantage to be secured from the bribery, if any. According to *Taishinin*'s precedent ruling, the relation with official duty should be *shokumukōi-jitai* (a behaviour itself as official duty), or *shokumukōi-ni-missetsu-kankei* (a behaviour in close relation to official duty). In this case, *shokumukōi-jitai* should be out of *Taishinin*'s consideration. The conviction of *shokumukōi-ni-missetsu-kankei* was dependent on the concrete circumstantial evidence in each case. Even the slightest damage to the holiness of official duty could constitute criminal offence of bribery. Nakano reiterated that there was no evidence to prove the damage which had been inflicted by all the appellants on the *shokumu-no-shinsei* (holiness or sanctity of official duty). Nothing had been adduced by the prosecutor as evidence to prove the essence of the corruptibility of *ben'eki* as *quid pro quo*.

It is noteworthy that two appellants lodged appeals against the junior courts' convictions for bribery. Hikata's acceptance of culinary entertainment from Nakano, Hige and Matsuda from September 1932 to October 1936 was erroneously identified by the junior courts as bribery. They insisted that *kyōō* (receptions) was for *shakō* (socializing) and *ikitōgō* (kindred spirits) among good friends, which had neither any convenience nor advantage to be acquired from Hikata for business, security or hygiene. All alleged *quid pro quo* was not in the scope of a judicial police officer's official duty.

Statutorily, Hikata had no power for the supervision of bribers' sex business. As confirmed by the junior courts' judgements, the Criminal Prevention Division merely had legal power to charge undesirables of criminal offence and arrest for wanted criminals but had no relation with the control of these licenced restaurants' business. The organization of Ebisu police station stipulated different police units for the district control of security, business, judicial, crime prevention, rescue and discipline. Each unit had its own scope of official duty. The supervision of restaurant business belonged to the official duty of administrative police under the Business Division, whose power included deploying policemen for petrol duty in red-light districts, imposing administrative penalties, suspension and even prohibition of business. It also handled sex workers' behaviour of public nuisance, such as soliciting customers in public area. The follow-up punitive action was taken by petrol police constable in police kiosk, *koban*. The control of Matsuda's mahjong club belonged to the Security Division. All these official duties had no relationship whatsoever with the Crime Prevention Division, in where Hikata only had official duties limited to judicial domain.

To substantiate the claim of friendship without corruption, character evidence for Hikata was stated. Since Autumn 1932, appellants Nakano and Hikata had known each other with *shiriai-kankei* (acquaintance relationship). Even so, Nakano all along had not sought any lenient police control for his business. In May or June 1932, several union members were arrested for soliciting customers. Hikata followed the criminal procedure of the Judicial Division for decision-making in their detention and release. Hikata had neither shown special favours nor partiality to arrestees. The whole chain of events was clearly recorded. As a matter of fact, Hikata had good integrity and character. Corruption should be kept secret but Nakano's good community relation with Ebisu Police Station was transparent and open, which was not a secret on many occasions of open culinary entertainments in public. On 25 January 1935, Nakano's social reception at a restaurant was actually a party for the police officers in the incoming and outgoing posting of Ebisu Police Station. Upon the next reception of the similar nature at another restaurant in Osaka, all attendees were senior police officers of the rank Head of Petrol or above. These gatherings had nothing to do with the control of licenced restaurant business. It should be a well-known fact that the whole chain of entertainments was irrelevant to Hikata's official duty of judicial police constable.

As to whether Hikata might have close working relation with the official duties of the Business Division or negotiation with it for future convenience, the uncertainty was *mihitsuteki-shokumu-kengen* (non-mandatory authority for official duty contingent upon uncertainty of future occurrence). It was therefore inappropriate to treat Hikata as currently having double power of administrative police. The officer-in-charge of the Business Division of Ebisu Police Station was Nakajima. Through the introduction of Nakano's son, he and Hikata knew each other and also had close friendship, who received the social receptions and gifts for *ochūgen* and *oseibo*. In case Nakano had corrupt intent, the target should be Nakajima, not Hikata.

8.6 Analysis of Appeal Grounds

The appeal strategy was reinforced by circumstantial character evidence to prove the integrity of Nakano and Nikata so that the appellants' grounds of appeals seemed very logical, lucid and reasonable. According to the appeal grounds, although Nakano maintained a good relationship with the senior officers of Ebisu Police Station, it should be considered the episodic and deviant behaviour with low frequency of an individual police office, which had little impact of severity on the organization and institutional structure. The appellants' three lawyers adopted a very clever strategy to deny corrupt *quid pro quo* between culinary and sex entertainments and the official duty of the Crime Prevention Division, thereby denying these two crucial constituent elements of bribery offence. As to the *hanzaiito* (guilty intention), unconditional receptions and social gatherings out of acquaintance relationship without damage to the sanctity of official duty. Two appellants added that the nature of the whole chain of events was not a behaviour intersecting with the police officers' official duty.

Two appellants attacked the prosecutor's weakness that no specific incident had been mentioned to confirm Hikata's criminal acts consequential on Nakano's entrustment or request. The most convincing circumstantial evidence was the two open and transparent social gatherings in Ebisu Police Station with the senior police officers' participation, while the prosecutor gave no concrete proof for criminal intent in the transparency of these gatherings. Therefore, the future corruptibility consequential on appellants' friendly relationship was a hard uncertainty for *Taishinin*'s judicial behaviour to confirm. The evidence was to two appellants' advantage and could justify the benefit of doubt to be granted in favour of the appellants.

8.7 *Taishinin*'s Ruling for Refusal

The following is a segment of the ruling issued by *Taishinin*:

> The Crime Prevention Division belongs to the judicial police, and the control of the restaurant business union and the mahjong club belongs to the administrative police[9]... In the end, judicial administration and other divisions shall be assigned to each unit based on the convenience of work and shall be divided according to the nature of the affairs of the unit[10]...In addition, the security guards and patrols of restaurants, the management of the associations and mahjong entertainment departments, etc., are handled by the police division system

[9] The original text in the judgement: 防犯係ハ司法警察ニ屬シ飲食店料理屋営業其ノ組合及麻雀倶樂部ノ取締ハ行政警察ニ屬スルコト論ヲ俟タスト雖凡ソ巡査ハ警察ニ關シテハ一般的権限ヲ有スルモノニシテ。

[10] The original text in the judgement:司法行政及其ノ他ノ細別ハ畢竟執務上ノ便宜ニ基キ各自ガ主トシテ擔任セル事務ノ性質ニ従ヒ之ガ分掌ヲ設ケタルニ過キス。

> for convenience[11]… the acceptance of hospitality offered in relation to it shall constitute a corruption offense.[12]

Taishinin mentioned its conceptual demarcation of two types of police powers was based on de facto police power, and the vague term *shokumujō-no-bengi* (convenience of work) was used to negate the strict categorization of police powers. Therefore, *Taishinin* stated it clearly in this judgement:

> For that reason, it is not the case that the general authority should be restricted, such as by the means of the Crime Prevention Division.[13]

8.8 Analysis of *Taishinin*'s Ruling

The prewar metropolitan police had basically five ranks of *keishi* (superintendent), *keibu* (police inspector), *keibuho* (lieutenant), *junsa-buchō* (head of petrol, sergeant) and *junsa* (constable) (Momose 1990, pp. 77–78). The Japanese term *junsa* has been used since June 1875 (Suzuki 2018, p. 290). Hikata was *junsa*, which meant his power was very limited. As analysed hereunder, prewar Japanese police officers, including *junsa,* had various de facto police powers which had not been authorized by the law. Though subject to the legal argument, *Taishinin* was correct in its judicial behaviour to criminalize two appellants by de facto police power instead of *de jure* power holding the legal right to do so.

At the beginning of its ruling, *Taishinin* endorsed that judicial police officers belonged to Criminal Prevention Division, while the administrative police officers were responsible for monitoring and control of restaurant business and mahjong club, so that Taishinin raised no objection to two appellants' appeal grounds in this regard. Then, *Taishinin* confirmed the relation between Hikata's official duty by *ippan-no-kengen* (general or common authority) of a police officer, and the entertainments of food and sex accepted.

For job convenience, each division in police structure held different de facto powers according to the ad hoc nature of prescribed responsibility. *Ippan-no-kengen* implied the authority of uncertain nature. *Taishinin*'s legal reasoning process then extend to criminalize that both administrative police power and judicial police power had overlapping area of general authority for convenience of enforcement. The Crime Prevention Division thus set up without limitation of such general authority. The intention of provision of culinary entertainment and reception to a petrol police constable of Crime Prevention Division was assumed to be seeking lenient control for restaurant business, trade union and mahjong club therefore led to the commission of

[11] The original text in the judgement: 従テ防犯係タル巡査ガ飲食店料理屋営業其ノ組合及麻雀倶樂部ノ經營者等ヨ警察取締上ノ便宜寛大ナル取扱。

[12] The original text in the judgement: 受ケ度旨ノ請託ノ下ニ饗應接待ヲ受タルニ於テハ瀆職罪テ構成スルモノトス。

[13] The original text in the judgement: 故ニ防犯係ニ従事シタルカ如キハ必スシモ一般的権限ヲ制限スルモノニ非ス。

corruption offence. *Taishinin* thereby rationalized the assumption (not confirmation) to link the bribers' guilty intent with Hikata's official duty.

Unlike the case in the last chapter about an administrative police officer's act for mediation in private capacity for dispute resolution, this Taishinin's judgement mentioned nothing about the possible *modus operandi* and means of abusing police power for lenient control or convenience. On the contrary, the appellants concretely narrated the character evidence of Hikata's impartiality and integrity in several incidents. Nakano substantiated his claim of his open community relation with the senior police officers. Whether this relation had hidden agenda to bring about a specific corruptibility was subject to corroboration with evidence, which was unavailable in the judgement. According to *quid pro quo* of a corruption case, all police officers who attended the two parties in Ebisu Police Station should have committed the acceptance of banquet bribe. The most controversial was that banquet bribes were provided in police station and attended by some senior police officers. One of whom was named Nakajima in the judgement, but he was not summoned by court to provided witness statement. All party attendees had no involvement in this police corruption of banquet bribe case. In other words, Taishinin's judicial behaviour did not shed light on this. The corrupt *quid pro quo* was based on *Taishinin*'s inference by assumption.

Taishinin maintained that it was not necessary to impose restrictions on the scope of general police duties.[14] Therefore, it used *ippan-no-kengen* to rationalize the linkage between official duty and culinary and sex entertainment.De facto power for law enforcement required a determination of accountability and job responsibility not only for Hikata but also his superiors who were, based on the evidential proof, in control of him.

Taishinin's term *ippan-no-kengen* (general or common power) implied uncertain de facto authority in the grey area of unspecific nature, which might or might not be relevant to the management of the red-light districts. In the view of such uncertain grey area, Nakano and Hikata might simply lack of awareness of Hikata's conflict of role or interest, which was a poor conscious of role in an organization instead of a criminal offence in prewar Japan. *Taishinin*'s judicial behaviour provided no clear feedback by concretely establishing *quid pro quo* and consideration of such mitigating factors. Its judicial behaviour of expansive legal interpretation is similar to criminalization by the vague *an'nei-chitsujo* (peace and order) in last chapter. Therefore, *Taishinin*'s judicial behaviour in refusal to this appeal still belongs to strict liability model.

Taishinin's employment of the term *ippan-no-kengen* as an umbrella term for criminalization in this case is an example of linguistic ambiguity. Its judgement failed to provide an explanation for the circumstances under which *ippan-no-kengen* might occur, be taken place or for any instances in which it had already occurred. A review of the extant literature reveals a paucity of broadly accepted definitions of *ippan-no-kengen* in Japanese studies, public administration studies, management studies and criminal justice studies. The possession of a particular role or rank within

[14] The original text in the judgement: 必スシモ一般的権限ヲ制限スルモノニ非ス。

the police organization does not inherently guarantee the individual's inclusion in *ippan-no-kengen*. This power is not a legitimate power analogous to statutory law enforcement authority, under which people are obligated to comply. The mediation of police officers in the previous chapter serves as an illustration of this phenomenon.

A police officer, who is under his superiors' supervision and management, has to exercise this vague *ippan-no-kengen* with superiors' consent to confer *ippan-no-kengen* beforehand or provide *ex post facto* endorsement for it based on principal-agent relation. It determines the legitimacy of *ippan-no-kengen.* If so, it means superior of the police constable may have negligence of supervision or recklessness to order. Otherwise, it is a police officer's personal *ultra vires* act by abusing his post.

The attitudinal model of judicial behaviour assumes that judges made judicial decisions based on the case facts against his beliefs and values. In this case, the attitudinal views subtly affected judicial behaviour than the law. *Taishinin* justices' usage of language is a highly significant way in which judicial behaviour can be shaped or conditioned by cognitive ramifications of words. Interplay of descriptive belief words and emotive words reflects beliefs and ideological preferences in *Taishinin*'s judicial behaviour.[15]

For a total of six times in this judgement, *Taishinin* stigmatized the appellants with the descriptive term *shushoku* (酒色wine and sex), while酒食 (same pronunciation *shushoku*) was used in the remaining receptions. It was a goal-oriented judicial behaviour to denounce the appellants' characters moralistically. The *kanji*色 refers to sex and prostitution instead of the literal meaning of colour. Traditionally, the meaning of 酒色 is negative on commenting a person's character of licentiousness, poor conduct and immoral sense of discipline. *Shokunihonki* recorded that in June 766 (*Tenpyō-jingo* 2), the prince had a lifestyle without any restraint, and greatly enjoyed drinking and women, which was the first time the negative word of 酒色 appeared in Japanese history.[16] As the consumption of酒色 in brothels was repeatedly mentioned for six times in the judgement, the judicial mindset of *Taishinin* was attitudinally hostile to the appellant Hikata. To *Taishinin*, a police officer's acceptance of sex and wine entertainment in brothels was doubtful and immoral. Or at least, it was not proper or decent.

In terms of freedom and equality in fair society studies, sex worker may have no dignity, but it is a means for well-being. Sex industry is a complex sociocultural and sociopolitical issue usually affected by low income, poor education, human trafficking and gender inequality. In prewar Japan, legality of sex industry could not mitigate negative social consciousness against it and its impacts of human trafficking and social hygiene issue (Masugi 2009, pp. 237–238). Such negative social consciousness can be read in a record of the House of Representatives of Imperial Diet in 1929. A politician Kawashima Shōjirō openly criticized against licenced prostitution with that human trafficking supplied prostitutes to it currently…in the

[15] On this see Solan (1995, p. 1076, pp. 1079–1980) and Probert (1959, p. 35, p. 41); Also see Bimston (2022, p. 213) and Cruse (2011, pp. 86–91).

[16] The Original text in *Shokunihonki*: 放縦不レ拘頗好酒色。In *Systematic National History Volume 2: Shokunihonki*, edited by Keizai Zasshisha, p. 455.

so-called brothel, underaged girls everywhere are fifteen, sixteen or even thirteen and fourteen.[17] Even today, *jinshin-torihiki* (human trafficking) for prostitution is still a criminal law issue in Japan (Ōno 2017, pp. 77–78). Prostitution under the package of licenced restaurant was still a *shūgyō* (ugly business) in prewar Japan. As equitable *dori*, specially licenced restaurant was not a decent place for normal culinary entertainment. As mentioned in Chap. 3, traditional Japanese judicial behaviour was usually based on equitable *dori* to soften the rigidity of statutory provision, which was from time to time consistent with social consciousness for or against a behaviour or institution. In addition to strict liability model, *Taishinin*'s judicial behaviour is also attitudinalism consequential on sex industry as an ugly business.

8.9 The Inconsistency of *Ippan* with Historical Facts

Ippan, of the term *ippan-no-kengen* in the judgement implied the vagueness of *Taishinin*'s judicial behaviour in distinguishing the grey area of authority of administrative police from that of judicial police. The truth is that the statutory authority of administrative police and judicial police had been clearly differentiated since the power struggle between the Ministry of Interior and the Ministry of Justice since 1872. As the law for the organizational structure of police was not that clear to protect state polity in Emperor Meiji's *Ten'nōsei-keisatsu* (imperial police under the Emperor), the struggle for the control of the police system occurred between these two ministries. In April 1872, while Etō Shinpei was appointed as the first Minister of Justice, *Shihōshō-shokusei-shōtei* (Ministry of Justice Official Charter) dated 3 August 1872 stipulated those local police should take up the duties of arrest and apprehension of fugitives. And Article 35 in Chapter Nine was for *hobou-shōtei* (Charter for captivity) in the *Shihōshokumu-Teisei* (Judicial Duty System), which statutorily stipulated that the duty of arrest should begin with searching for criminals and arresting them to end up in the hands of a judge.[18]

Two weeks after the release of *Shihōshōan-keisatsu-kisoku* (Department of Justice Proposed Police Regulations) in 1873, Home Ministry counter-proposed *Naimushō-Keisatsu* (Police of the Ministry of Interior) to be re-organized as administrative police.[19] In January 1874, nationwide police affairs in Japan was transferred from the Ministry of Home Affairs to the Ministry of Justice (Asakura 1969, pp. 192–193). As per Article 10 of *Kenjishokusei-shōtei-nami-shihōkeisatsu-kisoku* (Prosecutor's Office Charter and Judicial Police Regulations) in1874, the power of judicial police

[17] The Original text in Kawashima Shōjirō's accusation in the Proceedings of the 56th Imperial Diet House of Representatives Petition Committee: 現在公娼に於きましては...いわゆる淫売窟に居りまする所の女と云ふものは，十五歳，十六歳，甚しきは十三歳，十四歳と云ふ風な......In *Official Gazette Extra-supplement* dated 14 March 1929, edited by Cabinet Printing Bureau.

[18] The original text in *Shihōshokumu Teisei:* 捕亡の職務は罪犯を探索するに始め捕縛して裁判官に付するに終わる。

[19] On this see Uchida (1982, p. 30, p. 36, pp. 40–41).

should be limited to arrest and follow-up action thereafter. The Search for the criminal offenders belonged to the scope of administrative police's preventative powers.[20] Two types of police had identical status and were awarded the same militaristic and ultra-nationalistic imperial sixteen-petaled golden chrysanthemum crest of Emperor. They were instrumental for policing the neighbourhood in a totalitarian way and denying citizens' political, social and economic equality (Wildes 1953, pp. 655–658). From the very beginning, it was not a case of vague common or general authority, or *ippan-no-kengen* as *Taishinin* stated in the judgement.

Article 4 in Chap. 1 of *Gyōseikeisatsu-kisoku* (Administrative Police Regulations) in 1875 further clarified that it is the responsibility of the judicial police to search for and arrest those who violate the law for the follow-up of judicial proceedings. The authority of administrative police was clearly confirmed for crime prevention.[21] Prewar Japanese administrative police mainly acted as *hojoyaku* (an assistant officer) subordinated to public prosecutor (Katō 2015, p. 1462). Administrative police under Home Ministry was responsible to Emperor to control the imperial empire's internal affairs and social stability with police dictatorship. This is the reason why postwar police and law reforms had to consider imperial traditions resultant from the state polity structure (Oppler 1949, p. 292).

The judicial police officer appointment is now non-existent in the organization of National Police Agency. According to this analysis, *prima facie*, the appellant, judicial police constable Hikata had no statutory power to monitor the *yūkaku* and the mahjong club. The constituent element requirement in the doctrine of "no law, no crime and no punishment" was not met. *Taishinin* criminalized Hitaka by literalism of *ippan* is subject to argument. If Hikata did it, it was *ultra vires*.

8.10 De Facto or *Ultra Vires* Police Power for Governance

In actuality, prewar Japanese police wielded significant de facto authority, albeit without explicit legislative sanction to do so. Acts of executive branch of government may be declared invalid by the courts if they are beyond the authorities' legal powers. *Ippan-no-kengen* belonged to this type in case of no *ex post facto* endorsement or approval. Strictly speaking, such exercise of authority was *ultra vires* without *ex post facto* endorsement or approval (Tanaka 2020, p. 409). *Taishinin*'s *ippan-no-kengen* could conceptually be applied to rationalize a de facto police power of no legality-based paradigm. This is a double-edged legal sword of *Taishinin*'s judicial behaviour, which also had final say as to what constituted *ultra vires*. Nonetheless, what specific

[20] The original text in *Kenjishokusei-shōtei-nami-shihōkeisatsu-kisoku*: 司法警察ハ行政警察予防ノ力及ハスシテ法律ニ背ク者アル時其(その)犯人ヲ探索シテ之(これ)ヲ逮捕スルモノトス(第10条)。.

[21] The original text in *Gyōseikeisatsu-Kisoku*: 行政警察予防ノ力及ハスシテ法律ニ背ク者アルトキ其犯人ヲ探索逮捕スルハ司法警察ノ職務トス之ヲ行政警察ノ官ニ於(おい)テ行フトキハ検事章程並司法警察規則ニ照スヘシ。

elements of authority were in *ippan-no-kengen*? *Taishinin* gave no clear answer in its judgement.

Record check confirms that the scope of de facto power of prewar Japanese police was far more extensive that readers of this book think. The common de facto exercise of power without a legal paradigm included the following: The *eisei-keisatsu* (health or sanitary police) was a type of public health officer in Japan during the Edo period. The *suigai-keibi* are responsible for the protection of the populace from the threat of flooding. Since 1893, the administration of public health in rural areas had been de facto under the jurisdiction of the police, though this had not been formally recognized by statutory authority. Prior to this, no physician or nurse had been appointed to the prewar police organization (Shimizu 1976, p. 73). In the event that *Taishinin* did not interpret such power vaguely and elastically as *ippan*, but rather adhered to the doctrine of "no law, no crime, and no punishment", it would have been necessary for *Taishinin* to rule the performance of police duties related to health and flood protection as *ultra vires* (Matsuo 2018, p. 39). It is evident that *ippan* in *Taishinin*'s *ippan-no-kengen* reflected the reality of unclear scope of police power in prewar social conditions.

In his capacity as Supreme Commander for the Allied Powers, General MacArthur was taken aback by the extensive de facto authority wielded by the Japanese police, which was not subject to any statutory oversight and had no relevance to criminal investigations. The implementation of community policing initiatives had enabled the extension of de facto police power into all facets of citizens' lives. This encompassed the monitoring of financial and commercial institutions, including banks, restaurants, medical practitioners, barbers, masseurs and market stalls. Furthermore, community policing had been instrumental in the oversight of public health and hygiene, ranging from the prevention of venereal diseases to the biannual compulsory house cleaning, the distribution of emergency relief supplies and the resolution of domestic and social challenges. The scope of oversight encompassed the supervision of construction, repair, maintenance and fireproofing of buildings. It also included the implementation of game law, conservation of resources for environmental protection, settlement of labour disputes, regulation of unions, enforcement of factory legislation, monitoring of the neighbourhood, population, individuals' occupations, leisure activities and even family relations (Aldous 1997, pp. 24–25).

Even nowadays, it is hard to find another national police team of so many de facto authorities, which are originally *ultra vires* before *ex post facto* rationalization. Watanabe Yōzō designated this peculiar prewar occurrence as the doctrine of *Tennosei Hōchishugi* (Emperor Legalism), law enforcement officials functioned as the Emperor's proxies, tasked with the implementation and enforcement of the Emperor's directives. This system was designed to ensure the maintenance of social order and the promotion of collective welfare (Watanabe 1988, p. 33). The Emperor ideology (*tennosei*) is a concept that can be understood as the particular Japanese response to social and cultural strains in governance (Tipton 2012, pp. 105–106). The primary function of law enforcement was to support the monarchy rather than the general populace (Yamanaka 1994, p. 14).

In this case, flexibility was prioritized over statutory authorization. The substantial flexible, non-statutory, de facto prewar Japanese police duties and powers in community policing was evident. The term *ippan-no-kengen* is employed in this judgement, and its elements are not further clearly elaborated upon. Japanese community-oriented policing to facilitate extensive de facto power was typified by *koban*, which was a police box or kiosk. The *koban* ensures interactions between the police and citizens, thereby enabling the police to fulfil theirde facto duties in a positive relationship with the community (Tran 2017, p. 39). It facilitated mediation in last chapter. The utilization of *ippan-no-kengen* in this chapter constitutes a transgression against the statutory authority bestowed through the principal-agent paradigm within the state political structure. Principal might have no knowledge of it before the exercise of power. The typical example is mediation.[22] Chiba comments that this lenient attitudinal judicial behaviour exhibited equitable Confucian elements and was designated as a characteristic of *tendōsei* (nature of Heaven's way), which is a concept deeply rooted in traditional Japanese philosophy (Chiba 1997, p. 436).

8.11 *Honne* and *Tatemae*

From a legal perspective, *Taishinin*'s judicial behaviour to deal with prostitution case serves as a notable illustration of cultural interaction between Japan and other societies. *Honne* and *tatemae* are Japanese words that can be translated as "real and facade intention", respectively. In the context of the state polity, *Taishinin*'s hybrid judicial behaviour, incorporating both the strict liability model and the attitudinal model, was consistent with government policy. In the judgements, *Taishinin* imposed sanctions on civil servants, particularly law enforcement officers, for abusing their power and position to gain personal benefit from the sex industry. It is noteworthy that *Taishinin* refrained from any condemnation of the actions of brothels, sex entertainment establishments and pimps, who rely on the income of prostitutes to make a living.

It is evident that no formal Japanese government policy has been established to regulate the social management of prostitution nowadays, thereby hindering the development of the sex entertainment market. Conversely, legal frameworks have been instituted to regulate and constrain its market expansion. Prewar government had established licencing requirements for brothels under "specially licensed restaurant" normally as *tatemae*, but this *tatemae* discontinued now. The Japanese government has ceased to issue new special restaurant licences.

A possible rationale for *Taishinin*'s judicial behaviour to tolerate prostitution, as reflected in the contract law case, is that sex industry was a significant employer during the prewar Showa era. The underlying rationale behind these phenomena pertains to the deliberate incorporation of legal loopholes by law, which are designed to ensure the survival and well-being of sex workers. Despite its perceived moral

[22] On this see Takeda (2007).

deficiencies, *yūkaku* had a notable economic impact. A prominent brothel owner in Sendai exercised significant influence over the livelihoods of 3000 employees. As a *kōshōseido* (licenced prostitution system), the institution not only provided employment opportunities, but also stimulated the prices of real estate and land development in the vicinity of the red-light district.[23] A similar economic contribution has been observed in postwar Japan. In 2022, the number of businesses operating in the Japanese sex industry was estimated to be approximately 32,900. However, in 2021, law enforcement officials had only made 266 arrests in the sex entertainment sector.[24] The "traditional Japanese body" of *Taishinin*, characterized by its lenient judicial behaviour with regard to the sex industry, remains in the GHQ's codification of Anti-Prostitution Code.

The judicial system's capacity to enforce the law is often characterized by ambiguity and inefficiency. This phenomenon can be attributed, at least in part, to the actions of the legislative branch, which can impose constraints on the actions of the judicial branch (Haye 2007, p. 175). The built-in loopholes of Anti-Prostitution Code surprisingly bear flexibility similar to legal tolerance of sex industry in prewar Japanese society. An example is Article 3 of Anti-Corruption Code "nominally" stipulates prohibition of prostitution. No person shall engage in, or be the partner of, prostitution,[25] while Article 2 defines "prostitution" as sexual intercourse with an unspecified partner in exchange for compensation.[26] This article prohibits prostitution itself and becoming a partner of prostitution. Paradoxically there are no penalties for prostitution itself or becoming a partner of prostitution.

8.12 *Taishinin*'s Judicial Behaviour of Strict Liability Model and *Unvermeidbar*

During the trial, no one recorded any information about the appellant judicial police constable's use of *ippan-no-kengen* for the appellant brothel owner's benefit. Instead, it showed that the two appellants were close friends by talking about the events that happened between them. The hidden reason behind *Taishinin*'s legal actions in this case was to prevent actions that could endanger social peace. *Taishinin* supported criminalization based on strict liability. They did this to prevent crime, maintain public order and protect society. Because of the dangers to public safety that might damage the flexible legalism under Emperor, *Taishinin* had to find a fair balance

---

[23] On this see Onjō (2012, p. 74, p. 82).

[24] On this see Statista (2022 and 2023).

[25] The original text in Anti-Prostitution Code: 何人も、売春をし、又はその相手方となつてはならない。See e-Gov. Anti-Prostitution Code at https://elaws.e-gov.go.jp/document?lawid=331AC0000000118. Accessed 9 July 2023.

[26] The original text in Anti-Prostitution Code:この法律で「売春」とは、対償を受け、又は受ける約束で、不特定の相手方と性交することをいう。See e-Gov. Anti-Prostitution Code at https://elaws.e-gov.go.jp/document?lawid=331AC0000000118. Accessed 9 July 2023.

between the crime of accepting a bribe as a police officer and the public interest of the state in maintaining security. In *Taishinin*'s *ius puniendi* (right to punish), under the strict liability model of judicial behaviour, anyone who was not aware of the external elements of the bribery offence would still be convicted. Two people accused of a crime could not use a defence to show that they did not have the necessary intent to commit the crime, or that the crime was not foreseeable. The Meiji leader borrowed German laws. As a weapon in the fight against crime, *Taishinin*'s strict liability model of judicial behaviour in this case is acceptable under *unvermeidbar* (unavoidable) in German-style strict liability offence.[27]

8.13 Brief Remarks

Taishinin has demonstrated a consistent adherence to a hybrid judicial approach, encompassing the application of the strict liability model and the attitudinal model. A comparison of the present Japanese government's policy of social management and control with that of the sex industry in prewar Japan reveals a striking similarity. The prewar government, in conjunction with *Taishinin* as a social policy maker, maintained a policy of relatively limited oversight in the realm of the sex industry, eschewing the imposition of stringent restrictions on its development. *Taishinin*'s stance is characterized by a deliberate avoidance of criticism and negative commentary concerning the realm of sex entertainment and its workforce. According to the attitudinal model, *Taishinin*'s judicial behaviour is indicative of prevailing social attitudes toward the sex industry and adult entertainment.

Despite the prevalent stigma and social disapproval associated with the sex industry, it did not pose a particularly salient moral challenge or threat to the prewar state polity and *Taishinin*, which did not perceive sex industry as a significant legal jeopardy. State-sanctioned prostitution had not problematized Japanese males' pursuit of sexual gratification in itself since the Tokugawa bakufu. Today's advent of the internet has rendered the involvement of intermediaries or pimp unnecessary for direct interactions between clients and sex workers. Through internet, sex entertainment in the virtual "floating world" becomes a global fast way to make some cash.

It is unadvisable to infer the judicial behaviour of Japanese judges as being analogous to that of their Western counterparts following legal transplantation. This universality approach demonstrates an oversight of cultural relativism and social conditions (Gray 2022, p. 47). As discussed in Chap. 3, the Japanese judicial system has historically exhibited a lack of clear demarcation between legal principles and moral standards. This is due to the influence of the flexible equitable circumstantial *dori*, which is a concept that is intertwined with judicial behaviour and social conditions. In light of an understanding of this legal culture, it was unsurprising to read that the prewar Japanese police exercised a significant extent of de facto police powers

[27] See Green (2005, pp. 21–50).

in situations that were *ultra vires* in the perspective of common law jurisdiction. The prewar police had to play special role in rural areas with de facto power as a matter of *dori*. Otherwise, Japanese nationals there might have no government service.

In next chapter, an examination will be conducted in the historical relationship between *Taishinin* judges and the Ministry of Justice and *Taishinin*'s role in state polity.

References

Aldous, C. (1997) *The police in occupation Japan: control, corruption and resistance to reform.* Routledge.

Asakura, H. (1969) *Meiji Kansei Jiten (Dictionary of Meiji Government Official System).* Tokyodo.

Bimston, D. (2022) Linguistics in the Courtroom: Incorporating Considerations of Language and Context to Improve Criminal Court Consent Analysis. *Emory Law Journal*, Vol. 72 (1), 211-252.

Cabinet Printing Bureau. (1929) Kawashima Shōjirō: Dai Gojūrokkai Teikoku Gikai Shūgi-in Seigan Iinkai Giroku Sokki, Dai Kyū Kai, Shōwa 4-nen (The House of Representatives of the Imperial Diet. Shojiro Kawashima: Proceedings of the 56th Meeting of the Petition Committee of the House of Representatives of the Imperial Diet, shorthand, 9th, 1929). *Kanpō Gōgai (Official Gazette Extra-supplement)*, 14 March 1929, 2–3.

Chiba, M. (1997) Jibunka-ken ni okeru Kokyūhō to Kindaihō: Tokuni Kankoku to Nihon to no Hikaku (State-owned law and modern law in the cultural sphere of Chinese characters: a comparison between Korea and Japan). *Hokudai Hōgaku Ronshū (Hokkaido University Law Journal)*, Vol.47 (5), 430-447.

Cruse, A. (2011) *Meaning in Language: An Introduction to Semantics and Pragmatics (3rd edition).* Oxford University Press.

Frühstück, S. (2000) Managing the Truth of Sex in Imperial Japan. *The Journal of Asian Studies*, Vol. 59 (2), 332–358.

Fujino, Y. (2014) Sengo Nihon no Kōshō Seido Haishi ni okeru Keisatsu no Ninshiki : Naimushō Keihokyoku Hoan-kakari "Kōshō Seido Haishi Kankei Kianzuto" no Bunseki (Police Perceptions on the Abolition of the Licensed Prostitution System in Postwar Japan: An Analysis of the "Draft Document Related to the Abolition of the Licensed Prostitution System" by the Security Section of the National Security Bureau of the Ministry of Home Affairs). *Keiwa Gakuen Daigaku Jinbun Shakaikagaku Kenkyūjo Nenpō (Annual Report of Institute for Humanities and Social Sciences, Keiwagakuen University*, Issue 12, 41-57.

Garon, S. (1997) *Molding Japanese Minds: The State in Everyday Life.* Princeton. Princeton University Press.

Gray, G. P. (2022) The Commodification of Sex in Modern Japan: Outdated Attitudes and Overdue Reforms. In Schotanus. S. M. ed. *Gender Violence, the Law, and Society* (pp. 35–50). Emerald Publishing Limited.

Green, S. P. (2005) Six Senses of Strict Liability. In Simester, A. ed. *Appraising Strict Liability*, (pp. 1-20). Oxford University Press.

Haye, A. (2007) Prostitution in Japan: Social Management or Regulation. *Bōekifū: Chūbu Daigaku Kokusai Kankei Gakubu Ronshū (Trade Winds: Chubu University Faculty of International Relations Collected Paper)*, No. 2, 170–176.

Kasai, T., Kasai, J. (2017) Meiji Kōki ni okeru Ōsaka Kagai no Henbō to "Haru no Odori" Kyōen no Shutsugen (Transformation of Osaka Hanamachi in the Late Meiji Era and Appearance of 'Spring Dance' Competition). *Ningen Shakai Kankyō Kenkyū (Human Social and Environmental Research)*, No. 34, 187–198.

Katō, K. (2015) Gyōsei Keisatsu Katsudō to Hanzai no Jizen Sōsa Jō (Administrative Police Activity and the Investigation of Crimes before their Occurrence Vol.1). N*ihon Hōgaku (Journal of Japanese Law)*, Vol. 80 (4), 1457–1489.
Maeda, M. D. (2001) G.I. Joe meets geisha girls: Japan's postwar policies of legalized prostitution for US occupation forces. *Hitotsubashi Journal of Law and Politics*, No. 29, 41–48.
Maesaka, T. (1998.) *Abe Sada shuki (Abe Sada Note).* Chuokoronsha.
Masugi, Y. (2009) Jinshin Baibai Haijo Hōshin ni Miru Kindai Kōshō Seido no Yōsō (Aspects of the Modern Licensed Prostitution System as Seen in the "Elimination of Trafficking in Persons" Policy). *Ritsumeikan Daigaku Jinmon Kagaku Kenkyūjo Kiyō (Ritsumeikan University Research Institute for Humanities Bulletin).* No. 93, 237–268.
Matsuo, S. (2018) hōkōroku ni Miru Meiji no Keisatsu Katsudō no Ittan (A Part of Police Activities in the Meiji Era Seen in Shokorok). *Meijiki no Keisatsu ni Kansuru Shokōsatsu Keisatsu Seisaku Gakkai Shiryō (Various Considerations on the Police in the Meiji Era: Journal of the Society of Police Policy)*, No. 101. 26–35. Police Policy Society, Management and Operation Study Group.
Momose, T. (1990) *Jiten Shōwa Senzenki no Nihon (Encyclopedia of Showa and Prewar Japan: Institutions and Realities).* Yoshikawa Kobunkan.
Morrison, A. D. (1998) Teen Prostitution in Japan: Regulation of Telephone Clubs. *Vanderbilt Journal of Transnational Law*, Vol. 31 (2), 457- 497.
National Diet Library. *Birth of the Constitution of Japan, Prime Minister Shidehara's meeting with General MacArthur on 11 October 1945.* https://www.ndl.go.jp/constitution/e/shiryo/01/033/033_001l.html. Accessed 24 October 2025.
Nippon Yuransha. (1930) *Zenkoku Yūkaku Annai (Nationwide Red-light District Guidance).* Nippon Yuransha.
Nishimoto, H. (2016) *Tobita Shinchi no Hitobito: Kansai Shinchi Kansen Guide (The People of Tobita Shinchi: The Complete Guide to Kansai Shinchi).* Rokusaisha.
Onjō, A. (2012) Meijiki no Sendai-shi ni okeru Yūkaku Iten Mondai to Toshi Shakai (The Problem of Brothel Relocation and Urban Society in Sendai City in the Meiji Era). *Kūkan, Shakai, Chiri Shisō ((Spatial, Social and Geographic Thoughts)*, No. 20, 73–83.
Ōno, S. (2017) Nihon ni okeru Jinshin Torihiki no Mondai-ka: Jinshin Torihiki Gainen no Henshen o Tegakari ni (Human Trafficking Problem in Japan: Using the Changes in the Concept of Human Trafficking as a Clue). *Seisen Joshi Daigaku Jinbun Kagaku Kenkyūjo Kiyō (Seisen Women's University Research Institute for Humanities Bulletin)*, No. 38, 73–79.
Oppler, A. C. (1949) The Reform of Japan's Legal and Judicial System Under Allied Occupation *Washington Law Review*, Vol. 24 (3), 290–324.
Probert, W. (1959) Law and Persuasion: The Language Behavior of Lawyers. *University of Pennsylvania Law Review*, Vol. 108 (1), 35-58.
Shimizu, K. (1976) Shōwa Shoki no Kōshū Eisei ni Tsuite: Eisei Gyōsei Kikō, Kekkaku Yobō oyobi Karyūbyō Yobō (On public health in the early Showa period: health administration organization, prevention of tuberculosis and prevention of Hanryu disease). *Minzoku Eisei (Ethnic Hygiene)*, Vol. 42 (2), 72-86.
Solan, L. (1995) Judicial Decisions and Linguistic Analysis: Is There a Linguist in the Court. *Washington University Law Quarterly*, Vol. 73 (3), 1069-1080.
Sora News 24. (2016) *Same-sex prostitution business technically legal in Japan, goes untouched by police*, 28 April 2016. https://soranews24.com/2016/04/28/same-sex-prostitution-business-not-illegal-in-japan-untouched-by-police. Accessed 24 August 2022.
Statista. 2022. *Number of people arrested for violations of the Prostitution Prevention Law in the sex industry in Japan in 2021, by violation type.* https://www.statista.com/statistics/1197354/japan-number-arrests-breaches-sex-industry-by-violation-type/. Accessed 7 July 2023.
Statista. 2023. *Number of businesses operating in the sex industry in Japan from 2015 to 2022.* https://www.statista.com/statistics/1194705/japan-number-businesses-sex-industry/. Accessed 7 July 2023.
Suzuki, Y. (2018) Meiji Ishin to Kindai Keisatsu Seido (Meiji Restoration and Modern Police System). *Keisatsu Seisaku (Police Policy).* Vol. 20, 263-303.

Takeda, K. (2007) O-tentō-sama ga Miteiru (Heavenly Sama is Watching). *Gekkan Keizai (Monthly Economic Trend)*, Nippon Keidanren (Japan Business Federation), No.5: https://www.keidanren.or.jp/japanese/journal/200705.html. Accessed 21 October 2022.

Tanaka, M. (2020) Furansu ni okeru "Kōjo" to Jiyū o Meguru Kōsatsu: Furansu no Gyōsei Keisatsu no Arikata o Tegakari to shite (Public Order and Freedom in France: Consideration from the Role of the French Administrative Police). *Hitotsubashi Hōgaku (Hitotsubashi Law)*, Vol. 19 (2), 405-469.

Tipton, E. K. (2012) *The Japanese Police State: Tokko in Interwar Japan*. Bloomsbury Academic.

Tran, K. (2017) How Japan's Cultural Norms Affect Policing: A Side-By-Side Comparison with the United States. *Themis: Research Journal of Justice Studies and Forensic Science*, Vol. 5 (3), 37–62.

Uchida, M). (1982) Meiji Zenki ni okeru Gyōsei Keisatsu-teki Torishimari Hōrei no Keisei (Formation of Laws and Regulations for Administrative Police Control in the Early Meiji Era). *Waseda Hōgakkai-shi (Journal of Waseda Law Society)*, Vol. 33, 29–59.

Watanabe, Y. (1988) *Hō to Shakai no Shōwashi (Showa History of Law and Society)*. Iwanami Shoten.

Wildes, H. E. (1953) The Postwar Japanese Police. *Journal of Criminal Law and Criminology and Police Science*, Vol. 43 (5), 655-671.

Yamanaka, E. (1994) Nihon Kindai Hōron Josetsu: Nihon Kindai Hō no Rekishi to Hō Bunka (Introduction to Japanese Modern Law: History and Legal Culture of Japanese Modern Law). *Otemon Keizai Keiei Kenkyū (Otemon Economic and Management Review*, No. 1, 240–254.

Zheng, J. D. et al. (2021) Friend or foe? Social ties in bribery and corruption. *Experimental Economics*, Vol. 24, 854-882.

Chapter 9
Taishinin's Role and Judicial Behaviour in State Polity

9.1 Introduction

The analysis of the five cases in this book demonstrated an intricate interweaving of *Taishinin*'s position within the judicial system, the social dynamics of the state political sphere, the prevailing social conditions that fostered corruption and the prevailing traditional legal consciousness that was oriented against corruption. This chapter delves into the underlying rationales behind this intricate phenomenon.

9.2 *Taishinin's* Judicial Behaviour and the Imperial Rescripts

9.2.1 Consistency in Judicial Policy

Taishinin's judicial behaviour, which is predicated mainly on a strict liability model, is, in certain instances, supplemented by a strategic model, an attitudinal model and a historical institutionalist model. According to *Taishinin*, corruption constitutes a *mala prohibita* that poses a threat to the ethical and legal foundations of Japanese social relations. This consistent judicial behaviour constitutes a judicial policy that is congruent with traditional Japanese policy against corruption, as articulated in Chap. 3. The primary *hōishiki* (legal consciousness) that served as the impetus for *Taishinin*'s judicial policymaking was not founded on the principles of equality or human rights.[1] This approach does not solely align with the principles of justice or *dori*.[2] The objective of solidarity in social stratification is to establish a robust nation

[1] On this refer to contract law ruling in Chaps. 7 and 8.

[2] On this refer to small monetary amount of culinary entertainment in Chap. 6.

K. B. Wong and S. L. Fang, *Taishinin's Judicial Behaviour in Corruption Cases*,
https://doi.org/10.1007/978-981-95-5823-0_9

within a state political system.[3] As discussed in the preceding five chapters, the discipline exhibited by the corruption in regard to various categories of bureaucrats proved to be a pivotal factor in the maintenance of the hegemony of the prevailing top-down principal-agent power relations, which were structured in a vertical hierarchical manner. This chapter elucidates the underlying rationales that precipitated the judicial behaviour delineated in preceding chapters.

Both of *hō* and *ritsu* in *hōritsu* mean the same as the law, but *ritsu* was used traditionally for the feudalistic Japanese law.[4] The *rei* in *hōrei* is order or regulation in English but *hōrei* itself can be also translated as the same meaning. The Emperor's *rei* in prewar state polity was a source of the law. This conceptual influence of *rei* is still existing. Even today, the website of *e-GOV*, which is operated by Japanese government officially, still states that Japanese government treats laws, cabinet orders, ministry ordinances and regulations as *hōrei*.

In the state polity, the Emperor, the House of Peers the House of Representatives and the cabinet had power to issue laws in various forms. Under Article 9 of the Meiji Constitution, the Emperor could exercise his hegemonic prerogative to issue or caused to be issued orders necessary for the maintenance of the public peace and order, and for the promotion of the welfare of the subjects. *Chokurei* (Imperial Rescript or Decree) was a general term for the orders enacted by the Emperor. The legislative intent of Imperial Rescript was to strengthen the basis of the nation by cultivating the values of filiality and fraternal love, loyalty, sincerity and collective patriotism (Cluck 1985, pp. 129–130). Depending upon the issuing authorities, laws could be codified in the forms of Imperial Ordinances (or Decree), Prerogative Ordinances, Extraordinary Ordinances, Rescripts or Cabinet Ordinances.[5]

The prewar *Nihonhōrkenkyūkai* (Japan Jurisprudence Research Society) advocated judicial behaviours to follow the spirit of Imperial Rescripts upon exercise judicial power. Law could be substantially applied to Japanese subjects as an amplification of the Emperor's hegemonic moral relationship in their daily life. It asked the judicial institutions to interpret the state polity, morality and law for *kiso-bengi-shugi* (prosecution expediency) like a general legislative intent for all prewar Japanese laws. The Emperor was perceived as the origin of law and with his *toku* (virtue) for all institutions in the state polity.[6] The government officials' power in public administration institutions was given by the Emperor as a matter of such virtue.

9.2.2 *Kanri-Fukumu-Kiritsu and Kanri-Fukumu-Kiritsu*

According to Hiranuma Kiichirō, the eleventh *Taishinin* Chief Justice, law was historically a tool of judicial institution to help the Emperor's governance by virtue.

[3] On this see Matsuoka (2006, p. 126, p. 127, p. 134, p. 145).

[4] On this see Nishihara (1967, p. 62, p. 65).

[5] On this see Southgate (2000).

[6] On this see Japan Jurisprudence Research Society (1943, pp. 12–14).

Emperor's virtue in Imperial Rescript underpinned the spirit and organizational culture of anti-corruption (Hiranuma 1923, p. 12). Two Imperial Rescripts issued by the Emperor Meiji were found to be attitudinally consistent with *Taishinin*'s strict liability model of judicial behaviour in the previous chapters, namely *Kanri-fukumu-kiritsu* (Imperial Rescript of Discipline for Service of Civil Servants) dated 29 July 1887 and *Bunkanchōkairei* (Civil Official Disciplinary Order) dated 27 March 1899.[7] *Kanri-fukumu-kiritsu* and *Bunkan-chōkairei* were two Imperial Rescripts setting standards that all officials in government institutions in the state polity under Emperor, embedding social trust to bureaucrats under Emperor as a core cultural value and tradition (Shimizu 2020, p. 3–5). *Taishinin*'s judicial behaviours in the five judgements analysed in this book were under the shadow of *Kanri-fukumu-kiritsu* and *Bunkan-chōkairei.* In the perspective of historical institutionalist model, *Taishinin*'s judicial behaviour had mission to enforce it.

The first Imperial Rescript is *Kanri-fukumu-kiritsu* dated 29 July 1887. The legal consciousness of *Taishinin*'s judicial behaviour of strict liability model in respect of bureaucrats' integrity had similarity with elements in this Imperial Rescript, of which the first article stipulated that all government officials shall be loyal and diligent toward His Majesty the Emperor and His Majesty's Government and shall perform utmost for their respective duties in accordance with legal orders.[8]

The term s*okumu* (official duty) was used in Article 1 and had been the hottest term argued in previous *Taishinin* five judgements. Article 1 required all government officials to perform their utmost for the official duty,[9] but the scope of it was neither defined nor limited by this Article. Non-official duty is accordingly the most common appeal ground in *Taishinin* judgements. Article 3 stated that the government officials should place great importance on uprightness and anti-corruption, regardless of whether they are in charge of their duties or not. And government officials should not abuse their power of hegemony, whether inside or outside their duties, and should exercise it with caution and respect. The terms *tano* (corruption) and *iken* (hegemony) were found in Article 3.[10] All government officials were at the service of Emperor. This Imperial Rescript stipulated that government officials were obligated to comply with orders, maintain confidentiality and limit in their side jobs. During postwar law reform, this Imperial Rescript was revised on 2 May 1947 by deletion of all wordings relating to the state polity.

The second Imperial Rescript of relevance to *Taishinin*'s judicial behaviour was number 63 was *Bunkan-chōkairei* dated 27 March 1899, which clearly stipulated *igen* (dignity), *shinyō* (credibility or trustworthiness) and *shokumuj-no-gimu* (sense

[7] On the original text of *Kanri-fukumu-kiritsu* see *Compendium of laws and regulations* (*Meiji* 4) edited by Cabinet Gazette Bureau; See the original text of *Bunkanchōkairei* at https://www.digital.archives.go.jp/DAS/meta/Detail_F0000000000000017902. Accessed 2 October 2025.

[8] The original text in Kanrifukumukiritsu: 第一条、凡ソ官吏ハ天皇陛下及天皇陛下ノ政府ニ対シ忠順勤勉ヲ主トシ法律命令ニ従ヒ各其職務ヲ尽スヘシ。

[9] The original text in Kanrifukumukiritsu: 各其職務ヲ尽スヘシ。

[10] The original text in Kanrifukumukiritsu: 第三条、官吏ハ職務ノ内外ヲ問ハス廉耻ヲ重シ貪汚ノ所為アルヘカラス官吏ハ職務ノ内外ヲ問ハス威権ヲ濫用セス謹慎懇切ナルコトヲ務ムヘシ。

of obligation to official duty) were the core values in the government's organizational culture. Article 2 of it stated that the punishment of dismissal, salary reduction or reprimand were applicable to a government official's breach of obligation for official duty or its negligence, or behaviours leading to loss of the dignity and credibility of the government office, no matter inside and outside the office.[11]

9.2.3 *Kenpō-Kōfu-Chokugo and Boshin-Shōsho*

The Emperor's governance by virtue is further exemplified by the *Kenpō-kōfu-chokugo* (Imperial Rescript of Constitution Promulgation) dated 11 February 1889, in which the Emperor expected the loyalty and bravery of his subjects and the love of the country and the public martyrdom. He also treated his subjects as the immediate loyal decent descendants of ancestors.[12] In 1908, the Emperor's hegemony was further reaffirmed with by *Boshin-shōsho* (Boshin Imperial Edict), in which the Emperor expected his subjects' kindness and loyalty … disseminate mighty virtue of ancestors.[13] In 1929, Satomi Kishio, the founder of Japanese *kokutai* (state polity) studies, treated such consciousness as the law of personal coexistence and co-prosperity in prewar Japan. With absolute obedience and loyalty, the social expectation was that the Emperor, and his subjects were assumed to have the same mindset under the same social cohesiveness.[14]

Corruption was disobedience damaging social cohesiveness and breach of loyalty in Japanese legal culture. The control of selfishness against it is the *tenri* (principles of heaven) in terms of *giri-honshin* (principles of rightness inherently in one's mind). Japanese *giri* (moralistic principles of rightness) over *gimu* (obligations) and *ninjō* (humaneness) over *kenri* (rights) are at the expense of individualist freedom and social justice in prewar Japan. The core values emphasized in the aforesaid Imperial Rescripts and Edicts were reinforcing "the body of Japanese culture", which is mentioned in Chap. 3 of this book.[15] The transplantation of Western laws was like a jacket on this Japanese body. With such hegemonic *hōrei* issued by the Emperor, *Taishinin* could apply it with its strategic model of judicial behaviour to guide politics

---

[11] The original text in *Bunkanchōkairei*:第二条、官吏ノ懲戒ヲ受クヘキ場合左ノ如シ。一、職務上ノ義務ニ違背シ又ハ職務ヲ怠リタルトキ; 二、職務ノ内外ヲ問ハス官職上ノ威厳又ハ信用ヲ失フヘキ所為アリタルトキ。第三条、懲戒ハ左ノ如シ。一、免官。二、減俸。三、譴責。

[12] The original text in Kenpōkōfuchokugo: 臣民ノ忠實勇武ニシテ國ヲ愛シ公ニ殉ヒ以テ…我カ臣民ハ即チ祖宗ノ忠良ナル臣民ノ子孫ナル。https://www.digital.archives.go.jp/item/4151021.html. Accessed 2 October 2025.

[13] The original text in *Boshinshōsho*:我ガ忠良ナル臣民ノ協翼ニ倚藉シテ… 祖宗ノ威徳ヲ対揚セムコト。 https://www.archives.go.jp/exhibition/popup_jousetsu_20_1/popup_jousetsu_20_1_0401.html. Accessed 2 October 2025.

[14] On this see Satomi (1929, p. 231, pp. 271–275).

[15] On this see Tucker (2014, pp. 47–48); Also see Feldman (2004, pp. 46–48).

and influence norms and beliefs to the bureaucrats' incentives for a particular course of action.[16]

According to the Emperor's legislative intent in these *hōrei*, *Taishinin*'s hybrid judicial behaviour of strict liability model and strategic model in corruption cases was frequently establishing constituent elements for the goal of no infringement against Article 23 of the Meiji Constitution. As long as *Taishinin*'s judicial behaviour could meet this constitutional requirement, the judicial behaviour was legitimate to bind all Japanese nationals.

9.3 *Taishinin* and the Ministry of Justice

9.3.1 The First Minister of Justice

As the first Minister of Justice, Etō Shinpei also had similar family background of samurai of Saga domain. With similar socialization by a samurai family, judicial bureaucrats were willing to attack enemies in the name of the national need for the state polity (Beasley 1972, p. 390). Etō's legal knowledge of traditional Japanese law *ritsuryō* and its history was first indoctrinated by the traditional loyalist Edayoshi Shinyō in Saga domain. Edayoshi was a scholar famous for his *sonnōron* (advocation for conservative devotion and reverence for the emperor) (Hoshihara 2006, p. 214). The similar traditional cultural values indoctrinated in the samurai families were found among the bureaucrats leading Meiji legal reform. Duus describes it as a "revolution from above" during this period (Duus 1976, p. 73).

9.3.2 Saibansho-Kōseihō

Before *Saibansho-kōseihō* (Court Structure Code, or Judicial Organization Act), the full judicial autonomy of *Taishinin* from the Minister of Justice was doubtful in historical institutionalism perspective. Though early *Taishinin* was nominally a self-governing elite bureaucracy and its justices had very close career paths and advancement within the power of Ministry of Justice, the Chief Justice was lower than the Minister of Justice. Even after *Saibansho-kōseihō,* the undue influence of the Minister of Justice remained.

In February 1890, along with the promulgation of the Constitution of the Empire of Japan as the state polity, *Saibansho-kōseihō* was enacted by legal transplantation from the Germanic law. Superficially, it was packing Japanese judiciary to be more Westernized. Beneath this "Western jacket" of judiciary, the ultimate aim of legislative behaviour for *Saibansho-kōseihō* was to end extraterritoriality and take

[16] On this see Ramseyer and Rosenbluth (1995, pp. 39–40, pp. 160–166).

tariff sovereignty back. As per *Saibansho-kōseihō*, *Taishinin* was historically and institutionally handcuffed as merely the isolated highest court, and the courts of appeal, district courts and local courts had been firmly established under Article 135 (1). Article 135 (2) allowed *Taishinin* to have self-governance, but its governance and supervision were not extended to the lower courts, which were under the judicial administration of the Minister of Justice, which handcuffed *Taishinin*'s judicial administration of junior courts.

Chapter 5 of Articles 43 to 56 in *Saibansho-kōseihō* provides the details of *Taishinin*'s structure and power. As per Articles 43 and 44, *Taishinin* kept its Supreme Court status of the establishment of one or more than two civil and criminal divisions. *Taishinin* Chief Justice was appointed to direct the general affairs and supervise its own administrative affairs. In the organizational structure of *Taishinin*, each division had a director for the supervision and appropriation of duties. *Taishinin* Chief Justice was de facto appointed by the Emperor based on the recommendation of the Minister of Justice, while other judges were directly appointed by the Minister of Justice.

Articles 45 to 47 administratively authorized *Taishinin* Chief Justice to internally monitor manpower deployment under each division head annually. He could also designate division heads for the following year. At any time, *Taishinin* Chief Justice might transfer a division head or a division member to another division, subject to their consents. In the event that a justice's incapability to handle a case and no replacement, a deputy justice could be appointed for the urgent trials. *Taishinin* Chief Justice might notify the justice who headed the court of appeal in the judicial area where it was located, and the justice who headed the court of appeal might act as a deputy justice accordingly. In the event of re-structuring divisions, *Taishinin* Chief Justice had to ensure job arrangements in case of sick leave or annual leave in a judicial year as stipulated in Article 23. He had to arrange judge for relieving sick leave or emergency as per Article 24.[17]

Articles 48 to 50 were about procedural justice, stating that legal grounds to bring a trial at *Taishinin* for any litigation should be submitted through the lower courts. Judgement should be prepared for hearing a final appeal case. In case of conflictual opinions of different divisions on a judgement, the case should be brought to the attention of *Taishinin* Chief Justice who would hold a second hearing together with the relevant divisions according to the case nature.[18]

Article 50 empowered *Taishinin* to hear appeals against the judgement of the court of appeal and against the judgement of the first instance. *Taishinin* also heard criminal appeals against the decisions and orders of the court of appeal on the felonies listed in Chaps. 1 and 2 of the Penal Code, pretrial and trial for the crimes against imperial house punishable with the imprisonment or more severe punishment. Under Article 51, if *Taishinin* deemed it necessary to refer a case listed in Article 50, it could authorize the court of appeal or a district court to hold a hearing. In such case, the

[17] On the original text see *Saibansho-kōseihō* edited by Book Publishing Company 1890.

[18] Ibid.

justices of the court of appeal might join as division members of *Taishinin*, but the number should not be more than half of division members.[19]

As per procedural justice from Articles 52 to 56, *Taishinin*'s scope of jurisdictional power and arrangement for hearing were governed. Hearing had to be conducted by a *Taishinin* chamber composed of seven *Taishinin* justices, one of whom should be the presiding justice. In the case of joint hearing of two divisions, the number of attendance of justices should be at least two-thirds. The Chief Justice should approve the justice of the highest rank in it to be the director of such joint hearing. And a justice had the right to head his own division. Article 50 allowed *Taishinin* Chief Justice to order his subordinate, and the justices to conduct pretrial in preparation for a final trial. The Prosecution Bureau of *Taishinin* was permitted to have its own Director General of *Kenji-kyoku* (Public Prosecutor's Office).[20]

Article 70 was about the minimum eligibility for the post of *Taishinin* justice, who should have at least ten-year experience in judgeship or ten-year professorship of law at Imperial University. For a lawyer who had not been appointed as a judge before, he might not be appointed as an assistant judge of *Taishinin*. In order to provide the package for the nominal independence, *Saibansho-kōseihō* was amended in 1914, so that *Taishinin* Chief Justice became a direct appointment of the Emperor,[21] but the nomination was still made by the Minister of Justice.

Under *Saibansho-kōseihō*, judges and public prosecutors were appointed by the Emperor or his endorsement on the Minister of Justice's recommendation of candidate for such appointment according to Article 67 and 79(1). The Minister of Justice not only had power to make recommendations to appoint the Chief Justice (Article 68), but also the chief prosecutor (Article 79), the court secretary (Article 88) and even the bailiff (Article 95). The Minister of Justice also determined promotion, salary amount (Articles 76), change of organization of judiciary (Article 75), also the dismissal, disciplinary action and suspension of a judge (Article 78). The Minister had final judicial administration power and duty to monitor all courts and public prosecution office, except *Taishinin*. The Minister of Justice was considered omnipotent, omniscient and omnipresent according to *Saibansho-kōseihō*.

A close careful scrutiny of Articles 43 to 56 reveals something unusual. Though *Taishinin* Chief Justice held presiding judgeship for judiciary, his power of supervision and administration was limited to *Taishinin* only. Unlike the comprehensive power of the Minister of Justice over the whole judiciary, *Saibansho-kōseihō* even gave the Chief Justice no legal authority for recruiting and further promoting the career judges under his leadership. There was no statutory provision to select qualified judges of lower court or public prosecutors to be put into the pool of candidates for judges. This process was under the control and discretion of the Minister of Justice. Therefore, no legal provision was available to empower *Taishinin* Chief Justice for selection of non-career judge appointees and screening the whole process, which could ensure neither partisan nor political influence on such appointments. In

[19] Ibid.

[20] Ibid.

[21] On the amendment of *Saibansho-kōseihō* see Ministry of Finance (1914, p. 1).

terms of the whole judiciary under the Minister of Justice and the Meiji Constitution, *Taishinin* was like an isolated lame duck in state polity.

From the historical institutionalist viewpoint, the Minister of Justice could subtly affect all *Taishinin* Justices' judicial behaviour through the recommendation privilege. The whole prewar Japanese judiciary was dominated by the Minister of Justice with limited exemption granted to *Taishinin* under Article 135(2) of *Saibansho-kōseihō*. All *Taishinin* Chief Justices' working experiences and promotions were involved in this organizational hierarchy. Therefore, beliefs and values of the Ministry of Justice could be culturally assimilated to the working culture in the whole judiciary. The undue influence was thus not limited to the judge appointment. While all courts lower than *Taishinin* were under the administration of the Minister of Justice, his exercise of judicial administration power for three decades in the early Meiji era led to an accumulative deterrent effect of punishment and consolidated his influence on jurisdiction. Moreover, without the real separation of power, politicians and the Ministers could subtly manipulate judiciary by dismissal or posting arrangement, thereby affecting the group solidarity in judicial behaviour. The historical cognitive institutionalized influence of the Ministry's working culture on *Taishinin* justices could not be underestimated or eliminated. This was totally different from Article 6 of the postwar Constitution which stipulated the Emperor shall appoint the Chief Judge of the Supreme Court as designated by the cabinet.

As a judicial oligarchy administratively controlling all legal affairs, the Minister of Justice also headed *kensatsu* (public prosecutors or prosecution) to interpret law and make decisions to drop or indict a case internally. The higher status and power of public prosecutors in Japan is still a factor behind the current high conviction rate.[22] As the agents of the Minister of Justice in prewar Japan, prosecutors could sit along with the judge up on the stand in the court room. By such layout and body language, prosecutors showed contempt and hegemony to the defendant, instead of implying the intention to grant the benefit of doubt.[23] In criminal proceedings, benefit of doubt commonly belonged to the prosecutors, not the defendants. The prewar *Baishinhō* (Jury Code), which was codified on 18 April 1923 and suspended on 1 April 1943, was a legislative means to handle the expanding power of public prosecutors on judicial behaviour (Hayashi 2012, pp. 64–65). Out of 484 trials with jury, defendants in 81 cases were found not guilty. More than one of out of ten was deemed to be innocent according to the citizens' common sense (Okahara 1943, p. 16).

The Ministry of Justice took into consideration the determinative opinions of the procuracy with regard to the posting and appointment of judges. This action enabled the ministry to exert its influence on the substantive justice of the court and procedural justice through the procuracy. In the context of the state polity, the Minister of Justice wielded significant influence over both prosecutors and judges, subjecting them to the prevailing ideological preferences of the Minister. In cases of a sensitive nature that carried significant political implications, judges had to demonstrate a high degree of personal courage and judicial integrity when their actions were not aligned with

[22] On this see Gōhara (2020).

[23] On this see Nippon Communications Foundation (2019).

the policy directives of the Minister of Justice. The presiding judge might need to consider the possibility of a confrontation with the public prosecutor. The public prosecutor was under the command of the Minister of Justice, and his duty was to monitor the judicial behaviour of judges in an institutional manner (Oppler 1949, p. 305).

9.4 The Minister of Justice's Interventions

The research of Iwatani Juro confirmed that the Minister of Justice's domination and command to *Taishinin* existed in prewar Japan. He found that seven *Taishinin* justices in criminal cases had sought the directives and legal advice of the Ministry of Justice on thirty-seven criminal cases in 1879. The natures of these thirty-seven cases included preliminary case commentary and legal reasoning approach at preparation stage, and overview case analysis. In all thirty-seven cases, the Ministry was controlling *Taishinin*'s judicial behaviour to set judicial precedents for uniformity of court rulings thereafter. In one judgement on an abortion case delivered on 2 June 1879, the Ministry advised the punishment according to their status in social hierarchy. If the offender belonged to samurai or *kashizoku* (noble class), different punishments should be inflicted. Iwatani harshly criticized *Taishinin* as a puppet in noble judicial robe of the Ministry of Justice.[24]

During second Itō Hirofumi cabinet (1893–1894), the Minister of Justice Yamagata Aritomo and his successor Yoshikawa Akimasa dismissed seven *Taishinin* Justices and sixty-seven judges of junior courts. While *Taishinin* Justice Chiya Toshinori argued with the legality of such exercise of judicial administration power, he was punished by a reduction in rank to be a judge of Okinawa District Court in 1893. From 1898 to 1899, the Minister of Justice dismissed a total of eighty-eight judges of old generation. In view of the salary gap between judges and bureaucrats, judges asked for a salary increase during 1902 to 1903. However, the Minister, Kiyoura Keigo responded it with a cutting of thirty-six judges. Three *Taishinin* justices, Okamura Tamezō, Serizawa Seion and Iwata Mugi were punished by *kyūshoku* (suspended from duty or asked to have leave of absence). In 1913, the cabinet of Yamamoto Gonbee exercised the same judicial administration power to ask *Taishinin* justice, Inoue Seiichi and the Chief Justice of Hakodate Appeal Court Ichinose Yūzaburō to have suspensions. In 1921, the cabinet of Hara Takashi introduced mandatory retirement age. It was understandable that the large scale of dismissal of judges was partly for the replacement of judges of old generation. However, it unduly extended to *Taishinin* justices and some judges who had new legal education background, such as Ichinose Yūzaburō.[25]

---

[24] On this see Iwatani (1993, p. 15, p. 18, pp. 23–24, p. 52).

[25] On this see Shichinohe (2010, p. 72); Also see Kasumi (2021).

9.4.1 The Otsu Jiken

Kojima Korekata was the eighth *Taishinin* Chief Justice from May 1891 to August 1892. On 11 May 1891, the *Ōtsu Jiken* (Incident) happened. An attempt was made to assassinate the Russian Crown Prince Nicholas Alexandrevich in Otsu, Shiga Prefecture on 11 May 1891. The prince was not for sightseeing in Japan but out of his initiative to construct the eastern part of the Trans-Siberian Railway to Asia for potential colonial expansion. The Minister of Justice and the government cabinet openly intervened by advocating to convict and sentence the offender Tsuda Sanzo to death by the offence of *daigyakuzai* (high treason), in order to avoid a possible diplomatic tension. Kojima refused to do so for protecting *Taishinin*'s judicial independence upon sentencing (Mori 1971, p. 2).

It is considered that Kojima's vigorous protest against the government's interference in the judicial process triggered a wellspring of sense for judicial autonomy of *Taishinin*, but Ramseyer and Rosenbluth argue that the presiding judges in the courtroom for this case were pressurized by Meiji political oligarchs.[26] Two arguments make an ideological obfuscation on this case. While Kojima Korekata was not the presiding judge in this case, his presence upon sentencing also constituted a pressure on the judicial autonomy and independence of presiding judge, who was Kojima's subordinate. The circumstances also constituted an undue influence of Kojima. Most scholars overlooked it and mistakenly praised Kojima one-sidedly.[27]

9.4.2 The Hōkan Rōka Jiken

Rule of law triumphed in the dramatic confrontation between *Taishinin* and the Minister of Justice in the *Otsu* case, which likely led to the background of *Hanafuda Case*, or *Hōkan Rōka Jiken* in Japanese. *Hanafuda*, or *Rōka* was considered as a traditional card gambling game. In 1892, *Taishinin* Chief Justice, Kojima Korekata was discovered with this gambling behaviour in office involving some *Taishinin* judges. This case evinced the internal personnel conflicts in *Taishinin* and the possibility of the Ministry of Justice to try to get rid of Kojima behind the curtain. Gambling had to be caught red-handedly according to the law. In this complaint of *Taishinin* justices' gambling lodged by the Prosecutor General Matsuoka Yasuki on 17 June 1892 for *chōkai-saiban* (disciplinary trial), it was solely based on hearsay evidence. Although the disciplinary trial was therefore waived on 17 July 1892, Kojima resigned after being shamed openly in this incident.[28] The considerable factor in this case was that Matsuoka should have professional knowledge that hearsay evidence or oral evidence without corroboration was not acceptable as the evidence for proof, which should

---

[26] On this see Ramseyer and Rosenbluth (1995, pp. 76–78).

[27] On this see Ramseyer (1994); Also see Ramseyer (2001).

[28] On this see Odanaka (1969).

be a matter of legal common sense. It is noteworthy that even Australian newspaper reported this mysterious case.[29]

9.4.3 The Taisei Yokusan Kai Case

Under the Meiji Constitution, *Taishinin* had neither legal provision nor practice for judicial review. However, election invalidation lawsuits were first-instance cases at *Taishinin*. Articles 81–84 in Chapter 9 of prewar *Shūgiingiin-senkyohō* (House of Representatives Election Law) empowered *Taishinin* to declare an election null and void in case of violating electoral regulations. *Taishinin* had delivered several landmark judgements on it before the 1930s.[30]

Yokusan Seiji Taisei Kyōgikai (or *Taisei Yokusan Kai*, Yokusan Political System Council) was under government sponsorship to win the seats in the House of Representatives. *Yokusan* means lending your strength and assisting the Son of Heaven in politics. *Taisei Yokusan Kai* was claimed to be a voluntary association of thirty-three representatives from the military, business circles, agricultural organizations, members of both the House of Peers and the House of Representatives, and others were invited. They actually received funds from government to endorse and campaign for electoral candidates. The amount was about 5,000 *yen* from temporary military expenses (Miyashita 2022, p. 12). With such allowance, *Taisei Yokusan Kai* won about eighty per cent of the seats in the House of Representatives in April 1942.

In order to preside in an election invalidation litigation lodged by failed candidates against the electoral candidate of *Taisei Yokusan Kai* in Kagoshima's second district, *Taishinin* justice, Yoshida Hisa led a team of four justices to examine the Governor of Kagoshima Prefecture, Usuda Mitomo with a total of 187 witnesses. *Taishinin* finally ruled the election was invalid. As the *Taishinin* Chief Justice, Shimoyama Seiichi endorsed this ruling. Four days later, in respect of invalidation of electoral victory, Yoshida resigned under the pressure of the Minister of Justice, and the judgement was missing.

Until the end of the Pacific War, Yoshida had been under the surveillance of *Tokubetsu-kōtōkeisatsu* (Special Police) as a dangerous social undesirable.[31] The Ministry of Justice had to subdue *Taishinin*'s judicial behaviour of conflict with governance in the state polity. After his appointment was ended in 1946, Yoshida was decreed as a member of the House of Peers in the same year. He contributed his expertise to the draft of the new constitution.

---

[29] See *The Express and Telegraph* (12 September 1892) About *Japanese Gambling Scandal.* at https://trove.nla.gov.au/newspaper/article/208439362 - Accessed 15 September 2025.

[30] On the original text see *Shūgiingiin-senkyohō* edited by Criminal Affairs Bureau, Ministry of Justice, pp. 48–102.

[31] On this see Kiyonaga (2008, pp. 80–82, p. 97, pp. 152–153, p. 165).

9.5 Institutionalized Discrimination Against *Taishinin*

The institutionalist interventions and undue influence from the Minister of Justice on *Taishinin*'s judicial behaviour were under asymmetry power relationship. The ranking of the Minister of Justice was structurally higher than that of the *Taishinin* Chief Justice, though both were prestigious *kanri* instead of *kōri. Kanri* referred to the Emperor's bureaucrats under Article 10 of the Meiji Constitution, *Kōri* referred to officials of the local governments and special organizations under Meiji Constitution. In other words, *kōri* was an employee other than a bureaucrat of central government who handles state affairs. Among *kanri*, the highest rank was a *shinninkan* (direct appointed official) made by the Emperor at a ceremony held in the Imperial Palace. Under the Meiji Constitution, *shinnonian* included the Minister of State, the Admiral of the Army and Navy, the Chairman of the Privy Council, the *Taishinin* Chief Justice, the President of the Board of Auditors and the Ambassador Extraordinary and Plenipotentiary. Their letters of appointment required a countersignature from the Prime Minister. Without the recommendation of the Minister of Justice, *Taishinin* Chief Justice could not own the honour of direct appointment status.

Below *shinninkan*, the second rank was called *chokuninkan* as the imperial appointed officials, and the lower rank was *sōninkan* as the appointed officials. According to *Saibansho-shokuin-teiinrei* (Court Staff Quota Order) in1920, there were five imperial appointed judges with twenty-six appointed judges, one imperial appointed prosecutor to head the prosecution division with seven appointed prosecutors. Under the limitation with only thirty-six subordinates under *Taishinin* Chief Justice, *Taishinin* was structurally a mini institution, which limited collective bargaining for a fairer salary scale. In the historical institutionalist perspective, the salary scale of judges was intentionally and discriminatorily set lower than other judicial bureaucrats under the Ministry of Justice. According to *Kōtōkan-ninmei-itaru-houkyuurei* (Senior Official Appointment and Salary Order) dated 27 July 1891, the annual salary of a senior official of the Ministry of Justice was between 800 *yen* and 2,500 *yen*. The Minister got an annual salary of 6,000 *yen*, which is 1,000 *yen* higher than that of the *Taishinin* Chief Justice, which could be considered as a confirmation of the *Taishinin* Chief Justice's lower rank in the Meiji bureaucracy (Ono 2022, p. 327).

9.6 *Taishinin's Judicial Behaviour* and State Polity

9.6.1 Historically Designed Role

Article 52(1) of the Meiji Constitution in theory placed judiciary as a part of a bureaucratic system under the Emperor's command and domination like the Prussian absolute monarchism, while Article 57 guaranteed that the judicature should be exercised by the judiciary according to law enforced in the name of the Emperor.[32] Under Article 58, the Emperor could appoint a judge for life tenure, and no judges could be removed, suspended or dismissed or forced with a reduction of salary unless they were not able to perform duties due to the physical or mental issues, criminal convictions or disciplinary sanctions. Actually, this power of judicial administration was increasingly exercised by the Ministry of Justice in the name of the Emperor. From the late 1920s and 1930s, judges were judicial bureaucrats under increasingly strident ideological control of all extremes in the state polity. The independence of judges and prosecutors was under acceptable niche and strict monitor of the Ministry of Justice (Haley 2005, p. 18).

In the absence of provision of judicial review power by the Meiji Constitution, the judicial behaviour exhibited by *Taishinin* was characterized as a conservative judicial lame duck. *Taishinin* exhibited a judicial behaviour characterized by a lack of the capacity to challenge the state polity in a constitutionally compliant manner. This observation is supported by the provision of legal interpretations and explanations pertinent to the Meiji Constitution. Record check revealed that there were no Emperor's Imperial Rescripts that had been issued to delegate power of constitutional interpretation and explanation to *Taishinin*. *Taishinin* could not rule government's executive act to be unconstitutional. The legal status of the Emperor in the state polity was supreme and absolute above judiciary, which was totally different from today's Supreme Court of Japan. Therefore, *Taishinin* could not apply attitudinal or strategic model of judicial behaviour in order to hold political decisions to be constitutionally inconsistent. Although its judicial behaviour can be highly deliberative for consensus on the legitimacy and illegitimacy of a political decision or act,[33] *Taishinin* was deprived of constitutional power to provide better protection of people's constitutional rights, and more generally, to enforce the constitution against the maladministration of the prewar government (Mendes and Hubner 2014, pp. 101–102). On the contrary, *Taishinin* was a court with a special historical institutionalist role at the service of imperial house.

The Meiji Constitution prescribed all Japanese were *shinmin* (subjects, bureaucrats and ordinary people) under the Emperor, who was the son of the Heaven to rule and enlighten the world moralistically (Kuriyama 1891, pp. 8–9). The indoctrination of this consciousness to government officials was responding imperial sovereignty under Articles 1 and 10 of the Meiji Constitution, which has been repeatedly addressed in this book: Article 1 declared that the Empire of Japan shall be reigned over and governed by a line of Emperors unbroken for ages eternal[34]; Article 10 empowered Emperor to determine the organization of the different branches of the administration, and salaries of all civil and military officers, and appoints and

[32] The original text of Article 57 in the Meiji Constitution: 第五十七條司法權ハ天皇ノ名ニ於テ法律ニ依リ裁判所之ヲ行フ裁判所ノ構成ハ法律ヲ以テ之ヲ定ム。https://www.ndl.go.jp/constitution/etc/j02.html. Accessed 2 October 2025.

[33] On this see Eagan (2016).

[34] The original text in Meiji Constitution:大日本帝国ハ万世一系ノ天皇之ヲ統治ス。https://www.ndl.go.jp/constitution/etc/j02.html. Accessed 2 October 2025.

dismisses the same.[35] As the agents of the Emperor's power, government officials had status superior to the citizens and inherited traditional strict conduct and discipline, valued honour, integrity, pride and unmaterialistic affluence under the Emperor's command.[36] The hybrid of the attitudinal, strategic and strict liability model of *Taishinin*'s judicial behaviour in some corruption cases therefore took place under historical institutionalism.

9.6.2 Taishinin's Historical Institutionalist Role for Imperial House

As *Taishinin* had been designated a historical institutionalist role to protect the imperial house. Under Article 3 of the Meiji Constitution, the Emperor is sacred and inviolable. The origin of the Emperor's hegemony was his sacredness as the descendants of the Great Goddess Amaterasu as the core of the state polity. *Taishinin* had judicial role to protect and rationalize the Emperor's hegemonic governance as *tendō* (the Heaven's way) in traditional Japanese jurisprudence. Many articles in the Meiji Constitution were interdependent for the state polity, and directly or indirectly relating to *Taishinin*'s protection of the imperial house. Article 29 of the Meiji Constitution stipulated Japanese subjects shall, within the limits of the law, enjoy the liberty of speech, writing, publication, public meetings and associations. These basic underpinnings for constitutional monarchy were in fact at the mercy of the Emperor as an absolute monarchy emanating all powers structurally. Article 31 stipulated that the provisions contained in the Chapter II (Article 18–30 for rights and duties of the nationals) shall not affect the exercise of the powers appertaining to the Emperor, in the times of war or in cases of a national emergency. Article 57 stipulated the Judicature shall be exercised by the Courts of Law according to the law in the name of the Emperor. All these mean that *Taishinin*'s judicial behaviour should be in the name of the Emperor to protect the stability of social relations in the absolute *tennōsei* (emperorism).

Under the three-trial system, *Taishinin* had special judicial role for the final decision on interpreting the transplanted law, determining jurisdiction over the second appeals, and it also played a special role as the court of first instance and final appeal over crimes of *taigyakuzai* or *fukeizai* (crimes of disrespectful acts or blasphemy on the imperial family). *Taigyakuzai* and *fukeizai* can be traced in *Taihō-ritsuryō* in 701 and *Yōrō-ritsuryō* in 718, included in *hachigyaku* (the eight felony crimes) as the crimes of the highest seriousness such as *muhon* (rebellion) and *bōtaigyaku* (intending for high treason). It even included the plotting to destroy an imperial mountain tomb or the Imperial Palace.[37] Before the Meiji Constitution, Articles 116

[35] The original text in Meiji Constitution: 天皇ハ行政各部ノ官制及文武官ノ俸給ヲ定メ及文武官ヲ任免ス https://www.ndl.go.jp/constitution/etc/j02.html. Accessed 2 October 2025.

[36] On this see Akio (2010, p. 250, p. 252).

[37] On this see Arai (2013a, b).

to120 of the Penal Code 1880 punished these acts by the minimum penalty of six months to the maximum penalty of capital punishment.

Especially, the articles in the Penal Code 1907 for *Taishinin*'s protection of the imperial house addressed that its judicial behaviour was "Japanese body in Germanic jacket". In Germanic law, *taigyakuza* could be interpreted as *hochverrat,* but only the murders or attempted murders against the Emperor can be considered as *hochverrat* which could be punishable by the death penalty (Ichikawa 2019, p. 137). This is different from the traditional Japanese concept, in which *taigyakuzai* and *nairanzai* (insurrection) were interrelated. The aim of insurrection was conceptually assumed to overthrow government.[38] In this connection, only *Taishinin*'s jurisprudence could be applied to Articles 73 to 79 for judicial decision on *taigyakuzai* or *fukeizai.* These articles of prewar Penal Code not only punished *muhon* and *bōtaigyaku*, but also protected Japanese imperial house. *Taishinin* had been assigned a historical institutionalist role in the state polity to protect Shinto, enforce *fukeitsumi* against disrespectful acts or blasphemy on Japanese imperial family, which had sacredness under Imperial Shinto.

9.6.3 Taishinin and Kokka Shintō

Before the Meiji era, the historical development of Shintō lacked a definitive correlation with a nationwide religious law that was enforced by a national judicial system. Shintō is a native Japanese belief system comprising shrine rituals that predate historical records. The integration of shrine rituals with Shintō concepts is a pivotal moment in the development of nationwide doctrine during the early period of the Meiji Restoration, marking the inception of Shintoism as a widespread belief system. This phenomenon can be considered a form of "religionization" of Shintō, a term used to describe the adoption of religious elements into non-religious contexts. Consequently, Shintoism evolved into a national ideology, serving to unify the populace under the state. This ideology substantiated the sacredness of the Emperor, his legitimacy to rule, and his position within the state political structure. The promotion of ideological and spiritual unification through the medium of *Shintō kokkyō-ka-seisaku* (Policy of nationalization of Shintō) served to instill imperial nationalism into the Japanese populace. This state-sanctioned form of Shintō, which incorporated a national religious system, a theoretical and institutional organization of shrines, and Shintoism, is a prime example of the interweaving of religion and state in Japan.[39]

For the first time in Japanese legal history, prewar Penal Code designated *Taishinin* to have judicial power to criminalize and punish any disrespectful behaviour against the imperial Shintō shrines, including the imperial mausoleums. It was thus a form of socialization of the imperial Shintō by formal social control in support of governance. An example is the Ise Shrine representing the origin of sacredness of the

[38] Ibid.

[39] On this see Inoue (2024, p. 155, p. 256).

imperial house.[40] The Meiji government, born out of feudalism, had centralized power with overemphasis in the urban areas and feudal clique politics. The worship at Shintō shrines could keep the legitimacy and hegemony of the Emperor in both urban areas and the countryside (Mori, K. and Mori, N. 1967, p. 48). With the support of formal social control, Shintō rationalized Emperor's governance and integrated into state polity. For these political objectives, in 1882, the Meiji government set up *Kōten-kōkyūsho* (the Imperial Court Research Institute) as the organization for the training of the Shintō priesthood. It became postwar Kokugakuin University. *Kokka-Shintō* or State Shintōism legitimatized the state polity with imperial dynasty of an unparalleled, historical religious traditions and holy status for the legitimacy of the Emperor's reign. It was like an imagined national political community of a common public culture (Nakamura 2022, pp. 57–59). In 1936, the *Kyōgaku-sasshin-hyōgikai* (Education Revision Deliberative Committee) even subordinated everything under the Emperor by education, in which profound reverence on the part of generations of the Emperors was reiterated.[41] In 1940, on the occasion of the 2600th anniversary of Emperor's accession to the throne, *Kōten-kōkyūsho* was re-organized into the *Jiingīn* (Institute of Divinities) to ensure national consciousness under the religious sacredness of imperial house.[42]

All these developments were coordinated with *Taishinin*'s jurisprudence on *fukeizai. Taishinin* had an historical institutionalist role in the strategy to attain political goal of state Shintō, in addition to protection of Emperor's hegemonic powers and status under Articles 1 to 17 of Meiji Constitution. Other than *Taishinin*, no other court or institution owned similar jurisdiction and judicial functions in the perspective of historical institutionalist model of judicial behaviour. It is worthwhile to mention that though Articles 73 to 76 for *taigyakuzai* (crime of inflicting harm on the imperial family) and *fukeizai* had been deleted during postwar law reform, *nairanzai* (insurrection) under Articles 77–79 are still kept in postwar Penal Code for state security.

9.7 The Ultra-Nationalist *Taishinin* Chief Justices

Judges who were ambitious and opportunistic were tempted to modify their legal mindset and judicial conduct in a manner consistent with the presumptive intention of the government and the prevailing state of consciousness. Ultra-nationalism can be considered part of the attitudinal model of judicial behaviour. The ultra-nationalist Hiranuma Kiichirō is a prominent figure in the field. This case exemplifies the trajectory of a judicial bureaucrat from the Ministry of Justice who ascended to the position of prime minister.

---

[40] On this see Fuenaga (1943).

[41] On this see Teeuwen and Breen (2017, p. 75, p. 196).

[42] On this see Suzuki (2014, pp. 64–66).

9.7.1 Hiranuma Kiichirō

Hiranuma Kiichirō served as the fourteenth *Taishinin* Chief Justice from October 1921 to August 1923. He was an active proponent of ultra-nationalism. Since his entry into the Ministry of Justice in 1889, he had ascended steadily through the bureaucratic hierarchy. In the *Taishinin* trial of the *Kōtoku Incident* in 1910, the prosecutor argued against the conspiracy of Kotoku Shishi and other 26 anarchists within a Buddhist organization. The objective of this conspiracy, according to the prosecution, was to plan for high treason and assassinate the Meiji Emperor. Subsequently, there was an increase in the prevalence and complexity of pro-*kokutai* ultra-nationalist judicial behaviour. This behaviour included the implementation of stringent control measures over Buddhist organizations, with the objective of impeding the dissemination of potentially hazardous ideologies (Izumi 2002, p. 107).

In the second Yamamoto Gonnohyoe Cabinet, Hiranuma climbed his career ladder up from *Taishinin* Chief Justice to the Minister of Justice during 2 September 1923 to 27 December 1923, and he was honoured as a baron in 1926. His councillor service in the Privy Council started in 1924. With the support from the conservative bureaucrats and the ambitious military, he had been selected twice as the President of Privy Council in 1936 and 1945. His ultra-nationalism was evinced by his open advocation of *Ōseifukko* (Retro-Japanism by restoration of monarchy) and his presidency in the ultra-nationalist organization *Kokuhonsha* (National Foundation Society). The essence of his ultra-nationalism for the state polity was based on "a society as one single family" under the Emperor's governance: The imperial family made Japan's state polity become superior to other nations; Foreign ideas should be fused and harmonized with the unique Japanese way and be consistent with the Japan "body" as a familial hierarchical society. With these ultra-nationalist ideas, Hiranuma restructured the *Kokuhonsha* for the glorification of the state polity and enlightenment against foreign ideas. It advocated the affinities between the Fascist Italy and the Imperial Japan, condemned Jewish menace and the necessity to smash dangerous thoughts within Japan. After the February 26 Rebellion in 1936, *Kokuhonsha* was dissolved on 10 June. It accomplished its mission and had satisfaction over the elevation of the Japanese spirit in the aftermath of the Manchurian Incident.[43]

As a prominent right-wing Japanese politician, Hiranuma became the Prime Minister in 1939. He was the unique as he had been the *Taishinin* Chief Justice and was convicted as a Class-A war criminal being sentenced to life imprisonment by the International Military Tribunal for the Far East. Upon the trial of war crime at the Tribunal, *Kokuhonsha* was unsuccessfully defended as a society to support a proper and true understanding of the true nature and spirit of Japan. The declassified secret documents of the General Headquarters Supreme Commander for the Allied Powers confirmed that they categorized *Kokuhonsha* as a fascist organization and "thought" society.

[43] On this see Szpilman (1998, p. 107, pp. 121–122, pp. 127–128, p. 131).

9.7.2 Nagashima Hatasu

Nagashima Hatasu was a typical ultra-nationalist *Taishinin* Chief Justice with a historical institutionalist judicial behaviour model by supporting the government. He started his career in Yokohama Shōkin Bank after his graduation from the Law School of Tokyo University in 1906. In 1911, he debuted his judicial career as an assistant judicial officer in the Ministry of Justice. In September 1941, he replaced Motoji Shinkuma as *Taishinin* Chief Justice until 1944.

Taishinin under Nagashima Hatasu was knelling to the government by applying law to support government policy. In July 1943, his long article was published in *Hōritsushinpō (Law News)* under the title of *War and Law*, where he wrote: "The mobilization of men, minds and forces is driving the law to the ends of war. A law that lags behind the movement of people, minds, and things can only be rubbish wastepaper that has been discarded in a dustbin. The law must not lose its center but must take a sharp turn in this direction.[44]"

Another well-known case was Nagashima's nationalist attitude toward the government in the *Tōjō Ensetsu jiken* (*Tojo Speech Incident*). In February 1944, the Prime Minister Tojo Hideki openly delivered a speech to press the judiciary to cooperation with the wartime regime. Hosono Nagara was the Chief Justice of the Hiroshima Appeal Court, who accused Tojo's outcry to dominate judiciary as unconstitutional. Hosono sought apolitical and depoliticized judiciary as judicial independence. He insisted that freedom of judges' judicial behaviour should not be subject to the control of the Ministry of Justice (Miyamoto 2020, pp. 91–92). Unfortunately, as there was neither judge autonomy nor judicial self-administration, only a few judges supported Hosono to fight against the government pressure and Tōjō (Yasuhara 2018, pp. 14–15). Hosono drafted a protesting letter against such pressure and intended to hand it over to Tojo through Nagashima, but Nagashima silently kept it in his desk.[45] Nagashima's unwillingness to ensure freedom of judicial behaviour evinced that nationalist culture had been embedded in judiciary. Notwithstanding the status of *Taishinin* Chief Justice, it could be seen that Nagashima himself did not care about the judicial independence in the state polity.

9.8 Brief Remarks: True Judicial Independence Came Late

This chapter's findings reveal *Taishinin*'s role under the Minister of Justice. The Meiji Restoration and the accompanying judicial reform were the result of the efforts of a small group of intellectuals, primarily junior samurai from former feudal domains.

---

[44] The original text: 人と心と力の結集は法律を戦争の目的へと追い込みつつある。人と心と物の動きに立ち遅れた法律はただ屑籠に捨てられて顧みられない反古紙でしかありえない。法律は中心を失ってはならないが、この方向に向かって急転回して進まなければならない。See Kiyonaga (2008), pp. 113–114.

[45] On this see Kimidzuka (2018, p. 20); Also see Kiyonaga (2008, pp. 113–114).

The objective was strengthening Japan, which was in the process of modernization, to be independent from political pressure. The Penal Code, the Meiji Constitution and even the judiciary were the means by which the social structure of the state polity and the power of the state were maintained (Ramseyer and Rosenbluth 1998, p. 29).

During the outset of Meiji Restoration, there was a political intent for the legal system to defer to the government influence. Ramseyer and Rasmusen's research demonstrated that the Minister of Justice's power of judicial administration for career development could exert undue influence on judges who hold radical views or oppose the regime's policies (Ramseyer and Rasmusen 2001, p. 331). Meiji Constitution was therefore silent on judicial independence and the issue of check and balance of government power. The oligarchs could thereby regulate the legal system in a manner that benefited their political desire. This "Western jacket" was "fashionable" on "Japanese body" but not for citizens' challenge against state polity. This is evinced by Ito Hirofumi's open saying that "by the expression of legal measures of the administrative authorities, it must be understood that no suit can be brought against those measures that have been carried out in conformity with law or with the functionary power of the office in question… Inhabitants may petition the competent authorities but will not be allowed to bring an action before the Court of Administrative Litigation[46]".The administration of judicial power in the adjudication of cases had therefore been confined to those judicial officials selected and overseen by the Minister of Justice (Oba 2014, p. 26). Obedient judges got promotion. This chapter corroborates this assertion with the case studies of Hiranuma Kiichirō and Nagashima Hatasu.

From the outset, *Taishinin* had suffered from structural discriminatory treatment embedded in government design. *Taishinin*'s role was a product of this historical dilemma: both undue influence of oligarchs and such indigenous legal value as equitable *dōri* remained (refer Chap. 3 of this book), and yet *Taishinin* was an isolated final appeal court fashioned on European civil law system, particularly the Meiji Constitution and the Penal Code transplanted from Germanic jurisprudence. As a "Western jacket", the underlying objective of this discriminatory isolation was not for real rule of law but keeping legal justice under oligarchical influence and revising unequal treaties, particularly those pertaining to the consular jurisdiction of Western powers.[47]

In this connection, *Taishinin*'s consistent judicial behaviour of strict liability model, which had hybridity with attitudinal, strategic model and historical institutionalist model from time to time, was to punish corruption and discipline civil servants very strictly. It helped hegemonic governance and served protecting the image of oligarchy from being stigmatized. The strict liability model of judicial behaviour in the five cases in this book coincided with a particular urgency in early Showa era to shore up a national policy centred on the Imperial House, in which

---

[46] On the original words of Ito Hirofumi see *Political reorientation of Japan, September 1945 to September 1948, Vol. 1* edited by Supreme Commander for the Allied Power, p. 85.

[47] On this see Cassel (2012, pp. 179–185).

the civil service was urged to be an example in the national family and rid itself of corruption (MacNaughton and Wong 2017, p. 79).

It subtly guided *Taishinin*'s judicial behaviour in a manner that prioritized political objective beyond the mere pursuit of justice.[48] As demonstrated in *Taishinin*'s jurisprudence on *taigyakuzai* and *fukeizai*, which extended to the disrespect on *Kokka Shintō*. It facilitated state polity to function as a unified, seamless political apparatus without competitive alternatives. It is evident in this chapter that *Taishinin*'s judicial behaviour exhibited a profound adherence to the principles outlined in the Emperor's Imperial Rescripts with a primary objective being the preservation of the integrity of official duties. The vague wordings of "maintenance public peace and order" to plug loophole for police corruption were exactly copied from Article nine of Meiji Constitution (refer Chap. 7), which was promulgated by the Emperor. Under subtle influence of the Minister of Justice, *Taishinin*'s strict judicial behaviour was instrumental to the Emperor's governance. All powers were originated from His Majesty (Fukushima 1956, pp. 137–138). Corruption distorted this principal-agent relationship and could trigger civic and political unrest for competitive alternatives. Corruption had all along been perceived as one of the most serious threats to Japanese society historically (Rose 2001, p. 105).

Before the Constitution of Japan in 1947, there was no delinking the Emperor from the functions of the state polity and sovereignty, notwithstanding that true judicial independence was an essential cornerstone to the rule of law. In addressing this issue, Article 76, Paragraph 3 of the prevailing Constitution of Japan stipulates that all judges were designated to exercise their duties with complete autonomy of conscience, and are obligated to adhere strictly to the principles outlined in the Constitution and the prevailing laws. This principle underscores the imperative for judicial autonomy, ensuring that judges remain uninfluenced by external factors during the adjudication process. It effectively eliminated the potential for any interpretive ambiguity that might have been exploited in a manner analogous to that of the prewar Minister of Justice. The term "judge's conscience" is ambiguous and subject to interpretation. Its definition is contingent on specific circumstances and cultural context, rendering it a highly situational and cultural concept. Prewar *Taishinin*'s experience tells us that "conscience" refers to the trial judges' internal and external independence without restriction by any external institution or other judges in judiciary internally (Lin 1999, p. 192). In other words, court should have freedom of judicial behaviour with applicability of equitable *dōri* according to juridical facts in each court case. The two authors of this book would like to comment that true judicial independence came late after the promulgation of the postwar Constitution of Japan.

[48] On this see Ramseyer and Frances (1995, p. 39–40, pp. 160–166).

References

Akio, K. (2010) Public Service Ethics and Corruption in Japan. In Evan, M. B. et al. ed. *Public Administration in East Asia: Mainland China, Japan, South Korea, Taiwan.* CRC Press.

Arai, T. (2013a) Kodai Nihon no Muhen, Muhon ni tsuite (On Rebellion and Rebellion in Ancient Japan). *Nihon Hōgaku (Japan Legal Studies)*, Vol. 78 (1), 1-27.

Arai T. (2013b) Meiji Zenki no Hangyaku ni tsuite: Taigyaku-zai, Nairan-zai Kenkyū no Zentei to shite: Okumura Daisaku Kyōju Koki Kinen-gō Seiji, Keizai, Shakai ni Kansuru Sho-mondai (On the Rebellion in the Early Meiji Era: As Premises for Research on High Treason and Civil War: Professor Daisaku Okumura's commemorative issue related to politics, economy, and society). *Seikei Kenkyū (Political and Economic Research)*, Vol. 49 (4), 1351-1372.

Beasley, W. G. (1972) *The Meiji Restoration.* Stanford University Press.

Cassel, P. K. (2012) *Extraterritoriality and Imperial Power in Nineteenth-Century China and Japan: Grounds of Judgment.* Oxford:Oxford University Press.

Cluck, C. (1985) *Japan's Modern Myths: Ideology in the Late Meiji Period.* Princeton University Press.

Duss, P. (1976) *The Rise of Modem Japan.* Houghton Mifflin Company.

Eagan, Jennifer L. (2016). *deliberative democracy.* https://www.britannica.com/topic/deliberative-democracy . Accessed 1 September 2023.

Feldman, E. A. (2004) *The Ritual of Rights in Japan.* Cambridge University Press.

Fuenaga, M. (1943) *Amaterasu Ōmikami no Shingaku-teki Kenkyū (Theological study of Amaterasu Omikami).* Meisedo Shoten.

Fukushima, M. (1956) Meiji Zenhanki ni okeru Ie Seido no Keisei (Formation of the Family System in the First Half of the Meiji Era. *Hō Shakaigaku (Sociology of Law)*, Vol. 7-8, 123–206.

Gōhara, N. (2020) *"Japanese Prosecutors" Justice on Trial, 15 June 2020.* https://www.nippon.com/en/in-depth/a06802/# . Accessed 21 September 2022.

Haley, J. O. (2005) *The Japanese Judiciary: Maintaining Integrity, Autonomy and the Public Trust* https://papers.ssrn.com/sol3/papers.cfm?abstract_id=821466. Accessed 12 September 2025.

Hayashi, N. (2012) Kindaï Nihon no Shisō to Shihō (Ideological Justice in Modern Japan). R*itsumeikan Daigaku Jinmon Kagaku Kenkyūjo Kiyō (Bulletin of the Institute of Humanities, Ritsumeikan University)*, No. 97, 63–90.

Hiranuma, K. (1923) Hōchi ni Tsuite (About rule of law). *Keisei (Penal Administration)*, Vol. 36 (11), 2–18.

Hoshihara, D. (2006) Etō Shinpei no Meiji Ishin (Shinpei Eto's Meiji Restoration). *Waseda Review of Socio-science*, Vol. 12, 202–217.

Ichikawa, K. (2019) Taigyaku-zai ni okeru "Kahentoshita" to Bōgi-ron ("Kahentoshita" and Conspiracy Discussion in High Treason). *Ritsumeikan Hōgaku (Ritsumeikan Law)*, No. 385, 94–141.

Inoue, H. (2024) *Nihon no Jinja to Shintō (Japanese Shrines and Shintō).* Hozokan.

Iwatani, J. (1993) Kunrei o Oyogu Daishin'in - Meiji 12-nendai no Shihōken (The Supreme Court Seeing Instructions: Judicial Power in the 12th Years of the Meiji Era). *Keio University Law Research*, Vol. 66 (8), 1–58.

Izumi, K. (2002) Taigyaku Jiken to Shinshū Ōtani-ha (The Great Treason Incident and the Otani School of Shinshu). *Otani Daigaku Kenkyū Nempō(Otani University Research Annual Report)*, Vol. 54, 63–110.

Japan Jurisprudence Research Society. (1943) *Nihon Keiji Tetsuzuki Yōkō (Japan Criminal Procedure Guidelines).* Japan Jurisprudence Research Society.

Kasumi, N. (2021) *Yoshikawa Akimasa in Legal History Book*, No.54, Ministry of Justice, Minister's Secretariat, Judicial Legislation Department. https://www.moj.go.jp/content/001355 467.pdf Accessed 9 October 2022

Kimidzuka, M. (2018) Saibankan no Dokuritsu: Shihōken Kempō Soshōron Hoi (Independence of Judges: Judiciary Constitutional Litigation Supplement 2). *Yokohama Kokusai Shakai Kagaku Kenkyū(Yokohama International Social Science Research)*, Vol. 23 (1),19–57.

Kiyonaga, S. (2008) *Kotsu no Hanketsu (The Verdict of Grit)*. Shinchosha.

Kuriyama, G. (1891) *Hoken Daiki*. Chūō-dō.

Lin, L. (1999) Judicial Independence in Japan: A Re-investigation for China. *Columbia Journal of Asian Law*, Vol. 13 (2), 185-202.

MacNaughton, A, Wong, K. B. (2017) Corruption Judgments in Pre-War Japan: Locating the Influence of Tradition, Morality, and Trust on Criminal Justice. Corruption and the Secret of Law, pp. 77–97. https://doi.org/10.4324/9781315259208-4. Accessed 1st October, 2025.

Matsuoka, S. (2006) Nihonjin no Hōishiki ni tsuite (On Japanese Legal Awarenes). *Hōritsu Ronsō (Law Review)*, Volume 78, No. 2, 125-169.

Mendes, Conrado Hubner. 2014. Constitutional Courts and Deliberative Democracy. Oxford: Oxford University Press.

Miyamoto, H. (2020) Nihon Keiji Shiho no Kosō: Sairon 2 - Sengo Keiji Shiho Kaikaku no Sasetsu (Ancient layers and re-examination of Japanese criminal justice 2: The collapse of postwar criminal justice reform). *Kantō Gakuin Hōgaku (Kanto Gakuin Jurisprudence)*, Vol. 29 (2), 55-148.

Miyashita, M. (2022) Yokusan Senkyo Mukō Hanketsu o Kachitotta Taishū Seijika: Tomiyoshi Eiji Den (The populist politician who won the invalidation ruling of the sponsored election: The story of Eiji Tomiyoshi). *Kyūshū Chiku Kokuritsu Daigaku Kyōikukei Bunkei Kenkyū Ronshū (Kyushu National University Educational and Humanities Research Papers)*, Vol. 8 (2), No. 6.1–28.

Mori, J. (1971) Ōtsu Jiken to Shiga-ken (The Otsu Incident and Shiga Prefecture). *Hikone Ronsō (Hikone Essay Series)*, No. 153, 1–15.

Mori, K., Mori, N. (1967) Meiji Zenki no Seiji Shisō ni tsuite Oda Tamenori no Shisō o Chūshin to shite (On the Political Thought in the Early Meiji Era: Focusing on Oda Tametsuna's ideas). *Iwate Daigaku Kyōiku Gakubu Kenkyū Nenpō (Annual report of the Faculty of Education, University of Iwate)*, Vol. 27, 35-49.

Nakamura. T. (2022) Tennōsei Kokka to Gendai Nihon no Seiji Bunka: Chōetsu-teki Tennō no Sonzai to Fuhen-teki Kachi no Fuzai (The Imperial System and Modern Japanese Political Culture: The Existence of a Transcendent Emperor and the Absence of Universal Values). *Musashino Daigaku Seiji Keizai Kenkyūjo Nenpō (Musashino University Institute of Political Science and Economics Annual Report)*, Vol. 21, pp. 57-94.

Nippon Communications Foundation. 2019. *"Order in the Court: Explaining Japan's 99.9% Conviction Rate"*, 18 January 2019 https://www.nippon.com/en/japantopics/c05401/order-in-the-court-explaining-japan%E2%80%99s-99-9-convictionrate.html . Accessed 15 September 2022.

Nishihara, H. (1967) Keihō Seiteishi ni Arawareta Meiji Ishin no Seikaku (Characteristics of the Meiji Restoration that Appeared in the History of Criminal Law Enactment). *Hikaku Hōgaku (Comparative Law)*, Vol.3 (1), 51-94.

Oba, Y. (2014) Naikakuki Shihōshō Shokushō Keisei no Hōga (The germ of the formation of the Ministry of Justice during the Cabinet period). *Komazawa Shigaku (Komazawa History)*, No. 83, 23–47.

Odanaka, S. (1969) Shihōkan Rōka Jiken (Judicial Officer's Flower Incident). In Wagatsuma S. ed. *Nihon Seiji Saiban Shiroku: Meiji Go (Japanese Political Trial History Post-Meiji Period)* (pp. 176-194). Daiichi Hoki Publishing.

Okahara, M. (1943) Baishin-hō no Teishi ni Kansuru Hōritsu ni Tsuite (Regarding the Law Concerning the Suspension of the Jury Law). *Hōsōkai Zasshi (Bar Association Magazine)*, Vol. 21, No. 4, 10-24.

Ono, H. (2022) Hōritsuka to Saigai, Fukakōryoku 1 (Lawyers and Disasters, Force Majeure 1). *Dokkyō Hōgaku (Dokkyo Law Studies)*, Vol. 117, 285-344.

Oppler, A. C. (1949) The Reform of Japan's Legal and Judicial System Under Allied Occupation *Washington Law Review*, Vol. 24 (3), 290–324.

Ramseyer, M. J. (1994) The Puzzling (in) Dependence of the Courts: A Comparative Approach. *Journal of Legal Studies*, Vol. 23 (2), 721-747.

Ramseyer, M. J., Rosenbluth, M. F. (1995) *The Politics of Oligarchy: Institutional Choice in Imperial Japan*. Cambridge University Press.

Ramseyer, M. J. (2001) Rethinking Administrative Guidance. In Aoki, M., Saxonhouse, G. ed. *Finance, Governance and Competitiveness in Japan* (pp. 199-209). Oxford University Press.

Ramseyer, M. J, Rasmusen, E. B. (2001) Why are Japanese judges so conservative in politically charged cases. *The American Political Science Review*, Vol. 95 (2), 331-344.

Ramseyer, M. J, Rosenbluth, F. M. (1998) *The Politics of Oligarchy: Institutional Choice in Imperial Japan*. Cambridge University Press.

Rose, R. (2001) How People View Democracy: A Diverging Europe. *Journal of Democracy*, Vol. 12 (1), 93-106.

Satomi, K. (1929) *Emperor and Proletariat*. Ars Company.

Shimizu, Y. (2020) *The Origins of the Modern Japanese Bureaucracy*. Bloomsbury Publishing.

Shichinohe, K. (2010) Genkō Minpōten o Tsukutta Hitobito 12 Satei Iin 3, 4: Nanbu Mikio, Nakamura Motoyoshi, Gaiden 7: Rōkyū Shihōkan no Tōta (People Who Created the Current Civil Code 12 Appraisal Committee 3, 4: Mikao Nanbu, Motoyoshi Nakamura, Gaiden 7: Weeding Out Old Judicial Officials). *Hōgaku Seminar*, Vol. 55 (4), 70-72.

Southgate, J. 2000. *Materials for the study of Japanese law*. http://www.columbia.edu/~hds2/BIB95/ch22.htm. Accessed 13 September 2022.

Suzuki, N. (2014) Jingiin no Seiritsu Katei no Kenkyū (Study on the process of establishment of Institute of Divinities). *Meiji Seitoku Kinen Gakkai Kiyō Fukkan Dai 51-gō, Tokushū: Taishō Shōwa Zenki no Shintō to Shakai (Meiji Shotoku Memorial Society Bulletin Reprint No. 51, Special feature: Shintō and society in the Taisho and early Showa periods)*, 53–71.

Szpilman, C. W.A. (1998) Conservatism and its enemies in prewar Japan: The case of Hiranuma. Kiichiro and the Kokuhonsha. *Hitotsubashi Journal of Social Studies*, Vol. 30 (2), 101–133.

Teeuwen, M., John, B. (2017) *A social history of the Ise shrines: divine capital*. Bloomsbury Academic.

Tucker, J. A. (2014) The Meanings of Words and Confucian Political Philosophy: A Study of M atsunaga Sekigo's Ethics. In Huang, C. C., Tucker, J. A. ed. *Dao Companion to Japanese Confucian Philosophy* (pp. 31-68). Springer.

Yasuhara, H. (2018) Waga Kuni ni okeru Shihōken Dokuritsu no Jittai o Kangaeru (Thinking about the reality of judicial independence in Japan). *Seiji to Shiho: Nenpō Seijigaku (Politics and Judiciary :Annual Political Science)*, 13–23.

Chapter 10
Conclusive Evaluation of *Taishinin*'s Judicial Behaviour

In comparison with other academic disciplines, the development of judicial behaviour studies is relatively fragmented. The fragmentation of this field is attributable to the considerable difficulty in integrating its multidisciplinary approaches into a comprehensive academic paradigm. The endeavour to identify effective methods, techniques and strategies for teaching it as a cohesive pedagogy is a formidable task. This deficiency has impeded its integration into existing university curricula. Paradoxically, this deficit is also its asset. Absent a fixed research paradigm to guide the research process and determine its execution, researchers are at liberty to innovatively experiment with new empirical research methods and updated approaches. The multidisciplinary perspective in this book provides a critical, innovative, and alternative perspective on judicial behaviour. The backbone of it is based on court judgements and information on social conditions. Its interdisciplinarity collaborates with various judicial behaviour models to explore the question of the delicate role played by *Taishinin* before postwar legal reform. In the prewar state political system, the judiciary played a pivotal role in enforcing regulations, establishing norms and fortifying the government's capacity to maintain public order and political system. *Taishinin*'s role can be likened to that of a social engineer, providing a degree of legitimacy to the endeavour and Japanization of Western legal culture as Japanese body in Western culture.

Legislation and the rule of law are fundamental to judicial behaviour in any civilized fair society. Judicial behaviour is comprised of a multitude of components, including legal expertise, public sentiment and personal contemplations. A well-constructed comprehensive list of factors to be considered for evaluation of the fairness of judicial behaviour includes, but is not limited to, political beliefs, sensations, emotions, attitudes, representations, equity, cultural values, role in public administration and notions. This book demonstrates that these common variables are invariably embedded within different models of judicial behaviour, albeit often unacknowledged. For instance, the attitudinal model is more oriented towards cultural values.

K. B. Wong and S. L. Fang, *Taishinin's Judicial Behaviour in Corruption Cases*,
https://doi.org/10.1007/978-981-95-5823-0_10

The historical institutionalist model is characterized by its strong sociopolitical orientation. The strategic model is outcome oriented. The strict liability model is more closely aligned with the principles of public administration.

10.1 Judicial Behaviour in a Closed and Self-Contained System

Without sufficient empirically verifiable documentary record except court judgement, *Taishinin*'s judicialization in corruption cases can be regarded as a particular type of organizational behaviour taking place in a closed, self-contained system or a neatly ordered body of principles hierarchically arranged (Christensen and Charles 2007, p. 187). Nevertheless, the analysis of judicial behaviour is not entirely implausible. In addition to legislation and precedent, two authors of this book find that influences over *Taishinin*'s judicial behaviour include traditional Japanese strictness in anti-corruption and the philosophical attitudes of *Taishinin* justices. The concept of equity in the Japanese style is characterized by its historical institutionalism, which imposes limitations on *Taishinin*'s involvement in the state polity. Under pressure to provide judicial service that is timely, fair and a sense of sociopolitical responsibility, it has similarity with the working culture in organizational behaviour studies. Between the lines of a *Taishinin* judgement, it is possible to sense the shared values, beliefs and norms that shape *Taishinin* justices' legal reasoning, interaction with external and internal factors and decision-making in behavioural patterns. All these factors dictated *Taishinin*'s judicial behaviours as one of the main social engineers in prewar Japan.

The evaluation of judicial behaviour is regarded as a multifaceted endeavour, encompassing a range of criteria that are used to assess the quality of judges' judicial decision-making. The common criteria for judicial performance evaluation include, but are not limited to, the following: transparency, fairness, equity and social expectations. It can be graded as poor, reasonable, good, useful, desirable or equitable. While *Taishinin* existed as a closed and self-contained system of limited availability of information and under the occasional undue influence of Minister of Justice, this approach for evaluation is far from satisfactory.

10.2 Universality or Cultural Relativism for Evaluation of Judicial Behaviour

Japanese body in Western jacket is a phenomenon of interactions between two cultural relativisms, instead of international law of universality of applicability among all countries. The purpose of evaluation of judicial behaviour is to ascertain whether

Taishinin's judicial behaviour aligns with the overarching goal of justice by universality or cultural relativism. The universal application of the rule of law for evaluation is subject to the constraint of cultural relativism. The concept of Japanese cultural relativist *dōri* can be justified through rational analysis in the context of various judicial decisions, contingent upon distinct social circumstances and particular factors in an appeal case. Depending on the viewpoint, non-Japanese cultural relativists may comment *Taishinin*'s judicial behaviour is a judicial arbitrariness without judicial transparency and trustworthiness for rule of law.[1]

In the absence of universally agreed and well-constructed criteria to determine the performance of judicial behaviour, legal cultural value is logically reduced to a form of relativism, encompassing "ideas, values, attitudes, and beliefs of a particular group of people oriented towards law".[2] Judicial behaviour that is deemed acceptable within one legal culture may even be regarded as illegitimate in another, a phenomenon that can be attributed to the principle of cultural relativism. In contrast, the concept of rule of law is often considered to be analogous to the morality of law, typically intertwined with factors such as certainty, legality, legal values, cultural norms and the presence of independent and impartial courts. The fundamental rights in question are to be respected, as are the following: the checks and balances of powers, equality before the law and judicial transparency without arbitrariness.[3] The rule of law is a more universally acceptable concept that recognizes the superiority of the law over all forms of power, delivering four universal principles: social accountability under the law, law of fairness, transparent government and accessible and impartial justice. Rule of law is a precondition of individual liberty and any social life in the contemporary world (Raz 1988, pp. 400–429). In prewar Japan, the Minister of Justice's undue influence on *Taishinin*'s judicial behaviour reflects that law was not impartially superior over all form of power. It did not suit basic criteria of rule of law.

10.3 *Dōri* in *Taishinin*'s Judicial Behaviour as Cultural Relativism

Certainty of law is important because people have to understand where they stand, even if they do not believe in the fairness of law. Certainty is a key factor to ask for court's social accountability, but the applicability of cultural relativist *dōri* in *Taishinin*'s judicial behaviour is situational and dependent on judicial behaviour model. In comparison with *dōri*, *jōri* is like *naturalis ratio* in Latin and *natur der sache* in German. It refers to Japanese model of logic and reason of things as something like natural law and reasonableness. *Dōri* presents the common sense in Japanese cultural relativism, which is different from Western cosmopolitan civilization, though

---

[1] On this see Fuller and Kenneth (1978); Also see Hart and Sacks (1994).

[2] On this see Friedman (1985); also see Nelken (2004) and Llewellyn (1931).

[3] On this see Fuller (1964).

Western cosmopolitan civilization had gradually been popular in Japan before 1920s (Najita and Harootunian 1988, p. 735). Even *Taishinin*'s concept of *kenri* (right, on "*Taishinin*'s *kenri*" refer to Chap. 1) in judicial governance is neither individual right in English nor Germanic legal concept of *recht,* it is based on Japanese cultural relativism of *dōri.* Japanization of transplanted law concepts needs a time-consuming modification through judicial behaviour of *kakuchō-kaishaku* (expansive legal interpretation) of court to fit into "Japanese body" of her own traditional legal value and customs.

Taishinin's judicial behaviour did not occur within a self-subsistent legal system. The changeable judicial behaviour of *Taishinin* depended on *dōri* intertwining with social conditions and governance in state polity, instead of simply ideals of rule of law in the Western sense. This dynamic is more influenced by the prevailing social conditions and governance within the state polity than by the universal principle of rule of law. The aforesaid assertion is corroborated by the empirical evidence presented in Chaps. 4 through 9.

The flexible *Taishinin*'s judicial behaviour was officially consistent with cultural relativist judicial governance of prewar Japanese government in its *Saibanjimu-kokoroe* (Knowledge of Court Affairs) under *Dajōkan* Proclamation No. 103 on 8 June 1875. It clarified the judicial standards for trials. Articles 4 of it stated that case laws could be used as standards for judicial proceedings. Regarding trials, *jōri* (natural reason or principle, on "*dōri* and *jōri*" refer to Chap. 3) in Article 3 of it is still enforceable in postwar Japan statutorily, though it is applicable to civil law case only. *Jōri* has overlapping moralistic areas with *dōri.* Both *dōri* and *jōri* are hard to be applied universally, due to its evaluation on the basis of Japanese cultural relativism of common sense, good faith, public order and morals. Such evaluations are circumscribed in time and space. Different time and space might have different outcomes.

Inoue Shōichi, who graduated from the first intake of Law School of the Ministry of Justice in the Meiji era and had been the *Taishinin* Chief Justice from 1891 to 1912, stated that judicial decision-making was like a judge's trial seeking a solution. *Jōri* helped him solve a lot of court cases on the basis of French legal principles (Murakami 1994, p. 323). *Jōri* and *dōri* can be interpreted very expansively with abstract cultural relativist righteousness, honesty and social justice as the objective of a behaviour[4] (on "historical institutionalism" refer to Chap. 1).

Kabuto Kuninori was the Chief Justice of Osaka Appellate Court from 1898 to 1905. In the event that the legislation under consideration by a Japanese court was deemed to be inadequate, he proposed that the law in question be deemed non-existent rather than imperfect, with the understanding that this determination would be made solely on the basis of long-standing customs to ensure fairness.[5] It means priority is given to attitudinal judicial behaviour with reference to morality in old customary practices, such as elastic *jōri* and *dōri* instead of rigid legislation. The

---

[4] On this see Moribe (2004, p. 269, p. 276).

[5] The original text in the Autobiography of Kabuto Kuninori: 法律は不完全というよりも寧ろ皆無, 旧慣によるのみ。See Kabuto (1982, p. 178).

Japanese concept of law, writes Kawashima Takeyoshi, is like an heirloom samurai sword. It is to be treasured but not used unless and until no alternative (Kawashima 1967, p. 47). In terms of judicial behaviour analysis, this book proves Kawashima is correct. Fairness of judicial behaviour is under the impacts of equitable *jōri* and *dōri,* which are not totally determined by law terms in legislation, which is still dependent on legal reasoning process.

In order to comprehend *Taishinin*'s equitable cultural relativist *dōri* and *jōri* as a standard of fairness in *Taishinin*'s judicial behaviour, it is imperative to possess an objective understanding of the social conditions in each case. For this reason, background information is provided for each judgement analysis in this book. A thorough examination of the case background intertwining with the judicial behaviour of *Taishinin* in each judgement reveals the interface between particular social conditions in prewar Japan and *Taishinin*'s judicial behaviour. Examples of this kind in this book are the undefined scope of de facto police power of *ultra vires* nature, teachers' breach of social trust due to acceptance of cheap meal entertainments and *Taishinin*'s judicial behaviour tolerating prostitution by ruling in civil justice. The cultural relativist *dōri* in *Taishinin*'s judicial behaviour is still influencing today's Supreme Court of Japan. The most influential landmark ruling is the judicial activism by labelling breach of social trust as the victimized legal interest for corrupt behaviour. This ruling is still valid today.

10.4 Minister of Justice and *Taishinin*'s Cultural Relativism

Taishinin's cultural relativist judicial behaviour is not illogical. This book confirms that the judicial governance of the Minister of Justice had, in some cases, unduly or even openly influenced the judicial behaviour of *Taishinin.* Chap. 9 confirms the Minister of Justice's malfeasance in judges' posting, ultra-nationalist *Taishinin* Chief Justices and militaristic tendency in some *Taishinin* court judgements (Matsumoto 1962, p. 103). Furthermore, his judicial governance played a pivotal role in the process of Japanese legal transplantation, determining its course and ensuring its alignment with the principles of *kankō* (indigenous Japanese practices) as a source of *dōri* in legislation. This determination ensured the integration of foreign legal systems into the Japanese legal framework, fostering a relationship between international and domestic legal traditions.[6]

Kankō can be more equitable than rigid legislation. The *kan* in *kankō* or *kyūkan* (old custom) was customary practice or habitual practice. This is *kōjo-ryōzoku-no-gensoku* (public order and morality principles) beneficial to the entire order of life in Japan, and the manners and morals endorsed there as cultural relativism. Some *kankō* were codified as legislation drafted by the Minister of Justice, because *kankō* had been respected, accepted and well-followed as norms and *dōri* for a long time. For example, *kantsū* (or *fugi-mittsū,* deviant behaviour of adultery) was a *jūzai* (felony) punishable

[6] On this see Taguchi (2003, pp. 1–12).

by death penalty as per the law of Tokugawa bakufu's *kujikata-osadamegaki* (legal code), which supported traditional Japanese gender injustice as *dōri* that punishment for male might not be as severe as that for female. Moreover, Article 183 of prewar Penal Code statutorily continued this Japanese "body" of *kankō* in gender injustice that different punishments were conducted to males and females although adultery involved conspiracy of two parties. This Article 183 had existed for a long time until the law reform during the Occupation period. Taishinin had no judicial review power for inequitable legislation.

In addition to cultural relativism, Minister of Justice's domination to the small labour market of legal professionals as an undue influence on judicial behaviour is considerable. Only 133 of the 2043 judges and prosecutors had experience in private practice. Most fresh law department graduates competed in an initial civil service examination in order to have a job of security in the Ministry of Justice (George 1979, p. 812). To judges appointed under such circumstances, there was possibility of yielding to the undue influence of the Minister of Justice and succumbing to politicians' pressure (Takaaki 1984, p. 70). The Minister of Justice owned power to determine whether judicial bureaucrats, including prosecutor, could climb up from the hierarchy of *ku-saiban* (ward court), *chihō-saibansho* (District Court), *kōsoin* (Court of Appeals) and *Taishinin* at the peak. Prewar Ministry of Justice's governance in fact did not have much difference from other government departments. Judges and prosecutors could even be interchanged by posting arrangement (Setsuo 1991, p. 57). Two incidents of *Taishinin*'s struggle for more judicial independence from the Minister of Justice and government are therefore discussed in Chap. 9. Under the shadow of such judicial governance, the early judicial behaviour of *Taishinin* considered and applied rulings of junior courts, which were under the Minister of Justice's direct supervision and management (Ohkawa 2003, p. 111).

As per *Shihōshō-kansei* (Organization of Ministry of Justice) issued by Imperial Decree No. 100 dated 21 June 1890, the Minister of Justice did have power to monitor judicial administration and execution of court judgement, except *Taishinin*.[7] Other than some extreme cases, *Taishinin's* de facto coordination with the Ministry of Justice could ensure consistency in prewar social management, thereby forming uniformity of law enforcement for legal justice to achieve publicly essential goals.[8] The Minister of Justice was like a double-edged sword.

Corruption is not generally considered the final act in a criminal scheme. Rather, it is typically regarded as a means to another crime against criminal justice (Kratcoski and Edelbacher 2018, pp. 13–14). The etymology of justice in English term of criminal justice is derived from the Greek word *dike*, which conceptualizes the notion of all things being in their proper place or role. The analysis of *Taishinin*'s judicial behaviour for justice in the selected corruption cases reveals its contribution to the maintenance of a robust criminal justice system and the reinforcement of government's public order policy. Such actions, however, is not solely determined

[7] The original text in *Shihōshō-kansei*:司法大臣ハ司法上ノ行政…二関スル事務ヲ管理シ裁判ノ執行ヲ監査シ行政事務二付テ裁判所ヲ監督ス。Edited by Cabinet Gazette Bureau, p. 227.

[8] On this see Iwatani (1993, pp. 20–45).

by the principles of legal justice in the Western sense. It is important to note that ethical cultural relativist considerations were also pertinent in this context.[9]

10.5 Fair Society and Universality

As a contributor to the multidisciplinary fair society studies, this book includes the fair society model as a standard of universality. A court of law is not merely a venue for the administration of justice. A court's actions may also be perceived as part of a brutal and oppressive regime, particularly in instances where legal processes are not aligned with the principles of natural justice and fairness (Twining 2009, pp. 25–26). The universality of fairness represents a further refinement of justice, aimed at ensuring equality, well-being and freedom as pillars. In order to further evaluate *Taishinin*'s judicial behaviour, a further analysis with referral to fair society model is conducted hereunder (Kleinig 2008, p. 22). It concerns *Taishinin*'s judicial behaviour from the standpoint of universality in the context of fair society studies. This constitutes a novel new methodology for the evaluation of judicial behaviour.

10.5.1 Kobayashi's Multifaceted Framework of "Four-Dimensional Fairness"

The fundamental tenet of a fair society as a concept of universality is predicated on the premise of autonomous and egalitarian individuals engaging in cooperative endeavours within the framework of a nation-state.[10] Fairness is widely regarded as the fundamental value in human existence. The calculation of fairness in judicial behaviour is not possible through the application of a uniform formula. In the process of constructing an explanation, definition serves as a crucial instrument. It facilitates the articulation of representative conceptions, thereby enabling the identification of a set of criteria and conditions that characterize a particular phenomenon (Mark 2014, p. 17).

Kobayashi's theoretical framework encompasses a multifaceted concept of "four-dimensional fairness", defining and encompassing rule compliance, equal impartiality, ethical fidelity and benefit reciprocity. Rule compliance is defined as adherence to, or observance of, international and/or domestic environmental laws and regulations. Impartiality and equality are inextricably linked. The former is predicated on the latter. The notion of impartiality is predicated on the principle of equal respect for the fundamental rights of all individuals. Accordingly, ethical fidelity is the ethical uprightness of loyalty to the prevailing cultural practices and legal restrictions. Benefit reciprocity is defined as the analysis of the equilibrium between

[9] On this see Pollock (2019, pp. 53–55, pp. 60–62, p. 70).

[10] On this see Kolm (2004).

the provision and reception of benefits or happiness (Kobayashi and Ishido 2023, pp. 7–9). This well-constructed "four-dimensional fairness" model for evaluation of judicial behaviour can be universal and more objective.

10.5.2 Rule Compliance

Rule compliance is not only assurance in line with the required legal standards, but also unwritten ethical standards. Judicial behaviour of rule compliance is essential for both procedural and substantiative justice and maintaining a good judicial reputation intertwined with impartiality and equality in the "four-dimensional fairness" model.

While the landscape of rule compliance varies across different corruption cases, Taishinin's rule compliance to the basic constitutional requirement of "constituent element" was consistently the same. Both Articles 197 and 198 in prewar Penal Code had legislative silence on the quality and quantity of bribes and the nature and scope of a civil servant's official duty. Statutory mitigating or aggravating factors for criminality, and deterministic reference to customary practice for enhancement of evident ability and/or convict ability were non-available in statutes. Regarding these legislative shortcomings, *Taishinin*'s judicial behaviour in previous chapters had national-level rule compliance to *zaikeihōtei-shugi* (no law, no crime and no punishment, or *nullum crimen sine lege*) stipulated in Article 23 of the Meiji Constitution in 1889. This constitutional compliance legitimatized *Taishinin*'s expansive legal reasoning through the applicability of *dōri* for net-widening of criminalization. Judicial behaviour of rule compliance is important in the process of seeking legitimacy of power to be transformed to the legitimacy of *Taishinin*'s exercise constitutional right of trial, which is the premise of gathering support and respect from the citizens. A government's legitimate enforcement of *Taishinin*'s judicial decisions is analogous (Grossman 1984, p. 214).

Rule compliance includes ethical rule. It is important to note that *Taishinin*'s judicial behaviour was not entirely insulated from political exigencies or public opinion. It had incidents of political exigencies to disobey Minister of Justice's influence (on this refer to Chap. 9). While social trust is regarded as ethically well-accepted customary principle in Japan, *Taishinin*'s emphasis on it is imperative for the continuation of group stability and social solidarity.[11] Even in the judicial behaviour exhibited by the historical institutional model, characterized by its close working relations with the Ministry of Justice, *Taishinin* did not deviate from legislation and Minister of Justice's unwritten rule in prevailing judicial policy. *Taishinin*'s rule compliance was imperative to ensure the stability of social stratification and social relations within the state polity.[12]

---

[11] On this see Minami (1992, pp. 101–105).

[12] On this see Nakamura (1971, p. 10, pp. 15–16).

10.5.3 Impartiality and Equality

In the perspective of fair society, impartiality and equality are not neutrality, nor does it mean being apart from a trial. With due regard to litigant's rights and obligations in accordance with the law and natural justice, acquisition of relevant evidence and information collected, judicial transparency in procedural and substantiative justice and the right to refute and express opinions, the judicial behaviour should be characterized by equity and fairness, treating all parties equally. Impartiality and equality are thereby inextricably linked in judicial behaviour.

Japan's legal system is not predicated on case law, in contrast to the predominant approach observed in common law jurisprudence. Nevertheless, case law exerts a de facto influence on judicial behaviour. Even in today's Japan, *Taishinin*'s ruling of *shakai* (social) *shinrai* (trust) in the impartiality of civil servants' performance of official duty is still regarded as the *hōeki* (legal interest). It is still a "backbone" of landmark rulings in today's anti-bribery judicial behaviour,[13] and applicable to all with impartially and equally.

The common typology of *Taishinin*'s judicial behaviour in corruption and bribery case is usually along two lines of thinking. The first is corruption exchanges in unclear official duty, which covers but not limited to bribery between bureaucrats and bribers. It commonly involved gift-giving or *sharei* as token of appreciation or gratitude. The second is corruption involving possibility of rent-seeking by abuse of status, embezzlement or extortion which occurs among bureaucrats of authority (Ang 2020, p. 8). Typical examples are Tokyo City Assembly in Chaps. 4 and 5 and the ruling of social trust in Chap. 6. The hidden agenda behind *Taishinin*'s judicial behaviour in these cases is social deterrence that a civil servant should have alertness against whether a third party may cast doubt on impartiality in official duty. This alertness against another person's evaluation of behaviour is the typical core of Japanese shame culture. In Chap. 6, *Taishinin* corrected unfairness and inequality in market competition caused by bureaucrats' abuse of public power for private gain. At the cultural level, *Taishinin* redefined *sharei* and such customary gifting practice as *ochūgen*. This is a labelling process with which criminality of a behaviour is socially re-constructed by legal power.[14] As the final court of appeal, *Taishinin* showed its impartiality and equality to all Japanese national in the said cases. There is no status responsibility like the criminal justice in Tokugawa era.

10.5.4 Ethical Fidelity

For determination of judicial behaviour in terms of fair society, the third factor in Kobayashi's multifaceted concept of "four-dimensional fairness" is ethical fidelity. The concept of "ethical fidelity" in *Taishinin*'s judicial conduct was closely linked to

---

[13] On this see Mashahide and Fujimori (1997, pp. 127–128, p. 134).

[14] On this see Lanier and Henry (1998, p. 158, p. 180).

the social capital of trustworthiness. Fidelity is the most important element of ethical righteousness.

The cultural construction of moral principles for the assessment of criminal behaviour is not merely a product of rational thought and empirical evidence. This struggle can also be conceptualized as a confrontation between an established moral order and the threat of subversion to ethical order (Ferrell and Sanders 1995, pp. 147–148). In the Tokugawa bakufu's judicial practices, legal interpretation was informed by prevailing moral standards under *dōri*. The judicial precedents that were established with the intention of ensuring ethical conduct were duly respected (Bellah 1985, p. 24). The prewar anti-bribery legislation was derived from the Germanic Penal Code during Meiji Restoration. The efficacy and expeditiousness with which legal transplants are implemented is contingent upon two factors: the adaptation of the imported legal framework to local social conditions and the degree of familiarity among the population with the legal principles involved (Oto-Peralías and Romero-Ávila 2017, p. 9). In this regard, the absence of a clearly defined political orientation enabled the perpetuation of the Confucian-inspired value as *dōri* for social harmony (Glenn 2007, p. 318).

In this context, the corruption of bureaucrats had historically constituted an infringement on the ethics of the samurai class during the Tokugawa era (refer Chap. 3). Meiji Constitution was characterized by the absence of bourgeois ideology, which, in contrast to "feudal" ideology, did not challenge the established order. Meiji Restoration should not be considered a bourgeois revolution of elements against prevailing traditional ethics. *Taishinin*'s judicial behaviours have ethical uprightness in the prevailing social ethics. *Taishinin*'s judicial behaviours in previous judgements confirm its conceptual scope of fidelity encompassing bureaucrats' qualities, such as loyalty, fairness, integrity and conscientiousness.

The intensification of acts for public commitments over self-interest rationalized bureaucrats' exercise of power delegated from the divine Emperor. *Taishinin*'s judicial behaviour in corruption cases was not introduction of new values to prewar Japan but propagating and intensifying old values, especially loyalty to the divine Emperor as omnipotent God in government structure. It is noteworthy that the earliest word for government is *matsurigoto*, which originally meant divine worship of religious implications.[15] The integrity and allegiance exhibited by bureaucrats were not directed towards the individual authority of the Emperor, but rather towards the "status" of the institution itself. The death of Emperor Taisho and Emperor Meiji are examples. This status was embodied by the monarchy, characterized by uniformity, stability, centralization and absolute authority. The shift in leadership did not impact bureaucrats' perception of integrity, honesty and loyalty as fundamental qualities necessary to achieve a social objective. The selflessness and self-sacrifice are still highly honoured and glorified in the drama of *Akō rōshi* nowadays (Katsube 1992, pp. 83–85).

Feldman points out that the emphasis on traditional Japanese morality over legal obligations and humaneness over rights are at the expense of individualism and

[15] On this see Bellah (1985); Also see Takarajimasha (2004).

justice in prewar Japan (Feldman 2004, p. 32). *Taishinin*'s moralistic attitude and strict liability model of judicial behaviour against corruption were in line with ethical fidelity, which is ethical uprightness and loyalty to the prevailing cultural practices and legal restrictions. The criminal law reform in the Meiji era all along had not denied *wakon* (Japanese soul) under persuasion to the Western powers to cancel the unequal treaties (Haley 1991, p. 69). *Taishinin*'s ethical fidelity in its value laden judicial behaviours of strict liability model and attitudinal model were rational and socially acceptable under prewar social conditions.

10.5.5 Benefit Reciprocity

In Kobayashi's model, benefit reciprocity is a two-way win–win relationship of equilibrium where people benefit equally. This equilibrium is a combination and balance in a society that is fair to everyone. Reciprocity is a two-way redistribution of benefits. Citizens are obliged to exchange the receipt of benefits by his/her contribution to the collective survival in society equally. Legislation, taxation, social ethics, social welfare and judicial decision are common examples.

The imported laws were enforced in prewar Japan by the letter of the law. *Taishinin*'s judicial behaviour had to rationalize and soften its rigidity with indigenous legal understanding (Röhl 2005, p. 4). As judicial bureaucrats acting in the capacity of *tennō-no-kanri* (Emperor's official) to exercise his power through judicial behaviour, *Taishinin* served to safeguard the dominance of the state political system. This is confirmed by its cognitive consistency with citation of the Emperor's two Imperial Rescripts (on this refer to Chap. 3). In the context of the bureaucratic system and society, *Taishinin*'s emphasis on honesty in official duty and obedience aligned with the prevailing vertical structure of authority in prewar Japan (Nakane 1984, p. 103). The system functioned as a unified, seamless political machine, effectively controlling Japan without the presence of competitive alternatives. The most important is that judicial corruption is non-existent in *Taishinin*'s history. Though *Taishinin* is not a perfect legal institution but law enforcement under the shadow of Minister of Justice, it contributed social benefit of playing an active role in shaping prewar Japanese society and heralded many landmark decisions. Its judicial behaviour ensured Japanese subjects the promise of equal justice under law.

Prewar Japan is undoubtedly not a fair society, *Taishinin*'s judicial behaviour provided the first step toward benefit reciprocity under the domination of state political system. Many appeal grounds reflected improvement in Japanese legal consciousness and society's view of the judicial function, especially in the Keisei case and the compensation case (on this refer to Chaps. 4 to 5).

10.6 Conclusive Remarks: Not a Totalitarian Court

Corruption was a clear disparity in the treatment of nationals with regard to social status, political influence and access to public services. By referral to *Taishinin*'s judgements on it, *Taishinin*'s judicial behaviour models are identified. A comprehensive evaluation of *Taishinin*'s judicial behaviour within the framework of universality, cultural relativism and Kobayashi's "four-dimensional model" substantiates the conclusion that *Taishinin* did not function as a totalitarian court, although prewar state polity did not adequately align with the principles of a fair society and universal principle of rule of law. *Taishinin* was not exclusively dedicated to the ideal of rule of law in prewar Japan, but its strict equitable judicial behaviour served as a vocal advocate for social concerns regarding the imperative for stringent control of bribery and corruption.

The concept of justice is predicated on the principle of fairness. The principle of fairness is prioritized over that of justice.[16] Prewar Japan was not a civil society characterized by individualism, nor was it a fair society.[17] The social environment in prewar Japan was not conducive to the establishment of *Taishinin* as a court of full and true independence, particularly in the face of authoritarianism, militarism and State Shintoism. The state of prewar Japan was characterized by state political system, rather than as a government that promoted the core values of liberalism, namely the equal treatment of free individuals and the facilitation of fair social cooperation. Moreover, a comparative analysis of the Meiji Constitution and the postwar Japanese constitution can help identify significant disparities in the extent to which fundamental freedoms, rights and judicial independence were not guaranteed by the former. It is logically that *Taishinin*'s judicial behaviour could not create a situation which in turn generated a loud and persuasive message for true judicial independence.

References

Ang, Y. Y. (2020), *China's Gilded Age: The Paradox of Economic Boom and Vast Corruption.* Cambridge University Press.

Bellah, R. N. (1985) *Tokugawa Religion: The Culture Roots of Modern Japan.* Free Press.

Christensen, R. K., Charles, R. W. (2007) Law and Management: Comparatively Assessing the Reach of Judicialization. In Jos, C.N. et al. ed. *The Civil Service in the 21st Century: Comparative Perspectives* (pp. 185–200). Palgrave Macmillan.

Feldman, E. A. (2004) T*he Ritual of Rights in Japan.* Cambridge University Press.

Ferrell, J., Clinton, R. S. (1995) *Cultural Criminology.* Northeastern University Press.

Friedman, L. M. (1985) *The Legal System: A Social Science Perspective.* Russell Sage Foundation.

Fuller, L. L., Kenneth, I. W. (1978). The Forms and Limits of Adjudication. *Harvard Law Review,* Vol.92, 353–409.)

Fuller, L. L. (1964) *The Morality of Law. New Haven.* Yale University Press.

---

[16] On this see Rawls (1971).

[17] On this see Monji (1995).

George, B. J. J. (1979) The Japanese Judicial System: Thirty Years of Transition. *Loyola of Los Angeles Law Review*, Vol. 12 (4), 807–832.
Glenn, P. H. (2007) *Legal Traditions of the World*. Oxford University Press.
Grossman, J. B. (1984) Judicial Legitimacy and the Role of Courts: Shapiro's Courts. *American Bar Foundation Research Journal*, Vol. 9 (1), 214–22.
Haley, J. O. (1991) *Authority Without Power*. Oxford University Press.
Hart, H. M., Sacks, A. M. (1994) *The Legal Process: Basic Problems in the Making and Application of Law*. Foundation Press.
Iwatani, J. (1993) Kunrei o Oyogu Daishin'in - Meiji 12-nendai no Shihōken (The Supreme Court Seeing Instructions: Judicial Power in the 12th Years of the Meiji Era). *Keio University Law Research*, Vol. 66 (8), 1–58.
Kabuto, K. (1982) *Jirekifu (Autobiography)*. Iwanami Shoten.
Katsube, M. (1992) The Three Types of Bushido. In *Essay on Japan* (pp. 74–85). Maruzen.
Kawashima, T. (1967) *Nihonjin no Hō Ishiki (Japanese Legal Awareness)*. Iwanami Shinsho.
Kleinig, J. (2008) *Ethics and Criminal Justice*. Cambridge University Press.
Kolm, S. (2004) *Macrojustice: The Political Economy of Fairness*. Cambridge University Press.
Kobayashi, M., Ishido, H. (2023). Introduction: Multi-Layered and Multi-Dimensional Viewpoints towards a Fair Society. In Mizushima, J. et al. ed. *Social Fairness in a Post-Pandemic World* (pp. 1–17). Palgrave Macmillan.
Kratcoski, P. C., Maximilian, E. (2018) *Fraud and Corruption: Major Types, Prevention, and Control*. Springer International Publishing.
Lanier, M. M., Stuart, H. (1998) *Essential Criminology*. Westview Press.
Llewellyn, K. N. (1931) Some Realism about Realism: Responding to Dean Pound. Harvard Law Review Vol. 44, 1222-1264.
Mark, P. (2014) The Definition of Political Corruption. In Heywood, P. M. ed. *Routledge Handbook of Political Corruption* (p. 7). Routledge.
Matsumoto, T. (1962) Kōjo Ryōzoku no Gensoku no Seidoteki Kinō: Minpō Dai-kyūjūjō e no Hōshakaigaku-teki Sekkin (The Institutional Function of the Principle of Public Order and Morality: A Sociological Approach to Article 90 of the Civil Code). *Hō Shakaigaku (Sociology of Law)*, No. 13, 100–135.
Minami, H. (1992) *Ego of Japanese*. Iwanami Shoten.
Monji, M. (1995) *The Structure of Social Consciousness of Modern Japan*. Kitaifuhgasha.
Moribe, H. (2004) Shakai Kyōiku Hanrei ni okeru Jōri (Jōri in Social Education Case Laws). *Gunma Daigaku Kyōiku Gakubu Kiyō: Jinbun Shakai Kagaku-hen (Gunma University Faculty of Education Bulletin Humanities and Social Sciences)*, Vol. 53, 269–296.
Murakami, K. (1994) Meijiki ni okeru "Jōri" Saiban to Furansu-hō no Eikyō (The Influence of "Jōri " Trials and French Law in the Meiji Period). *Hōritsu Ronsō (Law Review)*, Vol. 67 (1), 321–329.
Najita, T., Harootunian, H. D. (1988) Japanese Revolt Against the West: Political and Cultural Criticism in the Twentieth Century. In Duus, P. ed. *The Cambridge History of Japan, Vol. 6: The Twentieth Century* (pp. 711–774). Cambridge University Press.
Nakamura, H. (1971) Shihō Seido to Nihon no Kindaika (Judicial System and Modernization of Japan). *Hikaku Hōgaku (Comparative Law Studies)*, Vol. 7 (1), 7–17.
Nakane, C. (1984) *Japanese Society*. University of California Press.
Nelken, D. (2004) Using the Concept of Legal Culture. *Australian Journal of Legal Philosophy*, Vol. 29, 1–26.
Ohkawa, S. (2003) Seigen Chōka Rishi ni Kansuru: Meiji Zenki Taishin'in Hanrei no Keisei (Regarding Excess Interest Limits: Formation of Judicial Precedents of the Supreme Court in the Early Meiji Era). *Ritsumeikan Hōgaku (Ritsumeikan Legal Studies)*, No. 1 (287), 110–191.
Oto-Peralías, D, Romero-Ávila, D. (2017) *Legal Traditions, Legal Reforms and Economic Performance: Theory and Evidence*. Springer.
Pollock, J. M. (2019) *Ethical Dilemmas and Decisions in Criminal Justice*. Cengage Learning.
Rawls, J. (1971) *A Theory of Justice*. The Belknap Press of Harvard University Press.

Raz, J. (1988) *The morality of freedom.* Oxford University Press
Röhl, W. (2005) *History of Law in Japan since 1868.* Koninklijke Brill NV.
Setsuo, M. (1991) Administrative Control of Japanese Judges. *Kobe University Law Review*, Issue 25, 45–61.
Taguchi, M. (2003) Josetsu: Nihonhō no Naka no Gaikokuhō (Introduction: Foreign Law in Japanese Law). in Institute of Comparative Law, Waseda University ed. *Nihonhō no Naka no Gaikokuhō: Kihonhō no Hikakuhōteki Kōsatsu (Foreign law in Japanese law Comparative legal considerations of the basic law)* (p. 112). Institute of Comparative Law, Waseda University.
Takaaki, H. (1984) The Role of the Supreme Court of Japan in the Field of Judicial Administration. *Washington Law Review*, Vol. 60 (1), 69–86.
Takarajimasha. (2004). *Read Nitobe's Bushido in English.* Takarajimasha.
Twining, W. (2009) *General Jurisprudence: Understanding Law from a Global Perspective.* Cambridge University Press.

Name Index

K. B. Wong and S. L. Fang, *Taishinin's Judicial Behaviour in Corruption Cases*,
https://doi.org/10.1007/978-981-95-5823-0

Subject Index

K. B. Wong and S. L. Fang, *Taishinin's Judicial Behaviour in Corruption Cases*,
https://doi.org/10.1007/978-981-95-5823-0

I

J

K

U

V

W

Y

FSC
www.fsc.org
MIX
Papier aus verantwortungsvollen Quellen
Paper from responsible sources
FSC® C105338

If you have any concerns about our products,
you can contact us on
ProductSafety@springernature.com

In case Publisher is established outside the EU,
the EU authorized representative is:
Springer Nature Customer Service Center GmbH
Europaplatz 3, 69115 Heidelberg, Germany

Printed by Libri Plureos GmbH
in Hamburg, Germany